250 Home Preserving favorites

250 Home Preserving favorites

Yvonne Tremblay

Robert ROSE

For complete cataloguing information, see page 374.

Disclaimer
The recipes in this book have been carefully tested by our kitchen and our tasters. To the best of our knowledge, they are safe and nutritious for ordinary use and users. For those people with food or other allergies, or who have special food requirements or health issues, please read the suggested contents of each recipe carefully and determine whether or not they may create a problem for you. All recipes are used at the risk of the consumer.

We cannot be responsible for any hazards, loss or damage that may occur as a result of any recipe use.

For those with special needs, allergies, requirements or health problems, in the event of any doubt, please contact your medical adviser prior to the use of any recipe.

Design and Production: Daniella Zanchetta/PageWave Graphics Inc.
Editors: Sue Sumeraj and Jennifer MacKenzie
Proofreader: Sheila Wawanash
Indexer: Gillian Watts
Photography: Colin Erricson
Food Styling: Kathryn Robertson
Prop Styling: Charlene Erricson

Cover image: Nectarine Plum Jam (page 124)

We acknowledge the financial support of the Government of Canada through the Book Publishing Industry Development Program (BPIDP) for our publishing activities.

Published by Robert Rose Inc.
120 Eglinton Avenue East, Suite 800, Toronto, Ontario, Canada M4P 1E2
Tel: (416) 322-6552 Fax: (416) 322-6936

Printed and bound in Canada

1 2 3 4 5 6 7 8 9 CPL 18 17 16 15 14 13 12 11 10

Contents

Introduction 8
Acknowledgments 10

A Primer on Preserving 13

Jams 39
    Single-Fruit Jams 44
    Mixed-Fruit Jams 88
    Micro-Mini Jams 159
    Special Jams, Spreads and Mincemeats 173
Conserves 199
Marmalades 227
Jellies 255
    Fruit Jellies 259
    Savory Jellies 281
Fruit Butters 307
Chutneys 323
Recipes Using Preserves 341

Jam Glam: Jar Decorations and Gift Ideas 370
Resources 372
Index 375

—o—o—o—

To my grandmother Margaret Stefan, whose kitchen was a
source of warmth for body and soul and of good things to eat.

And to my grandfather Nicholas Stefan, whom I admired
for his kind heart and strong principles.

Thank you both for many happy summers
on the farm in Saskatchewan.

Introduction

It all started on a hot summer day, when someone called Grandma to say that the fruit truck from British Columbia had arrived in town. Soon Grandpa returned to the farm, laden with cases of sweet cherries that needed to be canned right away. Out came the quart jars and canning pots, and the process (and processing) began. Luckily, cherries are not pitted for canned fruit, so it was not as much work as when peaches and pears arrived later in the summer. It was just one of those things that seemed a normal part of growing up to me. It was on this wheat farm in southern Saskatchewan (while on summer break from Thunder Bay, Ontario) that I learned to love to cook, with my grandmother and older cousin JoAnne. It gave me a taste for everything homemade (fresh-baked bread and baked goods, fresh-churned butter, country-fresh eggs and chicken, veggies from the garden, and so on).

That early canning experience provided the groundwork for my interest in jam-making, after my university years studying Food and Nutrition in Guelph, Ontario, when I moved to Toronto. Strawberry jam was my first. Eventually, a friend suggested that I enter some of my jams and jellies in the Royal Winter Fair, one of Canada's oldest agricultural fairs and certainly its biggest, held in Toronto each November. I call it "a big city fair with a country air." I thought it was pretty neat to be able to take your jams to a country fair in the middle of a big city. That year I won a first prize red rosette ribbon for my Rosemary Apple Cider Jelly (page 306). The next year I decided to go for Grand Champion Jam and Jelly Maker by entering all 10 categories for jams, jellies, marmalades and conserves. To my delight, I won Grand Champion that year, and have won three more times since. I am now affectionately known to family as "the jelly queen" (long may she reign!).

Somewhere during that time I was asked by an acquisitions editor for a publisher to develop and write original recipes for *Prizewinning Preserves* (2001), which contained many of my prizewinning jams, jellies, marmalades and so on. The next year, following another passion, I published *Thyme in the Kitchen: Cooking with Fresh Herbs*, after many years of teaching on that subject. (I have developed many recipes for jams and jellies that include fresh herbs; look for them in this book — more fresh summer tastes!)

I spent the summer of 2009 making delicious jams, jellies, marmalades and more to add over 120 new recipes to the ones from my first book, so what you're holding in your hands now is really like two books in one. Believe it or not, I am not tired of making jams and jellies. I have never been so sticky or had so much fun. I have included all-time favorites and added twists to come up with interesting new flavors too. You're gonna love 'em! My official tasters (friends and family) guarantee it.

Making wonderful preserves, for ourselves and to share, is satisfying. We do it not because we *have to* (as in previous generations) but because we *want to*. We enjoy picking berries, or we go to local markets and bring home too much fruit because it all looked so good. (Or is that just me?) We want to capture summer tastes to savor in the off-season. We want to reconnect with some of the simpler things in life, and feed our souls too. We want to give presents that reflect a part of ourselves. We love homemade. We love bread and jam.

So whether you're a beginner or a seasoned pro, there's something here for you — reliable, easy-to-follow recipes for scrumptious jams, jellies, conserves, marmalades, fruit butters and chutneys, as well as up-to-date preserving information. I hope many of these recipes will become winners with your family and friends.

Yvonne Tremblay
December 2009

Acknowledgments

First, to publisher Bob Dees (the "Robert" of Robert Rose publishing), who got me into this mess! *Thank you* for giving me the opportunity to add all these wonderful new creations to my first jams and jellies cookbook (*Prizewinning Preserves*, 2001). It was a "fruitful" summer, if you'll pardon the pun, busy developing 120+ new recipes, especially new fruit combinations. As I said to Bob later in the season, I am not out of ideas, just out of time. Even as I finished the manuscript, I kept thinking of recipes to add! Bob, your commitment to cookbook publishing results in better cooks and delicious eating.

Though my name is on the front of the book, there are others whose names deserve to be inside it, as you never do this kind of project completely on your own. I always say editors turn cooks into cookbook authors. Editor Sue Sumeraj kept on top of things for correctness and consistency as we merged recipes and copy from the first book with the new stuff. She also contributed great ideas for the charts, tips and extra information. And foodie colleague Jennifer MacKenzie ("queen of pickles"), author of *The Complete Book of Pickling* and co-author of *Complete Curry Cookbook*, *The Dehydrator Bible*, *The Complete Trail Food Cookbook* and *The Complete Root Cellar Book*, contributed her valuable canning expertise to the editing process. Thank you both for your professionalism and patience as we pulled it all together.

Thanks also to the top-notch creative team who turned my labors into a beautiful book: designer Daniella Zanchetta at PageWave Graphics, photographer Colin Erricson, food stylist Kathryn Robertson and prop stylist Charlene Erricson. To Gillian Watts, indexer extraordinaire, thank you for making everything so easy for readers to find. And to Marian Jarkovich, Director of Sales and Marketing for Robert Rose Inc., for her efforts to encourage book distribution and sales, as well as to MDG and Associates, public relations specialists, for getting the word out.

I am grateful to my fellow (and lady) preserve-makers for allowing me to include some of the recipes for their Royal Winter Fair prizewinning preserves in this book: Paul Barrie of East York, Ontario, who is teaching his son his tricks; Sharon Evans of Haliburton, Ontario, whose preserves grace the tables of cottage-country B&Bs; Barbara Mander of Mississauga, Ontario, who loves to give her jams in gift baskets; Larry McGuire of Hamilton, Ontario, who holds preserving bees with friends who have become addicted to his preserves; Shirley McMurray of Stoney Creek, Ontario, who sells her wine jellies in the Niagara region under the name The Jelly Crate (Shirley has a special outfit she wears when preserving: black leggings, a long black T-shirt, old running shoes and a cap); and Gayle Rowan of Haliburton, Ontario, who follows her own path, in life and to the woods, to pick wild berries for jams she sells under the name Wolfpath Products. I have so enjoyed speaking with each of them, learning how they got into preserving, what they like making most, and so on. I count myself in good company and am thrilled to include their wonderful recipes (all were tested for the book). Their love of jamming is inspiring and comes through in their jams, jellies and other preserves. For a list of their recipes, see Contributors, page 12.

Many thanks and hugs to two special foodie friends, Pat Moynihan and Wendi Hiebert, who always have a generous supply of moral support. Pat is a food consultant like me and a "bread-baking queen," and I am grateful for the three baking recipes she contributed to this book. Wendi is a food writer and food blogger in addition to her full-time job as Food and Nutrition Specialist for Egg Farmers of Ontario. Wendi loves chocolate and jumped — no, leapt — at the opportunity to develop a jam using cocoa. She also offered to help with adding metric equivalents to the recipes when timing was critical and I was overwhelmed with a looming deadline. Pat's and Wendi's recipes are listed under Contributors, page 12.

When it comes to Lise Ferguson, "thanks" is not good enough. There must be another word for "huge gratitude" — maybe greatitude! Lise worked with me on my first two books, and when I asked her to help me with this one too, she didn't run the other way. Lise can take my sometimes less-than-legible test sheets and magically transform them into readable recipes (she *does* read between the lines, literally). She says, "Just give me that," and I do! She typed all the new recipes, despite an aching head on many occasions. A night owl like me, she was there with funny emails just when I thought no one else was up and my energy was waning.

Lise's mom is none other than Carol Ferguson (the chip fell off the block!), former food editor of *Canadian Living* and *Homemakers* magazines and the author of *The New Canadian Basics Cookbook* and *The Canadian Living Cookbook*. I had the privilege of working with Carol at *Homemakers* for three years and learned a lot from her. She makes the best scones, and I bake them often to enjoy my jams on (occasionally with clotted cream, when I can get it). She has graciously contributed her recipe.

Thank you to my family, especially my cousin JoAnne for requesting recipes with passion fruit, and to my many friends, especially Sandra and Micki, who are always cheerleading in my corner, Sonja (who loves all things cherry) for black and red currants from her bushes, and Luisa for her calls and encouragement. Thanks also to my salsa dancing friends, especially Cindy, Margaret, Suzanne V., Tanya and Jaime, to my sailing buddies on *Defiant II* and to my friends Sylvia (whom I have known since we were five) and Suzanne L. They are my personal troupe of taste-testers, giving me their ideas and feedback (as well as empty jars back) and keep telling me I make the best jam in the world. Now you have to help me eat it all!

Special thanks to my good friend Tim, who gives two thumbs up to the hot pepper jellies. He has helped and supported me in many ways over the years. While I was in the final stages of the book, he helped me move into a new house, which he also renovated for me. Thank you for the beautiful kitchen I now get to cook in!

I would like to thank the companies who support us all in our preserving endeavors: Jarden Home Brands, encompassing the Bernardin and Ball brands (which supply canning jars, lids, pectin products and canning equipment), and Kraft Canada Inc. (makers of Certo pectins) for their commitment, their expertise and the contribution of a few of their recipes in the Special Jams, Spreads and Mincemeats section (pages 177–183). See the Resources (page 372) for their websites.

Hats (or oven mitts) off to the farmers who grow and harvest the quality fruits and vegetables that are the basis of exquisite preserves.

Finally, thank you for taking this book home with you. The fun is about to begin!

Contributors

Jams, Jellies and Marmalades

Paul Barrie: Red Fruit Jam (page 144), Rhubarb Pineapple Jam (page 146), Lime Marmalade (page 240)

Sharon Evans: Peach Orange Marmalade (page 249)

Wendi Hiebert: Chocolate Raspberry Jam (page 79)

Barbara Mander: Strawberry Pineapple Jam (page 152)

Larry McGuire: Peach Raspberry Jam (page 129), Seville Orange Marmalade (page 245), Christmas Plum Conserve (page 224)

Shirley McMurray: Cabernet Wine Jelly (page 293), Spiced Cranberry and Red Wine Jelly (page 295), Spiced Port Wine Jelly (page 296)

Gayle Rowan: Piña Colada Jam (page 71), Peach Pear Jam (page 127)

Recipes Using Preserves

Carol Ferguson: Cream Tea Scones (page 353)

Pat Moynihan: Empire Cookies (page 357), Pineapple Tartlets (page 363), Apricot Ladder Braid (page 365)

A Primer on Preserving

The Fundamentals 14
   Food Safety 14
   Nutrition 14
   Metric Measurements 15
   Equipment 15
   Utensils 16
   Where to Find Stuff 17
Getting Started 18
   Preparing, Sterilizing and Filling Jars 18
   Preparing Metal Lids 18
Test for the Setting Point 19
Using a Boiling Water Canner 20
   New Processing Times 20
   High Altitude Processing 21
Labeling and Storage 21
Yield 22
Tips for Successful Preserving 22
Terminology 23
Choosing and Preparing Fruit and Vegetables 24
   Fruit Seasonality 24
   Fruit and Vegetable Information 25
Produce Purchase Guide 32
Understanding Fruit's Natural Pectin 34
A Word or Two on Adding Flavors 36
Preparation Checklist 37

The Fundamentals

This section provides some useful and necessary information to help you succeed at making top-quality sweet preserves that will keep well.

Food Safety

When you're making preserves, keeping things sanitary is most important. Microbes — usually molds, yeasts and bacteria — are responsible for food spoilage. Spoilage ruins the flavor and consistency of preserves; more importantly, some toxins produced by the microbes can be lethal. It is never worth the risk to consume suspect food; discard food that has been kept too long, in which you can see moving bubbles, for which the seal has broken or in which there is obvious mold growth.

> It is not safe to simply remove mold from the preserves in a jar. If you find mold, discard the entire contents of the jar.

The high concentration of sugar found in jams, jellies and other sweet preserves is responsible for deterring the growth of molds. But molds will grow on the surface, as well as inside the preserve, in the presence of air. That is why processing in a boiling water canner is recommended, to provide an airtight seal and to kill any organisms that may get into the jar from utensils or the air during filling. Processing is even more important for low-sugar preserves or no-sugar spreads. Preserves may also be frozen, without processing, for safe long-term storage.

> It is no longer considered a safe practice to use paraffin wax on top of preserves.

Nutrition

While preserves are generally high in sugar, they contain almost no fat. Butter and margarine have about 100 kcal (calories) and 11 g of fat per tablespoon (15 mL). The same amount of most regular jams contains about 55 kcal and no fat, while no-sugar (artificially sweetened or no-sugar-added) spreads range from 10 to 15 kcal per tablespoon (15 mL). Jams made with light pectin crystals have 20% less sugar and 30% more fruit. Preserves contain no protein and are primarily carbohydrate from the fruit and the sugar.

Preserves retain a lot of the nutrients that were present in the fruit. Some of the vitamins are destroyed by heat and exposure to air when the fruit is cut; however, many vitamins, minerals and phytochemicals (plant compounds thought to be beneficial in the prevention of certain diseases) are retained. Preserves often contain the seeds and peels of fruits, which are good sources of fiber, as is the flesh itself. Pectin, whether from the fruit used or added commercial pectin, is a type of soluble fiber.

Preserves can be part of a nutritious meal plan, especially when you eat them on whole-grain breads (complex carbohydrates), which are also rich in fiber. Whole grains help to slow down the absorption of sugars (simple carbohydrates) into the bloodstream, which can be beneficial for those with blood-sugar problems. Eating simple carbohydrates with proteins works as well — try a little jam stirred into plain yogurt to sweeten it.

Of course, don't overdo it. Excess calories (calories over and above your energy needs) will all be converted to and stored as fat, no matter what foods they come from.

Metric Measurements

Metric measurements have been included for all the recipes. They are based on *equivalent* measurements developed for Canadian cooks by cooking professionals and home economists working for the Metric Commission when the metric system was first introduced, rather than on straight conversions from imperial to metric. For convenience, the numbers were designed to be even multiples of fives and tens. The recipes in this book were not tested in metric, so results may vary. For best results, use all imperial or all metric measures. Use tests for doneness, where possible, to ensure that the mixture has reached the setting point.

Equipment

- **Large, deep, heavy-bottomed pot.** Thin-bottomed pots will likely cause scorching, and pots that are too small will result in messy boilovers. Most sets of cooking pots include a large, wide pot or a Dutch oven with a lid. Other large pots, such as stockpots, may also be suitable. The bottom of the pot should have an extra layer of metal; it is usually aluminum or copper, which are good heat conductors. Do not use all-aluminum or all-iron pots.

> A Dutch oven is a very large pot, found in most cookware sets, that has two side handles and a lid. The name comes from early cast-iron Dutch cooking pots, which were used over an open fire, with hot coals sometimes being placed on the lid so the pot acted like an oven.

I like to use wide-mouth (large-diameter) pots for fruit butters, marmalades, conserves and chutneys. They allow for greater evaporation of water when you are cooking down the mixture to thicken it. The capacity of the pot I use is about 5½ quarts, or 22 cups (5.5 L). I have another pot that is a bit taller (deeper) and a little narrower in which I prefer to make jams and especially jellies: the jelly liquid often bubbles up high and could overflow a shorter pot; you need a pot with a depth at least four times that of the liquid. The one I use is 9½ inches (24 cm) in diameter and 6½ inches (16 cm) deep, and holds about 28 cups (7 L).

- **Large kettle.** Any large pot is good for sterilizing jars and for processing the preserves (see Using a Boiling Water Canner, page 20). For processing, the pot must be deep enough to allow water to cover jars by at least 1 inch (2.5 cm).

- **Canning jars with two-part lids.** Canning jars are made of special heat-resistant glass for boiling water canning. The lids consist of metal rings (also known as screw bands) and one-time-use metal lids with a sealing compound that needs to be softened before using. Most of the preserves in this book use 8-ounce (250 mL) jars (also called half-pint jars). I like these smaller jars because you open and use them up more quickly (thereby consuming a fresher product). In addition, you can try several kinds at the same time for more variety, and you have more jars to share. For popular jams for larger families, use the 16-ounce (500 mL) jars, as these preserves will be consumed more quickly. For savory preserves, such as wine, garlic, herb and pepper jellies, I like the smallest 4-ounce (125 mL) jars. They're great for gift-giving and for preserves eaten in smaller amounts.

- **Small saucepan.** This is used to heat metal jar lids to soften the sealing compound.

- **Bowls.** Large and small bowls are used for premeasured fruit, sugar, dried fruit, nuts, etc. Small glass plates or bowls can be placed in the freezer and used to check the setting point.

- **Knives.** You need a good-quality chef's knife for chopping and a paring knife for peeling and trimming. A knife sharpener keeps knives sharp so you can work faster and avoid cuts due to the knife slipping.

- **Cutting boards.** Have a large plastic cutting board, with a groove to catch juices, for chopping citrus fruit, pineapple, peaches, etc., as well as a wooden board for cutting onions, peppers, garlic, etc. for chutney (do not also use this cutting board for fruit, as the flavors will transfer).

- **Other equipment.** You'll get good use out of a food processor, a food mill, a colander, sieves, a kitchen scale and a plastic-coated apron.

> A food mill looks like a metal pot with small holes in the bottom and a crank with a bent metal blade that pushes soft foods through as the crank is turned clockwise. It is used to purée soft foods and to remove seeds and skins from tomatoes.

Utensils

- **Measures.** For accurate measuring, you need glass liquid measures and metal or plastic nesting measuring cups and spoons for dry ingredients. Do not measure sugar in a liquid measure, and do not measure liquids (water, juice, wine, etc.) in the cups used for dry ingredients. Fruit may be measured in either; I prefer a 4-cup (1 L) liquid measure for large quantities of fruit (once it is empty, use it for discarding skimmed material).

- **Spoons.** Wooden spoons are great for stirring, and ones with extra-long handles are ideal for avoiding hot splashes from bubbling preserves (I wrote "Magic Wand" on the handle of one of mine). Mark wooden spoon handles so you do not interchange those you use for sweet and savory preserves. Plastic or melamine spoons are not as good for the constant stirring of hot mixtures. Use a large metal spoon (stainless steel or chrome-plated) for skimming.

- **Ladle.** I prefer a ladle (stainless steel or chrome-plated) for transferring mixtures to jars.

- **Canning funnel.** Most of the canning funnels available today are plastic. They make it easier to ladle preserves into jars.

- **Magnetic wand.** This handy tool — a magnet attached to the end of a plastic wand — is used to lift prepared jar lids from hot water. You simply touch the magnet to the center of the metal lid, place the lid on top of the clean jar rim and detach with your finger. These wands are not expensive, and are sold directly by Jarden Home Brands if you cannot find them in a hardware or general merchandise store. (See Resources, page 372.)

- **Headspace gauge/bubble remover.** This handy plastic tool is used to measure the headspace (the distance from the top surface of the mixture to the jar rim) and to remove bubbles from inside the jar. (See Resources, page 372.)

- **Rubber spatula/scraper.** This is used to scrape sugar from the inside edges of the pot. Look for high-heat-resistant (silicone) spatulas in kitchen stores. A narrow spatula can be used to remove air bubbles.

- **Potato masher or pastry blender.** Use to crush fruit to release juices.

- **Kitchen timer.** A digital timer ensures accurate timing of boiling and cooking.

- **Candy or digital thermometer.** Use to test the temperature for the setting point.

- **Other utensils.** Cheesecloth, a jelly bag, a cherry pitter, a strawberry huller or wide drinking straw (to remove strawberry hulls), a vegetable peeler, a citrus zester, graters and a citrus juicer will all come in handy.

I place spare lids and rings, funnels and so on in plastic storage bags to keep them clean and together when not in use.

Where to Find Stuff

Hardware or general merchandise stores usually carry the full line of canning paraphernalia: jars, extra lids, magnetic wands, canning funnels and jar lifters, extra labels, etc. Many of these products, while not essential, do make canning easier and are worth the small investment.

The housewares sections of department and discount stores, specialty kitchen stores and supermarkets carry cookware, utensils and gadgets. If you can, spend the extra money for quality goods.

For more information on where to buy jars and some of the other supplies, see Resources, page 372.

Getting Started

Preparing, Sterilizing and Filling Jars

Wash jars in hot, soapy water; rinse well. Place jars in a large pot of water, tilting them to fill with water, then placing them upright on a rack. Add water to ensure they are covered, if necessary. Bring to a boil and boil for 10 minutes. Turn off heat and let the jars rest in hot water until ready to use. Lift jars from water with a jar lifter; drain water.

> Ensure that jars are well drained. They may be turned upside down onto a clean towel on the countertop.

Place hot jars upright on a dishcloth or tea towel and fill with the hot mixture. Use a ladle or a measuring cup with a pouring spout to transfer the hot mixture. A canning funnel helps to prevent dribbles.

> Jars may be washed in the dishwasher but will not be sterilized. The water in your dishwasher only gets as high as about 145°F (65°C), and jars must be at 212°F (100°C) for at least 10 minutes to be sterilized.

Jams, jellies, marmalades and spreads are filled to within 1/4 inch (0.5 cm) of the rim of the jar. This is based on 8-ounce (250 mL) or smaller jars. Increase to 1/2 inch (1 cm) if you're using 16-ounce (500 mL) jars; do not use jars larger than 16 ounces (500 mL). Chutneys, conserves, mincemeats and fruit butters are filled to within 1/2 inch (1 cm) of the rim. Do not overfill or underfill: if you overfill, the preserve may seep out and interfere with the seal; underfilling will leave more air in the jar than can be forced out during the processing time, resulting in a poor seal.

You can measure the headspace with a headspace gauge or a ruler.

To remove any air that may be trapped inside your mixture, slide a clean, non-metal utensil (such as a rubber spatula or a bubble remover) between the jar and the mixture. Move it gently so bubbles will rise to the surface. Thicker preserves such as butters, mincemeats and chutneys are especially prone to trapping air when jars are filled.

Carefully wipe the top rim of the jar with a clean, damp cloth or paper towel to ensure a good seal.

> To clean the rims of the jars, I use a clean paper towel dipped in the hot water the metal lids were prepared in.

Preparing Metal Lids

Set rings (screw bands) aside in a small bowl. Bring about 2 inches (5 cm) of water to a boil in a small saucepan. Reduce heat to medium, place lids in water and bring to a simmer. Do not let the lids boil. Once they have come to a simmer, remove the pot from the heat and keep them hot until ready to use. Make sure to prepare lids ahead so they are ready once your mixture is done. Lift each lid from the water using a magnetic wand or a non-metal utensil (metal tongs will scratch lids, which can result in rusting) and place on a filled jar that has had its rim wiped clean. Apply the ring and tighten with your fingertips just until the ring is snug, not as tight as it will go. Air needs to escape during processing to create the vacuum seal, so don't

> Do not let metal lids boil. Instructions used to call for boiling, but this is no longer done. Do, however, ensure that they are hot when placed on filled jars. If the water cools, the sealant will harden again and will not seal properly.

overtighten. On the other hand, if it's too loose, some of the contents may leak out.

After processing and cooling, lids will have a tight vacuum seal. Rings should be removed and jars and rings wiped well to remove any residues. If desired, rings may be reapplied once jars are dry. Do not overtighten, or you may disturb the seal.

Do not reuse metal lids. Once they have sealed a jar, the sealing compound will not work properly a second time. Used lids may be kept for preserves that will just be refrigerated or frozen, not processed or sealed. Unused lids may be reheated at a later time. Remove from water, let cool, dry and store them in a box or a plastic zip-lock bag. Metal rings can be reused if they are not rusted or dented.

> Discard any jars that have been chipped or scratched.

Test for the Setting Point

Testing whether a jam, jelly or marmalade made without added pectin will set once it cools can be tricky. There are several ways to test, and I always use the temperature method in combination with one of the other methods. Always remove the pot from the stove to stop the cooking while you test.

1. **Wrinkle (or plate) method.** Place about 2 tsp (10 mL) of jam, jelly or marmalade on a chilled small plate and place it in the freezer for a minute or two, until cooled to room temperature. A skin will form on top. If you gently push it with your finger or a fork, it will wrinkle if the mixture is done. I usually keep two or three plates chilled and ready.

> Tests for doneness for conserves, butters and chutneys are at the beginning of those chapters.

2. **Sheeting method.** Using a clean, dry, small metal spoon, remove some of the mixture from the pot. Tilt the spoon so the mixture runs over the side onto a dish. Early in the process, the drops will be runny; as the mixture continues to cook, the drops will start to come together. When the mixture is ready, the drops will join into one and sheet off the spoon in what looks like one layer.

3. **Temperature method.** Use a candy or digital thermometer. First test the boiling point of water, which will vary with altitude and the atmospheric conditions that day. Then take the temperature of the jam, jelly or marmalade. Make sure to place the thermometer in the center of the pot, not touching the bottom or the sides. The setting point is usually 8°F (4°C) above the boiling point of water as determined by your thermometer — there may be a 1° margin of error in its accuracy. At sea level, the setting temperature would be 220°F (104°C). As water evaporates from your mixture, it will increase in temperature. It may not seem to change too quickly at first but will increase more quickly as the jam gets closer to the setting point.

Using a Boiling Water Canner

Processing jars after you've filled them and applied the lids is important for the safe long-term room temperature storage of your preserves. Processing ensures that any microbes that got into your product while you were filling the jars are killed, and that you achieve a good vacuum seal that will be maintained for the duration of the jars' storage. While jars may seal (as verified by the lids curving inward) without processing, the strength of the vacuum is greater after processing.

Processing is done in a large pot of boiling water with a rack on which to place jars. You may use any large, deep pot with a rack, or place a round cake rack in the bottom of a pot. The pot needs to be deep enough to allow for 2 inches (5 cm) of boiling water above the jars.

Ensure that the water is boiling before you place your jars in the pot. Lower jars in carefully, ensuring that they do not tilt. Make sure to leave some space between the jars. Top off with additional hot water, if necessary, leaving at least 2 inches (5 cm) between the surface of the water and the top of the pot; remove water, if necessary, with a small saucepan or a heatproof glass measuring cup. Cover the pot and return to a boil over high heat. Begin timing once the water has returned to a boil.

Process for the specified time (see High Altitude Processing, page 21, for altitude adjustments). Remove jars with a jar lifter, *lifting them straight up* (do not tilt), and place them on a towel-lined surface, leaving some space around each jar. (I place a tea towel on a large tray.) Do not place jars on a cold surface. As the jars cool, you will hear the lids pop and see that they have been sucked downward. Check seals after cooling by pressing the center of the lids; they should not move.

It is not worth the risk of losing your preserves to skip the processing step. You have made an investment of your time and money. In addition, fruit may be out of season and you may have to wait another year until you are able to replace what you have lost.

Let rest until set; this may take up to 24 hours. Once jars have cooled, you may check for set by tilting the jar slightly. Jellies will not move when set; some jams and conserves have a softer set and may move slightly; marmalades may take up to a week to completely set. If the contents move easily, your preserves may not have set. (See the Trouble-Shooting section that appears in each chapter.)

Once the preserves have set, remove the jar rings. Wipe the jars well with a damp cloth, especially the area under the rings and inside the rings themselves (any sweet material left will likely grow mold, which may get into your jars). Once the jars are dry, you can replace the rings if you like. Do not overtighten or you may break the seal. Any unsealed jars must be refrigerated and used within 3 weeks.

New Processing Times

Home preserving experts have recently recommended increased processing times, as this ensures improved food safety (in case you have not been 100% careful to keep everything sterilized). Although in theory these increased processing times mean there's no longer a need to sterilize the jars (they just need to be hot), I still sterilize them anyway; it never hurts to be on the safe side.

Some sources say to sterilize jars by placing them in an oven at about 220°F (104°C) for 10 minutes. Jar manufacturers do not recommend this, as it may cause breakage.

All high-sugar preserves — jams, jellies, marmalades and conserves — in jars 8 ounces (250 mL) or smaller are processed for 10 minutes; pint (500 mL) jars are processed for 15 minutes. Most fruit butters and chutneys, which are lower in sugar, are processed for 15 minutes.

High Altitude Processing

If you live at an altitude above 1,000 feet (306 m), you'll need to adjust the processing times given in the recipes as follows:

- 1,000 to 3,000 feet (306 to 915 m): increase time by 5 minutes
- 3,001 to 6,000 feet (916 to 1,830 m): increase time by 10 minutes
- 6,001 to 8,000 feet (1,831 to 2,440 m): increase time by 15 minutes
- 8,001 to 10,000 feet (2,441 to 3,050 m): increase time by 20 minutes

Source: Courtesy of Jarden Corporation.

> No-cook preserves do not require sterilized containers or processing. Ladle the mixture into clean freezer containers or jars, leaving room for expansion. Cover tightly and freeze. Or store in the refrigerator for up to 3 weeks. The plastic lids that are available to fit standard canning jars are suitable for no-cook preserves.

Labeling and Storage

Label jars with the name of the contents and the date. If you're planning to store your jams in a box, you might want to place the labels on the top of the lid rather than on the side of the jar. That way, you can read them easily while the jars are in the box. The other benefit is that there's no need to pick the labels off the jars once they're emptied; after eating the preserve, just discard the metal lid, as it cannot be reused anyway.

Store sealed, labeled jars in a cool, dry, dark place. Warmth, temperature fluctuations, dampness or light will deteriorate the flavor and color of your preserves. The ideal storage temperature is 40°F to 50°F (4°C to 10°C). You may have a special cupboard for storage, or you can place the jars back in the box they came in. If you make a lot of jams, you may want to keep an inventory list of what is in each box. This helps a lot when you are trying to locate a particular jam. On the outside of the box, I mark whether it contains jams or jellies, etc.

Stored properly, your preserves will keep for more than a year, but I recommend that you try to use them up within a year.

> Once jars are opened, refrigerate them and use up the contents within 3 weeks.

Yield

The yield stated for each recipe is for the *minimum* number of standard canning jars the recipe will fill. You will often get more than the amount stated, depending on how accurately you measure, variability in the moisture content of the fruit, the diameter of the pot you use and variations in cooking time. The yield is meant to be a guideline for the number of jars and lids to prepare. I usually prepare at least one additional jar and lid in case I have extra preserve or one of my jars breaks. You can also put extra preserves in a small bowl, container or non-canning jar for sampling; once cooled, cover and refrigerate for up to 3 weeks. Or use a spare canning jar with a plastic lid (metal lids are not necessary if it is not being processed).

> Do not double recipes. Your pot may overflow, even if it does not look all that full. Also, cooking in too large a quantity may overcook fruit or prevent thickening/gelling.

Tips for Successful Preserving

1. Always follow guidelines for food safety and sterilization of jars and utensils.

2. Use reliable recipes and measure carefully.

3. Select ingredients of the best quality. Picking your own fruit is a good way to obtain quality, as is buying from farmers' markets. The smell of the fruit will give you an idea of its flavor. Fruit should have a strong, pleasant aroma (for example, peaches should smell very peachy). Avoid overripe fruit; however, some slightly underripe fruit is actually good, as its natural pectin levels are usually higher. Since underripe fruit may be less juicy, it should make up only a quarter of the total amount used.

4. Prepare fruits as outlined in the recipe: wash, stem, pit, chop well, etc. If the peel of a fruit is not normally eaten — as with kiwis, mangos and pineapple — remove it. For other fruits, peel if the recipe tells you to do so (peaches, for example, are usually peeled in preserves recipes, while apricots and plums are not.) For more details, see Fruit and Vegetable Information, page 25.

5. Follow product instructions for commercial pectins and do not interchange liquid pectin and powdered pectin (pectin crystals) in recipes.

6. Use the exact amount of sugar called for in the recipe; otherwise, your preserves may not set.

7. Time cooking carefully, preferably using a digital timer or the second hand on a clock. When the time is up, immediately remove the pot from the stove to stop the cooking. For preserves made without added commercial pectin, test for doneness or the setting point at the minimum time given. If the mixture is not ready, return it to the heat, bring it back to a boil, begin timing for another minute or two and test again; repeat until ready. Do not overcook or your preserves will be gluey.

8. Stir to prevent floating fruit. Certain preserves benefit from 5 to 8 minutes of stirring after they are removed from the heat. This helps suspend all the bits of fruit throughout the mixture, and keeps them from floating to the top of the jar. Occasionally, it may take 10 minutes or longer for the preserve to begin to set. You can fill a test jar to see if it is ready. If not, pour the mixture

> Floating can occur when ingredients have not been chopped finely enough. Peaches, pears, blueberries, cherries, strawberries and bell (sweet) peppers in particular have a tendency to float.

back into the pot and continue stirring. Now that the recommended processing time has been increased from 5 minutes to 10 or 15 minutes (depending on the size of the jar), I have found that some mixtures heat up and floating reoccurs. If that happens, wait until jars have sealed and have cooled slightly on the towel-lined surface, then gently twist them to try to resuspend the fruit bits. Do not shake or invert jars.

9. When filling the jars, make sure to leave the amount of headspace (the space between the top of the mixture and the rim of the jar) specified in the recipe.

10. Do not overtighten jar rings, either before or after processing.

11. Let jars rest at room temperature, undisturbed until set. Do not invert jars.

12. Remove rings and wipe away any stickiness, especially from jar threads and under rings. Store jars in a cool, dark, dry place. Use within a year for best quality.

Terminology

Boiling

- **Full boil, full rolling boil, hard boil:** A boil that cannot be stirred down, that bubbles constantly and vigorously.

- **Rapid boil:** A steady boil that bubbles well but can be stirred down.

- **Gentle boil:** A steady boil that is not too vigorous but is not as slow as simmering.

- **Simmer:** A constant, light bubbling over lower heat that slowly cooks the food.

Chopping

- **Coarsely chopped:** Cut into ½- to ¾-inch (1 to 2 cm) pieces.

- **Chopped:** Cut into roughly ½-inch (1 cm) pieces.

- **Finely chopped:** Cut into pieces smaller than ¼ inch (0.5 cm).

- **Diced:** Cut evenly into cubes of ½ inch (1 cm) or smaller.

- **Minced:** Cut into very fine pieces smaller than ⅛ inch (3 mm).

Other

- **Fingertip-tight:** To tighten the jar ring, with only your fingertips gripping it, just until the ring is snug, not as tight as it will go. If the ring is overtightened before processing, air will not be able to escape the jar during processing, and a good seal will not form. Tightening rings after processing is likely to disturb and weaken the seal.

- **Headspace:** The space left between the surface of the preserve and the top rim of the jar. It is important to leave the amount of space specified in the recipe to create the vacuum for a good seal. Contents from overfilled jars may seep out.

- **Setting point, set point, jelling point, gel point:** The point at which your preserve is done, at which the sugar, pectin and acid come together to create a gel and will set. There are various ways to test for the setting point; see details, page 19.

Choosing and Preparing Fruit and Vegetables

The flavor and ripeness of the produce you choose for preserving is the key to making good jams, jellies, etc. If a fruit or vegetable is the proper ripeness and is void of any blemishes, it will be fragrant and will taste great. And if all the produce you use looks beautiful and smells appetizing, the resulting preserve will be delicious. I choose the best I can find. If I cannot find what I am looking for, I either wait or make something else.

Use produce as soon as possible after bringing it home, rather than storing it for several days. If you do need to store it, choose a cool place, such as the crisper drawer, to prevent deterioration. When you're ready to use it, be meticulous in your handling and preparation. Handle tender fruits carefully to avoid bruising them. Wash all produce (even though you are going to cook it) to eliminate any dirt, insecticides and microbes. Wash even produce you are going to peel, such as citrus fruit, as you may have to place it on a cutting board to remove the peel. Trim away bad spots and discard leaves, hulls, stems and inedible seeds.

A good rule of thumb: If you need to peel it to eat it, then peel it to preserve with. (Citrus fruit for marmalades is an exception to this rule.)

When you find great-quality fruit or vegetables, freeze some for later use or for combination jams later in the season, or in winter months. Sometimes there is simply too much produce to deal with at one time. Mother Nature and weather conditions can make a real jumble out of the seasonality of fruit and vegetables, with several in season at the same time (so much produce, so little time!). I freeze rhubarb, currants and most berries so I have them on hand to make combination fruit preserves when they're out of season. I prefer to use tree fruit fresh in season.

For the ultimate convenience, be sure to make use of commercial frozen fruit, as it is sometimes less expensive, has often been cleaned, and is ready to use: strawberries have been hulled, stemmed and sliced; cherries have been pitted; peaches have been peeled, pitted and chopped; gooseberries have been bearded; currants have been stemmed and bearded and so on. You can often find out-of-season fruit as well. Winter is a great time for preserving.

Fruit Seasonality

Here are the approximate times when fruits start to appear in stores and markets. This is meant to be a rough guide of what to look for so you can plan what jams and jellies to make. Of course, it all depends on the weather.

- **Winter:** citrus fruit (January for Seville oranges), storage apples, imported apples and pears, kiwifruit from the southern hemisphere, exotic tropical fruit

- **Spring to early summer:** apricots, mangos, pineapple, rhubarb, U.S. strawberries

- **Early summer:** Canadian strawberries, sour (tart) cherries, cultivated blueberries, plumcots, apriums

- **Mid- to late summer:** peaches, small red and yellow plums, nectarines, raspberries, wild blueberries, blackberries, boysenberries, gooseberries, red currants, sweet cherries, unique regional berries, kiwifruit, limes, passion fruit, prickly pear, watermelon

- **Late summer:** apricots, black currants, blueberries (especially wild), blackberries, late-bearing raspberries and strawberries, nectarines, Italian and damson plums, Concord and Coronation grapes, figs, pears, green tomatoes, early apples, crabapples

- **Fall:** cranberries, apples, quince, pears, pomegranates

Locally grown fruit is usually best for quality and flavor, but we are fortunate to have produce from around the world to choose from. So if the spirit moves you, the fruit is nice and you're in the mood to make jam, go for it!

Fruit and Vegetable Information

Apples

Apples are used in a lot of preserves and are available year-round. For jams and fruit butters, choose apples that soften and lose their shape when cooked; for conserves and chutneys, choose apples that keep their shape when cooked (see box, below). Sometimes, a combination of both can be used. Older, less crisp apples may be used to make butters. Note that Red Delicious apples are good for eating, but are not recommended for cooking.

Apples That Soften

McIntosh, Paula Red, Cortland, Empire, Russet

Apples That Keep Their Shape

Golden Delicious, Jonagold, Ginger Gold, Crispin, Idared, Northern Spy, Spartan

---

For fruit butters, the peels are left on apples, and the stems, blossom ends and cores are removed. Otherwise, apples are peeled for preserving recipes.

Do not freeze apples for preserving, as they have to be frozen with sugar, which is suitable for pies but not for preserves. They also brown easily when frozen.

Apricots

Choose firm, ripe or slightly underripe fruit. Do not peel, but do discard pits. The skins add flavor, color and texture to jams and conserves.

Do not freeze apricots for preserving, as they would need to be peeled and have juice, sugar or syrup added.

Dried apricots have good flavor and are used to make fruit butters or are added to conserves and chutneys.

Bananas

Best used when ripe but still slightly firm. I prefer to use finely chopped bananas instead of mashed in jams and conserves.

Beets

Before use, scrub beets very well and trim off ends. Do not bother peeling them before cooking, as the skins come off easily afterwards.

Berries

Either fresh or frozen berries can be used for preserves. Frozen berries will produce more juice when thawed, so preserves may need slightly more cooking time.

If using fresh berries, choose firm, ripe, dry fruit. Store fresh berries (except cranberries; see page 26) in a single layer under a paper towel in the refrigerator, but do not store them for too long before using. Wash, rinse and drain all berries before use. For strawberries, remove hulls and stems after washing.

To freeze berries, first wash them and dry well on paper towels. Lay whole berries in a single layer on a baking sheet, freeze completely, then transfer to freezer bags or containers.

There are many regional berries that are terrific for preserves and may be substituted in recipes. Keep an eye out for berries that are native to your area, and make good use of them when they're in season.

Carrots

Peel and trim the ends before chopping or shredding.

Cherries

Both sweet and sour (tart) cherries may be used to make jams and conserves; use sour (tart) cherries for jelly. Choose firm, ripe, glossy fruit and store in the refrigerator. Before use, remove stems and pits. To pit cherries, you can either use a cherry pitter or halve the fruit and remove the pit with a paring knife. Some cherries come pitted, a big time-saver. Pitted cherries can be frozen using the same method used for berries (see page 25). If you have a large amount of cherries (they sometimes come in large pails), you may want to divide them into premeasured quantities.

Citrus Fruit
(Oranges, Grapefruit, Lemons, Limes)

Choose firm, deep-colored, glossy fruit with blemish-free rinds. The fruit should be heavy for its size. Store in the refrigerator in perforated plastic or mesh bags in the crisper drawer. Before using citrus fruit for marmalades, scrub rinds well with soapy water and rinse. Do not freeze citrus fruit to use for preserving. Any extra juice can be frozen in ice cube trays, then transferred to freezer bags and used for other recipes.

Crabapples

Crabapples make excellent jelly. Remove the stems and blossom ends. Do not peel or remove cores.

Cranberries

Choose firm, ripe, red fruit. Freeze when in season (September/October) by placing bags of whole berries inside a freezer bag to keep them from drying out.

Currants

Red and black currants are great for jams or jellies. Choose firm, ripe, dry fruit. Remove from stems before use. Black currants need

---

How to Section Citrus Fruit

Sectioning means removing all unwanted elements — skin, white pith and membranes — from citrus fruit, leaving only the juicy parts. Using a small serrated knife, trim the top and bottom off the fruit. Set on a cutting board, with one flat end down, and cut off the skin in curved strips, removing as much of the white pith as possible. Holding the fruit on its side, carefully insert the tip of the knife between the right side of a section of flesh and the membrane, then cut along the membrane. Repeat on the left side. Loosen the section with the knife and remove. Continue removing sections, folding empty membranes to one side like pages of a book, until all the flesh is removed.

---

their "beards" (blossom ends) snipped for jams, but that step is not necessary for jellies. To remove beards, use small scissors, such as curved manicure scissors (keep new ones aside just for this job), and snip close to the fruit. Freeze currants as you would berries (see page 25).

Dried Fruit

Dried fruit, such as apricots, cranberries, currants, dates, figs, prunes and raisins, should be plump and soft. Store at room temperature (68°F/20°C or less), in an area without excess humidity, in an airtight plastic bag, plastic container or glass container with as little air in it as possible to ensure that the fruit stays moist.

To plump dried fruit that has gotten too dried out, place it in a bowl, cover with hot water and let soak for about 10 minutes. Drain and dry on paper towels.

Fresh Figs

Trim off the tip and stem end. Figs can be peeled, if desired, but it is a tedious job and you lose a lot of the fruit. Cook well to soften the skin.

Garlic

"Head" refers to the whole bulb, and the cloves are the individual segments or wedges. Choose heads that are firm, with the outer paper intact and no signs of sprouting. Store in an unglazed clay garlic keeper, a paper bag or mesh netting in a dry place at a cool room temperature. Before chopping the cloves, remove the paper-like skins and trim the ends.

> The finer garlic is chopped, the hotter it will seem.

Ginger

Store unpeeled gingerroot (fresh ginger) in the refrigerator, wrapped in paper towels and sealed in a zip-lock bag. Or grate and freeze in small packages. Peel off the brown skin before grating or chopping.

Crystallized and candied ginger are the same thing: ginger that has been preserved and is coated with granulated sugar. It is available in supermarkets and bulk stores, and comes in slices or pieces.

Gooseberries

Choose firm, brightly colored green, red or white fruit. Remove "beards" by snipping off the blossom ends using small scissors, such as curved manicure scissors (keep new ones aside just for this job). Freeze as you would other berries (see page 25).

Grapes

Concord grapes are the most popular choice for jellies, but other grapes can also be used, such as Coronation grapes and, for jams, black, red or green seedless grapes. Choose firm grapes and remove stems before cooking. Use whole grapes to make juice for jelly, finely chopped grapes to make other preserves.

Kiwifruit

Either green or gold kiwifruit can be used in preserves. Choose firm, ripe fruit. Always peel kiwifruit before chopping it.

Lychees

Choose fruit that has a rough red shell. If the shell is brown, the fruit is past its prime. Keep unpeeled lychees in a perforated plastic bag in the refrigerator for up to 1 week. To use, peel and remove the pit. The flesh should be a translucent, milky white; if it is gray, throw it out. Peeled, pitted lychees can be frozen.

> ### How to Peel a Lychee
> Starting at one side of the stem and circling all the way around the fruit, score the skin with a sharp knife. Peel the two halves of the skin away from the white flesh. Pull the flesh away from the brown, nut-like seed, which will stay attached to the stem and skin. Discard skin, seed and stem.

Mangos

Choose firm, ripe fruit that gives slightly when pressed and is fragrant. (Alternatively, you can buy underripe mangos and ripen them at home in a paper bag at room temperature.) Always

> ### How to Peel and Pit a Mango
> Stand the mango on its stem end and slice along the wider sides, separating them from the pit. You will get two "cheeks" that you can scoop flesh from, or you can score the flesh in a grid pattern, push the skin from the bottom to pop pieces of flesh up, then cut them from the skin in small cubes. Cut or scrape the remaining flesh from the pit.

peel mangos and remove the pit. Ataulfo mangos, which are great for preserves because they have a tender texture and are less fibrous, are more available now. Look for frozen chopped mangos as well.

Melons

Choose melons that are fragrant at the stem end and heavy for their size. Store cantaloupe and honeydew at room temperature if using within a few days, or refrigerate for up to 3 weeks. Watermelon should be stored at room temperature. Watermelon keeps its crunch when cooked, so it is best to purée it for jams.

Nectarines

Choose firm fruit that is either ripe or slightly underripe (but without green areas). Do not peel nectarines for preserves, but do remove the pit. Nectarines are interchangeable with peaches in preserves recipes.

Onions

To prevent mold and sprouting, store onions in a dry, breathable container, such as a paper bag or a wicker basket, not in a plastic bag. Trim off the stem end and peel off dry or damaged outer layers before chopping.

Papayas

Choose fruit with smooth, wrinkle-free skin. Papayas can be ripened at home; they are ripe when the fruit gives slightly when pressed. They will keep in the refrigerator for several days after ripening. Before use, peel and cut in half; using a spoon, remove seeds from the center and discard.

Passion Fruit

Passion fruit can be yellow or dark purple, round or oval. The fruit is ready to use when the skin has no green and is slightly wrinkled in appearance. Whole fruit keeps for several weeks in the refrigerator. To use, cut in half and scoop out the edible seeds

and pulp. The fresh fruit is often expensive, but is well worth trying. You may also be able to find canned passion fruit pulp and seeds. Although passion fruit skins are high in pectin, they need to be boiled to extract it. The recipes in this book use only the interior.

Peaches

Choose firm fruit that is either ripe or slightly underripe (but without green areas). Peel and pit before using.

How to Peel Peaches

Bring a medium pot of water to a boil over high heat. Place peaches in water two at a time; boil for 20 to 30 seconds. Remove peaches with a slotted spoon and immediately immerse in a bowl of cold water. Repeat with remaining peaches. When peaches are cool enough to handle, slit down the side of the peel with a paring knife and slip off peel.

Pears

Pears are always picked underripe and must be ripened at home before use. To ripen, place in a paper bag and store at room temperature. Pears are ripe when the shoulders and neck yield to slight pressure. Always peel and core pears, except for use in some fruit butter recipes.

Peppers, Bell (Sweet)

Red, yellow, green or orange bell peppers are used to add color and taste to chutneys. Store peppers in a plastic bag in the refrigerator crisper. Before chopping, trim off the stem end and remove all seeds and membranes.

Peppers, Hot

Fresh chile peppers, such as jalapeños, habaneros, Scotch bonnets, Thai and so on, can all be used to add hotness to chutneys and jellies. Handle carefully, wearing gloves, and remove inner seeds and membranes before chopping. Chipotle peppers (smoked jalapeños) are also available, usually canned in adobo sauce.

Hot pepper flakes, dried chile peppers and crushed red chiles are all dried hot peppers. They can be used in place of fresh chile peppers to make hot pepper jelly and chutney. You can also use hot pepper sauce to turn up the heat.

Choose what pepper to use based on the level of heat you want to add.

The Scoville scale, named after the pharmacist who developed it, is used to measure the heat of a pepper. The higher the Scoville rating, the hotter the heat. For example, a bell pepper has a rating of 0, a jalapeño scores between 5,000 and 10,000, and a habanero can be anywhere from 100,000 to 500,000 Scoville units!

Pineapple

Choose a pineapple that is sweet and fragrant, with nice green leaves. Extra-sweet varieties are now available. To use, slice off the top and bottom, stand the fruit on end, pare off the skin in lengthwise pieces, remove the eyes, quarter lengthwise and remove the core.

Plumcots

These are a 50/50 cross of a plum with an apricot. There's no need to remove the peel, but do remove the pit before cooking. Other plum-apricot hybrids include pluots (75% plum, 25% apricot) and apriums (75% apricot, 25% plum).

Plums

Choose firm plums, either ripe or slightly underripe. Do not peel, but do remove the pit before cooking, unless you're using damson plums. The pits of damson plums separate naturally from the flesh while the fruit is boiling and can then be easily removed from the pot with a slotted spoon.

How to Remove the Pit from a Plum

Cut in half through the stem and twist to separate the halves. Repeat, cutting the half that still has the pit in half, then twisting the stone from the center. (This technique helps a lot when the pits are tightly imbedded in slightly underripe fruit.)

Pomegranates

Store whole fruit at room temperature for a few days, or for up to 3 months in a plastic bag in the refrigerator. To use, remove the small seeds (called "arils") from the leathery skins. Once separated from the membranes, the seeds can be refrigerated in an airtight container for several days or frozen for a few months (freeze as you would berries; see page 25). To juice a pomegranate, cut it in half and use a citrus juicer or reamer; strain to remove any seeds. One large pomegranate will yield about $\frac{1}{2}$ cup (125 mL) juice.

Prickly Pears

These are not actually pears at all, but the fruit of a cactus. Take care handling them, as they have tiny hair-like prickles that are irritating to the skin. The seeds are edible, but I prefer to remove them for preserves. The flesh is magenta.

How to Peel a Prickly Pear

Place prickly pears in a heatproof bowl and pour in boiling water to cover. Wearing rubber gloves, scrub skins with a brush to remove the tiny hair-like bristles. Rinse well. Using a sharp knife, cut the ends off and slit skins on one side from one end to the other. Peel back skin, rolling in one direction to release the pulp and seeds in one piece; collect all the pulp in a large bowl. Discard skins.

Quinces

Quinces are ripe when they have a fragrant aroma and the skins are yellow. It's not necessary to peel quince for jams or jellies, but wash well to remove any fuzz and discard the cores. Cook well to soften.

Rhubarb

Choose firm stalks that are not too large (large stalks become woody). For preserves, rhubarb is usually cut into $\frac{1}{2}$-inch (1 cm) pieces. To freeze, place chopped pieces in a freezer bag.

Rose Hips

These are the fruit of bush roses. Ideally, they are picked after the first frost, but it's okay to pick them earlier if you find deep red, shiny, plump ones. Remove the seeds, blossom ends and stems if making jam; for jelly-making, simply trim the ends. I personally use rose hips only for jelly, as the seeds can be a skin irritant and it can take a lot of time to remove them.

Shallots

This member of the onion family has a sweeter, milder flavor than a regular yellow cooking onion. Store whole for up to 6 months in a dry place that is low in temperature and humidity. To use, remove the dry, golden outer skin, trim the ends and finely dice.

Tomatoes

Green or red tomatoes can be used in chutneys and onion jam. Peel and/or seed if specified in the recipe.

Zucchini

Green or golden zucchini can be used in preserves. There's no need to peel, as zucchini has a thin, edible skin.

> Fruit-Fresh is an ascorbic acid color-keeper that prevents the natural enzymatic browning of fruit, especially apples, bananas and pears. Use according to package directions, either directly on fruit or dissolved in water.

Produce Purchase Guide

Use the following tables to figure out how much produce to buy for the recipes in this book. It's always best to purchase a little more than you think you need, just to make sure you've got enough for your recipe. You can always eat or freeze the extra!

FRESH FRUITS	QUANTITY	WEIGHT	PREPARED VOLUME
Apples	1 large	8 oz (250 g)	1 cup (250 mL) chopped; $\frac{2}{3}$ cup (150 mL) grated
Apricots	3 medium		1 cup (250 mL) chopped
Bananas	1 medium		$\frac{1}{2}$ cup (125 mL) chopped; $\frac{1}{3}$ cup (75 mL) mashed
Berries			
Blackberries		4 oz (125 g)	1 cup (250 mL) whole
Blueberries		4 oz (125 g)	1 cup (250 mL) whole; $\frac{1}{2}$ cup (125 mL) crushed
Boysenberries		4 oz (125 g)	1 cup (250 mL) whole
Cranberries	1 bag	12 oz (340 g)	3 cups (750 mL) whole
Elderberries		4 oz (125 g)	1 cup (250 mL) whole
Gooseberries		5 oz (150 g)	1 cup (250 mL) whole
Raspberries		4 oz (125 g)	1 cup (250 mL) whole
Saskatoon berries		4 oz (125 g)	1 cup (250 mL) whole
Strawberries		8 oz (250 g)	1 cup (250 mL) sliced; $\frac{1}{2}$ cup (125 mL) crushed
Cantaloupe	1 medium	4 lbs (2 kg)	4 cups (1 L) chopped
Cherries		8 oz (250 g)	1 cup (250 mL) chopped
Crabapples		4 oz (125 g)	1 cup (250 mL) whole
Currants (black and red)		6 oz (175 g)	1 cup (250 mL) whole
Figs	12	1 lb (500 g)	$2\frac{1}{2}$ cups (625 mL) chopped
Grapefruit	1 medium		1 cup (250 mL) chopped, with juices
Grapes (all varieties)		6 oz (175 g)	1 cup (250 mL)
Honeydew melon	1 medium	6 lbs (3 kg)	6 cups (1.5 L) chopped; 4 cups (1 L) puréed
Kiwifruit	3 medium		1 cup (250 mL) chopped
Lemons	1 medium		$\frac{1}{3}$ cup (75 mL) juice; 1 tbsp (15 mL) grated peel
Limes	1 medium		3 tbsp (45 mL) juice; 1 tsp (5 mL) grated peel
Mangos			
Regular	1 large		1 cup (250 mL) chopped
Ataulfo	1 medium		$\frac{3}{4}$ cup (175 mL) chopped
Nectarines	2 medium	8 oz (250 g)	1 cup (250 mL) chopped
Oranges	1 medium		$\frac{1}{3}$ cup (75 mL) juice; 4 tsp (20 mL) grated peel; $\frac{1}{2}$ cup (125 mL) chopped
Papaya	1 medium	2 lbs (1 kg)	2 cups (500 mL) chopped

FRESH FRUITS	QUANTITY	WEIGHT	PREPARED VOLUME
Passion fruit	6 or 7 medium		¾ cup (175 mL) pulp
Peaches	2 medium	8 oz (250 g)	1 cup (250 mL) chopped
Pears	2 large	1 lb (500 g)	1 cup (250 mL) chopped
Pineapple	1 medium	4 lbs (2 kg)	4 cups (1 L) chopped
Plumcots		8 oz (250 g)	1 cup (250 mL) chopped
Plums			
Black, red or yellow	3 or 4 large	8 oz (250 g)	1 cup (250 mL) chopped
Prune (blue)	4 medium	8 oz (250 g)	1 cup (250 mL) chopped
Shiro (small yellow, sugar plums)		12 oz (375 g)	1 cup (250 mL) chopped
Pomegranates	1 medium		½ cup (125 mL) juice, ¾ cup (175 mL) seeds
Watermelon	1 small		3½ cups (875 mL) purée

DRIED FRUITS	QUANTITY	WEIGHT	PREPARED VOLUME
Apricots		7 oz (210 g)	1 cup (250 mL) chopped
Cranberries		2 oz (60 g)	½ cup (125 mL)
Currants		2.7 oz (80 g)	½ cup (125 mL)
Dates		8 oz (250 g)	1 cup (250 mL) chopped
Figs	40	1 lb (500 g)	3 cups (750 mL) chopped
Raisins		3 oz (90 g)	½ cup (125 mL)

VEGETABLES	QUANTITY	WEIGHT	PREPARED VOLUME
Beets		3 lbs (750 g)	8 cups (2 L) chopped
Carrots	2 medium	5 oz (150 g)	1 cup (250 mL) shredded
Garlic	3 large heads		¼ cup (60 mL) minced or roasted
Gingerroot		1 oz (30 g)	1 tbsp (15 mL) finely grated
Onions			
Yellow (cooking)	1 medium		1 cup (250 mL) chopped
Red or white sweet	1 large		2 cups (500 mL) thinly sliced; 1½ cups (375 mL) chopped
Shallots	2 large		¾ cup (175 mL) finely chopped
Peppers			
Bell (sweet)	1 large	6 to 8 oz (175 to 250 g)	1¼ cups (300 mL) chopped
Habanero	5 to 6 large		½ cup (125 mL) minced
Jalapeño	1 medium		2 tbsp (30 mL) minced
Rhubarb		6 oz (175 g)	1 cup (250 mL) chopped
Tomatoes			
Green	7 large	3 lbs (1.5 kg)	7 cups (1.75 L) chopped
Plum (Roma)	15 medium	3 lbs (1.5 kg)	4 cups (1 L) chopped
Zucchini	one 6-inch (15 cm)	5 oz (150 g)	1 cup (250 mL) shredded

Understanding Fruit's Natural Pectin

Pectin is a type of soluble fiber and is highest in and under the skin of fruit, as well as in the seeds and flesh. Pectin, sugar and high acidity are necessary for the gelling of preserves. Some fruits have abundant natural pectin, so they do not require the addition of commercial pectin and do not need to be cooked for very long before they will set. Fruits lower in pectin must be cooked down to evaporate water and concentrate the pectin. High-pectin fruit can be combined with fruit that is lower in pectin to assist in gelling.

> Pectin comes from the Greek word *pektikos*, meaning "congealed." It was first isolated and described by Henri Braconnot in 1825. It is a soluble fiber that helps reduce blood cholesterol and has a prebiotic effect, increasing the healthy bacteria in the gut.

Commercial pectins are extracted from citrus fruit. Some preserves cannot be made without added commercial pectin, while some recipes include added pectin for speedier cooking and to make things easier for those who have trouble determining the setting point. The recipes in this book have it all worked out for you, but here are the general rules.

- For fruits that are naturally *high* in pectin, no added pectin is required for a good set. These can be paired with low-pectin fruit to boost overall pectin to adequate levels for setting.

- Fruits with *moderate* levels of pectin can be added to higher-pectin fruit combinations or cooked down to concentrate the levels.

- Fruits with *low* levels of pectin require pairing with high-pectin fruit, or need to have commercial pectin added. Wine jellies, spirited jellies and herb jellies also need added pectin.

Liquid pectin brands vary in their instructions on whether to boil after adding the pectin. If using Certo pectin in Canada, follow the package instructions, which say to boil hard for 1 minute first, then add the pectin and remove from the heat; do not boil for 1 minute after adding as instructed in the recipes in this book.

Pectin and Acid Content of Fruits

HIGH PECTIN	ACID
Apples, cooking (tart)	Low
Crabapples	High
Cranberries	High
Currants, black, red	High
Damson plums	High
Gooseberries	Medium
Grapefruit (especially in the peel)	High
Grapes (if underripe)	High
Kiwifruit	High
Lemons, limes (especially in the peel)	High
Oranges, Seville (especially in the peel)	High
Oranges, sweet (especially in the peel)	Low
Quinces	Low
Plums (sour)	High
Tangerines (especially in the peel)	Low

MEDIUM PECTIN	ACID
Apples, dessert (sweet)	Medium
Apricots	Medium
Blackberries	Medium
Blueberries	Medium
Boysenberries	High
Cherries, sweet	Medium
Cherries, sour (tart)	High
Elderberries	Medium
Grapes, Concord	Medium
Loganberries	High
Passion fruit pulp	High
Plums	Medium
Plumcots, sweet	Medium
Raspberries	Medium

LOW PECTIN	ACID
Bananas	Low
Figs	Low
Grapes, other	Medium
Guava, ripe	Low
Lychees	Low
Mangos, ripe	Low
Melons (cantaloupe, watermelon)	Low
Nectarines	Low
Papayas, ripe	Low
Peaches	Low
Pears	Low
Persimmon	Low
Pineapples	Medium
Pomegranates	Medium
Prickly pears	Low
Rose hips	Low
Rhubarb	High
Strawberries	Medium

Overripe fruit is lower in pectin and acid than ripe fruit. Underripe fruit is higher in acid and pectin and may be used in some preserves as a portion (no more than a quarter) of the overall fruit. Using too much underripe fruit increases acidity, causing preserves to set too quickly and too firmly, and can cause weeping (water oozing from the preserve).

A Word or Two on Adding Flavors

It is fun to add different flavors to jams, jellies and other preserves. Here is a brief overview of the flavorings you can use to accent or enhance the taste of the fruit. Just don't overdo it!

- **Almond:** almond liqueur, such as amaretto; almond extract; for conserves, whole almonds, toasted or untoasted

- **Balsamic vinegar:** to enhance preserves made with strawberries, figs, cherries, grapes, etc.

- **Black currant:** cassis liqueur, Ribena concentrate

- **Chocolate:** unsweetened cocoa powder, chocolate liqueur (crème de cacao is clear, so does not change the color)

- **Citrus:** citrus peel or zest; citrus juice; orange liqueur, such as Cointreau, Triple Sec or Grand Marnier; lemon liqueur, such as Limoncello

- **Coffee:** coffee-flavored liqueur, such as Kahlúa or Tia Maria; instant granules dissolved in a small amount of boiling water to make concentrated coffee

- **Floral:** lavender, rose water (gives a subtle hint of rose fragrance and flavor)

- **Fruit:** fruit extract, juice or concentrate; fruit liqueur or wine; dried fruits

- **Garlic:** fresh or roasted (do not use garlic powder)

- **Ginger:** ground ginger, fresh gingerroot, crystallized ginger

- **Heat:** fresh chile peppers (choose your hotness, from jalapeños to habaneros), dried and smoked chile peppers (such as chipotles), hot pepper flakes, hot pepper sauce

- **Herbs:** mints, lemon herbs, savory herbs (sage, rosemary, thyme), purple basil (infuse herbs in juice or wine, or chop and add to jellies, onion jams and chutneys); strong brewed herbal tea, such as mint or lemon balm

- **Honey, brown sugar:** for a change in taste from granulated sugar (can replace up to half of the granulated sugar)

- **Onions:** white or red sweet onions, yellow cooking onions, shallots (do not use onion powder)

- **Spices:** ground spices, whole spices such as cinnamon sticks, cardamom pods, cloves, star anise pods, cracked black pepper or whole peppercorns (some whole pieces can be left in after cooking)

- **Spirits:** rum, brandy, tequila, sherry, Campari, wine, peach or apple schnapps, cherry or peach brandy, lychee liqueur (Soho), melon liqueur (Midori), raspberry liqueur (Chambord), etc.

- **Teas:** black or green tea (regular or flavored), herbal teas

- **Vanilla:** vanilla extract, fresh vanilla bean

Preparation Checklist

Here is a handy checklist to photocopy and check off each time you make your preserves. It is a good tool for helping you get ready.

1. Read the recipe all the way through and check to make sure you have all the **supplies** you need, particularly new metal lids, enough sugar and the right type of pectin, if it's needed for the recipe. Check the expiry date on the pectin.

2. Prepare the **canning pot** (for processing jars). Fill it about two-thirds full with hot water. Cover and bring to a boil. The jar rack should be left out.

3. Place another large, deep **cooking pot** for the fruit on the stove burner (turned off).

4. Have a large **stainless steel spoon** ready for stirring and skimming off any foam. (You may use a wooden spoon for stirring, if desired, but do not use a spoon that has previously been used for savory dishes to stir fruit jams and jellies, in case the taste of onions, garlic or spices lingers on the spoon). Do not leave the spoon in the mixture while you are cooking, especially during the long-boil method. (Don't "cook" the spoon!)

5. Have your **jar funnel** and **jar lifter** ready.

6. Have **paper towels** ready to wipe jar lids after filling.

7. Prepare as many **new lids** as you'll need for the recipe, plus one more as a spare. Bring water to a boil in a **small saucepan** (about 2 inches/5 cm deep). Reduce heat to medium, place lids in water and bring to a simmer. Do not let the lids boil. Once they have come to a simmer, remove the pot from the heat and keep them hot until ready to use. Do not prepare too far ahead, or they will cool off too much. Place the same number of **rings** in a small bowl beside the stove. Have a **magnetic wand** ready to lift lids from hot water. (You can also use silicone-coated tongs, but be careful not to scratch the lids).

8. Prepare the **jars**. Jars must be clean and hot for filling. To sterilize, boil jars for 10 minutes in the large pot used for processing. Leave in hot water until ready to use.

9. Have an **oven mitt** ready to lift jars from the water. I use a mitt made of silicone, as the mitt often gets wet, and a wet mitt won't protect from the heat. Have an **apron**, preferably a plastic-coated one, ready to wear.

10. Place **pectin** (powdered or liquid) beside the stove. If using liquid pectin, have **scissors** ready to cut off the top of the pouch. Place the liquid pectin pouch in a 1-cup (250 mL) liquid measure or a tall glass to keep it upright.

11. Measure **sugar** into a large bowl and set it beside the stove.

12. Prepare and measure **fruit, vegetables and any other ingredients**.

13. Have a **timer** ready to time the cooking and processing.

14. Have a **tea towel** (and tray) ready to place jars on after processing.

15. Have **labels** and a pen ready to name and date jars.

16. Have yummy **bread** ready to try the jam on!

Jams

Jam is a spread made from one or more fruits, which are crushed or chopped and combined with sugar or a sugar substitute. They may be cooked or uncooked, and may be set by pectin that is naturally present in the fruit or by commercial pectin. Jams have a thick, spreadable consistency.

About Jams 39
A Word About Pectin and Sugar. 40
About Micro-Mini Jams 41
Tips for Successful Jams 41
Trouble-Shooting 42

Single-Fruit Jams 44
Mixed-Fruit Jams 88
Micro-Mini Jams. 159
Special Jams and Mincemeats. 173

About Jams

Jams range from simple one-fruit and sugar mixtures to multiple-fruit medleys and mixtures with spices or added liqueurs. We all seem to have a favorite, some personally appealing flavor that we savor on scones, English muffins, grainy breads or bagels. Maybe your favorite is something your mother or grandmother made that has special memories associated with it. Maybe it is something you picked up at a fair or market. Whatever your fancy, there is nothing like the fresh flavor of homemade jam.

This collection features jams made with and without added pectin, and includes some no-cook, low-sugar and no-sugar recipes, as well as some small batches made in the microwave. Some people find it easier to make jams with added liquid pectin or powdered pectin (also called pectin crystals) because the cooking time is shorter and these jams do not require testing for setting point. Even easier are the no-cook jams, which do not require any sterilization or hot water processing of the jars.

Many of the recipes here are brand-new creations, interesting combinations never before tried (see Mixed-Fruit Jams). I designed the recipes to be as easy to make as possible, with a smaller amount of fruit to prepare and less time at the stove. I have made as many as six jams in one day, so it should be no problem for you to make one. Jam-making can be done in stages: assembling ingredients, measuring sugar the day before, washing jars ahead and so on. Once you get organized, it goes very well.

I specifically developed the recipes not to yield excessively large quantities because I didn't want you to have to prepare too much fruit at one time. With a smaller yield, you can try a jam and see if you like it, or make a variety of different ones to have on hand or give as gifts.

Refer to the Produce Purchase Guide, page 32, to estimate the amount of fruit you'll need to purchase for these recipes.

A Word About Pectin and Sugar

Pectin is a natural substance that is high in soluble fiber. It is found in fruit, in varying levels. Some fruit is naturally high in pectin (see page 35) and will set well without added pectin. Some jams are cooked for a long time to concentrate the pectin that is naturally present. Commercial pectins are natural pectins extracted from apples and citrus fruit. When we use liquid pectin or powdered pectin (pectin crystals), we are giving low-pectin fruit a bit of a boost.

These jams were tested for sugar content using a refractometer, so no more sugar was added than was needed for a good set. Acidity was tested with a pH meter to ensure sufficient acid for gelling.

Commercial pectins come with recipes (see the leaflet inside the boxes) for most basic types of cooked jams: strawberry, raspberry, peach, etc. Commercial pectins are also used for no-cook jams, helping them retain vivid color and fresh-picked flavor. They are also necessary to help set fruit that is low in pectin of its own. Jams made with commercial pectin require more sugar but give a greater yield for the amount of fruit used.

No sugar needed and light pectins are special types called low-methoxy and help to thicken spreads with no sugar or low sugar or those that use sugar substitutes. While the texture of these spreads is not the same as that of regular jam, in some spread recipes I have combined small amounts of sugar with sugar substitutes such as Splenda and achieved good-quality results in both texture and flavor.

Always use the type of pectin specified in the recipe; otherwise, the jam probably won't set. For successful preserves, do not arbitrarily reduce the amount of sugar either.

About Micro-Mini Jams

I created micro-minis — petite batches of jam made in the microwave — to encourage people to try jam-making by starting with a few jars that can be made quickly, with minimal equipment, and then stored in the refrigerator. These unique recipes are ideal for people who love the taste of homemade jam but don't have the equipment or the room to store large pots. The micro-mini jam recipes start on page 159.

Tips for Successful Jams

1. Choose top-quality, firm, ripe fruit. Up to a quarter of your fruit can be underripe when you're making no-pectin-added jams, as underripe fruit is higher in pectin than ripe fruit. Be meticulous in your preparation of the fruit. Trim off any bad spots or blemishes, chop thoroughly and slice evenly.

2. Measure carefully.

3. When adding the sugar, stir well to ensure that it is completely dissolved, scraping down any that gets on the sides of the pot or the spoon handle. Undissolved sugar can crystallize in your jam. Heating the fruit a little before stirring in the sugar will help the sugar dissolve more quickly.

4. Stir and watch your jam. Pectin-added jams require a full boil, stirred constantly, for the entire cooking time. Simmered jams with natural pectin will thicken as they cook; reduce the heat as they thicken, stirring constantly to prevent scorching.

5. The timing for pectin-added jams should be exact; use a timer.

6. Check the expiration date on the box of pectin before beginning. Liquid pectin and powdered pectin are not interchangeable in recipes. Mix in pectin well.

7. For jams without added pectin, the timing will vary depending on the moisture and natural sugars in the fruit that year, how accurately you measure, how the fruit is chopped and the diameter of your pot. These jams must be tested to determine when they have reached the setting point (see Test for the Setting Point, page 19). Be sure to leave the test plate in the freezer long enough for the jam to cool and give an idea of the set. Do not put too much on the plate, just a spoonful. Always remove the pot from the heat to stop cooking the jam while you do the test. The mixture will usually feel quite viscous when stirred.

8. To prevent floating of the fruit pieces, especially strawberries, cherries, peaches and pears, stir the mixture slowly for 5 to 8 minutes after removing it from heat.

9. Skim any foam from the top of jam using a large metal spoon. (Not all jams will have foam.) Foam can interfere with your ability to fill jars to the proper level (the jam level becomes lower than needed for a good seal), as it is mostly air. Some recipes add butter to jam to prevent foaming; I do not like to do this.

> Please read A Primer on Preserving, pages 14 to 37. Things may have changed since you first started making preserves (such as the recent increase in processing time). If you are a beginner, there are a few important things you need to know before getting started. Many instructions are common to all preserves, so once you get it right for one, you'll sail through the others. In the primer, you will also find a handy Preparation Checklist (page 37).

Trouble-Shooting

PROBLEM: Jam does not set or is thin and runny.

Some jam will set as soon as it is cooled, while others may take up to 24 hours. If it does not set after this time, check your recipe. If it is a pectin-added jam, check the expiration date on the pectin box. You may wish to contact the manufacturer of the pectin, using the toll-free number or website on the box; they may have a solution for their particular product.

For a jam without added pectin, you may need to cook it a little longer. If the jars have all sealed properly, the contents are safe. Return the jam to the pot, discard the used lids and begin cooking and testing for the setting point. It may take only another couple of minutes after it begins to boil for it to reach the setting point. Stir constantly to prevent scorching. Then proceed with sterilized jars and new prepared lids.

PROBLEM: Jam is stiff or tough.

This can occur when fruit is high in natural pectin or when too much pectin is added. Likely the jam was overcooked. To salvage it, dilute it with fruit juice or a little liqueur and warm it in the microwave just before serving, to make it more spreadable.

PROBLEM: Jam has crystals.

Uncooked jam may develop crystals because it was not stirred well enough after the sugar was added. Fruit must be crushed well to extract juice and dissolve the sugar.

Cooked jams may crystallize because too much sugar was added (measure accurately, using a dry measure, and level the top with a straight edge or knife), or because there was undissolved sugar on the sides of the pan or the spoon handle. Stir well during cooking and scrape down the sides with a rubber scraper, if necessary.

Crystallization may also result from overcooking or from storage in a place that is too warm or has temperature fluctuations.

PROBLEM: Floating fruit.

Most fruit will break down during cooking, so this is not always a problem. Fruit will float if it is underripe or undercooked. Ensure that fruit is well crushed or finely chopped. Some fruits, especially strawberries, cherries, peaches and pears, are more likely to float than others. To prevent floating, stir the mixture slowly for 5 to 8 minutes after removing it from the heat. Then ladle jam into the first jar and wait about 30 seconds. If fruit pieces float, pour the mixture back into the pot and stir for a minute or two longer.

Single–Fruit Jams

The recipes in this section are perfect when you have a large bounty of a single seasonal fruit or for those times when you want to enjoy solo fruit flavor. I had some fun with them, adding flavor accents to make them anything but ordinary.

Dried Apricot Jam 46

Apricot Almond Jam 47

Brandied Apricot Jam 48

Black Currant Jam 49

Blackberry Jam 50

Seedless Blackberry Jam with Cassis 51

Wild Blueberry Jam with Grand Marnier 52

Boysenberry Jam 53

Sour Cherry Jam 54

Sweet Cherry Jam with Kirsch 55

Fig Jam 56

Dried Fig Jam 57

Double Ginger Jam 58

Gooseberry Jam 59

Spiced Black Grape Jam 60

Kiwi Jam 61

Spiced Mango Jam 62

Brandied Nectarine Jam 63

Spiced Peach Jam 64

Peach Lavender Jam 65

Pear Jam with Brown Sugar and Cinnamon 66

Honey Pear and Vanilla Bean Jam 67

Ginger Pear and Lime Jam 68

Ginger Pear Jam with Crème de Cacao 69

Pears and Port Jam 70

Piña Colada Jam 71

Plum Ginger Jam 72

Damson Plum Jam 73

Yellow Plum Jam 74

Plumcot Jam 75

Prickly Pear Jam with Triple Sec 76

Quince Jam 77

Raspberry Jam 78

Chocolate Raspberry Jam 79

Seedless Raspberry Lemon Verbena Jam 80

Rhubarb Jam 81

Saskatoon Berry Jam 82

Strawberry Jam 83

Strawberry Lavender Jam 84

Strawberry Jam with Rose Water 85

Strawberry Margarita Jam 86

Watermelon Jam 87

Dried Apricot Jam

Makes about six 8-ounce (250 mL) jars

The great thing about this jam is that it can be made when apricots are out of season. It has an intense apricot flavor.

— o o o —

Variation

Apricot Orange Jam: Add 2 tbsp (30 mL) finely grated orange rind to the apricots in the pot. Use 1½ cups (375 mL) orange juice in place of water for cooking. Add an orange-flavored liqueur, if desired.

It takes about 6 lbs (3 kg) of fresh apricots to make 1 lb (500 g) of dried apricots. California dried apricots are dried in halves (pits removed), while Turkish apricots are dried and sold whole, with the pit squeezed out. Dried California apricots are also a darker orange and have an intense, sweetly tart flavor.

1 lb	dried apricots	500 g
5½ cups	water, divided	1.375 L
¼ cup	lemon juice	60 mL
5 cups	granulated sugar	1.25 L
¼ cup	peach brandy, orange liqueur or amaretto (optional)	60 mL

1. Chop apricots into ½-inch (1 cm) pieces; measure 3 cups (750 mL). Place in a large bowl and add 4 cups (1 L) of the water. Cover and let stand overnight (or about 12 hours), until softened and plump.

2. Transfer soaked apricots with liquid to a large, deep, heavy-bottomed pot. Add the remaining water and lemon juice. Bring to a boil over high heat. Reduce heat and simmer, covered, for about 30 minutes or until apricots are softened.

3. Add sugar in a steady stream, stirring constantly. Bring to a boil over high heat, stirring constantly to dissolve sugar. Reduce heat to medium-high and boil rapidly, uncovered, stirring often, for 20 minutes.

4. Use a potato masher to further break down fruit. Reduce heat to medium-low and boil gently, stirring often, for about 10 minutes or until thickened. Test for setting point (for details, see page 19).

5. Remove from heat and skim off any foam. Stir in brandy (if using).

6. Ladle into sterilized jars to within ¼ inch (0.5 cm) of rim; wipe rims. Apply prepared lids and rings; tighten rings just until fingertip-tight.

7. Process jars in a boiling water canner for 10 minutes (for details, see page 20). Transfer jars to a towel-lined surface and let rest at room temperature until set. Check seals; refrigerate any unsealed jars for up to 3 weeks.

Apricot Almond Jam

Makes about six 8-ounce (250 mL) jars

A touch of almond really enhances the apricots in this jam.

— o o o —

Variations

Apricot Jam with Apricot Brandy: Replace the almond extract with 2 tbsp (30 mL) apricot brandy or amaretto. Stir in after skimming off foam.

Apricot Almond Jam with Poppy Seeds: Add 5 tsp (30 mL) poppy seeds with the almond extract.

Recipe Suggestions

Add as a glaze over French Apple Tarts (page 361) or use as a filling for Danish pastries.

Try the variation using poppy seeds and use it in place of marmalade to make the Apricot Ladder Braid (page 365) or the Fruit Loaf (page 356).

2 lbs	apricots	1 kg
3 tbsp	lemon juice	45 mL
1	package (1.75 oz/49 or 57 g) powdered pectin	1
5 cups	granulated sugar	1.25 L
1 tsp	almond extract	5 mL

1. Halve apricots and remove pits. Finely chop with a knife or by pulsing on and off in a food processor fitted with a metal blade (do not purée), using a spatula to scrape down sides. Measure $3\frac{1}{2}$ cups (875 mL).

2. In a large, heavy-bottomed pot, combine apricots and lemon juice. Stir in pectin until dissolved. Bring to a full boil over high heat, stirring constantly.

3. Add sugar in a steady stream, stirring constantly. Return to a full boil, stirring constantly to dissolve sugar. Boil hard for 1 minute.

4. Remove from heat and skim off any foam. Stir in almond extract.

5. Ladle into sterilized jars to within $\frac{1}{4}$ inch (0.5 cm) of rim; wipe rims. Apply prepared lids and rings; tighten rings just until fingertip-tight.

6. Process jars in a boiling water canner for 10 minutes (for details, see page 20). Transfer jars to a towel-lined surface and let rest at room temperature until set. Check seals; refrigerate any unsealed jars for up to 3 weeks.

Brandied Apricot Jam

*The apricot skins
intensify the flavor
and orange color of this
soft-set jam. The liqueur
may be omitted.*

—o o o—

Tip

You'll need about 5 lbs
(2.5 kg) of apricots for
this recipe.

Variation

Spiced Apricot Jam:
Omit the brandy and stir
in ¾ tsp (3 mL) ground
cinnamon and ¼ tsp
(1 mL) ground nutmeg
after skimming off any
foam.

8 cups	sliced or chopped apricots	2 L
4½ cups	granulated sugar	1.125 L
3 tbsp	brandy or apricot brandy	45 mL

1. Place apricots in a large, deep, heavy-bottomed pot. Add sugar in a steady stream, stirring constantly. Heat over medium heat, stirring constantly to dissolve sugar.

2. Increase heat to high and bring to a full boil, stirring constantly. Reduce heat to medium-high and boil rapidly, stirring often and reducing heat further as mixture thickens, for 20 to 25 minutes or until thickened. Test for setting point (for details, see page 19).

3. Remove from heat and skim off any foam. Stir in brandy.

4. Ladle into sterilized jars to within ¼ inch (0.5 cm) of rim; wipe rims. Apply prepared lids and rings; tighten rings just until fingertip-tight.

5. Process jars in a boiling water canner for 10 minutes (for details, see page 20). Transfer jars to a towel-lined surface and let rest at room temperature until set. Check seals; refrigerate any unsealed jars for up to 3 weeks.

> The kernels found inside apricot pits were once included in jam recipes, but are no longer considered safe, as they contain a toxic compound.

Black Currant Jam

**Makes about seven
8-ounce (250 mL) jars**

*Just black currants — a
solo performance with all
the berry flavor you enjoy.*

— ○ ○ ○ —

6 cups	black currants	1.5 L
4 cups	water	1 L
6 cups	granulated sugar	1.5 L

1. In a large, deep, heavy-bottomed pot, combine currants and water. Bring to a boil over high heat. Reduce heat and simmer, stirring occasionally, for 15 minutes or until softened. Use a potato masher to crush currants, if desired. Bring to a full boil over high heat, stirring constantly.

2. Add sugar in a steady stream, stirring constantly. Return to a full boil, stirring constantly to dissolve sugar. Reduce heat to medium-high and boil rapidly, stirring often and reducing heat further as mixture thickens, for 6 to 10 minutes or until thickened. Test for setting point (for details, see page 19).

3. Remove from heat and skim off any foam.

4. Ladle into sterilized jars to within 1/4 inch (0.5 cm) of rim; wipe rims. Apply prepared lids and rings; tighten rings just until fingertip-tight.

5. Process jars in a boiling water canner for 10 minutes (for details, see page 20). Transfer jars to a towel-lined surface and let rest at room temperature until set. Check seals; refrigerate any unsealed jars for up to 3 weeks.

> Black currants are used to make a liqueur called crème de cassis.

Blackberry Jam

*Blackberries have a lot
of natural pectin, so this
jam will set well without
added pectin. It is dark,
with a rich berry taste
and soft spread.*

— o o o —

Tips

You'll need about 2 lbs
(1 kg) of blackberries for this
recipe.

Blackberries can be frozen
for jam-making at a later
date. Freeze in a single
layer on a small baking
sheet or tray until solid, then
transfer to freezer bags or
containers.

8 cups	blackberries	2 L
1/2 cup	water	125 mL
1/4 cup	lemon juice	60 mL
4 cups	granulated sugar	1 L

1. In a large, deep, heavy-bottomed pot, combine blackberries, water and lemon juice. Bring to a boil over high heat. Reduce heat and simmer, stirring occasionally, for 5 minutes. Bring to a full boil over high heat, stirring constantly.

2. Add sugar in a steady stream, stirring constantly. Return to a full boil, stirring constantly to dissolve sugar. Reduce heat to medium-high and boil rapidly, stirring often and reducing heat further as mixture thickens, for 12 to 15 minutes or until thickened. Test for setting point (for details, see page 19).

3. Remove from heat and skim off any foam.

4. Ladle into sterilized jars to within 1/4 inch (0.5 cm) of rim; wipe rims. Apply prepared lids and rings; tighten rings just until fingertip-tight.

5. Process jars in a boiling water canner for 10 minutes (for details, see page 20). Transfer jars to a towel-lined surface and let rest at room temperature until set. Check seals; refrigerate any unsealed jars for up to 3 weeks.

Seedless Blackberry Jam with Cassis

*Blackberries are
abundant in natural
pectin, so this jam is
perfect for the long-
boil method. I prefer to
remove the seeds for
a smoother jam.*

— o o o —

Tips

You'll need about 2 lbs
(1 kg) of blackberries for this
recipe.

Juice and pulp tend to be
released more easily from
berries that have been
frozen.

8 cups	blackberries	2 L
2 tbsp	lemon juice	30 mL
3½ cups	granulated sugar	875 mL
¼ cup	crème de cassis	60 mL

1. In a large, flat dish, using a potato masher, crush blackberries. Press through a fine-mesh sieve (or use a food mill) to remove seeds. Measure 3½ cups (875 mL) pulp.

2. In a large, deep, heavy-bottomed pot, combine blackberry pulp and lemon juice. Bring to a boil over high heat, stirring constantly.

3. Add sugar in a steady stream, stirring constantly. Return to a boil, stirring constantly to dissolve sugar. Reduce heat to medium-high and boil rapidly, stirring often and reducing heat further as mixture thickens, for 5 to 7 minutes or until thickened. Test for setting point (for details, see page 19).

4. Remove from heat and skim off any foam. Stir in crème de cassis.

5. Ladle into sterilized jars to within ¼ inch (0.5 cm) of rim; wipe rims. Apply prepared lids and rings; tighten rings just until fingertip-tight.

6. Process jars in a boiling water canner for 10 minutes (for details, see page 20). Transfer jars to a towel-lined surface and let rest at room temperature until set. Check seals; refrigerate any unsealed jars for up to 3 weeks.

> Cassis (French for "black currant") is a short form for crème de cassis — black currant liqueur. There is no cream in it, though.

Wild Blueberry Jam with Grand Marnier

Makes about four 8-ounce (250 mL) jars

This recipe can be made with cultivated blueberries, but the intense flavor of wild ones makes this an extra-special jam. One year I made this jam with wild blueberries from Lac St-Jean, in Quebec, Canada, where there are many Tremblays, who are affectionately called "Les Bluets" (French for "blueberries").

— ○○○ —

Tip

I like to use Grand Marnier in this recipe for its sophisticated cognac flavor.

3 cups	wild blueberries	750 mL
¼ cup	water	60 mL
1 tbsp	lemon juice	15 mL
3½ cups	granulated sugar	875 mL
1	pouch (3 oz/85 mL) liquid pectin	1
3 tbsp	Grand Marnier or other orange liqueur	45 mL

1. In a large, deep, heavy-bottomed pot, combine blueberries, water and lemon juice. Bring to a boil over high heat. Reduce heat and simmer, covered, for 3 minutes. Use a potato masher to crush blueberries. Bring to a full boil over high heat, stirring constantly.

2. Add sugar in a steady stream, stirring constantly. Return to a full boil, stirring constantly to dissolve sugar.

3. Immediately stir in pectin; return to a full boil. Boil hard for 1 minute, stirring constantly.

4. Remove from heat and skim off any foam. Stir in liqueur.

5. Ladle into sterilized jars to within ¼ inch (0.5 cm) of rim; wipe rims. Apply prepared lids and rings; tighten rings just until fingertip-tight.

6. Process jars in a boiling water canner for 10 minutes (for details, see page 20). Transfer jars to a towel-lined surface and let rest at room temperature until set. Check seals; refrigerate any unsealed jars for up to 3 weeks.

Boysenberry Jam

Boysenberries are a hybrid berry — a cross between blackberries, raspberries and loganberries. If you like berry jams, give this one a try. It's one of my favorites. Frozen-fruit suppliers (see Resources, page 372) may sell boysenberries if they are not grown in your area.

— o o o —

Tip

For pictures of various unusual edible berries, visit www.garden.org/ediblelandscaping/?page=september_unusual.

| 7 cups | boysenberries | 1.75 L |
| 4 cups | granulated sugar | 1 L |

1. Place boysenberries in a large, deep, heavy-bottomed pot. Bring to a boil over high heat, stirring occasionally. Reduce heat and simmer, stirring often, for about 3 minutes or until berries begin to release some juice. Bring to a boil over high heat, stirring constantly.

2. Add sugar in a steady stream, stirring constantly. Return to a boil, stirring constantly to dissolve sugar. Reduce heat to medium-high and boil rapidly, stirring often and reducing heat further as mixture thickens, for 8 to 12 minutes or until thickened. Test for setting point (for details, see page 19).

3. Remove from heat and skim off any foam.

4. Ladle into sterilized jars to within $\frac{1}{4}$ inch (0.5 cm) of rim; wipe rims. Apply prepared lids and rings; tighten rings just until fingertip-tight.

5. Process jars in a boiling water canner for 10 minutes (for details, see page 20). Transfer jars to a towel-lined surface and let rest at room temperature until set. Check seals; refrigerate any unsealed jars for up to 3 weeks.

> Horticulturist Rudolph Boysen created this hybrid berry in 1923. It has the shape of a large raspberry, a dark purple color and a rich sweet-tart flavor.

Sour Cherry Jam

**Makes about five
8-ounce (250 mL) jars**

*Sour cherries make
delicious jam. The
addition of liqueur
heightens the flavor.
Great for gift-giving.*

— o o o —

Tips

The best cherry pitters have
a piece that holds the cherry
while the plunger pokes out
the pits.

You can use a food
processor to chop cherries;
just make sure all of the pits
are removed first, then pulse
a few times, scrape down
the sides and pulse again.
Do not purée.

4 cups	finely chopped pitted sour (tart) cherries	1 L
1 tbsp	lemon juice	15 mL
1	package (1.75 oz/49 or 57 g) powdered pectin	1
4½ cups	granulated sugar	1.125 L
2 tbsp	amaretto or cherry liqueur (optional)	30 mL

1. In a large, deep, heavy-bottomed pot, combine cherries and lemon juice. Stir in pectin until dissolved. Bring to a full boil over high heat, stirring constantly.

2. Add sugar in a steady stream, stirring constantly. Return to a full boil, stirring constantly to dissolve sugar. Boil hard for 1 minute.

3. Remove from heat and skim off any foam. Stir in liqueur (if using). Stir for 5 to 8 minutes to prevent floating fruit.

4. Ladle into sterilized jars to within ¼ inch (0.5 cm) of rim; wipe rims. Apply prepared lids and rings; tighten rings just until fingertip-tight.

5. Process jars in a boiling water canner for 10 minutes (for details, see page 20). Transfer jars to a towel-lined surface and let rest at room temperature until set. Check seals; refrigerate any unsealed jars for up to 3 weeks.

> Most sour (tart) cherries sold in North America are Montmorency. In Europe, cherries are grown in Turkey, Italy, Spain, Ukraine, Romania, Greece and the Baltic countries.

Sweet Cherry Jam with Kirsch

*I like to use dark red
sweet cherries such
as Bing for this recipe.
Rainier cherries (a Bing
and Van cherry cross
with a creamy yellow
flesh and a bright red
blush) may also be used.*

— ○○○ —

Tip
You'll need about 2 lbs
(1 kg) of cherries for this
recipe.

Variations
*Sweet Cherry Jam
with Balsamic Vinegar:*
Replace the lemon juice
with balsamic vinegar.

*Sweet Cherry Jam with
Vanilla:* Split 1 vanilla
bean lengthwise and
scrape out seeds with a
paring knife. Add bean
and seeds to pot after
stirring in pectin. Remove
bean before ladling jam
into jars.

*Spiced Sweet Cherry
Jam:* Add ½ tsp (2 mL)
ground cinnamon with
the sugar.

4 cups	finely chopped pitted sweet cherries	1 L
¼ cup	lemon juice	60 mL
1	package (1.75 oz/49 or 57 g) powdered pectin	1
4 cups	granulated sugar	1 L
¼ cup	cherry liqueur, such as Kirsch, or cherry brandy	60 mL

1. In a large, deep, heavy-bottomed pot, combine cherries and lemon juice. Stir in pectin until dissolved. Bring to a full boil over high heat, stirring constantly.

2. Add sugar in a steady stream, stirring constantly. Return to a full boil, stirring constantly to dissolve sugar. Boil hard for 1 minute.

3. Remove from heat and skim off any foam. Stir in liqueur.

4. Ladle into sterilized jars to within ¼ inch (0.5 cm) of rim; wipe rims. Apply prepared lids and rings; tighten rings just until fingertip-tight.

5. Process jars in a boiling water canner for 10 minutes (for details, see page 20). Transfer jars to a towel-lined surface and let rest at room temperature until set. Check seals; refrigerate any unsealed jars for up to 3 weeks.

Fig Jam

Makes about four 8-ounce (250 mL) jars

The purple-brown skins turn the jam red after cooking. Place a dollop on top of aged (old) Cheddar cheese on a cracker for a tasty treat.

—ooo—

Tips

You'll need about 2 lbs (1 kg) of figs (about 24 figs) for this recipe.

If desired, chop figs in a food processor fitted with a metal blade by pulsing on and off. Do not purée.

Variations

Fig Honey Jam: Replace ³⁄₄ cup (175 mL) of the sugar with an equal amount of liquid honey.

Spiced Fig Jam: Add ¹⁄₄ tsp (1 mL) ground cardamom, or ¹⁄₂ tsp (2 mL) ground cinnamon and ¹⁄₄ tsp (1 mL) ground nutmeg, with the lemon juice.

Fig Orange Jam: Replace 1 cup (250 mL) of the chopped figs with 1 tbsp (15 mL) grated orange rind and 1 cup (250 mL) chopped peeled oranges.

Fig Jam with Balsamic Vinegar: Replace the lemon juice with an equal amount of balsamic vinegar, or more to taste.

5 cups	finely chopped fresh dark figs, stems removed	1.25 L
¹⁄₂ cup	water	125 mL
¹⁄₄ cup	lemon juice	60 mL
3¹⁄₂ cups	granulated sugar	875 mL

1. In a large, deep, heavy-bottomed pot, combine figs and water. Bring to a boil over high heat. Reduce heat and simmer, covered, stirring occasionally, for about 10 minutes or until softened. Use a potato masher to break up skins.

2. Stir in lemon juice. Add sugar in a steady stream, stirring constantly. Bring to a boil over medium heat, stirring constantly to dissolve sugar. Reduce heat to medium-low and boil gently, uncovered, stirring often, for 10 to 12 minutes or until thickened. Test for setting point (for details, see page 19).

3. Remove from heat and skim off any foam.

4. Ladle into sterilized jars to within ¹⁄₄ inch (0.5 cm) of rim; wipe rims. Apply prepared lids and rings; tighten rings just until fingertip-tight.

5. Process jars in a boiling water canner for 10 minutes (for details, see page 20). Transfer jars to a towel-lined surface and let rest at room temperature until set. Check seals; refrigerate any unsealed jars for up to 3 weeks.

> To add chocolate flavor to this recipe (or any recipe), use unsweetened cocoa powder and follow the instructions for Chocolate Raspberry Jam on page 79.

Dried Fig Jam

This jam has a sweet, honey-like flavor. Try putting some in a warm salad dressing with cider vinegar, to go over mesclun mix with goat cheese (or blue cheese), sliced apples or pears and toasted walnuts.

— o o o —

Variations

Fig Honey Jam: Replace 1 cup (250 mL) of the sugar with an equal amount of liquid honey.

Spiced Fig Jam: Add 1/4 tsp (1 mL) ground cardamom with the lemon juice.

Fig Orange Jam: Discard liquid after soaking figs; instead, use 2 1/2 cups (625 mL) orange juice for cooking. Add 1 tbsp (15 mL) finely grated orange rind, if desired, with the lemon juice.

Fig Jam with Rum: Add 2 tbsp (30 mL) amber rum after removing jam from the heat.

1 1/4 lbs	dried figs	625 g
3 cups	boiling water	750 mL
3 tbsp	lemon juice	45 mL
3 3/4 cups	granulated sugar	925 mL

1. Place figs in a large heatproof bowl and cover with boiling water. Let stand for about 8 hours or overnight to soften. Drain, reserving soaking liquid.

2. Remove stems and coarsely chop figs. Place in a large, deep, heavy-bottomed pot. Measure 2 1/2 cups (625 mL) of the soaking liquid; add to pot. Stir in lemon juice.

3. Bring to a boil over high heat. Reduce heat and simmer, covered, stirring occasionally, for about 40 minutes or until softened.

4. In a food processor fitted with a metal blade, purée figs with liquid until smooth. Measure 4 cups (1 L) and return to pot.

5. Add sugar in a steady stream, stirring constantly. Bring to a full boil over high heat, stirring constantly to dissolve sugar. Reduce heat to medium-high and boil rapidly, uncovered, stirring often and reducing heat further as mixture thickens, for about 20 minutes or until thickened. Test for setting point (for details, see page 19).

6. Remove from heat and skim off any foam.

7. Ladle into sterilized jars to within 1/4 inch (0.5 cm) of rim; wipe rims. Apply prepared lids and rings; tighten rings just until fingertip-tight.

8. Process jars in a boiling water canner for 10 minutes (for details, see page 20). Transfer jars to a towel-lined surface and let rest at room temperature until set. Check seals; refrigerate any unsealed jars for up to 3 weeks.

> Golden, nutty-flavored Calimyrna figs and dark, sweet Mission figs are the two most common types of dried figs.

Double Ginger Jam

**Makes about four
8-ounce (250 mL) jars**

*Why settle for ginger
when you can have double
ginger? The small bits
of sweet crystallized
ginger add interesting
flavor bites.*

— ○ ○ ○ —

Tips

Supermarkets now carry
all-natural apple juice, which
is unfiltered and looks more
like apple cider, though it
may not be as tart. Shake
before using.

You'll need about 4 oz
(125 g) of gingerroot and
about 3½ oz (100 g) of
crystallized ginger for this
recipe.

2½ cups	all-natural apple juice (see tip, at left)	625 mL
¼ cup	finely grated gingerroot	60 mL
½ cup	finely chopped crystallized ginger	125 mL
2 tbsp	lemon juice	30 mL
3½ cups	granulated sugar	875 mL
1	pouch (3 oz/85 mL) liquid pectin	1

1. In a large, deep, heavy-bottomed pot, combine apple juice and grated ginger. Bring to a boil over high heat. Reduce heat and simmer, covered, for 10 minutes.

2. Stir in crystallized ginger and lemon juice. Add sugar in a steady stream, stirring constantly. Bring to a full boil over high heat, stirring constantly to dissolve sugar.

3. Immediately stir in pectin; return to a full boil. Boil hard for 1 minute, stirring constantly.

4. Remove from heat and skim off any foam. Stir for 5 to 8 minutes to prevent floating ginger.

5. Ladle into sterilized jars to within ¼ inch (0.5 cm) of rim; wipe rims. Apply prepared lids and rings; tighten rings just until fingertip-tight.

6. Process jars in a boiling water canner for 10 minutes (for details, see page 20). Transfer jars to a towel-lined surface and let rest at room temperature until set. Check seals; refrigerate any unsealed jars for up to 3 weeks.

> Crystallized ginger and candied ginger are the same thing. It is fresh ginger that has been preserved by cooking in a sugar syrup, then coated with sugar.

Gooseberry Jam

7 cups	gooseberries, beards removed	1.75 L
1/2 cup	water, cranberry cocktail or pomegranate juice	125 mL
4 1/2 cups	granulated sugar	1.125 L

Gooseberry jam has a unique flavor that is slightly tart, similar to rhubarb jam. Gooseberries have abundant natural pectin for a good set. Make this jam with green, red or white berries.

— o o o —

Tip

A small pair of curved manicure scissors (used only for food) are perfect for removing beards (blossom ends) from gooseberries and black currants.

Variations

Gingered Gooseberry Jam: Slice a 1-inch (2.5 cm) round piece of peeled gingerroot 1 1/2 inch (4 cm) long into about 6 rounds. Add to pot with gooseberries. Remove and discard before ladling jam into jars.

Rose Water Gooseberry Jam: Stir in 1/4 cup (50 mL) rose water with the sugar.

Spiced Gooseberry Jam: Add 1/2 tsp (2 mL) ground cardamom with the sugar.

1. In a large, deep, heavy-bottomed pot, combine gooseberries and water. Bring to a boil over high heat. Reduce heat and simmer, covered, stirring occasionally, for 5 minutes or until berries are softened. Crush any whole berries with back of spoon. Bring to a boil over high heat, stirring constantly.

2. Add sugar in a steady stream, stirring constantly. Return to a boil, stirring constantly to dissolve sugar. Reduce heat to medium-high and boil rapidly, uncovered, stirring often and reducing heat further as mixture thickens, for 10 to 12 minutes or until thickened. Test for setting point (for details, see page 19).

3. Remove from heat and skim off any foam.

4. Ladle into sterilized jars to within 1/4 inch (0.5 cm) of rim; wipe rims. Apply prepared lids and rings; tighten rings just until fingertip-tight.

5. Process jars in a boiling water canner for 10 minutes (for details, see page 20). Transfer jars to a towel-lined surface and let rest at room temperature until set. Check seals; refrigerate any unsealed jars for up to 3 weeks.

> Gooseberries may be frozen whole. Remove from stems, trim away blossom ends (beards) and place berries in freezer storage containers or plastic bags. Some markets that sell frozen fruit will have gooseberries.

Spiced Black Grape Jam

Makes about six 8-ounce (250 mL) jars

Not your ordinary grape jelly taste! This jam is mildly spiced and has an almost sweet cherry–like flavor with a lovely purple-red color.

— o o o —

Tip
For the freshest taste, grind cardamom seeds in a clean coffee or spice grinder, or using a mortar and pestle.

Variations
Balsamic Grape Jam: Replace the lemon juice with ⅓ cup (75 mL) balsamic vinegar.

Black Grape Orange Jam: Omit the cinnamon and use only the ¼ tsp (1 mL) nutmeg, if desired. Replace ⅔ cup (150 mL) of the chopped grapes with chopped peeled orange or orange segments.

2 lb	black seedless grapes	1 kg
¼ cup	lemon juice	60 mL
6 cups	granulated sugar	1.5 L
½ tsp	ground cinnamon	2 mL
¼ tsp	ground cardamom or ground nutmeg	1 mL
1	pouch (3 oz/85 mL) liquid pectin	1

1. Remove grapes from stems. In a food processor fitted with a metal blade, coarsely chop grapes, in batches, by pulsing on and off. Measure to make 3⅔ cups (900 mL).

2. In a large, deep, heavy-bottomed pot, combine grapes and lemon juice. Bring to a boil over high heat. Reduce heat and simmer, covered, stirring occasionally, for about 20 minutes or until grape skins are softened.

3. Add sugar in a steady stream, stirring constantly. Stir in spices. Bring to a full boil over high heat, stirring constantly to dissolve sugar.

4. Immediately stir in pectin; return to a full boil. Boil hard for 1 minute, stirring constantly.

5. Remove from heat and skim off any foam.

6. Ladle into sterilized jars to within ¼ inch (0.5 cm) of rim; wipe rims. Apply prepared lids and rings; tighten rings just until fingertip-tight.

7. Process jars in a boiling water canner for 10 minutes (for details, see page 20). Transfer jars to a towel-lined surface and let rest at room temperature until set. Check seals; refrigerate any unsealed jars for up to 3 weeks.

> Cardamom is common to East Indian cooking and Scandinavian baking (breads, cookies, cakes, etc.) and is aromatic and spicy-sweet. It is quickly making its way into North American spice cupboards and is definitely worth the money you spend for it. You will have had a hint of it if you have ever tried chai, an Indian tea made with milk and spices. Spiced Mango Jam (page 62) and Spiced Peach Jam (page 64) are also made with cardamom.

Kiwi Jam

*You can make this recipe
with traditional green
kiwis or the newer gold
kiwis, which have a
sweet, tropical flavor and
smooth, hairless, bronze-
colored skin.*

— o o o —

Tip
Premeasure the sugar into a
large bowl to make it easier
to add to the pot in a steady
flow while stirring constantly
to dissolve it.

5 cups	finely chopped or mashed peeled green or gold kiwifruit	1.25 L
2 tbsp	lemon juice	30 mL
1	package (1.75 oz/49 or 57 g) powdered pectin	1
5½ cups	granulated sugar	1.375 L
2 tbsp	lychee liqueur (optional)	30 mL

1. In a large, deep, heavy-bottomed pot, combine kiwis and lemon juice. Stir in pectin until dissolved. Bring to a full boil over high heat, stirring constantly.

2. Add sugar in a steady stream, stirring constantly. Return to a full boil, stirring constantly to dissolve sugar. Boil hard for 1 minute.

3. Remove from heat and skim off any foam. Stir in liqueur (if using). Stir for 5 to 8 minutes to prevent floating fruit.

4. Ladle into sterilized jars to within ¼ inch (0.5 cm) of rim; wipe rims. Apply prepared lids and rings; tighten rings just until fingertip-tight.

5. Process jars in a boiling water canner for 10 minutes (for details, see page 20). Transfer jars to a towel-lined surface and let rest at room temperature until set. Check seals; refrigerate any unsealed jars for up to 3 weeks.

Kiwifruit, also known as Chinese gooseberries, were brought to New Zealand (as seeds) from China in 1904 by teacher Isabel Fraser. Hayward Wright grew the first vines in 1928. New Zealand began exporting the fruit to England in 1952, naming it after their national symbol, a brown-feathered bird called a kiwi. In 1970, the Kiwifruit Marketing Board was formed and the Zespri brand was launched to indicate kiwis from New Zealand.

Spiced Mango Jam

Makes about five 8-ounce (250 mL) jars

Mangos are much more available and affordable than ever before, especially fragrant Ataulfo mangos, which used to be available only in ethnic markets. I buy them by the case when I find them sold that way, as it is more economical.

— o o o —

Variation

Mango Mint Jam: Omit the spices and brown sugar. Increase the granulated sugar to 5½ cups (1.375 L). Stir in ¼ cup (60 mL) finely chopped fresh mint leaves (spearmint or orange mint) after adding the pectin.

4 cups	finely chopped mangos	1 L
¼ cup	lemon juice	60 mL
½ tsp	ground cinnamon	2 mL
½ tsp	ground cardamom	2 mL
3½ cups	granulated sugar	875 mL
2 cups	packed brown sugar	500 mL
2	pouches (each 3 oz/85 mL) liquid pectin	2

1. In a large, deep, heavy-bottomed pot, combine mangos, lemon juice, cinnamon and cardamom. Bring to a full boil over high heat, stirring constantly.

2. Add granulated sugar in a steady stream, stirring constantly. Stir in brown sugar. Return to a full boil, stirring constantly to dissolve sugar.

3. Immediately stir in pectin; return to a full boil. Boil hard for 1 minute, stirring constantly.

4. Remove from heat and skim off any foam. Stir for 5 to 8 minutes to prevent floating fruit.

5. Ladle into sterilized jars to within ¼ inch (0.5 cm) of rim; wipe rims. Apply prepared lids and rings; tighten rings just until fingertip-tight.

6. Process jars in a boiling water canner for 10 minutes (for details, see page 20). Transfer jars to a towel-lined surface and let rest at room temperature until set. Check seals; refrigerate any unsealed jars for up to 3 weeks.

Mangos are fragrant and juicy when ripe. They are grown in tropical regions such as India, the West Indies, Mexico, Florida and Hawaii. Ataulfo mangos (also called champagne mangos), cultivated in Chiapas, Mexico, are almost fiberless. Mangos are rich in vitamins A, C and D. One large regular mango yields about 1 cup (250 mL) chopped; an Ataulfo mango yields about ¾ cup (175 mL) chopped.

Brandied Nectarine Jam

I like the way the peel of the nectarine adds to the overall flavor of jams and conserves. In addition, it takes less time, as you save the step of peeling.

— o o o —

Tip

You'll need about 3 lbs (1.5 kg) of nectarines (about 8 medium) for this recipe.

Variations

Spiced Nectarine Jam: Stir in 1 tsp (5 mL) ground cinnamon and 1/4 tsp (1 mL) ground nutmeg after stirring in the pectin.

Brandied Peach Jam: Use peeled peaches in place of the nectarines.

Bourbon Southern Peach Jam: Use peeled peaches in place of the nectarines and bourbon in place of the brandy.

4 cups	finely chopped unpeeled nectarines	1 L
3 tbsp	lemon juice	45 mL
1	package (1.75 oz/49 or 57 g) powdered pectin	1
4 1/2 cups	granulated sugar	1.125 L
1/4 cup	peach brandy, peach schnapps or apricot brandy	60 mL

1. In a large, deep, heavy-bottomed pot, combine nectarines and lemon juice. Stir in pectin until dissolved. Bring to a full boil over high heat, stirring constantly.

2. Add sugar in a steady stream, stirring constantly. Return to a full boil, stirring constantly to dissolve sugar. Boil hard for 1 minute.

3. Remove from heat and skim off any foam. Stir in brandy. Stir for 5 to 8 minutes to prevent floating fruit.

4. Ladle into sterilized jars to within 1/4 inch (0.5 cm) of rim; wipe rims. Apply prepared lids and rings; tighten rings just until fingertip-tight.

5. Process jars in a boiling water canner for 10 minutes (for details, see page 20). Transfer jars to a towel-lined surface and let rest at room temperature until set. Check seals; refrigerate any unsealed jars for up to 3 weeks.

> Nectarines are a close relative of the peach, with a thin, smooth skin and firm flesh. In jams, they are always used unpeeled.

Spiced Peach Jam

Makes about six 8-ounce (250 mL) jars

This jam features whole spices, which are left in the jam for extra flavor and interest.

— o o o —

Tip

How to Peel Peaches: Bring a medium pot of water to a boil over high heat. Place peaches in water two at a time; boil for 20 to 30 seconds. Remove peaches with a slotted spoon and immediately immerse in a bowl of cold water. Repeat with remaining peaches. When peaches are cool enough to handle, slit down the side of the peel with a paring knife and slip off peel. Cut peaches in half and remove pits.

Recipe Suggestion

Use this jam as a cake filling or to fill the Vanilla Jelly Roll (page 368).

Variation

Peach Jam: Omit the spices.

5 cups	finely chopped peeled peaches (see tip, at left)	1.25 L
12	whole cardamom pods	12
6	pieces (each 2 inches/5 cm) cinnamon stick	6
6	whole cloves	6
1	package (1.75 oz/49 or 57 g) powdered pectin	1
5 cups	granulated sugar	1.25 L

1. In a large, deep, heavy-bottomed pot, combine peaches, cardamom, cinnamon and cloves. Bring to a full boil over high heat. Boil for 3 minutes, stirring constantly. Turn off heat and let stand for 30 minutes, stirring occasionally.

2. Stir in pectin until dissolved. Bring to a full boil over high heat, stirring constantly.

3. Add sugar in a steady stream, stirring constantly. Return to a full boil, stirring constantly to dissolve sugar. Boil hard for 1 minute.

4. Remove from heat and skim off any foam. Stir for 5 to 8 minutes to prevent floating fruit.

5. Ladle into sterilized jars to within $\frac{1}{4}$ inch (0.5 cm) of rim. Make sure there are 2 cardamom pods, a piece of cinnamon stick and a clove in each jar. Wipe rims; apply prepared lids and rings. Tighten rings just until fingertip-tight.

6. Process jars in a boiling water canner for 10 minutes (for details, see page 20). Transfer jars to a towel-lined surface and let rest at room temperature until set. Check seals; refrigerate any unsealed jars for up to 3 weeks.

> Cardamom is a sweet spice commonly used in Scandinavian baking and East Indian cuisine. It can be found at most grocery stores, specialty food stores or bulk food stores. Store in a small glass bottle or jar to preserve the flavor.

Brandied Nectarine Jam (page 63)

Fig Jam (page 56)
and Kiwi Jam (page 61)

Apricot Almond Jam with
Poppy Seeds (variation, page 47)

Prickly Pear and Pear Jam (page 134)

Peach Lavender Jam

Makes about seven

3 tbsp	dried organic lavender flowers	45 mL
¼ cup	boiling water	75 mL
	finely chopped peeled peaches (see tip, page 64)	1 L
	lemon juice	60 mL
	granulated sugar	1.8 L
	pouches (each 3 oz/85 mL) liquid pectin	2

...ce lavender in a small heatproof bowl. Pour boiling ...ter over flowers; let steep for 20 minutes. Strain, ...erving liquid; discard lavender.

...a large, deep, heavy-bottomed pot, combine lavender ...usion, peaches and lemon juice. Bring to a full boil ...r high heat, stirring constantly.

...d sugar in a steady stream, stirring constantly. Return ...a full boil, stirring constantly to dissolve sugar.

...mediately stir in pectin; return to a full boil. Boil ...rd for 1 minute, stirring constantly.

...move from heat and skim off any foam. Stir for 5 to ...minutes to prevent floating fruit.

...dle into sterilized jars to within ¼ inch (0.5 cm) of ...m; wipe rims. Apply prepared lids and rings; tighten ...ngs just until fingertip-tight.

...ocess jars in a boiling water canner for 10 minutes ...r details, see page 20). Transfer jars to a towel-lined ...rface and let rest at room temperature until set. Check ...als; refrigerate any unsealed jars for up to 3 weeks.

Only use lavender that has been grown without pesticides or herbicides. Lavender will grow in the United States, the U.K. and many areas of Canada (check with a local nursery). It thrives in full sun and well-drained soil. Pick flower clusters just as flowers begin to open. Let dry, then store in a covered glass container. Leave whole for the best flavor preservation; crumble when using. Dried lavender flowers for culinary use are available at some specialty kitchen stores or at herb fairs and growers.

Original **CERTO** ®
LIQUIDE

TRUCS POUR BIEN RÉUSSIR LES CONFITURES

- On ne peut pas substituer les produits CERTO l'un pour l'autre ou pour une autre marque. Utilisez le produit CERTO mentionné dans la recette.

- Vérifiez toujours la date « meilleur avant » avant de commencer.

- Ne réduisez pas la quantité de sucre car elle aide à la gélification des confitures et des gelées.

- *Ne doublez pas les recettes.* Cela pourrait empêcher la confiture ou la gelée de gélifier.

- Mesurez les ingrédients avec précision. Les fruits ou les jus préparés devraient être mesurés dans une tasse à mesurer en verre après les avoir hachés ou écrasés. Le sucre devrait être mesuré dans une tasse à mesurer pour ingrédients secs.

- *Utilisez des fruits mûrs et fermes* ou des fruits surgelés non sucrés qui ont été dégelés au réfrigérateur. Les fruits trop mûrs ou en trop grande quantité affecteront la gélification. Mesurez avec le jus.

- Écrasez les petits fruits *avec un pilon à pommes de terre;* n'utilisez pas un robot culinaire.

Pear Jam with Brown Sugar and Cinnamon

Makes about five 8-ounce (250 mL) jars

Bartlett pears are a good choice for this amazing dark and delicious jam. I converted my friend Cindy, who thought she would not like pear jam, then asked to take the rest of the jar home. Make sure the pears are tender but not too soft.

— o o o —

Tips

You'll need about 4 lbs (2 kg) of pears (about 5 large) for this recipe.

Lemon juice (the amount in the recipe) or a small amount of ascorbic acid color-keeper (such as Fruit-Fresh) will prevent cut pears from browning. As you go, sprinkle a bit over chopped pears and stir in.

4 cups	finely chopped peeled pears	1 L
1/4 cup	lemon juice	60 mL
1	package (1.75 oz/49 or 57 g) powdered pectin	1
3 cups	granulated sugar	750 mL
2 cups	packed brown sugar	500 mL
1/2 tsp	ground cinnamon	2 mL

1. In a large, deep, heavy-bottomed pot, combine pears and lemon juice. Stir in pectin until dissolved. Bring to a full boil over high heat, stirring constantly.

2. Add granulated sugar in a steady stream, stirring constantly. Stir in brown sugar and cinnamon. Return to a full boil, stirring constantly to dissolve sugar. Boil hard for 1 minute.

3. Remove from heat and skim off any foam. Stir for 5 to 8 minutes to prevent floating fruit.

4. Ladle into sterilized jars to within 1/4 inch (0.5 cm) of rim; wipe rims. Apply prepared lids and rings; tighten rings just until fingertip-tight.

5. Process jars in a boiling water canner for 10 minutes (for details, see page 20). Transfer jars to a towel-lined surface and let rest at room temperature until set. Check seals; refrigerate any unsealed jars for up to 3 weeks.

Honey Pear and Vanilla Bean Jam

Makes about five 8-ounce (250 mL) jars

This delightful jam has lots of tiny vanilla seeds (known as the "caviar" of the vanilla bean) and a touch of honey.

— o o o —

Tips

You'll need about 4 lbs (2 kg) of pears (about 5 large) for this recipe.

Choose a vanilla bean that is moist, plump and dark chocolate brown to black in color. It should be moist enough to tie into a knot and not break or split. Longer beans will have more "caviar," the seeds that give the bean its flavor.

Variation

Honey Pear and Cardamom Jam: Replace the vanilla bean with ½ tsp (2 mL) ground cardamom.

4 cups	finely chopped peeled pears	1 L
¼ cup	lemon juice	60 mL
1	vanilla bean	1
4 cups	granulated sugar	1 L
½ cup	liquid honey	125 mL
2	pouches (each 3 oz/85 mL) liquid pectin	2

1. In a large, deep, heavy-bottomed pot, combine pears and lemon juice.

2. Split vanilla bean lengthwise and scrape out seeds with a paring knife. Add bean and seeds to pot. Bring to a full boil over high heat, stirring constantly.

3. Add sugar in a steady stream, stirring constantly. Stir in honey. Return to a full boil, stirring constantly to dissolve sugar.

4. Immediately stir in pectin; return to a full boil. Boil hard for 1 minute, stirring constantly.

5. Remove from heat and skim off any foam. Remove and discard vanilla bean. Stir for 5 to 8 minutes to prevent floating fruit.

6. Ladle into sterilized jars to within ¼ inch (0.5 cm) of rim; wipe rims. Apply prepared lids and rings; tighten rings just until fingertip-tight.

7. Process jars in a boiling water canner for 10 minutes (for details, see page 20). Transfer jars to a towel-lined surface and let rest at room temperature until set. Check seals; refrigerate any unsealed jars for up to 3 weeks.

> Vanilla is the second most expensive seasoning, after saffron.

Ginger Pear and Lime Jam

*Fresh gingerroot and
crystallized ginger are
both used to give this jam
its special flavor and bite.
Lime rind and juice give
it an interesting taste
sensation.*

—○○○—

Tip
You'll need about 4 lbs
(2 kg) of pears (about
5 large) for this recipe.

Variation
Pear Ginger Jam: Omit
the lime rind and replace
the lime juice with lemon
juice.

4 cups	finely chopped peeled pears	1 L
1/2 cup	minced crystallized ginger	125 mL
2 tbsp	grated gingerroot	30 mL
1 tbsp	grated lime rind	15 mL
1/4 cup	lime juice	60 mL
4 cups	granulated sugar	1 L

1. In a large, deep, heavy-bottomed pot, combine pears, crystallized ginger, grated ginger, lime rind and lime juice. Bring to a full boil over high heat, stirring constantly.

2. Add sugar in a steady stream, stirring constantly. Return to a full boil, stirring constantly to dissolve sugar. Reduce heat to medium-high and boil rapidly, stirring often and reducing heat further as mixture thickens, for 12 to 14 minutes or until thickened. Test for setting point (for details, see page 19).

3. Remove from heat and skim off any foam.

4. Ladle into sterilized jars to within 1/4 inch (0.5 cm) of rim; wipe rims. Apply prepared lids and rings; tighten rings just until fingertip-tight.

5. Process jars in a boiling water canner for 10 minutes (for details, see page 20). Transfer jars to a towel-lined surface and let rest at room temperature until set. Check seals; refrigerate any unsealed jars for up to 3 weeks.

> Although ginger is often called gingerroot, it is not a root but a creeping perennial tuber, a sort of horizontal stem from which other ginger plants can grow. It is indigenous to tropical Asia and other tropical areas, including Jamaica, and is cultivated in the United States, India and China.

Ginger Pear Jam
with Crème de Cacao

**Makes about six
8-ounce (250 mL) jars**

*Ginger, pears and a hint
of chocolate! The blend
of flavors is exquisite.*

—○○○—

Tip
You'll need about 6 large
pears for this recipe.

Recipe Suggestions
This jam is perfect to fill a
chocolate cake, crêpes or a
jelly roll (see Vanilla Jelly Roll,
page 368).

Warm it up and serve over
waffles; add a dollop of
whipped cream.

5 cups	finely chopped peeled pears	1.25 L
1/3 cup	minced crystallized ginger	75 mL
1 tbsp	finely grated gingerroot	15 mL
1 tbsp	lemon juice	15 mL
1	package (1.75 oz/49 or 57 g) powdered pectin	1
4 cups	granulated sugar	1 L
1/2 cup	crème de cacao liqueur	125 mL

1. In a large, deep, heavy-bottomed pot, combine pears, crystallized ginger, grated ginger and lemon juice. Stir in pectin until dissolved. Bring to a full boil over high heat, stirring constantly.

2. Add sugar in a steady stream, stirring constantly. Return to a full boil, stirring constantly to dissolve sugar. Boil hard for 1 minute.

3. Remove from heat and skim off any foam. Stir in liqueur. Stir for 5 to 8 minutes to prevent floating fruit.

4. Ladle into sterilized jars to within 1/4 inch (0.5 cm) of rim; wipe rims. Apply prepared lids and rings; tighten rings just until fingertip-tight.

5. Process jars in a boiling water canner for 10 minutes (for details, see page 20). Transfer jars to a towel-lined surface and let rest at room temperature until set. Check seals; refrigerate any unsealed jars for up to 3 weeks.

> Crème de cacao is a chocolate-flavored liqueur that is colorless, so it adds flavor without changing the color of the jam.

Pears and Port Jam

This jam tastes like classic pears poached in port.

— o o o —

Tip
You'll need about 6 large pears for this recipe.

Recipe Suggestion
Spoon some of this jam over a slice of Brie on a cracker, or use for Baked Brie (page 345).

5 cups	finely chopped peeled pears	1.25 L
¾ cup	port wine	175 mL
1 tbsp	finely grated lemon rind	15 mL
2 tbsp	lemon juice	30 mL
¼ tsp	ground allspice	1 mL
¼ tsp	ground cinnamon	1 mL
1	package (1.75 oz/49 or 57 g) powdered pectin	1
4½ cups	granulated sugar	1.125 L

1. In a large, deep, heavy-bottomed pot, combine pears, port, lemon rind, lemon juice, allspice and cinnamon. Stir in pectin until dissolved. Bring to a full boil over high heat, stirring constantly.

2. Add sugar in a steady stream, stirring constantly. Return to a full boil, stirring constantly to dissolve sugar. Boil hard for 1 minute.

3. Remove from heat and skim off any foam. Stir for 5 to 8 minutes to prevent floating fruit.

4. Ladle into sterilized jars to within ¼ inch (0.5 cm) of rim; wipe rims. Apply prepared lids and rings; tighten rings just until fingertip-tight.

5. Process jars in a boiling water canner for 10 minutes (for details, see page 20). Transfer jars to a towel-lined surface and let rest at room temperature until set. Check seals; refrigerate any unsealed jars for up to 3 weeks.

> Port, a sweet fortified wine, originated in northern Portugal and was shipped from the Portuguese city of Oporto. Tawny ports (a tawny color) are considered higher quality than ruby ports, as they are generally aged longer, but either is acceptable for this recipe. Cook with a port you would drink.

Piña Colada Jam

My friend Gayle Rowan (see Contributors, page 12) works part-time in a bar called McKeck's and thought piña colada flavor would be great as a jam. She was right!

— o o o —

Tip

In most supermarkets and specialty food stores, cream of coconut *syrup* is available in cans near the canned milk products or with beverage ingredients such as cordials. Do not confuse it with coconut *milk*, which is not sweet and is not recommended for making jams because of its high fat content.

Recipe Suggestions

This jam is perfect to warm and serve as a dip for Coconut Shrimp (page 347).

Use to fill a cake or crêpes.

3½ cups	puréed fresh pineapple	875 mL
1 cup	cream of coconut syrup (see tip, at left)	250 mL
⅓ cup	white rum	75 mL
¼ cup	lemon juice	60 mL
6½ cups	granulated sugar	1.625 L
2	pouches (each 3 oz/85 mL) liquid pectin	2

1. In a large, deep, heavy-bottomed pot, combine pineapple purée, cream of coconut, rum and lemon juice. Bring to a full boil over high heat, stirring constantly.

2. Add sugar in a steady stream, stirring constantly. Return to a full boil, stirring constantly to dissolve sugar. Boil hard for 3 minutes, stirring often.

3. Immediately stir in pectin; return to a full boil. Boil hard for 1 minute, stirring constantly.

4. Remove from heat and skim off any foam.

5. Ladle into sterilized jars to within ¼ inch (0.5 cm) of rim; wipe rims. Apply prepared lids and rings; tighten rings just until fingertip-tight.

6. Process jars in a boiling water canner for 10 minutes (for details, see page 20). Transfer jars to a towel-lined surface and let rest at room temperature until set. Check seals; refrigerate any unsealed jars for up to 3 weeks.

Plum Ginger Jam

**Makes about four
8-ounce (250 mL) jars**

*Ginger is becoming an
increasingly popular
flavor and is excellent
here with plums.*

— o o o —

Tips

You'll need about 2 lbs
(1 kg) of plums (about
15 medium) for this recipe.

To remove pits from plums,
cut in half through the stem
and twist to separate the
halves. Repeat, cutting the
half that still has the pit
in half, then twisting the
stone from the center. This
technique helps a lot when
the pits are tightly imbedded
in slightly underripe fruit.

Recipe Suggestion

Purée this jam to make a
delicious plum sauce for
dipping chicken fingers.

Variations

Plum Jam: Omit the
gingerroot.

*Plum Jam with Rose
Water:* Omit the
gingerroot and stir in
3 tbsp (45 mL) rose
water with the sugar.

5 cups	sliced pitted red plums	1.25 L
1¾ cups	water	425 mL
1 tbsp	lemon juice	15 mL
2 tsp	grated gingerroot	10 mL
5 cups	granulated sugar	1.25 L

1. In a large, deep, heavy-bottomed pot, combine plums and water. Bring to a boil over high heat, stirring occasionally. Reduce heat and simmer for about 20 minutes or until softened. Stir in lemon juice and ginger. Bring to a full boil over high heat, stirring constantly.

2. Add sugar in a steady stream, stirring constantly. Return to a full boil, stirring constantly to dissolve sugar. Reduce heat to medium-high and boil rapidly, stirring often and reducing heat further as mixture thickens, for 10 to 12 minutes or until thickened. Test for setting point (for details, see page 19).

3. Remove from heat and skim off any foam.

4. Ladle into sterilized jars to within ¼ inch (0.5 cm) of rim; wipe rims. Apply prepared lids and rings; tighten rings just until fingertip-tight.

5. Process jars in a boiling water canner for 10 minutes (for details, see page 20). Transfer jars to a towel-lined surface and let rest at room temperature until set. Check seals; refrigerate any unsealed jars for up to 3 weeks.

Damson Plum Jam

*Damson plums are
excellent for jams. When
they cook, the skin peels
back and the flesh softens
to release the pit. Look for
these plums at farmers'
markets in late August
to early September.*

— o o o —

Tip
Stirring sugar slowly and
thoroughly into the heated
fruit to dissolve it will prevent
crystallization later on.
Scrape down the sides of
the pot to ensure no crystals
are left.

7 cups	damson plums	1.75 mL
2½ cups	water	625 mL
5½ cups	granulated sugar	1.375 mL

1. In a large, deep, heavy-bottomed pot, combine plums and water. Bring to a boil over high heat. Reduce heat and boil gently for 15 minutes, stirring occasionally. Use a slotted spoon to remove pits (which have become loosened from fruit) and place them in a colander over a large bowl. Shake to drain extra pulp and skins from pits; add back to pot and discard pits.

2. Add sugar in a steady stream, stirring constantly. Bring to a boil over high heat, stirring constantly to dissolve sugar. Reduce heat to medium-high and boil rapidly, stirring often and reducing heat further as mixture thickens, for 8 to 12 minutes or until thickened. Test for setting point (for details, see page 19).

3. Remove from heat and skim off any foam.

4. Ladle into sterilized jars to within ¼ inch (0.5 cm) of rim; wipe rims. Apply prepared lids and rings; tighten rings just until fingertip-tight.

5. Process jars in a boiling water canner for 10 minutes (for details, see page 20). Transfer jars to a towel-lined surface and let rest at room temperature until set. Check seals; refrigerate any unsealed jars for up to 3 weeks.

Do not confuse damson plums with Italian plums, which are in season around the same time. Damsons are small and dark purple, and their pit is harder to remove. Because they are tart, they are not usually eaten raw. Italian plums are larger and purplish-black, and are freestone. They are sweeter, so are wonderful for eating raw.

Yellow Plum Jam

*The fragrant yellow plums
known as Shiro plums,
sometimes labeled "sugar
plums," range from the
size of a Ping-Pong ball to
that of a golf ball. If they
have a bit of red blush,
the jam will be a lovely
apricot color.*

— ○ ○ ○ —

Tip
You'll need about 4 lbs
(2 kg) of plums for this
recipe.

9 cups	chopped pitted firm ripe yellow plums	2.25 L
6 cups	granulated sugar	1.5 L

1. Place plums in a large, deep, heavy-bottomed pot. Add sugar in a steady stream, stirring constantly. Heat over medium heat, stirring constantly to dissolve sugar.

2. Increase heat to high and bring to a full boil, stirring constantly. Reduce heat to medium-high and boil rapidly, stirring often and reducing heat further as mixture thickens, for 20 to 22 minutes or until thickened. Test for setting point (for details, see page 19).

3. Remove from heat and skim off any foam.

4. Ladle into sterilized jars to within $1/4$ inch (0.5 cm) of rim; wipe rims. Apply prepared lids and rings; tighten rings just until fingertip-tight.

5. Process jars in a boiling water canner for 10 minutes (for details, see page 20). Transfer jars to a towel-lined surface and let rest at room temperature until set. Check seals; refrigerate any unsealed jars for up to 3 weeks.

> Plums are not peeled for preserves; the peels add color, flavor and nutritional benefits.

Plumcot Jam

*Plumcots are a new fruit
that appeared in the
supermarket when I was
developing recipes for
this book. They make a
terrific-tasting jam with
a deep red color and an
apricot-like aroma as
it cooks. Definitely try
them if you find them.*

— o o o —

Tip
You'll need about 2 lbs
(1 kg) of plumcots for this
recipe.

4 cups	chopped pitted plumcots	1 L
¼ cup	lemon juice	60 mL
5 cups	granulated sugar	1.25 L
1	pouch (3 oz/85 mL) liquid pectin	1
¼ cup	apricot or cherry brandy	60 mL

1. In a large, deep, heavy-bottomed pot, combine plumcots and lemon juice. Add sugar in a steady stream, stirring constantly. Heat over medium heat, stirring constantly to dissolve sugar. Increase heat to high and bring to a full boil, stirring constantly.

2. Immediately stir in pectin; return to a full boil. Boil hard for 1 minute, stirring constantly.

3. Remove from heat and skim off any foam. Stir in brandy.

4. Ladle into sterilized jars to within ¼ inch (0.5 cm) of rim; wipe rims. Apply prepared lids and rings; tighten rings just until fingertip-tight.

5. Process jars in a boiling water canner for 10 minutes (for details, see page 20). Transfer jars to a towel-lined surface and let rest at room temperature until set. Check seals; refrigerate any unsealed jars for up to 3 weeks.

Plumcots are a 50/50 cross of plums and apricots. They are small like apricots, with a fuzzy purple skin and apricot-colored flesh.

Prickly Pear Jam with Triple Sec

Makes about five 8-ounce (250 mL) jars

The sweetest varieties of prickly pears have magenta-colored flesh. The flavor and texture are like a cross between a watermelon and a papaya.

—ooo—

Tip

How to Peel a Prickly Pear: Place prickly pears in a heatproof bowl and pour in boiling water to cover. Wearing rubber gloves, scrub skins with a brush to remove the tiny hair-like bristles. Rinse well. Using a sharp knife, cut the ends off and slit skins on one side from one end to the other. Peel back skin, rolling in one direction to release the pulp and seeds in one piece; collect all the pulp in a large bowl. Discard skins.

15	prickly pears (approx.)	15
	Boiling water	
2 tbsp	lemon or lime juice	30 mL
1	package (1.75 oz/49 or 57 g) powdered pectin	1
4 cups	granulated sugar	1 L
3 tbsp	triple sec liqueur or undiluted orange juice concentrate	45 mL

1. Press prickly pears through a fine-mesh sieve to remove seeds; measure $3\frac{1}{2}$ cups (875 mL) pulp, including any juices.

2. In a large, heavy-bottomed pot, combine prickly pear pulp and lemon juice. Stir in pectin until dissolved. Bring to a full boil over high heat, stirring constantly.

3. Add sugar in a steady stream, stirring constantly. Return to a full boil, stirring constantly to dissolve sugar. Boil hard for 1 minute.

4. Remove from heat and skim off any foam. Stir in liqueur.

5. Ladle into sterilized jars to within $\frac{1}{4}$ inch (0.5 cm) of rim; wipe rims. Apply prepared lids and rings; tighten rings just until fingertip-tight.

6. Process jars in boiling water canner (for details, see page 20) for 10 minutes. Transfer jars to a towel-lined surface and let rest at room temperature until set. Check seals; refrigerate any unsealed jars for up to 3 weeks.

Also known as cactus pear (*tuna* in Spanish) as it is the fruit of a cactus, this fruit does indeed have tiny hair-like prickles and needs to be handled carefully, even in the store when you place them in a bag. Although the seeds are edible, I have removed them in my recipes as I find them a bit tough.

Quince Jam

Makes about six 8-ounce (250 mL) jars

You will find this fruit in special markets in October and November. It is not usually eaten raw, as it is too hard, sour and astringent, but it is ideal for jam. When cooked, the jam turns a pinkish-brown color.

— o o o —

Tip

To save time, use a grater to grate the peel and the flesh, working around the core; discard core. Or, if desired, remove cores and grate using the grating attachment on a food processor. The texture of the jam will resemble a fruit butter.

Marmelo is the Portuguese word for "quince," which is why quince jam was called marmalade. When ripe, quinces have yellow skin and a very fragrant aroma. Quinces are related to apples and pears and are rich in vitamin C.

5	large quinces, cored and finely chopped or grated	5
3 cups	water	750 mL
3 tbsp	lemon juice	45 mL
5¾ cups	granulated sugar	1.425 L

1. In a large, deep, heavy-bottomed pot, combine quinces, water and lemon juice, stirring well. Bring to a boil over high heat, stirring occasionally. Reduce heat and boil gently, stirring often, for about 10 to 15 minutes or until softened. If desired, use a potato masher to further break down the fruit. Bring to a boil over high heat, stirring constantly.

2. Add sugar in a steady stream, stirring constantly. Return to a boil, stirring constantly to dissolve sugar. Reduce heat to medium-high and boil rapidly, stirring often and reducing heat further as mixture thickens, for 30 to 35 minutes or until thickened. Test for setting point (for details, see page 19).

3. Remove from heat and skim off any foam.

4. Ladle into sterilized jars to within ¼ inch (0.5 cm) of rim; wipe rims. Apply prepared lids and rings; tighten rings just until fingertip-tight.

5. Process jars in boiling water canner for 10 minutes (for details, see page 20). Transfer jars to a towel-lined surface and let rest at room temperature until set. Check seals; refrigerate any unsealed jars for up to 3 weeks.

Variations

Quince Apple Jam: Replace about half of the chopped quinces with peeled chopped apples (choose apples that soften; see page 25).

Quince Jam with Brown Sugar or Honey: Replace 1 cup (250 mL) of the granulated sugar with an equal amount of packed brown sugar or liquid honey.

Quince Jam with Cardamom: Add ½ tsp (2 mL) each ground cardamom and ground cinnamon with the sugar.

Quince Jam with Rum: Add ¼ cup (60 mL) white rum after skimming off foam.

Raspberry Jam

**Makes about six
8-ounce (250 mL) jars**

This popular jam is a cinch to make. Take advantage of pick-your-own farms to get the best quality and price for raspberries. Freeze whole berries for later use.

— o o o —

Tip

Soho is the brand name for a very tasty lychee liqueur that goes well with many fruits. I first had it in a fresh fruit salad and decided to start adding it to some of my jams — I loved the result!

9 cups	raspberries	2.25 L
4½ cups	granulated sugar	1.125 L
3 tbsp	amaretto liqueur or lychee liqueur (optional)	45 mL

1. Place raspberries in a large, deep, heavy-bottomed pot. Add sugar in a steady stream, stirring constantly. Heat over medium heat, stirring constantly to dissolve sugar.

2. Increase heat to high and bring to a full boil, stirring constantly. Reduce heat to medium- high and boil rapidly, stirring often and reducing heat further as mixture thickens, for 10 to 12 minutes or until thickened. Test for setting point (for details, see page 19).

3. Remove from heat and skim off any foam. Stir in liqueur (if using).

4. Ladle into sterilized jars to within ¼ inch (0.5 cm) of rim; wipe rims. Apply prepared lids and rings; tighten rings just until fingertip-tight.

5. Process jars in a boiling water canner for 10 minutes (for details, see page 20). Transfer jars to a towel-lined surface and let rest at room temperature until set. Check seals; refrigerate any unsealed jars for up to 3 weeks.

Chocolate Raspberry Jam

**Makes about four
8-ounce (250 mL) jars**

*My friend Wendi (see
Contributors, page 12)
has a devout passion for
chocolate — she even
named her dog Cocoa.
So she enthusiastically
agreed to do some
experimenting with a
chocolate-flavored jam.
The results were excellent!*

— o o o —

Tips

Mixing the cocoa with a bit
of the sugar helps it to blend
in well.

For other ways to add
chocolate flavor to jams, see
page 36.

Variation

Raspberry Jam: Omit
the cocoa and skip
step 2, adding all of the
sugar in step 3. (See
page 78 for Raspberry
Jam made using the
long-boil method, with
no pectin added.)

5 cups	raspberries	1.25 L
2 tbsp	lemon juice	30 mL
4 cups	granulated sugar, divided	1 L
1/3 cup	unsweetened cocoa powder	75 mL
1	pouch (3 oz/85 mL) liquid pectin	1

1. In a large, deep, heavy-bottomed pot, combine raspberries and lemon juice, stirring well.

2. In a small bowl, combine 1/2 cup (125 mL) of the sugar and the cocoa; set aside.

3. Bring raspberries to a boil over high heat, stirring constantly. Add the remaining sugar in a steady stream, stirring constantly to dissolve sugar. Stir in cocoa mixture until well blended. Bring to a full boil, stirring constantly.

4. Immediately stir in pectin; return to a full boil. Boil hard for 1 minute, stirring constantly.

5. Remove from heat and skim off any foam.

6. Ladle into sterilized jars to within 1/4 inch (0.5 cm) of rim; wipe rims. Apply prepared lids and rings; tighten rings just until fingertip-tight.

7. Process jars in boiling water canner for 10 minutes (for details, see page 20). Transfer jars to a towel-lined surface and let rest at room temperature until set. Check seals; refrigerate any unsealed jars for up to 3 weeks.

Seedless Raspberry Lemon Verbena Jam

*Lemon verbena adds a
unique lemon taste that
is incomparable. You
will not find this herb
in supermarkets. I grew
mine in a pot from a
bedding plant that I
picked up at a nursery
in the spring.*

—o o o—

Tips

When using frozen fruit,
measure whole berries
before thawing. Let thaw
slightly before adding to
the pot.

If you strain the mixture a
second time, stir it gently
through the sieve — do not
push with a spatula or you
will get too many seeds
going through.

9 cups	raspberries	2.25 L
4¾ cups	granulated sugar	1.175 L
½ cup	loosely packed torn lemon verbena leaves	125 mL
1	pouch (3 oz/85 mL) liquid pectin	1

1. Place raspberries in a large, deep, heavy-bottomed pot; crush with a potato masher. Add sugar in a steady stream, stirring constantly. Stir in lemon verbena leaves. Let stand for 30 minutes.

2. Bring to a boil over high heat. Reduce heat and simmer for 5 minutes. Remove from heat and let foam subside. Strain through a fine-mesh sieve to remove the majority of the seeds and leaves. If desired, strain again, rinsing sieve between batches, to further remove seeds. Return to clean pot.

3. Bring to a full boil over high heat, stirring constantly.

4. Immediately stir in pectin; return to a full boil. Boil hard for 1 minute, stirring constantly.

5. Remove from heat and skim off any foam.

6. Ladle into sterilized jars to within ¼ inch (0.5 cm) of rim; wipe rims. Apply prepared lids and rings; tighten rings just until fingertip-tight.

7. Process jars in a boiling water canner for 10 minutes (for details, see page 20). Transfer jars to a towel-lined surface and let rest at room temperature until set. Check seals; refrigerate any unsealed jars for up to 3 weeks.

> Lemon verbena is a small shrub herb with long,
> pointed leaves. Like most herbs, it loves sun and
> well-drained soil. It is not winter-hardy, but plants can
> be taken indoors for the winter, as long as there is
> enough sun or you use grow lights. Avoid cold drafts
> and hot, humid places. Fresh or dried leaves can be
> used for herbal tea, or added to your favorite tea
> while it's steeping.

Rhubarb Jam

Rhubarb is a perennial vegetable, but is typically eaten as a fruit. If you cannot wait until spring, make this classic jam with greenhouse rhubarb.

— o o o —

Tip

This recipe can also be made with frozen rhubarb.

Variations

Rhubarb Jam with Mint: Add ¼ cup (60 mL) finely chopped fresh mint after stirring in the sugar.

Rhubarb Jam with Ginger: Add 1 tbsp (15 mL) finely grated gingerroot to the rhubarb before cooking.

Rhubarb Jam with Rose Water: Add 1 tbsp (15 mL) rose water after skimming off the foam.

6 cups	diced rhubarb (½-inch/1 cm pieces)	1.5 L
¾ cup	water	175 mL
1	package (1.75 oz/49 or 57 g) powdered pectin	1
5 cups	granulated sugar	1.25 L

1. In a large, deep, heavy-bottomed pot, combine rhubarb and water. Bring to a boil over high heat. Reduce heat and simmer, covered, for about 2 minutes or until rhubarb is tender.

2. Stir in pectin until dissolved. Bring to a full boil over high heat, stirring constantly.

3. Add sugar in a steady stream, stirring constantly. Return to a full boil, stirring constantly to dissolve sugar. Boil hard for 1 minute.

4. Remove from heat and skim off any foam.

5. Ladle into sterilized jars to within ¼ inch (0.5 cm) of rim; wipe rims. Apply prepared lids and rings; tighten rings just until fingertip-tight.

6. Process jars in boiling water canner for 10 minutes (for details, see page 20). Transfer jars to a towel-lined surface and let rest at room temperature until set. Check seals; refrigerate any unsealed jars for up to 3 weeks.

> Cultivated greenhouse rhubarb is worth buying, as it is generally redder in color and better quality than most garden rhubarb.

Saskatoon Berry Jam

Makes about six 8-ounce (250 mL) jars

6 cups	Saskatoon berries	1.5 L
3 tbsp	lemon juice	45 mL
5 cups	granulated sugar	1.25 L
1 tsp	ground cinnamon	5 mL
2	pouches (each 3 oz/85 mL) liquid pectin	2

These dark purple berries with large seeds grow wild in many parts of Canada, especially in the Prairies, but are cultivated as well. They have a distinctive taste you don't forget. My Aunt Alice, of North Battleford, Saskatchewan, suggested the addition of cinnamon, which she puts in a sauce she makes from Saskatoon berries.

—ooo—

Recipe Suggestion

Warm this jam, dilute it with a little water or orange juice and serve over pancakes or waffles.

1. In a large, deep, heavy-bottomed pot, combine berries and lemon juice; crush with a potato masher. Bring to a boil over high heat, stirring constantly. Reduce heat and simmer, covered, for 15 minutes or until berries are softened. Bring to a full boil over high heat, stirring constantly.

2. Add sugar in a steady stream, stirring constantly. Stir in cinnamon. Return to a full boil, stirring constantly to dissolve sugar.

3. Immediately stir in pectin; return to a full boil. Boil hard for 1 minute, stirring constantly.

4. Remove from heat and skim off any foam. Stir for 5 to 8 minutes to prevent floating fruit.

5. Ladle into sterilized jars to within $1/4$ inch (0.5 cm) of rim. Wipe rims and apply prepared lids and rings; tighten rings just until fingertip-tight.

6. Process jars in a boiling water canner for 10 minutes (for details, see page 20). Transfer jars to a towel-lined surface and let rest at room temperature until set. Check seals; refrigerate any unsealed jars for up to 3 weeks.

> The Saskatoon berry's name comes from the Cree *Mis-saskquah-toomina*. It was a staple food for the Aboriginal people and early European settlers. The shrub/small tree, native to North America, is a member of the apple family and can grow to about 20 feet (6 m) high. It is also known as serviceberry, Juneberry and shad bush. The nutritional profile is similar to that of blueberries.

Strawberry Jam

**Makes about five
8-ounce (250 mL) jars**

*Strawberry jam is one
of the most popular
preserves to make,
especially when local fruit
is in season. This recipe
uses the long-boil method,
with no added pectin.*

— ○○○ —

Tips

For 6 cups (1.5 L) crushed
strawberries, you'll need
about 12 cups (3 L) sliced.

The color of this jam starts
to deepen during cooking as
the setting point is reached.

Variations

*Strawberry Jalapeño
Jam:* Add ⅔ cup
(150 mL) finely minced
jalapeño peppers with
the strawberries.

Drunken Strawberry Jam:
Add 1 tsp (5 mL) orange
liqueur, Limoncello (Italian
lemon-flavored liqueur) or
lychee liqueur to each jar.

6 cups	crushed strawberries (see tip, page 86)	1.5 L
3 tbsp	lemon or lime juice	45 mL
5 cups	granulated sugar	1.25 L

1. In a large, heavy-bottomed pot, combine strawberries and lemon juice. Bring to a boil over high heat, stirring constantly.

2. Add sugar in a steady stream, stirring constantly. Bring to a full boil, stirring constantly to dissolve sugar. Reduce heat to medium-high and boil rapidly, stirring often and reducing heat further as mixture thickens, for 20 to 22 minutes or until thickened. Test for setting point (for details, see page 19).

3. Remove from heat and skim off any foam. Stir for 5 to 8 minutes to prevent floating fruit.

4. Ladle into sterilized jars to within ¼ inch (0.5 cm) of rim; wipe rims. Apply prepared lids and rings; tighten rings just until fingertip-tight.

5. Process jars in boiling water canner (for details, see page 20) for 10 minutes. Transfer jars to a towel-lined surface and let rest at room temperature until set. Check seals; refrigerate any unsealed jars for up to 3 weeks.

> Because of the long cooking to concentrate the natural pectin, the color of this jam will be darker than that of many strawberry jams. In addition, the yield is less for the amount of fruit than it would be for a pectin-added jam.

Strawberry Lavender Jam

Makes about seven 8-ounce (250 mL) jars

Lavender adds a touch of sweetness and aroma to strawberries in this quick-to-make jam.

— o o o —

Tips

If you leave the lemon juice out of strawberry jam, it will not set — strawberries are too low in acid.

For information about lavender, see page 65.

Variations

Strawberry Jam: Omit the lavender infusion. (See page 85 for Strawberry Jam made using powdered pectin and page 83 for the long-boil method, with no pectin added.)

Strawberry Balsamic Jam: Omit the lavender infusion and replace the lemon juice with balsamic vinegar.

3 tbsp	dried organic lavender flowers	45 mL
1/3 cup	boiling water	75 mL
3 1/2 cups	crushed strawberries (see tip, page 86)	875 mL
1/4 cup	lemon juice	60 mL
7 cups	granulated sugar	1.75 L
1	pouch (3 oz/85 mL) liquid pectin	1

1. Place lavender in a small heatproof bowl. Pour boiling water over flowers; let steep for 20 minutes. Strain, reserving liquid; discard lavender.

2. In a large, deep, heavy-bottomed pot, combine lavender infusion, strawberries and lemon juice. Add sugar in a steady stream, stirring constantly. Bring to a full boil over high heat, stirring constantly to dissolve sugar.

3. Immediately stir in pectin; return to a full boil. Boil hard for 1 minute, stirring constantly.

4. Remove from heat and skim off any foam. Stir for 5 to 8 minutes to prevent floating fruit.

5. Ladle into sterilized jars to within 1/4 inch (0.5 cm) of rim; wipe rims. Apply prepared lids and rings; tighten rings just until fingertip-tight.

6. Process jars in a boiling water canner for 10 minutes (for details, see page 20). Transfer jars to a towel-lined surface and let rest at room temperature until set. Check seals; refrigerate any unsealed jars for up to 3 weeks.

Strawberry Jam with Rose Water

Makes about six 8-ounce (250 mL) jars

Rose water adds a hint of exotic to strawberry jam. Just do an Internet search and you will find a myriad of other rose water recipes.

— ooo —

Tips

For 4 cups (1 L) crushed strawberries, you'll need about 8 cups (2 L) sliced.

Strawberries have a tendency to float after they are ladled into jars. Make sure to stir for at least 5 minutes after you skim off the foam. Do a test jar and wait a few minutes. If the berries start to float, pour the jam back into the pot and stir for a few minutes longer.

Variation

Strawberry Jam: Omit the rose water. (See page 84 for Strawberry Jam made using liquid pectin and page 83 for the long-boil method, with no pectin added.)

4 cups	crushed strawberries (see tip, page 86)	1 L
1/4 cup	lemon or lime juice	60 mL
1	package (1.75 oz/49 or 57 g) powdered pectin	1
6 1/4 cups	granulated sugar	1.55 L
3 tbsp	rose water, or to taste	45 mL

1. In a large, heavy-bottomed pot, combine strawberries and lemon juice. Stir in pectin until dissolved. Bring to a full boil over high heat, stirring constantly.

2. Add sugar in a steady stream, stirring constantly. Return to a full boil, stirring constantly to dissolve sugar. Boil hard for 1 minute.

3. Remove from heat and skim off any foam. Stir for 5 to 8 minutes to prevent floating fruit.

4. Ladle into sterilized jars to within 1/4 inch (0.5 cm) of rim; wipe rims. Apply prepared lids and rings; tighten rings just until fingertip-tight.

5. Process jars in boiling water canner (for details, see page 20) for 10 minutes. Transfer jars to a towel-lined surface and let rest at room temperature until set. Check seals; refrigerate any unsealed jars for up to 3 weeks.

> Rose water is a distillation of rose petals with an intense perfume-like flavor and the fragrance of real roses. I bought a small bottle (9 oz/270 mL) for $2.29 in the supermarket in the soft drinks and drink mixes section. (Maybe they should move it to the baking aisle!) It is used as a flavoring in fancy Greek pastries, puddings and cakes, and in many other recipes for Middle Eastern dishes and desserts.

Strawberry Margarita Jam

*If you like margaritas,
you'll love margarita jam!
The flavor is intoxicating.*

— o o o —

Tip

How to Crush Strawberries:
Use a square glass baking
dish placed on top of a
damp dish cloth (to prevent
movement). Use a potato
masher to crush berries,
one layer at a time. Crush
well to prevent floating fruit
in your jam (don't leave any
big chunks). Always remove
the white hulls from berries
when you are removing
the leaves. Hulls have no
flavor and a tough texture.
Measure the berries after
they're crushed.

Recipe Suggestions

Try this jam as a topping
for cheesecake.

Mix with cream cheese
and spread on bagels or
crackers.

3 cups	crushed strawberries (see tip, at left)	750 mL
¾ cup	lime juice	175 mL
⅔ cup	tequila	150 mL
¼ cup	orange liqueur, such as triple sec	60 mL
6 cups	granulated sugar	1.5 L
1	pouch (3 oz/85 mL) liquid pectin	1

1. In a large, deep, heavy-bottomed pot, combine strawberries, lime juice, tequila and liqueur. Add sugar in a steady stream, stirring constantly. Bring to a full boil over high heat, stirring constantly to dissolve sugar.

2. Immediately stir in pectin; return to a full boil. Boil hard for 1 minute, stirring constantly.

3. Remove from heat and skim off any foam. Stir for 5 to 8 minutes to prevent floating fruit.

4. Ladle into sterilized jars to within ¼ inch (0.5 cm) of rim; wipe rims. Apply prepared lids and rings; tighten rings just until fingertip-tight.

5. Process jars in a boiling water canner for 10 minutes (for details, see page 20). Transfer jars to a towel-lined surface and let rest at room temperature until set. Check seals; refrigerate any unsealed jars for up to 3 weeks.

Watermelon Jam

The small seedless watermelons you find in stores now are perfect for making this pretty salmon-pink jam.

— o o o —

Tip

If using a regular watermelon with seeds, remove the seeds before puréeing. Purée watermelon in batches in a food processor fitted with a metal blade. Transfer to a fine-mesh sieve and, using a rubber spatula, push pulp through to remove any small seeds.

4 cups	seedless watermelon purée (see tip, at left)	1 L
1/3 cup	lemon juice	75 mL
1	package (1.75 oz/49 or 57 g) powdered pectin	1
5½ cups	granulated sugar	1.375 L

1. In a large, deep, heavy-bottomed pot, combine watermelon purée and lemon juice. Stir in pectin until dissolved. Bring to a full boil over high heat, stirring constantly.

2. Add sugar in a steady stream, stirring constantly. Return to a full boil, stirring constantly to dissolve sugar. Boil hard for 1 minute.

3. Remove from heat and skim off any foam.

4. Ladle into sterilized jars to within $\frac{1}{4}$ inch (0.5 cm) of rim; wipe rims. Apply prepared lids and rings; tighten rings just until fingertip-tight.

5. Process jars in a boiling water canner for 10 minutes (for details, see page 20). Transfer jars to a towel-lined surface and let rest at room temperature until set. Check seals; refrigerate any unsealed jars for up to 3 weeks.

Mixed–Fruit Jams

Here's where you really get to create new tastes by combining fruits, either those that are in season at the same time, or some fresh and some frozen. You are sure to find new favorites to enjoy. I had so much fun mixing complementary flavors to give you maximum variety. Many of these jams have a wonderfully unique taste that is nothing like the individual fruits used to make them. The recipes often match fruits that are low in natural pectin with those that have more, or combine fruits for an interesting blend of colors. For information on adding other flavors, see page 36.

Apple Berry Jam 90
Apricot Cranberry Jam. 91
Apricot Kiwi Jam 92
Apricot Yellow Plum Jam with Apricot Brandy 93
Apricot Raspberry Jam 94
Black Currant Apple Jam. 95
Black and Red Currant Jam. 96
Black Currant Rhubarb Jam. 97
Blackberry Apple Jam 98
Blackberry Blueberry Jam 99
Blackberry Orange Jam. 100
Blueberry Banana Jam. 101
Blueberry Orange Amaretto Jam 102
Bumbleberry Jam 103
Sour Cherry Apricot Jam 104
Sweet Cherry and Blueberry Jam. 105
Sweet Cherry Cran-Raspberry Jam 106
Sour Cherry Pear Jam 107
Sweet Cherry and Black Plum Jam 108
Sour Cherry Raspberry Jam. 109
Cherries Jubilee Jam 110
Fig Orange Jam. 111
Fig Strawberry Jam with Balsamic Vinegar. 112
Five Berry Jam. 113
Gooseberry Orange Jam 114
Honey-Do Citrus Jam 115
Kiwi Banana Orange Jam. 116
Kiwi Mango Jam 117
Kiwi Pineapple Orange Jam. 118

Kiwi Raspberry Jam. 119
Kiwi Watermelon Jam 120
Mango Orange Jam with Mint Green Tea 121
Mango Passion Fruit Jam 122
Nectarine Blueberry Jam 123
Nectarine Plum Jam 124
Peach Sour Cherry Jam. 125
Spiced Peach Cranberry Jam 126
Peach Pear Jam 127
Peach Pomegranate Jam. 128
Peach Raspberry Jam 129
Pineapple Mango Jam. 130
Damson Plum Raspberry Jam 131
Red Plum Rhubarb Jam. 132
Plumcot Orange Jam. 133
Prickly Pear and Pear Jam. 134
Raspberry Blackberry Jam. 135
Raspberry Blueberry Jam 136
Raspberry Gooseberry Red Currant Jam 137
Raspberry Lychee Jam with Lychee Liqueur. 138
Raspberry Mango Jam 139
Raspberry Plum Jam 140
Raspberry Red Currant Jam 141
Raspberry Rhubarb Jam 142
Red Currant Orange Jam. 143
Red Fruit Jam 144
Rhubarb Orange Ginger Jam. 145
Rhubarb Pineapple Jam 146
Strawberry Cantaloupe Jam. 147
Strawberry Gooseberry Jam 148
Strawberry Red Grapefruit Jam 149
Strawberry Kiwi Jam 150
Strawberry Mango Daiquiri Jam. 151
Strawberry Pineapple Jam. 152
Strawberry Raspberry Jam 153
Strawberry Red Currant Jam 154
Strawberry Rhubarb Orange Jam. 155
Three-Berry Blend Jam 156
Watermelon Raspberry Jam. 157
Winter Berry Jam. 158

Apple Berry Jam

*This soft-spreading jam
is not too sweet and has
lovely berry flavors. It is
ideal to make when you
have little bits of fruit
left over and there's not
enough for any one jam.*

—o o o—

Tips

Grating the apples instead
of chopping them will save
you time when making
this recipe.

For 2 cups (500 mL)
crushed strawberries,
you'll need about 4 cups
(1 L) sliced.

2	large apples, peeled and grated or finely chopped	2
2 cups	crushed strawberries (see tip, page 86)	500 mL
2 cups	raspberries	500 mL
2 cups	red currants or gooseberries, beards removed	500 mL
2 tbsp	lemon juice	30 mL
5 cups	granulated sugar	1.25 L

1. In a large, deep, heavy-bottomed pot, combine apples, strawberries, raspberries, red currants and lemon juice. Bring to a boil over high heat, stirring occasionally. Reduce heat and simmer, stirring occasionally, for about 7 minutes or until softened.

2. Add sugar in a steady stream, stirring constantly. Increase heat to high and bring to a full boil, stirring constantly to dissolve sugar. Reduce heat to medium-high and boil rapidly, stirring often and reducing heat further as mixture thickens, for 12 to 15 minutes or until thickened. Test for setting point (for details, see page 19).

3. Remove from heat and skim off any foam.

4. Ladle into sterilized jars to within $1/4$ inch (0.5 cm) of rim; wipe rims. Apply prepared lids and rings; tighten rings just until fingertip-tight.

5. Process jars in a boiling water canner for 10 minutes (for details, see page 20). Transfer jars to a towel-lined surface and let rest at room temperature until set. Check seals; refrigerate any unsealed jars for up to 3 weeks.

Apricot Cranberry Jam

**Makes about five
8-ounce (250 mL) jars**

*This looks like strawberry
jam and has a pleasant
tartness.*

— o o o —

Tips

You'll need about 2 lbs
(1 kg) of apricots for this
recipe. You can use a food
processor fitted with a metal
blade to chop them. Pulse
in an on-off manner, but do
not purée. Scrape down
the sides with a spatula a
couple of times.

If using frozen cranberries,
measure while still frozen
and let thaw before adding
to the pot.

This jam has a tendency to
spatter; reduce the heat if
necessary and stir frequently
to avoid scorching.

Variation

*Apricot Cranberry Jam
with a Hint of Orange:*
Add 2 tbsp (30 mL) finely
grated orange rind with
the fruit in step 1.

3½ cups	coarsely chopped apricots	875 mL
3 cups	cranberries	750 mL
5¼ cups	granulated sugar	1.3 L
3 tbsp	orange liqueur or apricot brandy (optional)	45 mL

1. In a large, deep, heavy-bottomed pot, combine apricots and cranberries. Bring to a boil over high heat, stirring constantly.

2. Add sugar in a steady stream, stirring constantly. Bring to a full boil, stirring constantly to dissolve sugar. Reduce heat to medium-low and boil gently, stirring often and reducing heat further as mixture thickens, for 8 to 12 minutes or until thickened. Test for setting point (for details, see page 19).

3. Remove from heat and skim off any foam. Stir in liqueur (if using).

4. Ladle into sterilized jars to within ¼ inch (0.5 cm) of rim; wipe rims. Apply prepared lids and rings; tighten rings just until fingertip-tight.

5. Process jars in a boiling water canner for 10 minutes (for details, see page 20). Transfer jars to a towel-lined surface and let rest at room temperature until set. Check seals; refrigerate any unsealed jars for up to 3 weeks.

Apricot Kiwi Jam

*Apricots and kiwis
combine to make a
great-looking and
great-tasting jam.*

Tips

You'll need about 2 lbs
(1 kg) of apricots for this
recipe.

Ripe kiwifruit will give slightly
when gently pressed.
If fruit is hard, you can
speed ripening by placing
it in a plastic bag with an
apple and store at room
temperature. The ethylene
gas given off by the apple
will help to ripen the kiwi.

3 cups	finely chopped apricots	750 mL
2 cups	finely chopped kiwifruit	500 mL
1	package (1.75 oz/49 or 57 g) powdered pectin	1
5½ cups	granulated sugar	1.375 L

1. In a large, deep, heavy-bottomed pot, combine apricots and kiwis. Stir in pectin until dissolved. Bring to a boil over medium heat; boil gently for 2 minutes, stirring constantly.

2. Add sugar in a steady stream, stirring constantly. Increase heat to high and bring to a full boil, stirring constantly to dissolve sugar. Boil hard for 1 minute.

3. Remove from heat and skim off any foam. Stir for 5 to 8 minutes to prevent floating fruit.

4. Ladle into sterilized jars to within $1/4$ inch (0.5 cm) of rim; wipe rims. Apply prepared lids and rings; tighten rings just until fingertip-tight.

5. Process jars in a boiling water canner for 10 minutes (for details, see page 20). Transfer jars to a towel-lined surface and let rest at room temperature until set. Check seals; refrigerate any unsealed jars for up to 3 weeks.

> It is understood that if we normally eat the peel of a fruit (as with apricots), then we don't peel it for a recipe. A fruit such as kiwifruit, on the other hand, is peeled. Peaches (and occasionally tomatoes) are the exception to this rule — even though the skins are edible, peaches are peeled for preserves. For more fruit preparation information, see page 24.

Apricot Yellow Plum Jam with Apricot Brandy

Makes about six 8-ounce (250 mL) jars

A tasty pairing of mid-summer tree fruits with a dousing of brandy.

— ○ ○ ○ —

Tips

You'll need about 1 1/2 lbs (750 g) of apricots and 1 1/4 lbs (625 g) of plums for this recipe.

This jam has a tendency to spatter; reduce the heat if necessary and stir frequently to avoid scorching.

2 1/2 cups	finely chopped apricots	675 mL
2 cups	finely chopped yellow plums	500 mL
1	package (1.75 oz/49 or 57 g) powdered pectin	1
6 1/2 cups	granulated sugar	1.625 L
1/4 cup	apricot brandy or amaretto	60 mL

1. In a large, deep, heavy-bottomed pot, combine apricots and plums. Stir in pectin until dissolved. Bring to a boil over high heat, stirring constantly.

2. Add sugar in a steady stream, stirring constantly. Bring to a full boil, stirring constantly to dissolve sugar. Boil hard for 1 minute.

3. Remove from heat and skim off any foam. Stir in apricot brandy.

4. Ladle into sterilized jars to within 1/4 inch (0.5 cm) of rim; wipe rims. Apply prepared lids and rings; tighten rings just until fingertip-tight.

5. Process jars in a boiling water canner for 10 minutes (for details, see page 20). Transfer jars to a towel-lined surface and let rest at room temperature until set. Check seals; refrigerate any unsealed jars for up to 3 weeks.

Apricot Raspberry Jam

**Makes about six
8-ounce (250 mL) jars**

*Straining the raspberries
more than once will make
the smoothest "virtually
seedless" jam.*

—ooo—

Tip

You'll need about 2 lbs
(1 kg) of apricots for this
recipe. To finely chop, use
a food processor fitted
with a metal blade, pulsing
on and off and being sure
not to purée them. Or use
a knife.

Recipe Suggestion

Spoon into baked mini tart
shells or use in a linzertorte
(a pastry that features jam).

Variations

If you do not want a
seedless jam, use 4 cups
(1 L) raspberries and do
not strain.

Apricot Blackberry Jam:
Replace the raspberries
with blackberries.

5 cups	raspberries	1.25 L
3 cups	finely chopped apricots	750 mL
1	package (1.75 oz/49 or 57 g) powdered pectin	1
5½ cups	granulated sugar	1.375 L

1. Thaw raspberries slightly if frozen. Press through a fine-mesh sieve to remove seeds; if necessary, repeat to remove additional seeds. Measure 1½ cups (375 mL) pulp.

2. In a large, deep, heavy-bottomed pot, combine raspberry pulp and apricots. Stir in pectin until dissolved. Heat over medium heat, stirring constantly.

3. Add sugar in a steady stream, stirring constantly. Increase heat to high and bring to a full boil, stirring constantly to dissolve sugar. Boil hard for 1 minute.

4. Remove from heat and skim off any foam. Stir for 5 to 8 minutes to prevent floating fruit.

5. Ladle into sterilized jars to within ¼ inch (0.5 cm) of rim; wipe rims. Apply prepared lids and rings; tighten rings just until fingertip-tight.

6. Process jars in a boiling water canner for 10 minutes (for details, see page 20). Transfer jars to a towel-lined surface and let rest at room temperature until set. Check seals; refrigerate any unsealed jars for up to 3 weeks.

Black Currant Apple Jam

Black currants and apples combine well to produce great flavor and texture. This jam is a good choice when you have a smaller quantity of berries available.

— o o o —

Tip
You'll need about 1 lb (500 g) of apples (3 or 4 medium) for this recipe. Varieties of apples that soften when cooked include McIntosh, Cortland, Empire and Russet. See page 25 for more details.

Recipe Suggestion
Stir several large spoonfuls of jam into desserts such as apple crisp, apple pie or bread pudding.

3 cups	black currants, beards removed	750 mL
¾ cup	water	175 mL
4 cups	coarsely grated peeled apples that soften	1 L
4 cups	granulated sugar	1 L

1. In a large, deep, heavy-bottomed pot, combine currants and water. Bring to a boil over high heat. Reduce heat and simmer, stirring occasionally, for 5 minutes or until slightly softened. Use a potato masher to crush currants, if desired.

2. Stir in apples. Increase heat to high and bring to a boil, stirring constantly. Reduce heat and boil gently, stirring occasionally, for about 10 minutes or until apples are softened.

3. Add sugar in a steady stream, stirring constantly. Increase heat to high and bring to a full boil, stirring constantly to dissolve sugar. Reduce heat to medium-high and boil rapidly, stirring often and reducing heat further as mixture thickens, for 12 to 14 minutes or until thickened. Test for setting point (for details, see page 19).

4. Remove from heat and skim off any foam.

5. Ladle into sterilized jars to within ¼ inch (0.5 cm) of rim; wipe rims. Apply prepared lids and rings; tighten rings just until fingertip-tight.

6. Process jars in a boiling water canner for 10 minutes (for details, see page 20). Transfer jars to a towel-lined surface and let rest at room temperature until set. Check seals; refrigerate any unsealed jars for up to 3 weeks.

Black and Red Currant Jam

*The strong taste of black
currants is modified
here by the red currants,
giving you the best of
both fruits and resulting
in a deep red color.*

— o o o —

Tip
Use small manicure
scissors to remove the
beards (blossom ends)
from black currants.

4 cups	black currants, beards removed	1 L
4 cups	red currants	1 L
1/2 cup	water	125 mL
4 1/2 cups	granulated sugar	1.125 L

1. In a large, deep, heavy-bottomed pot, combine black currents, red currants and water. Bring to a boil over high heat. Reduce heat and simmer, covered, stirring occasionally, for 15 minutes or until softened. Use a potato masher to crush currants, if desired.

2. Add sugar in a steady stream, stirring constantly. Increase heat to high and bring to a full boil, stirring constantly to dissolve sugar. Reduce heat to medium-high and boil rapidly, stirring often and reducing heat further as mixture thickens, for 10 to 12 minutes or until thickened. Test for setting point (for details, see page 19).

3. Remove from heat and skim off any foam.

4. Ladle into sterilized jars to within 1/4 inch (0.5 cm) of rim; wipe rims. Apply prepared lids and rings; tighten rings just until fingertip-tight.

5. Process jars in a boiling water canner for 10 minutes (for details, see page 20). Transfer jars to a towel-lined surface and let rest at room temperature until set. Check seals; refrigerate any unsealed jars for up to 3 weeks.

> Black and red currants both contain generous amounts of natural pectin, so none needs to be added to preserves made with them.

Black Currant Rhubarb Jam

**Makes about five
8-ounce (250 mL) jars**

*You might be able to make
this lovely combination
jam with fruits right from
your own backyard!*

— o o o —

Tip

If using frozen fruit, measure
while still frozen and let thaw
before adding to the pot.

4 cups	black currants, beards removed	1 L
2 cups	water	500 mL
3 cups	chopped rhubarb (½-inch/1 cm pieces)	750 mL
5 cups	granulated sugar	1.25 L

1. In a large, deep, heavy-bottomed pot, combine currants and water. Bring to a boil over high heat. Reduce heat and simmer, stirring occasionally, for 15 minutes or until softened. Use a potato masher to crush currants, if desired.

2. Stir in rhubarb. Add sugar in a steady stream, stirring constantly. Increase heat to high and bring to a full boil, stirring constantly to dissolve sugar. Reduce heat to medium-high and boil rapidly, stirring often and reducing heat further as mixture thickens, for 4 to 7 minutes or until thickened. Test for setting point (for details, see page 19).

3. Remove from heat and skim off any foam.

4. Ladle into sterilized jars to within ¼ inch (0.5 cm) of rim; wipe rims. Apply prepared lids and rings; tighten rings just until fingertip-tight.

5. Process jars in a boiling water canner for 10 minutes (for details, see page 20). Transfer jars to a towel-lined surface and let rest at room temperature until set. Check seals; refrigerate any unsealed jars for up to 3 weeks.

Blackberry Apple Jam

**Makes about five
8-ounce (250 mL) jars**

*Apples make a nice
addition to jams, giving
a great texture and taste.
Here, they accent the
flavor of the blackberries
and make the jam less
seedy overall.*

— o o o —

Tips

Varieties of apples that
soften when cooked include
McIntosh, Cortland, Empire
and Russet. See page 25
for more details.

Instead of chopping apples,
peel but do not core. Grate
by hand on the coarse side
of a box grater, turning
apple until core is reached;
discard core. Alternatively,
cut apples into wedges
and remove cores, then
use the grater attachment
on a food processor. Work
quickly to prevent apples
from browning, or combine
them with the lemon juice as
you go.

You'll need about 1¼ lbs
(625 g) of blackberries for
this recipe.

Variation

*Blackberry Apple Jam
with Apple Liqueur:* Add
¼ cup (60 mL) apple
liqueur after skimming off
foam.

5 cups	chopped peeled apples that soften	1.25 L
2 tbsp	lemon juice	30 mL
5 cups	blackberries	1.25 L
4 cups	granulated sugar	1 L

1. In a large, deep, heavy-bottomed pot, combine apples and lemon juice. Bring to a boil over high heat, stirring constantly. Reduce heat and simmer, covered, stirring occasionally, for 5 minutes or until apples are softened.

2. Add blackberries; crush using a potato masher. Increase heat to high and bring to a boil, stirring constantly.

3. Add sugar in a steady stream, stirring constantly. Bring to a full boil, stirring constantly to dissolve sugar. Reduce heat to medium-high and boil rapidly, stirring often and reducing heat further as mixture thickens, for 5 to 8 minutes or until thickened. Test for setting point (for details, see page 19).

4. Remove from heat and skim off any foam.

5. Ladle into sterilized jars to within ¼ inch (0.5 cm) of rim; wipe rims. Apply prepared lids and rings; tighten rings just until fingertip-tight.

6. Process jars in a boiling water canner for 10 minutes (for details, see page 20). Transfer jars to a towel-lined surface and let rest at room temperature until set. Check seals; refrigerate any unsealed jars for up to 3 weeks.

Blackberry Blueberry Jam

Black and blue is a good thing in this jam, which has rich berry flavors.

— o o o —

Tips

A 4.4 oz (125 g) container of blueberries or blackberries will yield about 1 cup (250 mL).

Stir often and reduce heat if needed to keep jam from scorching. If you think the bottom has scorched or is beginning to, immediately remove pot from heat. Transfer contents to another pot or a large bowl, without scraping the bottom. If the mixture does not smell scorched, you may have saved it in time. Be sure to taste a cooled sample before filling jars. Clean the pot and continue (or use a new pot).

3 cups	blackberries	750 mL
3 cups	blueberries	750 mL
1/2 cup	water	125 mL
2 tbsp	lemon juice	30 mL
3 cups	granulated sugar	750 mL

1. In a large, deep, heavy-bottomed pot, combine blackberries, blueberries, water and lemon juice. Bring to a boil over high heat. Reduce heat and simmer for 5 minutes, stirring often. Use a potato masher to further break down fruit.

2. Add sugar in a steady stream, stirring constantly. Increase heat to high and bring to a full boil, stirring constantly to dissolve sugar. Reduce heat to medium-high and boil rapidly, stirring often and reducing heat further as mixture thickens, for 7 to 9 minutes or until thickened. Test for setting point (for details, see page 19).

3. Remove from heat and skim off any foam.

4. Ladle into sterilized jars to within 1/4 inch (0.5 cm) of rim; wipe rims. Apply prepared lids and rings; tighten rings just until fingertip-tight.

5. Process jars in a boiling water canner for 10 minutes (for details, see page 20). Transfer jars to a towel-lined surface and let rest at room temperature until set. Check seals; refrigerate any unsealed jars for up to 3 weeks.

Blackberry Orange Jam

**Makes about five
8-ounce (250 mL) jars**

*I love the flavor of orange
added to the blackberries.
For an upscale jam, add
an orange liqueur.*

— o o o —

Tip

You'll need about 1½ lbs
(750 g) of blackberries for
this recipe.

Variation

*Seedless Blackberry
Orange Jam:* In a
large saucepan, over
medium-high heat, cook
blackberries and ½ cup
(125 mL) water for
5 minutes. Press through
a fine-mesh sieve to
remove seeds; proceed
with recipe.

4	large oranges	4
6 cups	blackberries	1.5 L
2 tbsp	lemon juice	30 mL
4½ cups	granulated sugar	1.125 L
¼ cup	orange liqueur (optional)	60 mL

1. Using a fine grater, remove 2 tbsp (30 mL) orange rind; set aside. Peel oranges and remove all pith, seeds and membranes. Chop the fruit and measure to make 2⅔ cups (650 mL), including juices.

2. In a large, deep, heavy-bottomed pot, combine orange rind, oranges, blackberries and lemon juice. Bring to a boil over high heat. Reduce heat and simmer, covered, for 5 minutes, stirring occasionally. Use a potato masher to further break down fruit.

3. Add sugar in a steady stream, stirring constantly. Increase heat to high and bring to a full boil, stirring constantly to dissolve sugar. Reduce heat to medium-high and boil rapidly, stirring often and reducing heat further as mixture thickens, for 5 minutes or until thickened. Test for setting point (for details, see page 19).

4. Remove from heat and skim off any foam. Stir in liqueur (if using).

5. Ladle into sterilized jars to within ¼ inch (0.5 cm) of rim; wipe rims. Apply prepared lids and rings; tighten rings just until fingertip-tight.

6. Process jars in a boiling water canner for 10 minutes (for details, see page 20). Transfer jars to a towel-lined surface and let rest at room temperature until set. Check seals; refrigerate any unsealed jars for up to 3 weeks.

> Grand Marnier liqueur was created in France in 1880 by Alexandre Marnier-Lapostolle. It is made from a blend of true cognacs (brandy distilled from white wine from the Cognac region) and distilled bitter orange essence.

Blueberry Banana Jam

Makes about six 8-ounce (250 mL) jars

This jam is great spooned over pancakes and waffles, or served with bran muffins.

— o o o —

Tip

For a chunkier jam, finely chop bananas rather than mashing.

4 cups	blueberries	1 L
1⅔ cups	mashed ripe bananas	400 mL
2 tbsp	lemon juice	30 mL
1	package (1.75 oz/49 or 57 g) powdered pectin	1
5 cups	granulated sugar	1.25 L

1. In a large, deep, heavy-bottomed pot, combine blueberries, bananas and lemon juice. Stir in pectin until dissolved. Bring to a full boil over high heat, stirring constantly.

2. Add sugar in a steady stream, stirring constantly. Return to a full boil, stirring constantly to dissolve sugar. Boil hard for 1 minute.

3. Remove from heat and skim off any foam.

4. Ladle into sterilized jars to within ¼ inch (0.5 cm) of rim; wipe rims. Apply prepared lids and rings; tighten rings just until fingertip-tight.

5. Process jars in a boiling water canner for 10 minutes (for details, see page 20). Transfer jars to a towel-lined surface and let rest at room temperature until set. Check seals; refrigerate any unsealed jars for up to 3 weeks.

> Use bananas that are fully ripe (with no green on the skins) but not too soft and mushy.

Blueberry Orange Amaretto Jam

The inspiration for this jam comes from a hot drink called blueberry tea that includes amaretto and orange liqueurs. Use wild blueberries for the best flavor. Great for gift-giving.

— o o o —

Variation

Blueberry Jam: Omit the oranges and liqueur; increase the blueberries to 4 cups (1 L).

4	large oranges	4
3 cups	blueberries	750 mL
1/4 cup	lemon juice	60 mL
6 cups	granulated sugar	1.5 L
2	pouches (each 3 oz/85 mL) liquid pectin	2
1/4 cup	amaretto or orange liqueur	60 mL

1. Using a fine grater, remove 2 tbsp (30 mL) orange rind; set aside. Peel and section oranges, removing all pith, seeds and membranes, and chop the fruit, reserving any juices.

2. Place blueberries in a large, deep, heavy-bottomed pot. Use a potato masher to crush about one-third of the berries to release some of their juice. Stir in orange rind, oranges with juice and lemon juice. Bring to a boil over high heat, stirring occasionally.

3. Add sugar in a steady stream, stirring constantly. Bring to a full boil over high heat, stirring constantly to dissolve sugar.

4. Immediately stir in pectin; return to a full boil. Boil hard for 1 minute, stirring constantly.

5. Remove from heat and skim off any foam. Stir in amaretto.

6. Ladle into sterilized jars to within 1/4 inch (0.5 cm) of rim; wipe rims. Apply prepared lids and rings; tighten rings just until fingertip-tight.

7. Process jars in a boiling water canner for 10 minutes (for details, see page 20). Transfer jars to a towel-lined surface and let rest at room temperature until set. Check seals; refrigerate any unsealed jars for up to 3 weeks.

Bumbleberry Jam

Bumbleberry isn't a type of berry; it's an interesting mix of fruits that first appeared in a pie. There are different versions, some including apples, others without rhubarb.

— o o o —

Tip
Freeze premeasured amounts of chopped rhubarb, as well as whole strawberries, to make this jam later in the summer when the other berries are plentiful.

1 cup	crushed strawberries (see tip, page 86)	250 mL
1 cup	raspberries	250 mL
1 cup	blueberries	250 mL
1 cup	blackberries	250 mL
1 cup	chopped rhubarb (1/2-inch/1 cm pieces)	250 mL
5 cups	granulated sugar	1.25 L
1	pouch (3 oz/85 mL) liquid pectin	1

1. In a large, deep, heavy-bottomed pot, combine strawberries, raspberries, blueberries, blackberries and rhubarb. Bring to a boil over high heat, stirring constantly. Reduce heat and simmer for about 10 minutes or until rhubarb is softened.

2. Add sugar in a steady stream, stirring constantly. Increase heat to high and bring to a full boil, stirring constantly to dissolve sugar.

3. Immediately stir in pectin; return to a full boil. Boil hard for 1 minute, stirring constantly.

4. Remove from heat and skim off any foam. Stir for 5 to 8 minutes to prevent floating fruit.

5. Ladle into sterilized jars to within 1/4 inch (0.5 cm) of rim; wipe rims. Apply prepared lids and rings; tighten rings just until fingertip-tight.

6. Process jars in a boiling water canner for 10 minutes (for details, see page 20). Transfer jars to a towel-lined surface and let rest at room temperature until set. Check seals; refrigerate any unsealed jars for up to 3 weeks.

Sour Cherry Apricot Jam

*Cherries pair well with
fresh apricots in this
fabulous jam.*

— o o o —

Tips

Pit and freeze cherries to
have on hand when apricots
come into season.

You'll need about 2 lbs
(1 kg) of apricots for this
recipe.

4 cups	halved pitted sour (tart) cherries	1 L
4 cups	chopped apricots	1 L
1/4 cup	lemon juice	60 mL
4 cups	granulated sugar	1 L

1. In a large, deep, heavy-bottomed pot, combine cherries, apricots and lemon juice. Bring to a boil over high heat, stirring occasionally. Reduce heat and simmer, covered, for 5 minutes.

2. Add sugar in a steady stream, stirring constantly. Increase heat to high and bring to a full boil, stirring constantly to dissolve sugar. Reduce heat to medium-high and boil rapidly, uncovered, stirring often and reducing heat further as mixture thickens, for 15 to 20 minutes or until thickened. Test for setting point (for details, see page 19).

3. Remove from heat and skim off any foam.

4. Ladle into sterilized jars to within 1/4 inch (0.5 cm) of rim; wipe rims. Apply prepared lids and rings; tighten rings just until fingertip-tight.

5. Process jars in a boiling water canner for 10 minutes (for details, see page 20). Transfer jars to a towel-lined surface and let rest at room temperature until set. Check seals; refrigerate any unsealed jars for up to 3 weeks.

Sweet Cherry and Blueberry Jam

Makes about five 8-ounce (250 mL) jars

Cherries and blueberries partner well and make a delectable combination to serve over pancakes, waffles or crêpes. Warm slightly and thin with a little water, maple syrup or orange liqueur.

1½ lbs	sweet cherries	750 g
3 cups	blueberries	750 mL
2 tbsp	lemon juice	30 mL
1	package (1.75 oz/49 or 57 g) powdered pectin	1
4½ cups	granulated sugar	1.125 L

1. Remove stems and pits from cherries. Using a food processor fitted with a metal blade, finely chop cherries by pulsing on and off, scraping down sides (be careful not to purée). Place in a large, deep, heavy-bottomed pot.

2. In food processor, finely chop blueberries by pulsing on and off, scraping down sides (be careful not to purée). Add to cherries in pot.

3. Stir in lemon juice. Bring to a boil over high heat; reduce heat and simmer for 3 minutes, stirring constantly.

4. Stir in pectin until dissolved. Bring to a full boil over high heat, stirring constantly.

5. Add sugar in a steady stream, stirring constantly. Return to a full boil, stirring constantly to dissolve sugar. Boil hard for 1 minute.

6. Remove from heat and skim off any foam. Stir for 5 to 8 minutes to prevent floating fruit.

7. Ladle into sterilized jars to within ¼ inch (0.5 cm) of rim; wipe rims. Apply prepared lids and rings; tighten rings just until fingertip-tight.

8. Process jars in a boiling water canner for 10 minutes (for details, see page 20). Transfer jars to a towel-lined surface and let rest at room temperature until set. Check seals; refrigerate any unsealed jars for up to 3 weeks.

> Rainier and Bing cherries are both varieties of sweet cherries, and this recipe can be made with either. A cross between the Bing and Van cultivars, Rainer cherries are creamy yellow with a reddish blush. They were created in 1952 at Washington State University by Harold Fogle.

Sweet Cherry Cran-Raspberry Jam

This lovely red jam uses sweet cherries to contrast with the tartness of the cranberries.

——○○○——

Tip
You'll need about 1⅓ lbs (650 g) of cherries for this recipe. There should be 3 cups (750 mL) of cranberries in a 12-oz (340 g) package.

Recipe Suggestion
Place some of this jam in the center of the batter when you're spooning muffin batter into tins.

3 cups	sweet cherries, halved and pitted	750 mL
3 cups	cranberries	750 mL
3 cups	raspberries	750 mL
4½ cups	granulated sugar	1.125 L

1. In a large, deep, heavy-bottomed pot, combine cherries, cranberries, raspberries and sugar. Cover and let stand for 2 hours.

2. Bring to a boil over medium heat, stirring constantly to dissolve sugar. Increase heat to high and bring to a full boil, stirring constantly. Reduce heat to medium-high and boil rapidly, stirring often and reducing heat further as mixture thickens, for 25 to 30 minutes or until thickened. Test for setting point (for details, see page 19).

3. Remove from heat and skim off any foam.

4. Ladle into sterilized jars to within ¼ inch (0.5 cm) of rim; wipe rims. Apply prepared lids and rings; tighten rings just until fingertip-tight.

5. Process jars in a boiling water canner for 10 minutes (for details, see page 20). Transfer jars to a towel-lined surface and let rest at room temperature until set. Check seals; refrigerate any unsealed jars for up to 3 weeks.

Sour Cherry Pear Jam

Makes about five 8-ounce (250 mL) jars

This jam should be named "Cheery Pear." The sour cherry flavor nicely offsets the sweetness of the pears.

— o o o —

Tips

You'll need 2 or 3 medium pears for this recipe.

Pears are one of few fruits that are picked when they are underripe and ripen fully afterwards. To speed ripening, place them in a paper bag at room temperature for a couple of days. Pears are ready to use when they give slightly when pressed along their neck and shoulders.

2½ cups	finely chopped peeled pears	625 mL
2 cups	chopped pitted sour (tart) cherries	500 mL
2 tbsp	lemon juice	30 mL
1	package (1.75 oz/49 or 57 g) powdered pectin	1
4½ cups	granulated sugar	1.125 L
2 tbsp	cherry liqueur	30 mL

1. In a large, deep, heavy-bottomed pot, combine pears, cherries and lemon juice. Bring to a boil over high heat, stirring occasionally. Reduce heat and simmer, covered, for about 2 minutes or until pears are tender.

2. Stir in pectin until dissolved. Increase heat to high and bring to a full boil, stirring constantly.

3. Add sugar in a steady stream, stirring constantly. Return to a full boil, stirring constantly to dissolve sugar. Boil hard for 1 minute.

4. Remove from heat and skim off any foam. Stir in liqueur. Stir for 5 to 8 minutes to prevent floating fruit.

5. Ladle into sterilized jars to within ¼ inch (0.5 cm) of rim; wipe rims. Apply prepared lids and rings; tighten rings just until fingertip-tight.

6. Process jars in a boiling water canner for 10 minutes (for details, see page 20). Transfer jars to a towel-lined surface and let rest at room temperature until set. Check seals; refrigerate any unsealed jars for up to 3 weeks.

> There are several different cherry liqueurs, including Kirsch (a clear brandy flavored with cherry juice and pits), cherry brandy (made from fermented cherries) and Cherry Herring (a cherry liqueur from Denmark.)

Sweet Cherry
and Black Plum Jam

**Makes about seven
8-ounce (250 mL) jars**

*Use black (deep red)
sweet cherries and black
plums for a deep (colored)
and delicious jam!*

— o o o —

Tips

You'll need about 10 large
plums for this recipe. To
remove pits from plums, cut
in half through the stem and
twist to separate the halves.
Repeat, cutting the half
that still has the pit in half,
then twisting the stone from
the center. This technique
helps a lot when the pits are
tightly imbedded in slightly
underripe fruit.

Use a food processor
fitted with a metal blade
to finely chop the cherries
and the plums. Chop each
separately, pulsing on and
off, scraping down sides
and being sure not to purée
them. Or use a knife.

1½ lbs	sweet cherries, such as Bing, finely chopped	750 g
1½ lbs	black plums, finely chopped	750 g
3 tbsp	lemon juice	45 mL
1	package (1.75 oz/49 or 57 g) powdered pectin	1
6¼ cups	granulated sugar	1.55 L
⅓ cup	cherry brandy (optional)	75 mL

1. In a large, deep, heavy-bottomed pot, combine cherries, plums and lemon juice. Stir in pectin until dissolved. Bring to a boil over high heat, stirring constantly. Reduce heat and simmer for 3 minutes, stirring often.

2. Add sugar in a steady stream, stirring constantly. Increase heat to high and bring to a full boil, stirring constantly to dissolve sugar. Boil hard for 1 minute.

3. Remove from heat and skim off any foam. Stir in cherry brandy (if using.)

4. Ladle into sterilized jars to within ¼ inch (0.5 cm) of rim; wipe rims. Apply prepared lids and rings; tighten rings just until fingertip-tight.

5. Process jars in a boiling water canner for 10 minutes (for details, see page 20). Transfer jars to a towel-lined surface and let rest at room temperature until set. Check seals; refrigerate any unsealed jars for up to 3 weeks.

Sour Cherry Raspberry Jam

*This jam features larger
pieces of cherry suspended
in raspberry jam.*

— o o o —

Tip

This recipe would be great
with a little chocolate flavor
added! For details, see
page 36.

Recipe Suggestion

Try this as a filling for
chocolate cake or jelly
roll (see Vanilla Jelly Roll,
page 368).

Variation

*Cherry Blackberry or
Cherry Black Raspberry
Jam:* Replace raspberries
with blackberries or black
raspberries.

3 cups	halved pitted sour (tart) cherries	750 mL
2½ cups	raspberries	625 mL
2 tbsp	lemon juice	30 mL
1	package (1.75 oz/49 or 57 g) powdered pectin	1
4 cups	granulated sugar	1 L

1. In a large, deep, heavy-bottomed pot, combine cherries, raspberries and lemon juice. Stir in pectin until dissolved. Bring to a full boil over high heat, stirring constantly.

2. Add sugar in a steady stream, stirring constantly. Return to a full boil, stirring constantly to dissolve sugar. Boil hard for 1 minute.

3. Remove from heat and skim off any foam. Stir for 5 to 8 minutes to prevent floating fruit.

4. Ladle into sterilized jars to within $1/4$ inch (0.5 cm) of rim; wipe rims. Apply prepared lids and rings; tighten rings just until fingertip-tight.

5. Process jars in a boiling water canner for 10 minutes (for details, see page 20). Transfer jars to a towel-lined surface and let rest at room temperature until set. Check seals; refrigerate any unsealed jars for up to 3 weeks.

Cherries Jubilee Jam

*This jam is named after
the famous dessert, which
uses cherries, red currant
jam and cherry brandy.*

— o o o —

Recipe Suggestion

Add a little water or orange
juice to this jam, warm and
brush over a fruit flan or pour
over vanilla ice cream. It also
works well with crêpes.

3 cups	red currants	750 mL
3 cups	finely chopped pitted sweet cherries	750 mL
3½ cups	granulated sugar	875 mL
2 tbsp	cherry brandy (optional)	30 mL

1. Place currants in a large, deep, heavy-bottomed pot and crush with a potato masher. Stir in cherries. Bring to a boil over high heat, stirring constantly. Reduce heat and simmer, covered, for 5 minutes.

2. Add sugar in a steady stream, stirring constantly. Increase heat to high and bring to a full boil, stirring constantly to dissolve sugar. Reduce heat to medium-high and boil rapidly, stirring often and reducing heat further as mixture thickens, for 10 to 12 minutes or until thickened. Test for setting point (for details, see page 19).

3. Remove from heat and skim off any foam. Stir in cherry brandy (if using).

4. Ladle into sterilized jars to within ¼ inch (0.5 cm) of rim; wipe rims. Apply prepared lids and rings; tighten rings just until fingertip-tight.

5. Process jars in a boiling water canner for 10 minutes (for details, see page 20). Transfer jars to a towel-lined surface and let rest at room temperature until set. Check seals; refrigerate any unsealed jars for up to 3 weeks.

> Cooked jams may crystallize because too much sugar was added (measure accurately, using a dry measure, and level the top with a straight edge or knife), or because there was undissolved sugar on the sides of the pan or the spoon handle. Stir well during cooking and scrape down the sides with a rubber scraper, if necessary. Crystallization may also result from overcooking or from storage in a place that is too warm or has temperature fluctuations. (For more information on storage, see page 21.)

Fig Orange Jam

You will see fig jams, including some with orange, in the cheese section of some supermarkets. That's because fig jam is excellent over sharp cheese or goat cheese on crackers.

——— o o o ———

Tips

You'll need about 1¼ lbs (625 g) of figs for this recipe. You can use brown- or green-skinned fresh figs, or a combination.

To prepare figs, trim both ends and cut in half lengthwise through the stem. Using a sharp paring knife, remove the stem by making V-shaped cut in each half. To save time, you can chop trimmed figs in a food processor by pulsing on and off. Do not purée.

Recipe Suggestion

Spread some of this jam on a whole pork tenderloin near the end of cooking.

2	large oranges	2
3 cups	finely chopped fresh figs (see tips, at left)	750 mL
3 cups	granulated sugar	750 mL
¼ cup	liquid honey	60 mL

1. Using a fine grater, remove 1 tbsp (15 mL) orange rind; set aside. Peel oranges and remove all pith, seeds and membranes. Chop the fruit and measure to make 1 cup (250 mL), including juices.

2. In a large, deep, heavy-bottomed pot, combine orange rind, oranges, figs and sugar. Let stand for 1 hour.

3. Bring to a boil over high heat, stirring constantly to dissolve sugar. Stir in honey. Reduce heat to medium-low and boil gently, stirring often and reducing heat further as mixture thickens, for 15 to 20 minutes or until thickened. (If fig skins seem tough after 15 minutes, use a potato masher to further break down fruit, or use an immersion blender.) Test for setting point (for details, see page 19).

4. Remove from heat and skim off any foam.

5. Ladle into sterilized jars to within ¼ inch (0.5 cm) of rim; wipe rims. Apply prepared lids and rings; tighten rings just until fingertip-tight.

6. Process jars in a boiling water canner for 10 minutes (for details, see page 20). Transfer jars to a towel-lined surface and let rest at room temperature until set. Check seals; refrigerate any unsealed jars for up to 3 weeks.

Variations

Fig Orange Jam with Toasted Sesame Seeds: Stir in 1 tbsp (15 mL) toasted sesame seeds after skimming off foam. Stir for about 5 minutes to prevent floating.

Spiced Fig Orange Jam: Add ½ tsp (2 mL) ground cinnamon and a pinch of cloves after stirring in the sugar.

Fig Strawberry Jam with Balsamic Vinegar

**Makes about five
8-ounce (250 mL) jars**

*Figs and strawberries
make congenial partners.*

— o o o —

Tips

For 3 cups (750 mL)
crushed strawberries, you'll
need about 6 cups (1.5 L)
sliced.

You'll need about 1 lb
(500 g) of figs for this
recipe. To prepare figs,
trim both ends and cut in
half lengthwise through the
stem. Using a sharp paring
knife, remove the stem by
making V-shaped cut in
each half. To save time, you
can chop trimmed figs in a
food processor by pulsing
on and off. Do not purée.

If you have balsamic vinegar
syrup, use 2 tbsp (30 mL)
in place of the vinegar.

3 cups	crushed strawberries (see tip, page 86)	750 mL
2 cups	finely chopped fresh dark figs (see tip, at left)	500 mL
1/3 cup	balsamic vinegar, or to taste	75 mL
1 tbsp	lemon juice	15 mL
5 1/2 cups	granulated sugar	1.375 mL

1. In a large, deep, heavy-bottomed pot, combine strawberries, figs, vinegar and lemon juice. Bring to a boil over high heat, stirring constantly.

2. Add sugar in a steady stream, stirring constantly. Bring to a full boil, stirring constantly to dissolve sugar. Reduce heat to medium and boil gently, stirring often and reducing heat further as mixture thickens, for 18 to 22 minutes or until thickened. Use a potato masher to further break down figs. Test for setting point (for details, see page 19).

3. Remove from heat and skim off any foam.

4. Ladle into sterilized jars to within 1/4 inch (0.5 cm) of rim; wipe rims. Apply prepared lids and rings; tighten rings just until fingertip-tight.

5. Process jars in a boiling water canner for 10 minutes (for details, see page 20). Transfer jars to a towel-lined surface and let rest at room temperature until set. Check seals; refrigerate any unsealed jars for up to 3 weeks.

> Fresh figs are ripe when they are slightly soft and starting to bend at the neck. They do not keep well and can be stored in the refrigerator for only 2 to 3 days. (Dried figs can be stored in an airtight container at room temperature for up to 8 months.)

Five Berry Jam

This wonderful five-berry combination has a deep burgundy color, a bit of tartness and undertones of black currant. It's great when you have small amounts of berries left over from making other jams. At home, I call this jam "Five Star" because the berries are all stars.

— o o o —

Tips

The beards (blossom ends) of the black currants and gooseberries must be snipped from the ends before use. A small pair of manicure scissors is the perfect tool for this task.

Freeze summer berries as they come into season, so you have them on hand when you feel like making jam. Premeasure in 2-cup (500 mL) amounts, if desired.

2 cups	raspberries	500 mL
2 cups	blackberries	500 mL
2 cups	black currants, beards removed	500 mL
2 cups	red currants	500 mL
2 cups	gooseberries, beards removed	500 mL
5 cups	granulated sugar	1.25 L

1. In a large, deep, heavy-bottomed pot, combine raspberries, blackberries, black currants, red currants and gooseberries. Bring to a boil over high heat, stirring constantly. Reduce heat and simmer for 5 minutes, stirring constantly.

2. Add sugar in a steady stream, stirring constantly. Increase heat to high and bring to a full boil, stirring constantly to dissolve sugar. Reduce heat to medium-high and boil rapidly, stirring often and reducing heat further as mixture thickens, for 5 to 8 minutes or until thickened. Test for setting point (for details, see page 19).

3. Remove from heat and skim off any foam.

4. Ladle into sterilized jars to within $\frac{1}{4}$ inch (0.5 cm) of rim; wipe rims. Apply prepared lids and rings; tighten rings just until fingertip-tight.

5. Process jars in a boiling water canner for 10 minutes (for details, see page 20). Transfer jars to a towel-lined surface and let rest at room temperature until set. Check seals; refrigerate any unsealed jars for up to 3 weeks.

Gooseberry Orange Jam

Oranges give a pleasant flavor boost and perk up the color of the gooseberries.

— o o o —

Tips

I like this jam with green gooseberries, but you can use any color, or a mixture.

Use small manicure scissors to remove the beards (blossom ends) from gooseberries.

2	large oranges	2
5 cups	gooseberries, beards removed	1.25 L
4 cups	granulated sugar	1 L

1. Using a fine grater, remove 1 tbsp (15 mL) orange rind; set aside. Peel and section oranges, removing all pith, seeds and membranes, and chop the fruit, reserving any juices.

2. In a large, deep, heavy-bottomed pot, combine orange rind, oranges with juice, and gooseberries. Bring to a boil over high heat, stirring constantly. Reduce heat and simmer for 5 minutes or until gooseberries are softened. Crush any whole berries with back of spoon.

3. Add sugar in a steady stream, stirring constantly. Increase heat to high and bring to a full boil, stirring constantly to dissolve sugar. Reduce heat to medium-high and boil rapidly, stirring often and reducing heat further as mixture thickens, for 10 to 12 minutes or until thickened. Test for setting point (for details, see page 19).

4. Remove from heat and skim off any foam.

5. Ladle into sterilized jars to within $1/4$ inch (0.5 cm) of rim; wipe rims. Apply prepared lids and rings; tighten rings just until fingertip-tight.

6. Process jars in a boiling water canner for 10 minutes (for details, see page 20). Transfer jars to a towel-lined surface and let rest at room temperature until set. Check seals; refrigerate any unsealed jars for up to 3 weeks.

Honey–Do Citrus Jam

I called this jam honey-do because I wanted to try one made with both honeydew melon and honey. At first I didn't like it and was thinking maybe honey-don't, but then I added some citrus and it's marvelous.

— o o o —

Honeydew melon has light green flesh and, along with cantaloupe, is a member of the muskmelon family. Watermelon, on the other hand, is actually from the gourd family and is related to cucumbers.

1	honeydew melon	1
¾ cup	water	175 mL
2 or 3	large oranges	2 or 3
¼ cup	lemon juice	60 mL
¼ cup	lime juice	60 mL
1	package (1.75 oz/49 or 57 g) powdered pectin	1
1 cup	liquid honey	250 mL
5½ cups	granulated sugar	1.375 L
¼ cup	Triple Sec, other orange liqueur or melon liqueur (optional)	60 mL

1. Cut melon in half; scoop out seeds with a spoon and discard. Using a serrated knife, cut off peel. Chop fruit into 1-inch (2.5 cm) chunks.

2. In a large, deep, heavy-bottomed pot, combine melon and water. Bring to a boil over medium heat. Reduce heat and simmer, covered, for about 20 minutes or until softened. Use a potato masher to further break down melon so there are no lumps (or purée in food processor). Measure exactly 4 cups (1 L); return to clean pot.

3. Cut five strips of rind from 1 of the oranges, each about 3 inches by 1 inch (7.5 by 2.5 cm). Cut all oranges in half and squeeze out juice; measure 1 cup (250 mL). Add orange rind strips, orange juice, lemon juice and lime juice to pot.

4. Stir in pectin until dissolved. Bring to a boil over high heat, stirring constantly.

5. Stir in honey. Add sugar in a steady stream, stirring constantly. Return to a full boil, stirring constantly to dissolve sugar. Boil hard for 1 minute

6. Remove from heat, remove orange rind and skim off any foam. Stir in liqueur (if using). Stir for 5 to 8 minutes to prevent floating fruit.

7. Ladle into sterilized jars to within ¼ inch (0.5 cm) of rim; wipe rims. Apply prepared lids and rings; tighten rings just until fingertip-tight.

8. Process jars in a boiling water canner for 10 minutes (for details, see page 20). Transfer jars to a towel-lined surface and let rest at room temperature until set. Check seals; refrigerate any unsealed jars for up to 3 weeks.

Kiwi Banana Orange Jam

Makes about six 8-ounce (250 mL) jars

This combination of refreshing flavors makes a wonderful "good morning" jam.

— o o o —

Tip

You'll need about 6 medium kiwis and about 5 bananas for this recipe.

Variation

Kiwi Papaya Orange Jam: Replace the bananas with papaya.

3	large oranges	3
2 cups	chopped kiwifruit	500 mL
2½ cups	finely chopped firm ripe bananas	625 mL
2 tbsp	lemon juice	30 mL
1	package (1.75 oz/49 or 57 g) powdered pectin	1
4¾ cups	granulated sugar	1.175 L

1. Using a fine grater, remove 1 tbsp (15 mL) orange rind; set aside. Peel oranges and remove all pith, seeds and membranes. Chop the fruit and measure to make 1½ cups (375 mL), including juices.

2. In a large, deep, heavy-bottomed pot, combine orange rind, oranges, kiwis, bananas and lemon juice. Stir in pectin until dissolved. Bring to a boil over high heat, stirring constantly.

3. Add sugar in a steady stream, stirring constantly. Return to a full boil, stirring constantly to dissolve sugar. Boil hard for 1 minute.

4. Remove from heat and skim off any foam. Stir for 5 to 8 minutes to prevent floating fruit.

5. Ladle into sterilized jars to within ¼ inch (0.5 cm) of rim; wipe rims. Apply prepared lids and rings; tighten rings just until fingertip-tight.

6. Process jars in a boiling water canner for 10 minutes (for details, see page 20). Transfer jars to a towel-lined surface and let rest at room temperature until set. Check seals; refrigerate any unsealed jars for up to 3 weeks.

Kiwi Mango Jam

This jam has a beautiful color and an exquisite taste. It's delicious in cheesecake — both stirred into the batter and spooned over the top of the finished cake.

— o o o —

Tip

You'll need about 6 large kiwis and 3 or 4 medium mangos for this recipe.

3 cups	chopped kiwifruit	750 mL
3 cups	chopped mangos	750 mL
2 tbsp	lemon juice	30 mL
1	package (1.75 oz/49 or 57 g) powdered pectin	1
5 cups	granulated sugar	1.25 L

1. In a large, deep, heavy-bottomed pot, combine kiwis, mangos and lemon juice. Stir in pectin until dissolved. Bring to a full boil over high heat, stirring constantly.

2. Add sugar in a steady stream, stirring constantly. Return to a full boil, stirring constantly to dissolve sugar. Boil hard for 1 minute.

3. Remove from heat and skim off any foam. Stir for 5 to 8 minutes to prevent floating fruit.

4. Ladle into sterilized jars to within $\frac{1}{4}$ inch (0.5 cm) of rim; wipe rims. Apply prepared lids and rings; tighten rings just until fingertip-tight.

5. Process jars in a boiling water canner for 10 minutes (for details, see page 20). Transfer jars to a towel-lined surface and let rest at room temperature until set. Check seals; refrigerate any unsealed jars for up to 3 weeks.

> A kiwi contains almost twice the vitamin C of an orange and about 20% more potassium than a banana and is a source of both soluble and insoluble fiber.

Kiwi Pineapple Orange Jam

*This jam has a beautiful
light green and orange
color and a nice
fresh flavor.*

— o o o —

Tips

To section oranges, use a
sharp knife to cut off ends;
stand on one end. Cut
off and discard rind and
white pith. Cut between
membranes to remove
the flesh.

If desired, add 1 tbsp
(15 mL) finely grated orange
rind to this recipe; grate
before peeling and add
with the chopped oranges.

You'll need about 8 large
kiwis for this recipe.

3	medium oranges	3
3 cups	finely chopped kiwifruit	750 mL
1	can (8 oz/227 mL) or 1 cup (250 mL) crushed pineapple, including juice	1
1/4 cup	lime juice	60 mL
1	package (1.75 oz/49 or 57 g) powdered pectin	1
5 1/2 cups	granulated sugar	1.375 L

1. Peel and section oranges, removing all pith, seeds and membranes, and chop the fruit, reserving any juices.

2. In a large, deep, heavy-bottomed pot, combine oranges with juice, kiwis, pineapple with juice and lime juice. Stir in pectin until dissolved. Bring to a full boil over high heat, stirring constantly.

3. Add sugar in a steady stream, stirring constantly. Return to a full boil, stirring constantly to dissolve sugar. Boil hard for 1 minute.

4. Remove from heat and skim off any foam. Stir for 5 to 8 minutes to prevent floating fruit.

5. Ladle into sterilized jars to within 1/4 inch (0.5 cm) of rim; wipe rims. Apply prepared lids and rings; tighten rings just until fingertip-tight.

6. Process jars in a boiling water canner for 10 minutes (for details, see page 20). Transfer jars to a towel-lined surface and let rest at room temperature until set. Check seals; refrigerate any unsealed jars for up to 3 weeks.

Kiwi Raspberry Jam

Makes about five 8-ounce (250 mL) jars

This jam has a lovely fresh flavor! I enjoy these two fruits together with yogurt and desserts, so try some stirred into plain or vanilla yogurt, as a cheesecake topping, or as a cake filling.

— o o o —

Tip

You'll need about 8 large kiwis for this recipe. If desired, you can slice kiwis into several pieces and pulse in a food processor fitted with a metal blade to finely chop.

Variations

Kiwi Blackberry Jam: Replace the raspberries with blackberries.

Golden Kiwi Raspberry Jam: Replace green kiwifruit with gold kiwifruit.

3 cups	finely chopped kiwifruit	750 mL
2 cups	raspberries	500 mL
1 tbsp	lime or lemon juice	15 mL
1	package (1.75 oz/49 or 57 g) powdered pectin	1
4 cups	granulated sugar	1 L

1. Place kiwis in a large, deep, heavy-bottomed pot. In a shallow dish, use a potato masher to crush raspberries. Add raspberries and lime juice to pot. Stir in pectin until dissolved. Bring to a full boil over high heat, stirring constantly.

2. Add sugar in a steady stream, stirring constantly. Return to a full boil, stirring constantly to dissolve sugar. Boil hard for 1 minute.

3. Remove from heat and skim off any foam. Stir for 5 to 8 minutes to prevent floating fruit.

4. Ladle into sterilized jars to within 1/4 inch (0.5 cm) of rim; wipe rims. Apply prepared lids and rings; tighten rings just until fingertip-tight.

5. Process jars in a boiling water canner for 10 minutes (for details, see page 20). Transfer jars to a towel-lined surface and let rest at room temperature until set. Check seals; refrigerate any unsealed jars for up to 3 weeks.

Kiwi Watermelon Jam

**Makes about five
8-ounce (250 mL) jars**

*I just thought this
would make a nice-
looking jam — small
wedges of green kiwi,
with its tiny black seeds,
in a pink jelly. I was
right — and it tastes
great too!*

— o o o —

Tips

You'll need about 6 medium kiwis for this recipe.

Watermelon tends to stay crisp even after cooking, so I recommend puréeing it in a food processor fitted with a metal blade or a blender rather than finely chopping it by hand. You'll need about 3 cups (750 mL) chopped to start with. Be sure to remove any seeds before puréeing.

2 cups	chopped kiwifruit	500 mL
2 cups	puréed watermelon	500 mL
1/4 cup	lemon juice	60 mL
1	package (1.75 oz/49 or 57 g) powdered pectin	1
5 1/2 cups	granulated sugar	1.375 L

1. In a large, deep, heavy-bottomed pot, combine kiwis, watermelon and lemon juice. Stir in pectin until dissolved. Bring to a full boil over high heat, stirring constantly.

2. Add sugar in a steady stream, stirring constantly. Return to a full boil, stirring constantly to dissolve sugar. Boil hard for 1 minute.

3. Remove from heat and skim off any foam. Stir for 5 to 8 minutes to prevent floating fruit.

4. Ladle into sterilized jars to within 1/4 inch (0.5 cm) of rim; wipe rims. Apply prepared lids and rings; tighten rings just until fingertip-tight.

5. Process jars in a boiling water canner for 10 minutes (for details, see page 20). Transfer jars to a towel-lined surface and let rest at room temperature until set. Check seals; refrigerate any unsealed jars for up to 3 weeks.

Mango Orange Jam with Mint Green Tea

Makes about five 8-ounce (250 mL) jars

This jam has a nice aroma and a subtle mint flavor. I used mint-flavored green tea, but feel free to try this jam with other herbal teas that you like.

— ooo —

Tips

You'll need 2 medium mangos for this recipe. Or you can use about 1¼ lbs (625 g) of frozen chopped mango. Measure the volume while frozen, then let thaw before adding to the pot.

If desired, add 1 tbsp (15 mL) finely grated orange rind to this recipe; grate before peeling and add with the chopped oranges.

Variations

Mango Orange Jam: Replace the tea with 1 cup (250 mL) orange juice.

Mango Orange Mint Jam: To the above variation, add ¼ cup (60 mL) finely chopped orange mint or spearmint with the fruit.

5	mint green tea bags	5
1 cup	boiling water	250 mL
2	large oranges	2
2 cups	finely chopped mangos	500 mL
1 tbsp	lemon juice	15 mL
1	package (1.75 oz/49 or 57 g) powdered pectin	1
4 cups	granulated sugar	1 L

1. In a liquid measuring cup, pour water over tea bags; let steep for 5 minutes. Remove bags (squeezing is okay) and discard; add enough water to measure 1 cup (250 mL).

2. Peel oranges and remove all pith, seeds and membranes. Finely chop the fruit and measure to make 1 cup (250 mL), including juices.

3. In a large, deep, heavy-bottomed pot, combine oranges, mangos, lemon juice and prepared tea. Bring to a boil over high heat, stirring constantly. Reduce heat to medium and cook for 2 minutes, stirring constantly.

4. Stir in pectin until dissolved. Increase heat to high and bring to a full boil, stirring constantly.

5. Add sugar in a steady stream, stirring constantly. Return to a full boil, stirring constantly to dissolve sugar. Boil hard for 1 minute.

6. Remove from heat and skim off any foam. Stir for 5 to 8 minutes to prevent floating fruit.

7. Ladle into sterilized jars to within ¼ inch (0.5 cm) of rim; wipe rims. Apply prepared lids and rings; tighten rings just until fingertip-tight.

8. Process jars in a boiling water canner for 10 minutes (for details, see page 20). Transfer jars to a towel-lined surface and let rest at room temperature until set. Check seals; refrigerate any unsealed jars for up to 3 weeks.

Mango Passion Fruit Jam

Passion fruit can be expensive, so I like to combine it with another fruit. Here, mangos complement it well.

— o o o —

Tips

You'll need about 4 mangos and 6 or 7 passion fruit for this recipe.

If desired, use a food processor fitted with a metal blade to chop the mangos; pulse on and off to chop, but do not purée. Scrape down the sides with a spatula a couple of times.

Passion fruit is ripe when the rind no longer has any green and the outer skin becomes wrinkled. To prepare, cut in half around the middle and use a spoon to scoop out the seeds and jelly-like pulp, both of which are edible; discard the shells.

Variation

Peach Passion Fruit Jam: Replace all or half of the mangos with peeled peaches.

3½ cups	finely chopped mangos	875 mL
¾ cup	passion fruit pulp	175 mL
¼ cup	lemon juice	60 mL
5½ cups	granulated sugar	1.375 L
2	pouches (each 3 oz/85 mL) liquid pectin	2

1. In a large, deep, heavy-bottomed pot, combine mangos, passion fruit and lemon juice.

2. Add sugar in a steady stream, stirring constantly. Bring to a full boil over high heat, stirring constantly to dissolve sugar.

3. Immediately stir in pectin; return to a full boil. Boil hard for 1 minute, stirring constantly.

4. Remove from heat and skim off any foam. Stir for 5 to 8 minutes to prevent floating fruit.

5. Ladle into sterilized jars to within ¼ inch (0.5 cm) of rim; wipe rims. Apply prepared lids and rings; tighten rings just until fingertip-tight.

6. Process jars in a boiling water canner for 10 minutes (for details, see page 20). Transfer jars to a towel-lined surface and let rest at room temperature until set. Check seals; refrigerate any unsealed jars for up to 3 weeks.

Nectarine Blueberry Jam

**Makes about five
8-ounce (250 mL) jars**

*This is an easy jam to
make, as there is no
peeling of fruit. Use
wild blueberries if you
can get them.*

— o o o —

Tips

You'll need 4 or 5 large
nectarines for this recipe.

If using frozen berries,
measure while still frozen
and let thaw before adding
to the pot.

Variation

Peach Blueberry Jam:
Replace the nectarines
with peeled peaches
(see tip, page 129).

3 cups	finely chopped nectarines	750 mL
2 cups	blueberries	500 mL
1 tbsp	finely grated lemon rind (optional)	15 mL
3 tbsp	lemon juice	45 mL
1	package (1.75 oz/49 or 57 g) powdered pectin	1
4½ cups	granulated sugar	1.125 L

1. Place nectarines in a large, deep, heavy-bottomed pot. In a shallow dish, use a potato masher to crush blueberries. Add to nectarines in pot, along with lemon rind (if using) and lemon juice. Stir in pectin until dissolved. Bring to a boil over high heat, stirring constantly.

2. Add sugar in a steady stream, stirring constantly. Bring to a full boil, stirring constantly to dissolve sugar. Boil hard for 1 minute.

3. Remove from heat and skim off any foam.

4. Ladle into sterilized jars to within $\frac{1}{4}$ inch (0.5 cm) of rim; wipe rims. Apply prepared lids and rings; tighten rings just until fingertip-tight.

5. Process jars in a boiling water canner for 10 minutes (for details, see page 20). Transfer jars to a towel-lined surface and let rest at room temperature until set. Check seals; refrigerate any unsealed jars for up to 3 weeks.

Nectarine Plum Jam

*The peels of these
summer tree fruits add
color and flavor to this
scrumptious jam.*

Tip
You'll need about 4 large
nectarines and about
5 medium plums for this
recipe.

Variation
Peach Plum Jam:
Replace the nectarines
with peeled peaches
(see tip, page 129).

2½ cups	finely chopped nectarines	625 mL
2 cups	finely chopped red plums	500 mL
2 tbsp	lemon juice	30 mL
1	package (1.75 oz/49 or 57 g) powdered pectin	1
4½ cups	granulated sugar	1.125 L

1. In a large, deep, heavy-bottomed pot, combine nectarines, plums and lemon juice. Bring to a boil over high heat, stirring constantly. Reduce heat and simmer, covered, for 3 minutes, stirring often.

2. Stir in pectin until dissolved. Increase heat to high and bring to a full boil, stirring constantly.

3. Add sugar in a steady stream, stirring constantly. Return to a full boil, stirring constantly to dissolve sugar. Boil hard for 1 minute.

4. Remove from heat and skim off any foam. Stir for 8 to 10 minutes to prevent floating fruit.

5. Ladle into sterilized jars to within ¼ inch (0.5 cm) of rim; wipe rims. Apply prepared lids and rings; tighten rings just until fingertip-tight.

6. Process jars in a boiling water canner for 10 minutes (for details, see page 20). Transfer jars to a towel-lined surface and let rest at room temperature until set. Check seals; refrigerate any unsealed jars for up to 3 weeks.

Peach Sour Cherry Jam

**Makes about six
8-ounce (250 mL) jars**

*Sour cherries are a nice
complement to the sweet
ambrosia of peaches.*

— o o o —

Tips

You'll need 7 to 9 large
peaches and about 1 lb
(500 g) of cherries for this
recipe.

Freeze pitted sour (tart)
cherries early in the season
to use later. If using frozen
cherries, measure while still
frozen, then let thaw and
drain well before chopping.

Variations

*Nectarine Sour Cherry
Jam:* Replace the
peaches with unpeeled
nectarines.

*Peach Sour Cherry Jam
with Vanilla:* Split 1 vanilla
bean lengthwise and
scrape out seeds with a
paring knife. Add bean
and seeds to pot with
the fruit. Remove bean
after skimming off foam.

3 cups	finely chopped peeled peaches (see tip, page 129)	750 mL
2 cups	finely chopped pitted sour (tart) cherries	500 mL
2 tbsp	lemon juice	30 mL
1	package (1.75 oz/49 or 57 g) powdered pectin	1
5½ cups	granulated sugar	1.375 L
2 tbsp	cherry brandy (optional)	30 mL

1. In a large, deep, heavy-bottomed pot, combine peaches, cherries and lemon juice. Bring to a boil over high heat. Reduce heat and simmer, covered, for 3 minutes, stirring occasionally.

2. Stir in pectin until dissolved. Bring to a full boil over high heat, stirring constantly.

3. Add sugar in a steady stream, stirring constantly. Return to a full boil, stirring constantly to dissolve sugar. Boil hard for 1 minute.

4. Remove from heat and skim off any foam. Stir in cherry brandy (if using). Stir for 8 to 10 minutes to prevent floating fruit.

5. Ladle into sterilized jars to within $\frac{1}{4}$ inch (0.5 cm) of rim; wipe rims. Apply prepared lids and rings; tighten rings just until fingertip-tight.

6. Process jars in a boiling water canner for 10 minutes (for details, see page 20). Transfer jars to a towel-lined surface and let rest at room temperature until set. Check seals; refrigerate any unsealed jars for up to 3 weeks.

Spiced Peach Cranberry Jam

Makes about five 8-ounce (250 mL) jars

This refreshing jam has just a hint of spice to accent the fruit flavors. Pick up frozen cranberries to make this jam when peaches are in season.

— o o o —

Tip
There should be 3 cups (750 mL) of cranberries in a 12-oz (340 g) package.

Variation
Spiced Nectarine Cranberry Jam: Replace the peaches with unpeeled nectarines.

4 cups	chopped peeled peaches (see tip, page 129)	1 L
3 cups	cranberries	750 mL
1/2 tsp	ground cinnamon	2 mL
1/4 tsp	ground nutmeg	1 mL
4 1/2 cups	granulated sugar	1.125 L

1. In a large, deep, heavy-bottomed pot, combine peaches, cranberries, cinnamon and nutmeg. Bring to a boil over high heat, stirring occasionally.

2. Add sugar in a steady stream, stirring constantly. Bring to a full boil, stirring constantly to dissolve sugar. Reduce heat to medium-high and boil rapidly, stirring often and reducing heat further as mixture thickens, for 15 to 18 minutes or until thickened. Test for setting point (for details, see page 19).

3. Remove from heat and skim off any foam.

4. Ladle into sterilized jars to within 1/4 inch (0.5 cm) of rim; wipe rims. Apply prepared lids and rings; tighten rings just until fingertip-tight.

5. Process jars in a boiling water canner for 10 minutes (for details, see page 20). Transfer jars to a towel-lined surface and let rest at room temperature until set. Check seals; refrigerate any unsealed jars for up to 3 weeks.

Peach Pear Jam

Makes about eight 8-ounce (250 mL) jars

Gayle Rowan (see Contributors, page 12) adds a touch of peach to bring a sparkle to pear jam. Her jams are sold under the Wolfpath label in the Haliburton, Ontario, area.

— ooo —

Tip

Use a fork to crush fully ripe pears in a small, flat dish. Do not purée, or you will get mush; you want some small, lumpy bits. As you go, transfer crushed pears to a 4-cup (1 L) glass measure and stir in the lemon juice to prevent browning.

3½ cups	crushed peeled pears (see tip, at left)	875 mL
½ cup	crushed peeled peaches (see tip, page 129)	125 mL
¼ cup	lemon juice	60 mL
7½ cups	granulated sugar	1.875 L
2	pouches (each 3 oz/85 mL) liquid pectin	2

1. In a large, deep, heavy-bottomed pot, combine pears, peaches and lemon juice. Bring to a boil over high heat, stirring constantly. Reduce heat and boil gently for 1 minute to soften fruit.

2. Add sugar in a steady stream, stirring constantly. Increase heat to high and bring to a full boil, stirring constantly to dissolve sugar.

3. Immediately stir in pectin; return to a full boil. Boil hard for 1 minute, stirring constantly.

4. Remove from heat and skim off any foam. Stir for 5 to 8 minutes to prevent floating fruit.

5. Ladle into sterilized jars to within ¼ inch (0.5 cm) of rim; wipe rims. Apply prepared lids and rings; tighten rings just until fingertip-tight.

6. Process jars in a boiling water canner for 10 minutes (for details, see page 20). Transfer jars to a towel-lined surface and let rest at room temperature until set. Check seals; refrigerate any unsealed jars for up to 3 weeks.

> The amount of red on a peach has to do with the variety and is not always a sign of ripeness.

Peach Pomegranate Jam

*Pomegranate has
gained popularity for its
antioxidant effect. I liked
the convenience of using
bottled juice for this jam,
but if you prefer, you can
extract juice from the
fresh fruit (see tip, below).*

— o o o —

Tips

To juice a pomegranate,
cut it in half and use a citrus
juicer or reamer; strain to
remove any seeds. One
medium pomegranate yields
about ½ cup (125 mL) juice.

You'll need 8 to 10 peaches
for this recipe.

Variation

*Nectarine Pomegranate
Jam:* Use unpeeled
nectarines in place of
the peaches.

2 cups	unsweetened 100% pomegranate juice	500 mL
3½ cups	finely chopped peeled peaches (see tip, page 129)	875 mL
1 tbsp	lemon juice	15 mL
1	package (1.75 oz/49 or 57 g) powdered pectin	1
4½ cups	granulated sugar	1.125 L

1. In a medium pot, bring pomegranate juice to a boil over high heat. Boil for 7 to 8 minutes or until juice is reduced to 1 cup (250 mL). If it measures less, add water to make 1 cup (250 mL).

2. In a large, deep, heavy-bottomed pot, combine reduced pomegranate juice, peaches and lemon juice. Bring to a full boil over high heat. Reduce heat and simmer, covered, for 3 minutes, stirring often.

3. Stir in pectin until dissolved. Increase heat to high and bring to a full boil, stirring constantly.

4. Add sugar in a steady stream, stirring constantly. Return to a full boil, stirring constantly to dissolve sugar. Boil hard for 1 minute.

5. Remove from heat and skim off any foam. Stir for 5 to 8 minutes to prevent floating fruit.

6. Ladle into sterilized jars to within ¼ inch (0.5 cm) of rim; wipe rims. Apply prepared lids and rings; tighten rings just until fingertip-tight.

7. Process jars in a boiling water canner for 10 minutes (for details, see page 20). Transfer jars to a towel-lined surface and let rest at room temperature until set. Check seals; refrigerate any unsealed jars for up to 3 weeks.

Shut Cookies (page 359) with
Peach Sour Cherry Jam (page 125)

Orange Passion Fruit
Micro-Mini Jam (page 168)

Peach Papaya Orange Spread (page 185)
and Raspberry Pear Spread (page 189)

Cherry Profusion Conserve (page 212)

Peach Raspberry Jam

Makes about seven 8-ounce (250 mL) jars

Larry McGuire of Hamilton, Ontario (see Contributors, page 12), says he loves to make jams because they have tastes you can only get from your own kitchen. He shares his treasures as family Christmas gifts. This one is great stirred into plain yogurt.

— o o o —

Tip

How to Peel Peaches: Bring a medium pot of water to a boil over high heat. Place peaches in water two at a time; boil for 20 to 30 seconds. Remove peaches with a slotted spoon and immediately immerse in a bowl of cold water. Repeat with remaining peaches. When peaches are cool enough to handle, slit down the side of the peel with a paring knife and slip off peel. Cut peaches in half and remove pits.

3½ cups	chopped peeled peaches (see tip, at left)	875 mL
2 cups	raspberries	500 mL
¼ cup	lemon juice	60 mL
7 cups	granulated sugar	1.75 L
2	pouches (each 3 oz/85 mL) liquid pectin	2

1. In a large, deep, heavy-bottomed pot, combine peaches, raspberries and lemon juice. Bring to a boil over high heat, stirring constantly.

2. Add sugar in a steady stream, stirring constantly. Bring to a full boil, stirring constantly to dissolve sugar.

3. Immediately stir in pectin; return to a full boil. Boil hard for 1 minute, stirring constantly.

4. Remove from heat and skim off any foam.

5. Ladle into sterilized jars to within ¼ inch (0.5 cm) of rim; wipe rims. Apply prepared lids and rings; tighten rings just until fingertip-tight.

6. Process jars in a boiling water canner for 10 minutes (for details, see page 20). Transfer jars to a towel-lined surface and let rest at room temperature until set. Check seals; refrigerate any unsealed jars for up to 3 weeks.

Pineapple Mango Jam

I love the fresh, tropical taste this jam has. Use Ataulfo mangos if they are available, as their flavor and texture are superior.

—o o o—

Tip
You'll need about 4 Ataulfo mangos or 2 regular mangos for this recipe.

Recipe Suggestion
Use jam to make glaze for roasted ham: Mix together ¼ cup (60 mL) jam and 1 tsp (5 mL) Dijon mustard.

Variation
Pineapple Papaya Jam: Replace the mangos with papaya.

2 cups	finely chopped fresh pineapple (or well-drained canned crushed pineapple)	500 mL
2 cups	finely chopped mangos	500 mL
¼ cup	lime juice	60 mL
4½ cups	granulated sugar	1.125 L
1	pouch (3 oz/85 mL) liquid pectin	1
	Grenadine or amber rum (optional)	

1. In a large, deep, heavy-bottomed pot, combine pineapple, mangos and lime juice. Bring to a boil over high heat, stirring constantly. Reduce heat and simmer, stirring often, for 6 to 8 minutes or until pineapple is softened. If desired, use an immersion blender or a potato masher to break up any large pieces.

2. Add sugar in a steady stream, stirring constantly. Increase heat to high and bring to a full boil, stirring constantly to dissolve sugar.

3. Immediately stir in pectin; return to a full boil. Boil hard for 1 minute, stirring constantly.

4. Remove from heat and skim off any foam.

5. Add about 2 tsp (10 mL) grenadine (if using) to each jar. Ladle jam into sterilized jars to within ¼ inch (0.5 cm) of rim; wipe rims. Apply prepared lids and rings; tighten rings just until fingertip-tight.

6. Process jars in a boiling water canner for 10 minutes (for details, see page 20). Transfer jars to a towel-lined surface and let rest at room temperature until set. Check seals; refrigerate any unsealed jars for up to 3 weeks.

> Grenadine syrup is non-alcoholic, made from pomegranates and sweetened with sugar. It gets its name from the island of Grenada, where pomegranates are grown. You will find it in the carbonated drinks section of the supermarket.

Damson Plum Raspberry Jam

Makes about six 8-ounce (250 mL) jars

This pairing with raspberries makes a tasty variation on Damson Plum Jam (page 73), and is good when you have a small number of plums left over.

— ooo —

4 cups	damson plums	1 L
1½ cups	water	375 mL
3 cups	raspberries	750 mL
4½ cups	granulated sugar	1.125 L

1. In a large, deep, heavy-bottomed pot, combine plums and water. Bring to a boil over high heat. Reduce heat and simmer for 15 minutes, stirring occasionally. Use a slotted spoon to remove pits (which have become loosened from fruit) and place them in a colander over a large bowl. Shake to drain extra pulp and skins from pits; add back to pot and discard pits.

2. Stir in raspberries. Increase heat to high and bring to a full boil, stirring constantly.

3. Add sugar in a steady stream, stirring constantly. Return to a full boil, stirring constantly to dissolve sugar. Reduce heat to medium-high and boil rapidly, stirring often and reducing heat further as mixture thickens, for 8 to 12 minutes or until thickened. Test for setting point (for details, see page 19).

4. Remove from heat and skim off any foam.

5. Ladle into sterilized jars to within ¼ inch (0.5 cm) of rim. Wipe rims and apply prepared lids and rings; tighten rings just until fingertip-tight.

6. Process jars in a boiling water canner for 10 minutes (for details, see page 20). Transfer jars to a towel-lined surface and let rest at room temperature until set. Check seals; refrigerate any unsealed jars for up to 3 weeks.

> Damson plums are small, oval, bluish-purple plums that are extremely tart. They're not a plum for fresh eating, but they're ideal for preserves. Look for them at farmers' markets in late August to early September.

Red Plum Rhubarb Jam

*This jam has a gorgeous
pinky red color and a
pleasantly tart flavor with
a slightly softer set.*

— o o o —

Tips

You'll need 10 to 12 large
plums and about 1½ lbs
(750 g) of rhubarb for this
recipe.

To coarsely chop the plums,
cut them in half, remove pits
and cut into several pieces.
Chop in a food processor
fitted with a metal blade,
pulsing on and off and
scraping down the sides
with a spatula. Be careful
not to purée them.

Recipe Suggestions

Stir several large spoonfuls
of this jam into apples for
a pie or crisp.

This jam is excellent as
a topping for crêpes or
cheesecake.

4 cups	coarsely chopped red plums	1 L
4 cups	chopped rhubarb (½-inch/1 cm pieces)	1 L
½ cup	water or unsweetened orange juice	125 mL
2 tbsp	lemon juice	30 mL
4 cups	granulated sugar	1 L

1. In a large, deep, heavy-bottomed pot, combine plums, rhubarb, water and lemon juice. Bring to a boil over high heat, stirring constantly. Reduce heat and simmer, covered, stirring often, for about 15 minutes or until rhubarb is softened.

2. Add sugar in a steady stream, stirring constantly. Increase heat to high and bring to a full boil, stirring constantly to dissolve sugar. Reduce heat and boil gently, uncovered, stirring often and reducing heat further as mixture thickens, for 20 to 25 minutes or until thickened. Test for setting point (for details, see page 19).

3. Remove from heat and skim off any foam.

4. Ladle into sterilized jars to within ¼ inch (0.5 cm) of rim; wipe rims. Apply prepared lids and rings; tighten rings just until fingertip-tight.

5. Process jars in a boiling water canner for 10 minutes (for details, see page 20). Transfer jars to a towel-lined surface and let rest at room temperature until set. Check seals; refrigerate any unsealed jars for up to 3 weeks.

> Plums grow on every continent except Antarctica.

Plumcot Orange Jam

Makes about six 8-ounce (250 mL) jars

I love this new plum-apricot hybrid, which appeared in my supermarket this summer. Here, I have blended plumcots with oranges. If desired, add a bit of liqueur to make the jam a bit more upscale.

— o o o —

Tips

You'll need about 2 lbs (1 kg) of plumcots for this recipe. There's no need to peel plumcots (or plums) when making jam — or for any other cooking, for that matter — so they're not just a time-saver but have added good taste and nutrition too.

Use a food processor fitted with a metal blade to chop plumcots, if desired, by pulsing on and off several times and scraping down the sides with a spatula. Be sure not to purée.

3	large oranges	3
3 cups	finely chopped plumcots or plums	750 mL
1/4 tsp	ground nutmeg (optional)	1 mL
6 cups	granulated sugar	1.5 L
1	pouch (3 oz/85 mL) liquid pectin	1
1/4 cup	Triple Sec or other orange liqueur (optional)	60 mL

1. Using a fine grater, remove 2 tbsp (30 mL) orange rind; set aside. Peel oranges and remove all pith, seeds and membranes. Chop the fruit and measure to make 1 1/2 cups (375 mL), including juices.

2. In a large, deep, heavy-bottomed pot, combine orange rind, oranges, plumcots and nutmeg (if using). Bring to a boil over medium heat, stirring constantly. Reduce heat and simmer, covered, for 5 minutes, stirring occasionally.

3. Add sugar in a steady stream, stirring constantly. Increase heat to high and bring to a full boil, stirring constantly to dissolve sugar.

4. Immediately stir in pectin; return to a full boil. Boil hard for 1 minute, stirring constantly.

5. Remove from heat and skim off any foam. Stir in liqueur (if using).

6. Ladle into sterilized jars to within 1/4 inch (0.5 cm) of rim; wipe rims. Apply prepared lids and rings; tighten rings just until fingertip-tight.

7. Process jars in a boiling water canner for 10 minutes (for details, see page 20). Transfer jars to a towel-lined surface and let rest at room temperature until set. Check seals; refrigerate any unsealed jars for up to 3 weeks.

Prickly Pear and Pear Jam

**Makes about five
8-ounce (250 mL) jars**

*Prickly pears are not
pears but the fruit of
a cactus. I thought it
would be fun to try
pairing them with
pears, and it's a great
combination! The jam
has a lovely light peach
color and excellent flavor.*

— o o o —

Tips

You'll need about 3 lbs
(1.5 kg) of pears (about
6 large) for this recipe.

How to Peel a Prickly Pear:
Place prickly pears in a
heatproof bowl and pour
in boiling water to cover.
Wearing rubber gloves,
scrub skins with a brush
to remove the tiny hair-like
bristles. Rinse well. Using
a sharp knife, cut the ends
off and slit skins on one side
from one end to the other.
Peel back skin, rolling in one
direction to release the pulp
and seeds in one piece;
collect all the pulp in a large
bowl. Discard skins.

8	prickly pears (approx.), peeled	8
	Boiling water	
3 cups	finely chopped peeled Bartlett pears	750 mL
2 tbsp	lime or lemon juice	30 mL
1	package (1.75 oz/49 or 57 g) powdered pectin	1
5½ cups	granulated sugar	1.375 L

1. Press prickly pears through a fine-mesh sieve to remove seeds; measure 1¾ cups (425 mL), including any juices.

2. In a large, deep, heavy-bottomed pot, combine prickly pear pulp, pears and lime juice. Stir in pectin until dissolved. Bring to a full boil over high heat, stirring constantly.

3. Add sugar in a steady stream, stirring constantly. Return to a full boil, stirring constantly to dissolve sugar. Boil hard for 1 minute.

4. Remove from heat and skim off any foam. Stir for 5 to 8 minutes to prevent floating fruit.

5. Ladle into sterilized jars to within ¼ inch (0.5 cm) of rim; wipe rims. Apply prepared lids and rings; tighten rings just until fingertip-tight.

6. Process jars in a boiling water canner for 10 minutes (for details, see page 20). Transfer jars to a towel-lined surface and let rest at room temperature until set. Check seals; refrigerate any unsealed jars for up to 3 weeks.

Variations

Prickly Pear and Pear Jam with Ginger: Add 2 tbsp (30 mL) grated fresh gingerroot to the fruit and lime juice.

Prickly Pear and Pear Jam with Honey: Replace 1 cup (250 mL) of the sugar with 1 cup (250 mL) liquid honey.

Raspberry Blackberry Jam

5 cups	blackberries	1.25 L
4 cups	raspberries	1 L
3¾ cups	granulated sugar	925 mL

Makes about five 8-ounce (250 mL) jars

The addition of blackberries enriches the flavor of the raspberries in this lovely-textured jam.

— o o o —

Variations

Raspberry Blackberry Jam with Chambord: After skimming off foam, stir in ¼ cup (60 mL) Chambord or other raspberry liqueur.

Seedless Raspberry Blackberry Jam: Once jam has reached the setting point, working in batches, pour though a fine-mesh sieve placed over a large bowl; discard seeds and rinse sieve between batches. If desired, pass though additional times to further remove seeds that may have slipped through. Return to pot and bring to a boil, stirring constantly. Remove from heat and ladle into jars. Of course, the yield will be less.

1. In a large, deep, heavy-bottomed pot, combine blackberries and raspberries. Bring to a boil over high heat, stirring constantly.

2. Add sugar in a steady stream, stirring constantly. Bring to a full boil, stirring constantly to dissolve sugar. Reduce heat to medium-high and boil rapidly, stirring often and reducing heat further as mixture thickens, for 10 to 15 minutes or until thickened. Test for setting point (for details, see page 19).

3. Remove from heat and skim off any foam.

4. Ladle into sterilized jars to within ¼ inch (0.5 cm) of rim; wipe rims. Apply prepared lids and rings; tighten rings just until fingertip-tight.

5. Process jars in a boiling water canner for 10 minutes (for details, see page 20). Transfer jars to a towel-lined surface and let rest at room temperature until set. Check seals; refrigerate any unsealed jars for up to 3 weeks.

Raspberry Blueberry Jam

**Makes about four
8-ounce (250 mL) jars**

*I made a delicious pie
with these two berries
one summer, so I thought
I would try them together
as a jam. Superb!*

— ○ ○ ○ —

Tip

If using frozen fruit, measure while still frozen and let thaw before adding to the pot.

Recipe Suggestion

This jam is a great choice to stir into plain yogurt or to top a cheesecake.

3 cups	raspberries	750 mL
2 cups	blueberries	500 mL
2 tbsp	lemon juice	30 mL
3¾ cups	granulated sugar	925 mL

1. In a large, deep, heavy-bottomed pot, combine raspberries, blueberries and lemon juice. Using a potato masher, crush about half the berries to release some of their juice. Bring to a boil over high heat, stirring constantly.

2. Add sugar in a steady stream, stirring constantly. Bring to a full boil, stirring constantly to dissolve sugar. Reduce heat to medium-high and boil rapidly, stirring often and reducing heat further as mixture thickens, for 10 to 12 minutes or until thickened. Test for setting point (for details, see page 19).

3. Remove from heat and skim off any foam.

4. Ladle into sterilized jars to within ¼ inch (0.5 cm) of rim; wipe rims. Apply prepared lids and rings; tighten rings just until fingertip-tight.

5. Process jars in a boiling water canner for 10 minutes (for details, see page 20). Transfer jars to a towel-lined surface and let rest at room temperature until set. Check seals; refrigerate any unsealed jars for up to 3 weeks.

Raspberry Gooseberry Red Currant Jam

These three berries usually arrive midsummer. This jam has a lovely red color, with a slightly tart taste.

— o o o —

Tip
Use small manicure scissors to remove the beards (blossom ends) from gooseberries.

4 cups	gooseberries, beards removed	1 L
3 cups	red currants	750 mL
3 cups	raspberries	750 mL
6½ cups	granulated sugar	1.625 L

1. In a large, deep, heavy-bottomed pot, combine gooseberries and red currants. Bring to a boil over high heat, stirring constantly. Reduce heat and simmer, stirring occasionally, for 10 minutes or until softened.

2. Stir in raspberries. Increase heat to high and bring to a boil, stirring constantly.

3. Add sugar in a steady stream, stirring constantly. Bring to a full boil, stirring constantly to dissolve sugar. Reduce heat to medium-high and boil rapidly, stirring often and reducing heat further as mixture thickens, for 6 to 10 minutes or until thickened. Test for setting point (for details, see page 19).

4. Remove from heat and skim off any foam.

5. Ladle into sterilized jars to within ¼ inch (0.5 cm) of rim; wipe rims. Apply prepared lids and rings; tighten rings just until fingertip-tight.

6. Process jars in a boiling water canner for 10 minutes (for details, see page 20). Transfer jars to a towel-lined surface and let rest at room temperature until set. Check seals; refrigerate any unsealed jars for up to 3 weeks.

> Gooseberries are botanically related to red and black currants. One bush will produce 8 to 10 lbs (3.5 to 4.5 kg) of fruit per year.

Raspberry Lychee Jam with Lychee Liqueur

Makes about five 8-ounce (250 mL) jars

This turned out to be one of my favorite new jams. The addition of the aromatic lychee liqueur (Soho) dramatically enhances the lychee fruit flavor. Try this, especially if you are fond of raspberry jams.

— o o o —

Tip

How to Peel a Lychee Fruit:
Starting at one side of the stem and circling all the way around the fruit, score the skin with a sharp knife. Peel the two halves of the skin away from the white flesh. Pull the flesh away from the brown, nut-like seed, which will stay attached to the stem and skin. Discard skin, seed and stem.

Variation

Strawberry Lychee Jam:
Replace the raspberries with 5 cups (1.25 L) sliced strawberries. Crush with a potato masher before adding to pot.

1 lb	lychee fruit, peeled and seeds removed (see tip, at left)	500 g
5 cups	raspberries	1.25 L
1/4 cup	lemon juice	60 mL
1	package (1.75 oz/49 or 57 g) powdered pectin	1
4 cups	granulated sugar	1 L
1/4 cup	lychee liqueur	60 mL

1. Purée lychee flesh using a food processor fitted with a metal blade, or chop very finely using a sharp knife. Measure to make $1\frac{1}{3}$ cups (325 mL). Place in a large, deep, heavy-bottomed pot. Stir in raspberries and lemon juice.

2. Stir in pectin until dissolved. Bring to a boil over high heat, stirring constantly.

3. Add sugar in a steady stream, stirring constantly. Bring to a full boil, stirring constantly to dissolve sugar. Boil hard for 1 minute.

4. Remove from heat and skim off any foam. Stir in liqueur.

5. Ladle into sterilized jars to within 1/4 inch (0.5 cm) of rim; wipe rims. Apply prepared lids and rings; tighten rings just until fingertip-tight.

6. Process jars in a boiling water canner for 10 minutes (for details, see page 20). Transfer jars to a towel-lined surface and let rest at room temperature until set. Check seals; refrigerate any unsealed jars for up to 3 weeks.

> Lychees (pronounced lee-chees) are the fruit of a tropical Asian evergreen tree. They are also known as alligator strawberries. They are fragrant, with a sweet taste and a texture like the inside of a grape. Lychees are rich in vitamin C.

Raspberry Mango Jam

*Fragrant, sweet mangos
are a delicious accent
to the tartness of
raspberries.*

— o o o —

Tips

You'll need 5 or 6 Ataulfo
mangos or about 3 regular
mangos for this recipe.

*How to Peel and Pit a
Mango:* Stand the mango on
its stem end and slice along
the wider sides, separating
them from the pit. You will
get two "cheeks" that you
can scoop flesh from, or you
can score the flesh in a grid
pattern, push the skin from
the bottom to pop pieces
of flesh up, then cut them
from the skin in small cubes.
Cut or scrape the remaining
flesh from the pit.

Recipe Suggestion

This jam makes a terrific
filling for Low-Fat Raspberry
Mango Frozen Cake
(page 367).

2 cups	raspberries	500 mL
2 cups	finely chopped mangos	500 mL
2 tbsp	lemon juice	30 mL
5 cups	granulated sugar	1.25 L
1	pouch (3 oz/85 mL) liquid pectin	1

1. In a large, deep, heavy-bottomed pot, combine raspberries, mangos and lemon juice. Bring to a boil over high heat, stirring constantly.

2. Add sugar in a steady stream, stirring constantly. Bring to a full boil, stirring constantly to dissolve sugar.

3. Immediately stir in pectin; return to a full boil. Boil hard for 1 minute, stirring constantly.

4. Remove from heat and skim off any foam. Stir for 5 to 8 minutes to prevent floating fruit.

5. Ladle into sterilized jars to within $\frac{1}{4}$ inch (0.5 cm) of rim; wipe rims. Apply prepared lids and rings; tighten rings just until fingertip-tight.

6. Process jars in a boiling water canner for 10 minutes (for details, see page 20). Transfer jars to a towel-lined surface and let rest at room temperature until set. Check seals; refrigerate any unsealed jars for up to 3 weeks.

Raspberry Plum Jam

*Tasty little yellow plums
(sometimes labeled "sugar
plums") combine with
ever-popular raspberries
in this delightful jam.
This recipe may be also
be made with red plums.*

— o o o —

Tips

Using fruit such as plums
in combination with
raspberries or other berries
automatically cuts down on
the amount of seeds.

You'll need about 1½ lbs
(750 g) of plums for this
recipe.

2 cups	raspberries	500 mL
2 cups	finely chopped yellow or red plums	500 mL
¼ cup	lemon juice	60 mL
5 cups	granulated sugar	1.25 L
1	pouch (3 oz/85 mL) liquid pectin	1

1. In a large, deep, heavy-bottomed pot, combine raspberries, plums and lemon juice. Bring to a boil over high heat, stirring constantly.

2. Add sugar in a steady stream, stirring constantly. Bring to a full boil, stirring constantly to dissolve sugar.

3. Immediately stir in pectin; return to a full boil. Boil hard for 1 minute, stirring constantly.

4. Remove from heat and skim off any foam. Stir for 5 to 8 minutes to prevent floating fruit.

5. Ladle into sterilized jars to within ¼ inch (0.5 cm) of rim; wipe rims. Apply prepared lids and rings; tighten rings just until fingertip-tight.

6. Process jars in a boiling water canner for 10 minutes (for details, see page 20). Transfer jars to a towel-lined surface and let rest at room temperature until set. Check seals; refrigerate any unsealed jars for up to 3 weeks.

> The small, round, yellow plums are called Shiro plums. They range from the size of a Ping-Pong ball to that of a golf ball, and have a slight reddish blush. They are usually available during the month of August.

Raspberry Red Currant Jam

2 cups	red currants	500 mL
5 cups	raspberries	1.25 L
5¼ cups	granulated sugar	1.3 L

Makes about five 8-ounce (250 mL) jars

This is a beautiful red jam with lots of raspberry flavor and a hint of tartness from the red currants. Stir into your favorite baked cheesecake batter or serve with cream cheese and bagels.

— o o o —

Tip
Use the tines of a fork to strip currants from stems.

1. Place currants in a large, deep, heavy-bottomed pot and crush with a potato masher. Stir in raspberries. Bring to a boil over high heat, stirring constantly. Reduce heat and simmer, covered, for 5 minutes.

2. Add sugar in a steady stream, stirring constantly. Increase heat to high and bring to a full boil, stirring constantly to dissolve sugar. Reduce heat to medium-high and boil rapidly, stirring often and reducing heat further as mixture thickens, for 12 to 15 minutes or until thickened. Test for setting point (for details, see page 19).

3. Remove from heat and skim off any foam.

4. Ladle into sterilized jars to within ¼ inch (0.5 cm) of rim; wipe rims. Apply prepared lids and rings; tighten rings just until fingertip-tight.

5. Process jars in a boiling water canner for 10 minutes (for details, see page 20). Transfer jars to a towel-lined surface and let rest at room temperature until set. Check seals; refrigerate any unsealed jars for up to 3 weeks.

Raspberry Rhubarb Jam

**Makes about five
8-ounce (250 mL) jars**

*Two favorite flavors are
natural partners in this
delicious jam.*

—ooo—

Tip

Choose rhubarb that is
crisp. To store, wrap tightly
in plastic and refrigerate for
up to 3 days. Or cut into
½ inch (1 cm) pieces and
freeze, if desired.

Recipe Suggestion

Use this jam to make Easy
Coffee Cake (page 355).

2 cups	raspberries	500 mL
2 cups	chopped rhubarb (½-inch/1 cm pieces)	500 mL
2 tbsp	lemon juice	30 mL
6 cups	granulated sugar	1.5 L
1	pouch (3 oz/85 mL) liquid pectin	1

1. In a large, deep, heavy-bottomed pot, combine raspberries, rhubarb and lemon juice. Bring to a boil over high heat, stirring constantly. Reduce heat and simmer for 3 minutes, stirring occasionally.

2. Add sugar in a steady stream, stirring constantly. Increase heat to high and bring to a full boil, stirring constantly to dissolve sugar.

3. Immediately stir in pectin; return to a full boil. Boil hard for 1 minute, stirring constantly.

4. Remove from heat and skim off any foam.

5. Ladle into sterilized jars to within ¼ inch (0.5 cm) of rim; wipe rims. Apply prepared lids and rings; tighten rings just until fingertip-tight.

6. Process jars in a boiling water canner for 10 minutes (for details, see page 20). Transfer jars to a towel-lined surface and let rest at room temperature until set. Check seals; refrigerate any unsealed jars for up to 3 weeks.

Red Currant Orange Jam

Red currants and oranges make a tasty pairing in this vibrant jam.

— ○○○ —

Recipe Suggestion

Heat jam slightly and press through a sieve to remove seeds. Use to glaze a fruit flan or tart, or drizzle over cheesecake.

4	large oranges	4
5 cups	red currants	1.25 L
4½ cups	granulated sugar	1.125 L

1. Using a fine grater, remove 2 tbsp (30 mL) orange rind; set aside. Peel and section oranges, removing all pith, seeds and membranes, and chop the fruit, reserving any juices.

2. Place currants in a large, deep, heavy-bottomed pot and crush with a potato masher. Stir in orange rind and oranges with juice. Bring to a boil over high heat, stirring constantly. Reduce heat and simmer, covered, for 5 minutes.

3. Add sugar in a steady stream, stirring constantly. Increase heat to high and bring to a full boil, stirring constantly to dissolve sugar. Reduce heat to medium-high and boil rapidly, stirring constantly and reducing heat further as mixture thickens, for 7 to 10 minutes or until thickened. Test for setting point (for details, see page 19).

4. Remove from heat and skim off any foam.

5. Ladle into sterilized jars to within ¼ inch (0.5 cm) of rim; wipe rims. Apply prepared lids and rings; tighten rings just until fingertip-tight.

6. Process jars in a boiling water canner for 10 minutes (for details, see page 20). Transfer jars to a towel-lined surface and let rest at room temperature until set. Check seals; refrigerate any unsealed jars for up to 3 weeks.

Red Fruit Jam

*A blend of three fruits
produces wonderful
flavor and color in this
unique recipe from Paul
Barrie (see Contributors,
page 12). "I think this is
my very best jam. A little
shot of Kirsch at the end
really gives it a special
flavor," he says.*

1½ cups	chopped pitted sour (tart) cherries	375 mL
1½ cups	crushed red currants	375 mL
1½ cups	crushed raspberries	375 mL
3 cups	granulated sugar	750 mL
1 tbsp	Kirsch or cherry brandy (optional)	15 mL

1. In a large, deep, heavy-bottomed pot, combine cherries, currants and raspberries. Bring to a boil over high heat, stirring constantly. Reduce heat and simmer for 15 minutes, stirring often.

2. Add sugar in a steady stream, stirring constantly. Increase heat to high and bring to a full boil, stirring constantly to dissolve sugar. Reduce heat to medium-high and boil rapidly, stirring often and reducing heat further as mixture thickens, for 5 to 10 minutes or until thickened. Test for setting point (for details, see page 19).

3. Remove from heat and skim off any foam. Stir in Kirsch (if using).

4. Ladle into sterilized jars to within ¼ inch (0.5 cm) of rim; wipe rims. Apply prepared lids and rings; tighten rings just until fingertip-tight.

5. Process jars in a boiling water canner for 10 minutes (for details, see page 20). Transfer jars to a towel-lined surface and let rest at room temperature until set. Check seals; refrigerate any unsealed jars for up to 3 weeks.

Rhubarb Orange Ginger Jam

*Orange gives a lovely
color and flavor to
rhubarb jam. I've added
a little snap of ginger for
those who love the taste,
but it can be omitted.*

— ○ ○ ○ —

3	medium oranges	3
4 cups	chopped rhubarb (½-inch/1 cm pieces)	1 L
4½ cups	granulated sugar	1.125 L
¼ cup	minced crystallized ginger	60 mL

1. Using a fine grater, remove 2 tbsp (30 mL) orange rind; set aside. Peel and section oranges, removing all pith, seeds and membranes, and chop the fruit, reserving any juices.

2. In a large, deep, heavy-bottomed pot, combine rhubarb, orange rind and oranges with juice. Bring to a boil over high heat, stirring constantly. Reduce heat and simmer for 5 minutes.

3. Add sugar in a steady stream, stirring constantly. Stir in ginger. Increase heat to high and bring to a full boil, stirring constantly to dissolve sugar. Reduce heat to medium-high and boil rapidly, stirring constantly and reducing heat further as mixture thickens, for 10 to 15 minutes or until thickened. Test for setting point (for details, see page 19).

4. Remove from heat and skim off any foam.

5. Ladle into sterilized jars to within ¼ inch (0.5 cm) of rim; wipe rims. Apply prepared lids and rings; tighten rings just until fingertip-tight.

6. Process jars in a boiling water canner for 10 minutes (for details, see page 20). Transfer jars to a towel-lined surface and let rest at room temperature until set. Check seals; refrigerate any unsealed jars for up to 3 weeks.

Rhubarb Pineapple Jam

*Paul Barrie (see
Contributors, page 12)
graciously allowed me to
share this exquisite, tangy
jam recipe with you.*

— o o o —

Tip

If desired, use extra-sweet
gold pineapple in this
recipe in place of canned.
Remove the peel and core,
then pulse flesh in a food
processor fitted with a metal
blade until finely chopped.
Measure 2¼ cups (550 mL).

3 cups	chopped rhubarb (½-inch/1 cm pieces)	750 mL
1	can (19 oz/540 mL) crushed pineapple, including juice	1
1	package (1.75 oz/49 or 57 g) powdered pectin	1
5½ cups	granulated sugar	1.375 L
2 tbsp	apricot brandy or peach schnapps (optional)	30 mL

1. In a large, deep, heavy-bottomed pot, combine rhubarb and pineapple. Bring to a boil over high heat, stirring constantly. Reduce heat and simmer, covered, for about 2 minutes or until rhubarb is tender.

2. Stir in pectin until dissolved. Increase heat to high and bring to a full boil, stirring constantly.

3. Add sugar in a steady stream, stirring constantly. Return to a full boil, stirring constantly to dissolve sugar. Boil hard for 1 minute.

4. Remove from heat and skim off any foam. Stir in apricot brandy (if using). Stir for 5 to 8 minutes to prevent floating fruit.

5. Ladle into sterilized jars to within ¼ inch (0.5 cm) of rim; wipe rims. Apply prepared lids and rings; tighten rings just until fingertip-tight.

6. Process jars in a boiling water canner for 10 minutes (for details, see page 20). Transfer jars to a towel-lined surface and let rest at room temperature until set. Check seals; refrigerate any unsealed jars for up to 3 weeks.

Strawberry Cantaloupe Jam

**Makes about six
8-ounce (250 mL) jars**

*I prefer melons
combined with other
fruit, and cantaloupe
and strawberries seem
perfect for each other.*

— o o o —

Tip

For 1¾ cups (425 mL)
crushed strawberries,
you'll need about 3½ cups
(875 mL) sliced. For
convenience, you can use
frozen sliced strawberries.
Thaw before crushing.
Strawberries should be
crushed well; otherwise,
they might float in the jar.

Variation

*Strawberry Cantaloupe
Jam with Mint:* Add
¼ cup (60 mL) chopped
fresh mint (spearmint,
orange mint or pineapple
mint) to the fruit and
lemon juice.

1	medium cantaloupe	1
1¾ cups	crushed strawberries (see tip, page 151)	425 mL
¼ cup	lemon or lime juice	60 mL
1	package (1.75 oz/49 or 57 g) powdered pectin	1
5½ cups	granulated sugar	1.375 L

1. Cut cantaloupe in half lengthwise. Using a spoon, scoop out seeds. Cut each half into 4 wedges; cut off rind. Chop flesh into 1-inch (2.5 cm) chunks, trimming off any green parts; measure 4 cups (1 L). Using a food processor fitted with a metal blade, purée cantaloupe until smooth, scraping down sides with a spatula; measure 2¾ cups (675 mL).

2. In a large, deep, heavy-bottomed pot, combine cantaloupe purée, strawberries and lemon juice. Stir in pectin until dissolved. Bring to a boil over high heat, stirring often.

3. Add sugar in a steady stream, stirring constantly. Bring to a full boil, stirring constantly to dissolve sugar. Boil hard for 1 minute.

4. Remove from heat and skim off any foam.

5. Ladle into sterilized jars to within ¼ inch (0.5 cm) of rim; wipe rims. Apply prepared lids and rings; tighten rings just until fingertip-tight.

6. Process jars in a boiling water canner for 10 minutes (for details, see page 20). Transfer jars to a towel-lined surface and let rest at room temperature until set. Check seals; refrigerate any unsealed jars for up to 3 weeks.

> The word "cantaloupe" comes from the commune Cantalupo in Sabina, in the Sabine Hills near Tivoli, Italy. Seeds were brought to North America by Christopher Columbus.

Strawberry Gooseberry Jam

**Makes about five
8-ounce (250 mL) jars**

*In this jam, gooseberries
provide the pectin needed
for setting. A little orange
rind adds an extra
touch of flavor.*

— o o o —

Tip

The beards (blossom ends)
of the gooseberries must
be snipped from the ends
before use. A small pair of
manicure scissors is the
perfect tool for this task.

4 cups	gooseberries, beards removed	1 L
4 cups	sliced strawberries	1 L
2 tbsp	grated orange rind (optional)	30 mL
4 cups	granulated sugar	1 L

1. In a large, deep, heavy-bottomed pot, combine gooseberries and strawberries. Bring to a boil over high heat, stirring constantly. Reduce heat and simmer for 5 minutes, stirring occasionally. Stir in orange rind (if using).

2. Add sugar in a steady stream, stirring constantly. Increase heat to high and bring to a full boil, stirring constantly to dissolve sugar. Reduce heat to medium-high and boil rapidly, stirring often and reducing heat further as mixture thickens, for 10 to 15 minutes or until thickened. Crush any whole gooseberries with back of spoon. Test for setting point (for details, see page 19).

3. Remove from heat and skim off any foam.

4. Ladle into sterilized jars to within $\frac{1}{4}$ inch (0.5 cm) of rim; wipe rims. Apply prepared lids and rings; tighten rings just until fingertip-tight.

5. Process jars in a boiling water canner for 10 minutes (for details, see page 20). Transfer jars to a towel-lined surface and let rest at room temperature until set. Check seals; refrigerate any unsealed jars for up to 3 weeks.

Strawberry Red Grapefruit Jam

Makes about five 8-ounce (250 mL) jars

This jam has a lovely color and fresh grapefruit fragrance.

— o o o —

Tips

"Sections" refer to only the fleshy part of the fruit, not the inner membranes. For instructions on sectioning citrus fruit, see page 26.

If desired, you can use a food processor fitted with a metal blade to chop the grapefruit by pulsing on and off. Do not use the food processor for strawberries, as they easily become puréed — a potato masher works best, crushing the berries while leaving some texture.

Variation

Strawberry Citrus Jam: Replace 1 cup (250 mL) of the chopped grapefruit with chopped oranges and add 1 tbsp (15 mL) grated orange rind.

2 cups	crushed strawberries (see tip, page 151)	500 mL
2 cups	finely chopped sectioned red or pink grapefruit, with juices	500 mL
3 tbsp	lemon juice	45 mL
6½ cups	granulated sugar	1.625 L
1	pouch (3 oz/85 mL) liquid pectin	1

1. In a large, deep, heavy-bottomed pot, combine strawberries, grapefruit with juices and lemon juice. Bring to a full boil over high heat, stirring constantly.

2. Add sugar in a steady stream, stirring constantly. Return to a full boil, stirring constantly to dissolve sugar.

3. Immediately stir in pectin; return to a full boil. Boil hard for 1 minute, stirring constantly.

4. Remove from heat and skim off any foam. Stir for 5 to 8 minutes to prevent floating fruit.

5. Ladle into sterilized jars to within ¼ inch (0.5 cm) of rim; wipe rims. Apply prepared lids and rings; tighten rings just until fingertip-tight.

6. Process jars in a boiling water canner for 10 minutes (for details, see page 20). Transfer jars to a towel-lined surface and let rest at room temperature until set. Check seals; refrigerate any unsealed jars for up to 3 weeks.

Strawberry Kiwi Jam

*Strawberries and kiwis
have complementary
flavors and give this jam
a nice texture. Stir it into
your favorite cheesecake
batter or enjoy with
cream cheese and bagels.*

— o o o —

Tips

For 2 cups (500 mL)
crushed strawberries, you'll
need about 4 cups (1 L)
sliced. You'll also need
about 6 medium kiwis for
this recipe.

When cleaning strawberries,
always remove the white hull
from the inside. It is tough
and has no flavor.

2 cups	crushed strawberries (see tip, page 151)	500 mL
2 cups	finely chopped kiwifruit	500 mL
1	package (1.75 oz/49 or 57 g) powdered pectin	1
3½ cups	granulated sugar	875 mL

1. In a large, deep, heavy-bottomed pot, combine strawberries and kiwis. Stir in pectin until dissolved. Bring to a full boil over high heat, stirring constantly.

2. Add sugar in a steady stream, stirring constantly. Return to a full boil, stirring constantly to dissolve sugar. Boil hard for 1 minute.

3. Remove from heat and skim off any foam. Stir for 5 to 8 minutes to prevent floating fruit.

4. Ladle into sterilized jars to within $\frac{1}{4}$ inch (0.5 cm) of rim; wipe rims. Apply prepared lids and rings; tighten rings just until fingertip-tight.

5. Process jars in a boiling water canner for 10 minutes (for details, see page 20). Transfer jars to a towel-lined surface and let rest at room temperature until set. Check seals; refrigerate any unsealed jars for up to 3 weeks.

Strawberry Mango Daiquiri Jam

Makes about five 8-ounce (250 mL) jars

This jam has all the fun and flavor of a daiquiri, a rum-based drink made with lime juice and sometimes other fruits.

— o o o —

Tips

For 2 cups (500 mL) crushed strawberries, you'll need about 4 cups (1 L) sliced. You'll also need 2 or 3 Ataulfo mangos or 1 regular mango for this recipe.

How to Crush Strawberries: Use a square glass baking dish placed on top of a damp dish cloth (to prevent movement). Use a potato masher to crush berries, one layer at a time. Crush well to prevent floating fruit in your jam (don't leave any big chunks). Always remove the white hulls from berries when you are removing the leaves. Hulls have no flavor and a tough texture. Measure the berries after they're crushed.

2 cups	crushed strawberries (see tip, at left)	500 mL
1 cup	finely chopped or mashed ripe mangos	250 mL
½ cup	lime juice	125 mL
½ cup	white rum	125 mL
5½ cups	granulated sugar	1.375 L
1	pouch (3 oz/85 mL) liquid pectin	1

1. In a large, deep, heavy-bottomed pot, combine strawberries, mangos, lime juice and rum. Bring to a full boil over high heat, stirring constantly.

2. Add sugar in a steady stream, stirring constantly. Return to a full boil, stirring constantly to dissolve sugar.

3. Immediately stir in pectin; return to a full boil. Boil hard for 1 minute, stirring constantly.

4. Remove from heat and skim off any foam. Stir for 5 to 8 minutes to prevent floating fruit.

5. Ladle into sterilized jars to within ¼ inch (0.5 cm) of rim; wipe rims. Apply prepared lids and rings; tighten rings just until fingertip-tight.

6. Process jars in a boiling water canner for 10 minutes (for details, see page 20). Transfer jars to a towel-lined surface and let rest at room temperature until set. Check seals; refrigerate any unsealed jars for up to 3 weeks.

> Daiquiris were first created in a bar in Santiago, Cuba, near a beach named Daiquiri. They were then brought to New York by Americans who were working in Cuba and became popular in the U.S. in the 1940s.

Strawberry Pineapple Jam

Makes about six 8-ounce (250 mL) jars

This recipe was contributed by Barbara Mander (see Contributors, page 12). She learned jam-making from her mother and in high-school home economics classes. Most of her jams are eaten at home, but she often gives them as gifts, in decorated baskets.

—ooo—

Tip

Remove the pithy center core from strawberries before crushing. It has no flavor and a tough texture. After washing the berries, place a large straw at the tapered end of the strawberry and push into fruit towards the stem. The green calyx and the core will pop out with minimal strawberry waste.

2 cups	crushed strawberries (see tip, page 151)	500 mL
2 cups	finely chopped fresh pineapple	500 mL
7 cups	granulated sugar	1.75 L
1	pouch (3 oz/85 mL) liquid pectin	1

1. In a large, deep, heavy-bottomed pot, combine strawberries and pineapple. Bring to a boil over high heat, stirring constantly.

2. Add sugar in a steady stream, stirring constantly. Bring to a full boil, stirring constantly to dissolve sugar.

3. Immediately stir in pectin; return to a full boil. Boil hard for 1 minute, stirring constantly.

4. Remove from heat and skim off any foam. Stir for 5 to 8 minutes to prevent floating fruit.

5. Ladle into sterilized jars to within $\frac{1}{4}$ inch (0.5 cm) of rim; wipe rims. Apply prepared lids and rings; tighten rings just until fingertip-tight.

6. Process jars in a boiling water canner for 10 minutes (for details, see page 20). Transfer jars to a towel-lined surface and let rest at room temperature until set. Check seals; refrigerate any unsealed jars for up to 3 weeks.

Strawberry Raspberry Jam

Makes about five 8-ounce (250 mL) jars

Here are two all-time favorite fruits in one incredible jam!

—o o o—

Tip

For 3 cups (750 mL) crushed strawberries, you'll need about 6 cups (1.5 L) sliced. Strawberries should be crushed well; otherwise, they might float in the jar.

3½ cups	raspberries	875 mL
3 cups	crushed strawberries (see tip, page 151)	750 mL
⅓ cup	lemon juice	75 mL
4½ cups	granulated sugar	1.125 L

1. In a large, deep, heavy-bottomed pot, combine raspberries, strawberries, lemon juice and sugar; let stand for 10 minutes.

2. Bring to a boil over medium heat, stirring constantly to dissolve sugar. Increase heat to high and bring to a full boil, stirring constantly. Reduce heat to medium-high and boil rapidly, stirring often and reducing heat further as mixture thickens, for 15 to 18 minutes or until thickened. Test for setting point (for details, see page 19).

3. Remove from heat and skim off any foam. Stir for 5 to 8 minutes to prevent floating fruit.

4. Ladle into sterilized jars to within ¼ inch (0.5 cm) of rim; wipe rims. Apply prepared lids and rings; tighten rings just until fingertip-tight.

5. Process jars in a boiling water canner for 10 minutes (for details, see page 20). Transfer jars to a towel-lined surface and let rest at room temperature until set. Check seals; refrigerate any unsealed jars for up to 3 weeks.

> Modern-day strawberries derive from a cross between two strawberry varieties, one from North America and one from South America.

Strawberry Red Currant Jam

**Makes about four
8-ounce (250 mL) jars**

*This jam has an
excellent flavor, but
I prefer to remove the
red currant seeds.*

— o o o —

Tip

If you like, you can use
frozen sliced strawberries
in this recipe. One 20-oz
(600 g) bag should do it.
Measure before thawing.

4 cups	red currants	1 L
5 cups	sliced strawberries	1.25 L
3½ cups	granulated sugar	875 mL

1. Place currants in a large, deep, heavy-bottomed pot and crush with a potato masher. Bring to a boil over high heat, stirring constantly. Reduce heat and simmer, covered, for 3 minutes, stirring occasionally. Crush with the potato masher. Press fruit through a fine-mesh sieve placed over a bowl, using a spatula to push the pulp through; discard seeds and return pulp to pot. Stir in strawberries and crush well with the potato masher.

2. Add sugar in a steady stream, stirring constantly. Bring to a boil over high heat, stirring constantly to dissolve sugar. Reduce heat to medium and boil gently, uncovered, stirring often and reducing heat further as mixture thickens, for about 7 minutes or until thickened. Test for setting point (for details, see page 19).

3. Remove from heat and skim off any foam.

4. Ladle into sterilized jars to within ¼ inch (0.5 cm) of rim; wipe rims. Apply prepared lids and rings; tighten rings just until fingertip-tight.

5. Process jars in a boiling water canner for 10 minutes (for details, see page 20). Transfer jars to a towel-lined surface and let rest at room temperature until set. Check seals; refrigerate any unsealed jars for up to 3 weeks.

Strawberry Rhubarb Orange Jam

Orange peel provides an interesting flavor in this classic jam. It can be left out if you want to make straight Strawberry Rhubarb Jam.

— o o o —

Tip

One pound (500 g) of strawberries equals about 3¾ cups (925 mL) of whole medium berries and yields about 3 cups (750 mL) sliced berries or about 1½ cups (375 mL) crushed berries.

4 cups	chopped rhubarb (½-inch/1 cm pieces)	1 L
3 cups	chopped strawberries	750 mL
¼ cup	lemon juice	60 mL
3 tbsp	finely grated orange rind	45 mL
4½ cups	granulated sugar	1.125 L

1. In a large, deep, heavy-bottomed pot, combine rhubarb, strawberries, lemon juice and orange rind. Bring to a boil over high heat, stirring constantly.

2. Add sugar in a steady stream, stirring constantly. Bring to a full boil, stirring constantly to dissolve sugar. Reduce heat to medium-high and boil rapidly, stirring often and reducing heat further as mixture thickens, for 20 to 25 minutes or until thickened. Test for setting point (for details, see page 19).

3. Remove from heat and skim off any foam.

4. Ladle into sterilized jars to within ¼ inch (0.5 cm) of rim; wipe rims. Apply prepared lids and rings; tighten rings just until fingertip-tight.

5. Process jars in a boiling water canner for 10 minutes (for details, see page 20). Transfer jars to a towel-lined surface and let rest at room temperature until set. Check seals; refrigerate any unsealed jars for up to 3 weeks.

Three-Berry Blend Jam

**Makes about five
8-ounce (250 mL) jars**

*If you can't make up your
mind which one to use,
have all your favorite
berries in one jam!*

— o o o —

Tips

For 1⅔ cups (400 mL)
crushed strawberries,
you'll need about 2½ cups
(625 mL) sliced.

This jam may also be made
with 8 cups (2 L) frozen field
berry mix.

3 cups	raspberries	750 mL
2 cups	blueberries	500 mL
1⅔ cups	crushed strawberries (see tip, page 151)	400 mL
2 tbsp	lemon juice	30 mL
1	package (1.75 oz/49 or 57 g) powdered pectin	1
4 cups	granulated sugar	1 L

1. In a large, deep, heavy-bottomed pot, combine raspberries, blueberries, strawberries and lemon juice. Bring to a boil over high heat, stirring constantly. Reduce heat to medium-low and boil gently for 2 minutes, stirring occasionally. Use a potato masher to crush blueberries.

2. Stir in pectin until dissolved. Bring to a full boil over high heat, stirring constantly.

3. Add sugar in a steady stream, stirring constantly. Return to a full boil, stirring constantly to dissolve sugar. Boil hard for 1 minute.

4. Remove from heat and skim off any foam.

5. Ladle into sterilized jars to within ¼ inch (0.5 cm) of rim; wipe rims. Apply prepared lids and rings; tighten rings just until fingertip-tight.

6. Process jars in a boiling water canner for 10 minutes (for details, see page 20). Transfer jars to a towel-lined surface and let rest at room temperature until set. Check seals; refrigerate any unsealed jars for up to 3 weeks.

Watermelon Raspberry Jam

Makes about six 8-ounce (250 mL) jars

This pretty jam features refreshing watermelon taste with a hint of raspberry.

— ○ ○ ○ —

Tips

One small seedless watermelon should be enough for this recipe. If using a regular watermelon with seeds, remove the seeds before puréeing. Purée watermelon in batches in a food processor fitted with a metal blade. Transfer to a fine-mesh sieve and, using a rubber spatula, push pulp through to remove any small seeds.

If using frozen raspberries, measure while they're frozen, then let thaw before adding to the pot.

3½ cups	seedless watermelon purée (see tip, at left)	875 mL
2 cups	raspberries	500 mL
2 tbsp	lemon juice	30 mL
1	package (1.75 oz/49 or 57 g) powdered pectin	1
5 cups	granulated sugar	1.25 L

1. In a large, deep, heavy-bottomed pot, combine watermelon purée, raspberries and lemon juice. Stir in pectin until dissolved. Bring to a full boil over high heat, stirring constantly.

2. Add sugar in a steady stream, stirring constantly. Return to a full boil, stirring constantly to dissolve sugar. Boil hard for 1 minute.

3. Remove from heat and skim off any foam.

4. Ladle into sterilized jars to within ¼ inch (0.5 cm) of rim; wipe rims. Apply prepared lids and rings; tighten rings just until fingertip-tight.

5. Process jars in a boiling water canner for 10 minutes (for details, see page 20). Transfer jars to a towel-lined surface and let rest at room temperature until set. Check seals; refrigerate any unsealed jars for up to 3 weeks.

> Watermelon is not actually a melon — it is from the gourd family and is related to cucumbers. Use only the pink part for this jam.

Winter Berry Jam

*This jam is meant to be
dead easy — no fruit to
prep. Use frozen berry
mix (or your own frozen
berries) and frozen
cranberries to make this
incredible jam in the
throes of winter. It's sure
to cheer you up, and is a
perfect project for the day
of a snowstorm. If you
have a bread machine, put
on some bread to bake
while you make the jam.*

— o o o —

Tip

To save even the time it
takes to measure, I used
a 1¼-lb (600 g) bag of
frozen field berry mix and
a 10 oz (300 g) bag of frozen
cranberries to make this jam.

6 cups	frozen mixed berries (such as blackberries, blueberries, raspberries and strawberries), thawed	1.5 L
3 cups	cranberries	750 mL
4 cups	granulated sugar	1 L

1. In a large, deep, heavy-bottomed pot, combine mixed berries and cranberries. Bring to a boil over high heat, stirring constantly.

2. Add sugar in a steady stream, stirring constantly. Bring to a full boil, stirring constantly to dissolve sugar. Reduce heat and simmer, covered, for 5 minutes, stirring occasionally. Use a potato masher to crush berries.

3. Increase heat to medium and boil gently, uncovered, stirring often and reducing heat as mixture thickens, for 8 to 10 minutes or until thickened. Test for setting point (for details, see page 19).

4. Remove from heat and skim off any foam.

5. Ladle into sterilized jars to within ¼ inch (0.5 cm) of rim; wipe rims. Apply prepared lids and rings; tighten rings just until fingertip-tight.

6. Process jars in a boiling water canner for 10 minutes (for details, see page 20). Transfer jars to a towel-lined surface and let rest at room temperature until set. Check seals; refrigerate any unsealed jars for up to 3 weeks.

> Cranberries and most other berries (not including strawberries) have a high pectin level. Therefore, no added pectin is needed for a good set.

Micro–Mini Jams

Very small batches of jam, cooked in the microwave.

About Micro-Minis 159

Chocolate Banana Micro-Mini Jam. 162
Blackberry Blueberry Micro-Mini Jam. 163
Blueberry Micro-Mini Jam 164
Blueberry Mango Micro-Mini Jam. 165
Sweet Cherry Micro-Mini Jam 166
Cranberry Orange Micro-Mini Jam 167
Orange Passion Fruit Micro-Mini Jam. 168
Peach Micro-Mini Jam. 169
Raspberry Micro-Mini Jam. 170
Strawberry Banana Micro-Mini Jam 171
Strawberry Rhubarb Micro-Mini Jam 172

About Micro-Minis

Yes, you can make real jam in the microwave. There are a few guidelines to follow for success and to prevent sticky, messy boilovers.

I designed these recipes specifically for the following scenarios:

- You don't have the equipment for traditional jam-making.

- You like the homemade flavor of jams but want to make them on demand, for personal consumption or for only one or two people.

- You don't have room to store large canning pots and other equipment (jars, lids, a jar lifter, etc.).

- You don't have time to make bigger batches of jam, including the time to clean and prepare a large amount of fruit.

- You only have a small amount of fruit on hand.

If you have never made jam before, this is a perfect starting place. You can try it out, enjoy the sweet taste of success and perhaps move on to bigger and better things in the future! You will see how easy and quick it really is. In most cases, it will take less than 30 minutes, from start to finish. Of course, if you do not have a microwave, you can still make these jams in a large, heavy-bottomed pot, such as a Dutch oven. Follow the same steps, stirring often while boiling. The cooking time will be similar to that in the microwave, maybe a minute or two longer. Make sure to test for the setting point.

Once you learn the basic principles of jammin', you can apply the technique to the various recipes.

As with other jams, you will have to measure carefully, stir a lot, test for the setting point, and so on, but as these recipes make only two or three jars (each 8 ounces/250 mL), it won't be necessary to sterilize the jars or process the jams in a boiling water canner. Simply refrigerate and eat 'em up within 3 weeks (they probably won't last that long). Try the variations, too.

While making other jams using powdered pectin, I thought, Why not use just a measured portion and not the whole box? Just buy a box or two and pour into a small dish or jar. Each box contains about 5 tbsp (75 mL). These small batches take 2 to 3 tbsp (25 to 45 mL) of powdered pectin, depending on the type of fruit used. The Blackberry Blueberry and Cranberry Orange micro-mini jams did not need additional pectin, as blackberries and cranberries have enough for setting.

So have fun with these! You can definitely do it!

Here are my tips and recommendations:

1. Use a large microwave with a turntable. These recipes were tested in a 1200-watt microwave. If wattage is higher, cook on Medium-High (70%) power. If wattage is lower, the cooking time will be longer.

2. Measure your ingredients before you start.

3. Do not double the batches. Make another batch if you have more fruit.

4. Use a 16-cup (4 L) microwave-safe bowl, such as Pyrex. An 8-cup (2 L) glass measure is not big enough — I know, I tried it! If you use a smaller bowl, you are likely to have a boilover, make a big mess and lose most of your jam. The sloped sides of a bowl work better than a straight-sided container.

5. **Do not cover** the bowl, except briefly at the beginning of a recipe, where specified, to partially cook the fruit so it is easier to crush or when it needs a bit of precooking to soften.

6. Take care when lifting the bowl from the microwave. Use oven mitts. The mixtures will be hot, and there may be very hot steam as well. Have a safe place nearby to set the bowl down for stirring. You will have to do frequent stirrings for even cooking. Be safe: don't have kids or pets running around while you do this.

7. I use a silicone spatula to stir with and to scrape down the sides. (Jam will start to thicken on the sides of the bowl first.) They have high heat resistance.

8. The test for the setting point is the same as for larger batches of jam. For details, see page 19. When cooking, the mixture will start to look like a very thick fruit sauce; test at this time.

9. Some fruits, such as peaches and strawberries, have a tendency to float — especially if they have not been chopped finely or crushed enough — because air gets trapped in the cells. Stirring for a few minutes at the end of cooking allows the mixture to begin to thicken as it cools, and pieces become suspended.

10. Use any type of clean glass jar with a good lid. Do not use plastic containers.

11. It helps to have a wide-mouth canning funnel for filling jars. Look for one in the kitchen section of hardware stores.

12. There's no need to leave a specific headspace when filling the jars, as you will not be processing them. Headspace is necessary only for creating a vacuum seal.

13. There's no need to use new lids; any clean, non-rusted lids or plastic storage lids will do.

Chocolate Banana Micro-Mini Jam

Great on peanut butter sandwiches!

— o o o —

Tips

You'll need about 4 bananas for this recipe.

Bananas should be fully ripe and yellow in color, firm but slightly softened. Toss the bananas with the lemon juice as you chop to prevent browning. Remove any stringy bits and bruised spots.

Scrape down the sides of the bowl every time you stir for even cooking and to ensure that all of the sugar gets dissolved.

1 1/2 cups	finely chopped ripe bananas	375 mL
1 tbsp	lemon juice	15 mL
3 tbsp	powdered pectin	45 mL
3/4 cup	granulated sugar	175 mL
1/2 cup	packed golden brown sugar	125 mL
1/2 tsp	vanilla extract	2 mL
1 tbsp	melted dark (bittersweet) chocolate (about 1 oz/30 g)	15 mL

1. In a 16-cup (4 L) microwave-safe bowl, combine bananas and lemon juice.

2. Stir in pectin until dissolved.

3. Stir in granulated sugar and brown sugar.

4. Microwave on High for 2 minutes; stir and scrape down sides of bowl. Microwave on High again for 2 minutes; stir and scrape down sides of bowl. Repeat in 1-minute intervals for another 2 to 4 minutes, or until jam froths up and thickens; stir and scrape down sides each time.

5. Test for setting point (for details, see page 19). Microwave in additional 1-minute intervals as needed.

6. Remove from microwave. Stir slowly until foam subsides; skim off any remaining foam. Stir in vanilla. Fold in melted chocolate just until combined (it should have streaks of chocolate).

7. Ladle into clean jars; wipe rims. Apply metal lids and rings or use plastic lids; tighten until snug. Transfer to a towel-lined surface and let rest at room temperature until set. Refrigerate for up to 3 weeks.

> Adding chocolate to a refrigerator jam such as this one is fine, but it is not a good idea to add chocolate to a jam that gets processed, as chocolate is too high in fat. Eat this jam within 3 weeks (if it lasts that long in your house).

Blackberry Blueberry Micro–Mini Jam

Makes about two 8-ounce (250 mL) jars

Blackberries provide the pectin needed to set this jam. Enjoy the rich berry taste.

— ○○○ —

Tip

A heat-resistant silicone spatula is great for scraping down the sides of the bowl when stirring.

1½ cups	blueberries	375 mL
1 cup	blackberries	250 mL
1¾ cups	granulated sugar	425 mL

1. In a 16-cup (4 L) microwave-safe bowl, combine blueberries and blackberries. Partially cover bowl with plastic wrap, leaving a gap for some of the steam to escape. Microwave on High for 3 minutes or until hot. Remove and discard plastic. Using a potato masher, crush berries.

2. Stir in sugar until dissolved.

3. Microwave, uncovered, on High for 2 minutes; stir and scrape down sides of bowl. Microwave on High again for 2 minutes; stir and scrape down sides of bowl. Repeat in 1-minute intervals for another 2 to 4 minutes, or until jam froths up and thickens; stir and scrape down sides each time.

4. Test for setting point (for details, see page 19). Microwave in additional 1-minute intervals as needed.

5. Remove from microwave. Stir slowly until foam subsides; skim off any remaining foam.

6. Ladle into clean jars; wipe rims. Apply metal lids and rings or use plastic lids; tighten until snug. Transfer to a towel-lined surface and let rest at room temperature until set. Refrigerate for up to 3 weeks.

Blueberry Micro–Mini Jam

For the ultimate blueberry jam, make this recipe using wild blueberries and spike it with Grand Marnier!

— o o o —

Variations

Blueberry Micro-Mini Jam with Maple Syrup: Replace 1/4 cup (60 mL) of the sugar with pure maple syrup and omit the liqueur.

Blueberry Orange Micro-Mini Jam: Replace 3/4 cup (175 mL) of the blueberries with 1/2 cup (125 mL) finely chopped peeled orange segments (seeds, pith and membranes removed). Add 1 tsp (5 mL) grated orange rind to the fruit, if desired.

2 1/2 cups	blueberries	625 mL
2 tbsp	lemon juice	30 mL
2 tbsp	powdered pectin	30 mL
1 1/2 cups	granulated sugar	375 mL
1 tbsp	Grand Marnier (or other orange liqueur) or amaretto (optional)	15 mL

1. Place blueberries in a 16-cup (4 L) microwave-safe bowl. Partially cover bowl with plastic wrap, leaving a gap for some of the steam to escape. Microwave on High for 2 minutes (3 minutes if using frozen berries) or until hot. Remove and discard plastic. Using a potato masher, crush berries. Stir in lemon juice.

2. Stir in pectin until dissolved.

3. Stir in sugar until dissolved.

4. Microwave, uncovered, on High for 2 minutes; stir and scrape down sides of bowl. Microwave on High again for 2 minutes; stir and scrape down sides of bowl. Repeat in 1-minute intervals for another 2 to 4 minutes, or until jam froths up and thickens; stir and scrape down sides each time.

5. Test for setting point (for details, see page 19). Microwave in additional 1-minute intervals as needed.

6. Remove from microwave. Stir slowly until foam subsides; skim off any remaining foam. Stir in liqueur (if using).

7. Ladle into clean jars; wipe rims. Apply metal lids and rings, or use plastic lids; tighten until snug. Transfer to a towel-lined surface and let rest at room temperature until set. Refrigerate for up to 3 weeks.

Blueberry Mango Micro-Mini Jam

Makes about three
8-ounce (250 mL) jars

This is a terrific fruit combination, excellent stirred into yogurt or warmed and served over pancakes, waffles or crêpes.

— o o o —

Variation

Blueberry Peach Micro-Mini Jam: Replace the mango with chopped peeled peaches.

2¼ cups	blueberries	550 mL
1 cup	finely chopped mango	250 mL
2 tbsp	lemon juice	30 mL
2 tbsp	powdered pectin	30 mL
2 cups	granulated sugar	500 mL

1. Place blueberries in a 16-cup (4 L) microwave-safe bowl. Partially cover bowl with plastic wrap, leaving a gap for some of the steam to escape. Microwave on High for 2 minutes (3 minutes if using frozen berries) or until hot. Remove and discard plastic. Using a potato masher, crush berries. Stir in mango and lemon juice.

2. Stir in pectin until dissolved.

3. Stir in sugar until dissolved.

4. Microwave, uncovered, on High for 2 minutes; stir and scrape down sides of bowl. Microwave on High again for 2 minutes; stir and scrape down sides of bowl. Repeat in 1-minute intervals for another 2 to 4 minutes, or until jam froths up and thickens; stir and scrape down sides each time.

5. Test for setting point (for details, see page 19). Microwave in additional 1-minute intervals as needed.

6. Remove from microwave. Stir slowly until foam subsides; skim off any remaining foam.

7. Ladle into clean jars; wipe rims. Apply metal lids and rings, or use plastic lids; tighten until snug. Transfer to a towel-lined surface and let rest at room temperature until set. Refrigerate for up to 3 weeks.

Sweet Cherry Micro–Mini Jam

Makes about two 8-ounce (250 mL) jars

Make this jam whenever you have a craving for cherries. I love it with the chocolate liqueur, but you might also try adding melted chocolate (see variation, below).

— o o o —

Tips

You'll need about 1¼ lbs (625 g) of cherries for this recipe.

Some fruits are more prone to floating (strawberries, peaches, pears and cherries) and benefit from 2 to 3 minutes of stirring. This allows jam to begin to set, which prevents fruit bits from floating to the top of the jar.

Variation

Cherry Chocolate Micro-Mini Jam: Melt 1 oz (30 g) of good-quality dark (bittersweet) chocolate and stir into cooked jam before adding the liqueur.

4 cups	sweet cherries	1 L
1 tbsp	lemon juice	15 mL
2 tbsp	powdered pectin	30 mL
1¾ cups	granulated sugar	375 mL
1 tbsp	cherry brandy, crème de cacao or amaretto liqueur (optional)	15 mL

1. Stem, pit and coarsely chop cherries. Place in a 16-cup (4 L) microwave-safe bowl. Partially cover bowl with plastic wrap, leaving a gap for some of the steam to escape. Microwave on High for 3 minutes or until hot. Remove and discard plastic. Using a potato masher, slightly crush cherries. Stir in lemon juice.

2. Stir in pectin until dissolved.

3. Stir in sugar until dissolved.

4. Microwave, uncovered, on High for 2 minutes; stir and scrape down sides of bowl. Microwave on High again for 2 minutes; stir and scrape down sides of bowl. Repeat in 1-minute intervals for another 2 to 4 minutes, or until jam froths up and thickens; stir and scrape down sides each time.

5. Test for setting point (for details, see page 19). Microwave in additional 1-minute intervals as needed.

6. Remove from microwave. Stir slowly until foam subsides; skim off any remaining foam. Stir in liqueur (if using). Stir slowly for 2 to 3 minutes to prevent floating fruit.

7. Ladle into clean jars; wipe rims. Apply metal lids and rings, or use plastic lids; tighten until snug. Transfer to a towel-lined surface and let rest at room temperature until set. Refrigerate for up to 3 weeks.

Cranberry Orange Micro–Mini Jam

Makes about two 8-ounce (250 mL) jars

Cranberries provide the pectin needed to set this jam. It has a tart flavor with a touch of orange.

—ooo—

Variations

Cranberry Orange Micro-Mini Marmalade: For marmalade taste and texture, replace the finely grated orange rind with 1 to 2 tbsp (15 to 30 mL) thinly sliced orange rind, without any white pith.

Cran-Apple Micro-Mini Jam: Replace the chopped orange and orange rind with 2 cups (500 mL) finely chopped peeled apples that soften (see page 25).

Cran-Raspberry Micro-Mini Jam: Replace the chopped orange and orange rind with 2 cups (500 mL) raspberries.

1½ cups	cranberries	375 mL
1 cup	chopped orange	250 mL
2 tsp	finely grated orange rind (optional)	10 mL
2 cups	granulated sugar	500 mL

1. In a 16-cup (4 L) microwave-safe bowl, combine cranberries, chopped orange and orange rind (if using). Partially cover bowl with plastic wrap, leaving a gap for some of the steam to escape. Microwave on High for 3 minutes or until hot. Remove and discard plastic. Using a potato masher, crush berries.

2. Stir in sugar until dissolved.

3. Microwave, uncovered, on High for 2 minutes; stir and scrape down sides of bowl. Microwave on High again for 2 minutes; stir and scrape down sides of bowl. Repeat in 1-minute intervals for another 2 to 4 minutes, or until jam froths up and thickens; stir and scrape down sides each time.

4. Test for setting point (for details, see page 19). Microwave in additional 1-minute intervals as needed.

5. Remove from microwave. Stir slowly until foam subsides; skim off any remaining foam.

6. Ladle into clean jars; wipe rims. Apply metal lids and rings or use plastic lids; tighten until snug. Transfer to a towel-lined surface and let rest at room temperature until set. Refrigerate for up to 3 weeks.

Orange Passion Fruit Micro–Mini Jam

Passion fruit are expensive, but this small-batch jam allows you to indulge without breaking the bank.

— o o o —

Tips

You'll need about 6 passion fruit for this recipe.

Passion fruit is ripe when the rind no longer has any green and the outer skin becomes wrinkled. To prepare, cut in half around the middle and use a spoon to scoop out the seeds and jelly-like pulp, both of which are edible. Discard the shells.

For these microwave jams, which aren't processed in a boiling water canner, you can use plastic storage lids for standard mason jars in place of metal lids and rings.

Variations

Mango Passion Fruit Jam: Replace the orange juice with mango juice or nectar.

Pomegranate Passion Fruit Jam: Replace the orange juice with pure pomegranate juice.

1¼ cups	orange juice	300 mL
¾ cup	passion fruit pulp	175 mL
1 tbsp	lemon juice	15 mL
3 tbsp	powdered pectin	45 mL
2 cups	granulated sugar	500 mL

1. In a 16-cup (4 L) microwave-safe bowl, combine orange juice, passion fruit and lemon juice.

2. Stir in pectin until dissolved.

3. Stir in sugar.

4. Microwave on High for 2 minutes; stir and scrape down sides of bowl. Microwave on High again for 2 minutes; stir and scrape down sides of bowl. Repeat in 1-minute intervals for another 2 to 3 minutes, or until jam froths up and thickens; stir and scrape down sides each time.

5. Test for setting point (for details, see page 19). Microwave in additional 1-minute intervals as needed.

6. Remove from microwave. Stir slowly until foam subsides; skim off any remaining foam.

7. Ladle into clean jars; wipe rims. Apply metal lids and rings, or use plastic lids; tighten until snug. Transfer to a towel-lined surface and let rest at room temperature until set. Refrigerate for up to 3 weeks.

Peach Micro–Mini Jam

*Just peachy! Add a few
teaspoons of peach
brandy or amaretto,
if desired.*

— o o o —

Tip
You'll only need to buy 2 or
3 peaches, depending on
whether they are medium
or large.

Variations
*Spiced Peach Micro-Mini
Jam:* Add $\frac{1}{2}$ tsp (2 mL)
ground cinnamon and
$\frac{1}{4}$ tsp (1 mL) ground
nutmeg with the sugar.

*Peach Plum Micro-Mini
Jam:* Replace 1 cup
(250 mL) of the peaches
with finely chopped red
plums (no need to peel
them). Add $\frac{1}{4}$ tsp (1 mL)
ground ginger with the
sugar, if desired.

2 cups	finely chopped peeled peaches (see tip, page 129)	500 mL
2 tbsp	lemon juice	30 mL
2 tbsp	powdered pectin	30 mL
2¾ cups	granulated sugar	675 mL

1. In a 16-cup (4 L) microwave-safe bowl, combine peaches and lemon juice. Partially cover bowl with plastic wrap, leaving a gap for some of the steam to escape. Microwave on High, stirring twice, for 4 minutes or until hot. Remove and discard plastic. Stir in lemon juice.

2. Stir in pectin until dissolved.

3. Stir in sugar until dissolved.

4. Microwave, uncovered, on High for 2 minutes; stir and scrape down sides of bowl. Microwave on High again for 2 minutes; stir and scrape down sides of bowl. Repeat in 1-minute intervals for another 2 to 4 minutes, or until jam froths up and thickens; stir and scrape down sides each time.

5. Test for setting point (for details, see page 19). Microwave in additional 1-minute intervals as needed.

6. Remove from microwave. Stir slowly until foam subsides; skim off any remaining foam. Stir for 2 to 3 minutes to prevent floating fruit.

7. Ladle into clean jars; wipe rims. Apply metal lids and rings, or use plastic lids; tighten until snug. Transfer to a towel-lined surface and let rest at room temperature until set. Refrigerate for up to 3 weeks.

Raspberry Micro–Mini Jam

Makes about two 8-ounce (250 mL) jars

Raspberry is one of my favorite jams. This recipe works great with frozen berries; just remember to measure while they're still frozen.

— o o o —

Variations

Raspberry Kiwi Micro-Mini Jam: Replace 1 cup (250 mL) of the raspberries with ¾ cup (175 mL) finely chopped peeled ripe kiwifruit.

Raspberry Chocolate Micro-Mini Jam: Melt 1 oz (30 g) good-quality dark (bittersweet) chocolate and stir into cooked jam after skimming off any foam.

Raspberry Micro-Mini Jam with Lychee Liqueur: Stir in 1 tbsp (15 mL) lychee liqueur after skimming off any foam.

3½ cups	raspberries	875 mL
2 tbsp	lemon juice	30 mL
2 tbsp	powdered pectin	30 mL
1¾ cups	granulated sugar	425 mL

1. Place raspberries in a 16-cup (4 L) microwave-safe bowl. If using frozen raspberries, partially cover bowl with plastic wrap, leaving a gap for some of the steam to escape. Microwave on High for 2 minutes to thaw slightly. Remove and discard plastic. For both frozen and fresh berries, using a potato masher, crush berries. Stir in lemon juice.

2. Stir in pectin until dissolved.

3. Stir in sugar.

4. Microwave, uncovered, on High for 2 minutes; stir and scrape down sides of bowl. Microwave on High again for 2 minutes; stir and scrape down sides of bowl. Repeat in 1-minute intervals for another 2 to 4 minutes, or until jam froths up and thickens; stir and scrape down sides each time.

5. Test for setting point (for details, see page 19). Microwave in additional 1-minute intervals as needed.

6. Remove from microwave. Stir slowly until foam subsides; skim off any remaining foam.

7. Ladle into clean jars; wipe rims. Apply metal lids and rings, or use plastic lids; tighten until snug. Transfer to a towel-lined surface and let rest at room temperature until set. Refrigerate for up to 3 weeks.

Strawberry Banana Micro–Mini Jam

Makes about two 8-ounce (250 mL) jars

My friend Cindy taste-tested some of the jams, including this one, which she just adored. So of course I sent her home with a jar. Everyone finds their own favorite.

—o o o—

Tips

For 1 cup (250 mL) crushed strawberries, you'll need about 2 cups (500 mL) sliced.

You can use fresh or frozen strawberries for this jam. Crush them with a potato masher in a shallow dish, then measure 1 cup (250 mL). If using frozen berries, let them thaw before crushing.

1 cup	crushed strawberries	250 mL
1 cup	mashed ripe bananas	250 mL
2 tbsp	lemon juice	30 mL
2 tbsp	powdered pectin	30 mL
1½ cups	granulated sugar	375 mL

1. In a 16-cup (4 L) microwave-safe bowl, combine strawberries, bananas and lemon juice.

2. Stir in pectin until dissolved.

3. Stir in sugar.

4. Microwave on High for 2 minutes; stir and scrape down sides of bowl. Microwave on High again for 2 minutes; stir and scrape down sides of bowl. Repeat in 1-minute intervals for another 1 to 2 minutes, or until jam froths up and thickens; stir and scrape down sides each time.

5. Test for setting point (for details, see page 19). Microwave in additional 1-minute intervals as needed.

6. Remove from microwave. Stir slowly until foam subsides; skim off any remaining foam. Stir slowly for 2 to 3 minutes to prevent floating fruit.

7. Ladle into clean jars; wipe rims. Apply metal lids and rings, or use plastic lids; tighten until snug. Transfer to a towel-lined surface and let rest at room temperature until set. Refrigerate for up to 3 weeks.

Strawberry Rhubarb Micro–Mini Jam

*This classic fruit combo
has a lovely tart flavor.
Spoon some into
plain yogurt.*

— ○○○ —

Tips

For 1 cup (250 mL) crushed
strawberries, you'll need
about 2 cups (500 mL)
sliced.

You can use fresh or
frozen strawberries for this
jam. Crush them with a
potato masher in a shallow
dish, then measure 1 cup
(250 mL). If using frozen
berries, let them thaw
before crushing.

Variation

*Bumbleberry Micro-
Mini Jam:* Replace the
strawberries with crushed
mixed field berries,
such as blueberries,
blackberries, strawberries
and raspberries.

1½ cups	chopped rhubarb (½-inch/1 cm pieces)	375 mL
2 tbsp	water	30 mL
1 cup	crushed strawberries	250 mL
1 tbsp	lemon juice	15 mL
2 tbsp	powdered pectin	30 mL
2 cups	granulated sugar	500 mL

1. In a 16-cup (4 L) microwave-safe bowl, combine rhubarb and water. Partially cover bowl with plastic wrap, leaving a gap for some of the steam to escape. Microwave on High for 2 minutes or until hot. Remove and discard plastic. Drain off any liquid or blot with a paper towel. Stir in strawberries and lemon juice.

2. Stir in pectin until dissolved.

3. Stir in sugar until dissolved.

4. Microwave, uncovered, on High for 2 minutes; stir and scrape down sides of bowl. Microwave on High again for 2 minutes; stir and scrape down sides of bowl. Repeat in 1-minute intervals for another 2 to 4 minutes, or until jam froths up and thickens; stir and scrape down sides each time.

5. Test for setting point (for details, see page 19). Microwave in additional 1-minute intervals as needed.

6. Remove from microwave. Stir slowly until foam subsides; skim off any remaining foam. Stir slowly for 2 to 3 minutes to prevent floating fruit.

7. Ladle into clean jars; wipe rims. Apply metal lids and rings, or use plastic lids; tighten until snug. Transfer to a towel-lined surface and let rest at room temperature until set. Refrigerate for up to 3 weeks.

Special Jams, Spreads and Mincemeats

Some of the no-cook recipes in this section are made with a regular amount of sugar; a couple use a pectin specially devised for lower-sugar recipes. Of the cooked spreads in this section, two are made with a sugar substitute and others with a combination of sugar and an alternative sweetener. Also included here are onion jams and mincemeats.

About No-Cook Jams 174
About No-Sugar and Low-Sugar Spreads 174
A Note About Sugar 175
About Onion Jams 175
About Mincemeats 175

No-Cook Jams
Blueberry Orange No-Cook Jam 176
Peach Blueberry No-Cook Jam 177
Strawberry Banana No-Cook Jam 178
Strawberry Maple No-Cook Jam 179

Light No-Cook Jams
Peach Raspberry Light No-Cook Jam 180
Raspberry Kiwi Light No-Cook Jam 181

No-Sugar Spreads
Blackberry Apple Spread 182
Tropical Tango Spread 183

Low-Sugar Spreads
Mixed Berry Apple Spread 184
Peach Papaya Orange Spread 185
Pear Spread with Brown Sugar and Cinnamon 186
Raspberry Blueberry Spread 187
Raspberry Peach Spread 188
Raspberry Pear Spread 189
Micro-Mini Peach Spread with Stevia 190
Banana Orange and Date Conserve 191

continued…

Onion Jams

    Orange Onion Jam with Sage and Thyme 192

    Tomato Orange Jam with Basil and Saffron 194

    Strawberry Onion Jam with Balsamic Vinegar
        and Rosemary 196

Mincemeats

    Carrot Apple Mincemeat 197

    Pear and Apple Mincemeat 198

About No-Cook Jams

No-cook jams retain their fresh fruit flavor and are thickened by adding commercial pectin in liquid or powdered form. I have included a variety of recipes from Kraft Foods and Bernardin, who make these special products. Each pectin product has its own recipe leaflet containing numerous recipes, found inside the box. You may contact the companies directly using their toll-free numbers or websites (see Resources, page 372).

No-cook jams (which used to be called freezer jams) may be refrigerated for up to 3 weeks or frozen for up to 8 months. Because the jams will be kept at cold temperatures, you do not need to sterilize the containers; just wash them with soapy water, rinse and dry with a clean towel. Ball (in the U.S.) and Bernardin (in Canada) make plastic lids that fit their canning jars and are perfect for no-cook jams.

> Refer to the Produce Purchase Guide, page 32, to estimate the amount of fruit and/or vegetables you'll need to purchase for these recipes.

About No-Sugar and Low-Sugar Spreads

No-sugar pectins allow you to make jams with artificial sweeteners. The texture of no-sugar and low-sugar spreads may be a little different from that of regular jams, and they usually have a softer spread. Those made with a sugar substitute, such as Splenda or stevia, will not taste the same as if sugar were used. These spreads will not keep as long either. However, if you must watch your sugar intake carefully, they can be a reasonable alternative.

You will find the jams featured here to be very tasty. I found in my experimentation that a combination of 1 cup (250 mL) granulated or brown sugar and 1 cup (250 mL) Splenda No Calorie Sweetener is heat-stable and produces excellent results. It creates a spread with a fairly good texture and taste. These spreads may also be made with the sweetener alone (increase to 1½ cups/375 mL, or to taste) and no sugar.

These spreads are best eaten on a whole-grain, high-fiber bread that delays digestion and slows the entry of any sugars into the bloodstream. Eating a small amount of protein, such as cheese or yogurt, will also have this effect. Severe cases of diabetes may require the use of alternative sweeteners alone, with no sugar at all.

When choosing an artificial sweetener, always check the product information to see if it can take the high heat needed for cooked spreads.

> Stevia, a sweetener derived from the leaves of a plant, is gaining popularity and distribution in supermarkets. It is about 300 times sweeter than sugar. Add stevia to taste in recipes using no-sugar-needed pectin. Splenda (sucralose) is derived from sugar (sucrose) and is about 600 times sweeter than sugar. Both of these sweeteners are heat-stable and can be used in preserves.

A Note About Sugar

Sugar is responsible for working with the pectin and acid to create the structure needed for gelling. It also acts as a preservative (it prevents spoilage), inhibiting mold growth and helping to maintain the beautiful color of the fruit. Always use the exact amount of sugar or sweetener called for in the recipe. If you reduce it, the jam may not set nor keep.

> You can substitute 1 cup (250 mL) liquid honey for 1 cup (250 mL) of the granulated sugar in recipes with normal amounts of sugar, if desired.

About Onion Jams

Onion jams make a tasty condiment to serve with meats. Add to meat glazes or sauces, or use on top of sharp-tasting cheeses (such as Cheddar) or soft cheeses (such as Brie or Camembert). You will see onion jam listed on restaurant menus as onion confit. (*Confiture* is the French word for jam.) For these onion jams, unlike other jams, jars are filled to within ½ inch (1 cm) of rim and are processed for 15 minutes.

About Mincemeats

I have included a couple of recipes for fruit mixtures that are not really jams but minced fruit; they are ideal for making tarts. Use your favorite pastry recipe, fill with mincemeat and bake. If desired, cut a small top from the pastry with a scalloped-edge or small star cutter, place over the filling and sprinkle with granulated sugar before baking. Or cut a larger round to completely cover the filling and pinch to bottom pastry to enclose; cut small slits in the top and sprinkle with granulated sugar or, for a glossy finish, brush with egg yolk beaten with 1 tsp (5 mL) milk.

Blueberry Orange No-Cook Jam

Orange is a wonderful flavor accent to blueberries in this fresh-tasting jam.

— o o o —

Tips

Before measuring, use a potato masher to crush blueberries one layer at a time in a shallow dish. If desired, they may be pulsed in a food processor, but do not purée. If using frozen berries, thaw slightly first, but drain off any excess juice to help jam set properly.

"Sections" refer to only the fleshy part of the fruit, not the inner membranes. For instructions on sectioning citrus fruit, see page 26.

2 cups	crushed blueberries	500 mL
1 tbsp	finely grated orange rind (optional)	15 mL
1½ cups	finely chopped sectioned oranges, with juice	375 mL
4¾ cups	granulated sugar	1.175 L
¾ cup	water	175 mL
1	package (1.75 oz/49 or 57 g) powdered pectin	1

1. In a large bowl, combine blueberries, orange rind and oranges with juice. Stir in sugar; mix well. Let stand for 10 minutes.

2. In a small saucepan, whisk together water and pectin. Bring to a boil over high heat; boil hard for 1 minute, whisking constantly. Remove from heat.

3. Stir prepared pectin into fruit mixture; stir for 3 minutes or until most of the sugar is dissolved.

4. Ladle into jars or plastic freezer containers to within ½ inch (1 cm) of rim to allow for expansion; wipe rims. Cover with tight lids and let rest at room temperature until set (may take up to 24 hours). Refrigerate for up to 3 weeks or freeze for up to 8 months.

Peach Blueberry No-Cook Jam

Fragrant fresh peaches and wild blueberries get a chance to show off in this tasty jam. Stir some into pancake batter or bake into the center of muffins. (Recipe courtesy Kraft Canada Inc.)

— o o o —

Tip
You'll need 4 to 6 medium peaches for this recipe.

2 cups	finely chopped peeled peaches (see tip, page 180)	500 mL
1 cup	crushed blueberries	250 mL
1/4 cup	lemon juice	60 mL
5 cups	granulated sugar	1.25 L
3/4 cup	water	175 mL
1	package (1.8 oz) Sure Jell or (57 g) Certo powdered pectin	1

1. In a large bowl, combine peaches, blueberries and lemon juice. Stir in sugar; mix well. Let stand for 10 minutes.

2. In a small saucepan, whisk together water and pectin. Bring to a boil over high heat; boil hard for 1 minute, whisking constantly. Remove from heat.

3. Stir prepared pectin into fruit mixture; stir for 3 minutes or until most of the sugar is dissolved.

4. Ladle into jars or plastic freezer containers to within 1/2 inch (1 cm) of rim to allow for expansion; wipe rims. Cover with tight lids and let rest at room temperature until set (may take up to 24 hours). Refrigerate for up to 3 weeks or freeze for up to 8 months.

Strawberry Banana No-Cook Jam

A little of this jam in your breakfast shake will get you going in the morning! Also try stirring some into plain yogurt or serving over ice cream. (Recipe courtesy Bernardin Ltd.)

— ○ ○ ○ —

Tip

For 1½ cups (375 mL) crushed strawberries, you'll need about 3 cups (750 mL) sliced. You'll also need 2 to 3 medium bananas for this recipe.

1½ cups	crushed strawberries (see tip, page 151)	375 mL
¾ cup	well-mashed ripe banana	175 mL
4½ cups	granulated sugar	1.125 L
1	pouch (3 oz/85 mL) Ball or Bernardin liquid pectin	1
½ cup	lemon juice	125 mL

1. In a large bowl, combine strawberries and bananas. Stir in sugar; mix well. Let stand for 10 minutes.

2. Stir in pectin. Add lemon juice; stir for 3 minutes or until most of the sugar is dissolved.

3. Ladle into jars or plastic freezer containers to within ½ inch (1 cm) of rim to allow for expansion; wipe rims. Cover with tight lids and let rest at room temperature until set (may take up to 24 hours). Refrigerate for up to 3 weeks or freeze for up to 8 months.

Strawberry Maple No-Cook Jam

Makes about six 8-ounce (250 mL) jars

This Certo recipe has a lovely maple flavor and a soft set. Serve it slightly warmed and spooned over pancakes and waffles. Try it on crêpes or over ice cream too. (Recipe courtesy Kraft Canada Inc.)

—ooo—

1	large orange	1
1¾ cups	crushed strawberries (see tip, page 151)	425 mL
¾ cup	pure maple syrup	175 mL
¼ cup	lemon juice	60 mL
3¼ cups	granulated sugar	800 mL
¾ cup	water	175 mL
1	package (1.8 oz) Sure Jell or (57 g) Certo powdered pectin	1

1. Peel and section orange, removing all pith, seeds and membranes, and finely chop the fruit, reserving any juices.

2. In a large bowl, combine strawberries, orange with juice, maple syrup and lemon juice. Stir in sugar; mix well. Let stand for 10 minutes.

3. In a small saucepan, whisk together water and pectin. Bring to a boil over high heat; boil hard for 1 minute, whisking constantly. Remove from heat.

4. Stir prepared pectin into fruit mixture; stir for 3 minutes or until most of the sugar is dissolved.

5. Ladle into jars or plastic freezer containers to within ½ inch (1 cm) of rim to allow for expansion; wipe rims. Cover with tight lids and let rest at room temperature until set (may take up to 24 hours). Refrigerate for up to 3 weeks or freeze for up to 8 months.

Peach Raspberry Light No-Cook Jam

Makes about five 8-ounce (250 mL) jars

Enjoy fresh fruit flavors in this no-cook jam. Use it to fill an angel food cake (sliced into three layers) and serve with vanilla frozen yogurt or raspberry or mango ice for a light, low-fat dessert. (Recipe courtesy Kraft Canada Inc.)

— o o o —

Tip

How to Peel Peaches: Bring a medium pot of water to a boil over high heat. Place peaches in water two at a time; boil for 20 to 30 seconds. Remove peaches with a slotted spoon and immediately immerse in a bowl of cold water. Repeat with remaining peaches. When peaches are cool enough to handle, slit down the side of the peel with a paring knife and slip off peel. Cut peaches in half and remove pits.

2 cups	finely chopped peeled peaches (see tip, at left)	500 mL
1¾ cups	crushed raspberries	425 mL
3¼ cups	granulated sugar, divided	800 mL
1	package (1.8 oz) Sure Jell or (49 g) Certo Light powdered pectin	1

1. In a large bowl, combine peaches and raspberries.

2. In a separate bowl, combine ¼ cup (60 mL) of the sugar and pectin. Gradually add to fruit, stirring well. Let stand for 30 minutes, stirring occasionally.

3. Stir in remaining sugar; stir for 3 minutes or until most of the sugar is dissolved.

4. Pour into jars or plastic freezer containers to within ½ inch (1 cm) of rim to allow for expansion; wipe rims. Cover with tight lids and let rest at room temperature until set (may take up to 24 hours). Refrigerate for up to 3 weeks or freeze for up to 8 months.

Raspberry Kiwi Light No-Cook Jam

Makes about six 8-ounce (250 mL) jars

I love to eat these fruits together fresh, and they make a delicious jam. Serve with vanilla frozen yogurt or raspberry ice, and angel food or light pound cake. (Recipe courtesy Kraft Canada Inc.)

— o o o —

Tip

For 3 cups (500 mL) crushed raspberries, you'll need 6 to 7 cups (1.5 to 1.75 L) whole berries. You'll also need about 3 kiwis for this recipe.

3 cups	crushed raspberries	750 mL
1 cup	finely chopped kiwifruit	250 mL
3¼ cups	granulated sugar, divided	800 mL
1	package (1.8 oz) Sure Jell or (49 g) Certo Light powdered pectin	1

1. In a large bowl, combine raspberries and kiwis.

2. In a separate bowl, combine ¼ cup (60 mL) of the sugar and pectin. Gradually add to fruit, stirring well. Let stand for 30 minutes, stirring occasionally.

3. Stir in remaining sugar; stir for 3 minutes or until most of the sugar is dissolved.

4. Pour into jars or plastic freezer containers to within ½ inch (1 cm) of rim to allow for expansion; wipe rims. Cover with tight lids and let rest at room temperature until set (may take up to 24 hours). Refrigerate for up to 3 weeks or freeze for up to 8 months.

Blackberry Apple Spread

*To save time, this tasty
spread can also be
made using 4 cups (1 L)
unsweetened applesauce;
skip step 1. (Recipe
courtesy Bernardin Ltd.)*

— o o o —

Tip

The combined weight of
your apples should be about
2½ lbs (1.25 kg). Varieties
of apples that soften when
cooked include McIntosh,
Cortland, Empire and
Russet. See page 25 for
more details.

7	medium apples that soften	7
2 cups	water, divided	500 mL
2 cups	blackberries, lightly crushed	500 mL
1 tbsp	finely grated lemon rind	15 mL
¼ cup	lemon juice	60 mL
1	package (1.75 oz/49 g) Ball or Bernardin No Sugar Needed pectin	1
1¾ cups	artificial sweetener (a type that measures equivalent to sugar)	425 mL

1. Slice unpeeled apples into 8 wedges each, removing stem and blossom ends. Place in a Dutch oven or a large, heavy-bottomed pot with 1 cup (250 mL) of the water; bring to a boil over high heat. Reduce heat and simmer, covered, for 10 minutes or until apples are softened. Press apples through a sieve into a bowl; discard peels and cores. Measure exactly 4 cups (1 L) apple pulp; return to clean pot.

2. Stir in blackberries, lemon rind, lemon juice and ¾ cup (175 mL) of the remaining water. Very slowly whisk in pectin. Bring to a full boil over high heat, stirring constantly. Boil hard for 1 minute, stirring constantly. Remove from heat.

3. In a small bowl, dissolve sweetener in the remaining ¼ cup (60 mL) water; stir into fruit. Stir for 2 minutes.

4. Ladle into sterilized jars to within ¼ inch (0.5 cm) of rim; wipe rims. Apply prepared lids and rings; tighten rings just until fingertip-tight.

5. Process jars in a boiling water canner for 10 minutes (for details, see page 20). Transfer jars to a towel-lined surface and let rest at room temperature until set. Check seals; refrigerate any unsealed jars for up to 3 weeks.

Tropical Tango Spread

Makes about four 8-ounce (250 mL) jars

Try this exotic-tasting spread on toast or banana bread. (Recipe courtesy Bernardin Ltd.)

— o o o —

Tip
You'll need 3 or 4 mangos and 2 or 3 bananas for this recipe.

2 cups	puréed mangos	500 mL
1 cup	mashed ripe bananas (not puréed)	250 mL
2 cups	orange juice, divided	500 mL
2 tbsp	lemon juice	30 mL
1	package (1.75 oz/49 g) Ball or Bernardin No Sugar Needed pectin	1
1 cup	artificial sweetener (a type that measures equivalent to sugar)	250 mL
1 tsp	vanilla extract	5 mL
1 tsp	rum extract	5 mL

1. In a Dutch oven or a large, heavy-bottomed pot, combine mangos, bananas, 1¾ cups (425 mL) of the orange juice and the lemon juice.

2. Very slowly stir in pectin. Bring to a full boil over high heat, stirring constantly. Boil hard for 1 minute, stirring constantly. Remove from heat.

3. In a small bowl, dissolve sweetener in the remaining ¼ cup (60 mL) orange juice; stir into fruit, along with vanilla and rum extract. Stir for 2 minutes.

4. Ladle into sterilized jars to within ¼ inch (0.5 cm) of rim; wipe rims. Apply prepared lids and rings; tighten rings just until fingertip-tight.

5. Process jars in a boiling water canner for 10 minutes (for details, see page 20). Transfer jars to a towel-lined surface and let rest at room temperature until set. Check seals; refrigerate any unsealed jars for up to 3 weeks.

Mixed Berry Apple Spread

*This recipe allows you
to use whatever mix
of berries you have.
Apples give it a nice
spreadable texture.*

— o o o —

Tips

Varieties of apples that
soften when cooked include
McIntosh, Cortland, Empire
and Russet. See page 25
for more details.

To prevent browning, toss
apples with lemon juice after
chopping.

This spread may also
be made with just the
sweetener (increase to
1½ cups/375 mL, or
to taste) and no sugar.

6 cups	mixed berries (such as raspberries, blackberries, strawberries and blueberries)	1.5 L
3 cups	chopped peeled apples that soften	750 mL
1 tbsp	lemon juice	15 mL
1	package (1.75 oz/49 g) no-sugar-needed pectin	1
1 cup	Splenda No Calorie Sweetener	250 mL
1 cup	granulated sugar	250 mL

1. Combine berries in a large, deep, heavy-bottomed pot. Use a potato masher to crush berries. Stir in apples and lemon juice; bring to a boil over medium-low heat. Boil for 3 to 4 minutes or until apples are softened.

2. Stir in pectin until dissolved. Bring to a full boil over high heat, stirring constantly.

3. Stir in sweetener until dissolved. Add sugar, stirring constantly. Return to a full boil, stirring constantly to dissolve sugar. Reduce heat to medium and boil rapidly for 3 minutes, stirring constantly.

4. Remove from heat and skim off any foam.

5. Ladle into sterilized jars to within ¼ inch (0.5 cm) of rim; wipe rims. Apply prepared lids and rings; tighten rings just until fingertip-tight.

6. Process jars in boiling water canner for 10 minutes (for details, see page 20). Transfer jars to a towel-lined surface and let rest at room temperature until set. Check seals; refrigerate any unsealed jars for up to 3 weeks.

Peach Papaya Orange Spread

This spread has a lovely color and a fresh taste.

— o o o —

Tips

You'll need about 2 lbs (1 kg) of papaya for this recipe.

If desired, use a whisk to blend in the pectin, sugar and sweetener.

This spread may also be made with just the sweetener (increase to 1½ cups/375 mL, or to taste) and no sugar.

Variation

Mango Papaya Orange Spread: Replace the peaches with mangos.

2 cups	crushed peeled peaches (see tip, page 180	500 mL
2 cups	finely chopped or mashed papaya	500 mL
1 cup	orange juice	250 mL
3 tbsp	lemon or lime juice	45 mL
1	package (1.75 oz/49 g) no-sugar-needed pectin	1
1 cup	Splenda No Calorie Sweetener	250 mL
1 cup	granulated sugar	250 mL

1. In a large, deep, heavy-bottomed pot, combine peaches, papaya, orange juice and lemon juice.

2. Stir in pectin until dissolved. Bring to a full boil over high heat, stirring constantly.

3. Stir in sweetener until dissolved. Add sugar, stirring constantly. Return to a full boil, stirring constantly to dissolve sugar. Reduce heat to medium and boil rapidly for 3 minutes, stirring constantly.

4. Remove from heat and skim off any foam.

5. Ladle into sterilized jars to within ¼ inch (0.5 cm) of rim; wipe rims. Apply prepared lids and rings; tighten rings just until fingertip-tight.

6. Process jars in boiling water canner for 10 minutes (for details, see page 20). Transfer jars to a towel-lined surface and let rest at room temperature until set. Check seals; refrigerate any unsealed jars for up to 3 weeks.

> With this type of pectin, no sugar needs to be added. Or you can use only a sugar substitute (one that can take heat), with no sugar at all. I prefer to blend the two for the best texture and taste.

Pear Spread with Brown Sugar and Cinnamon

Makes about five 8-ounce (250 mL) jars

This spread has the texture of pear butter and a hint of vanilla and spice.

— o o o —

Tips

You'll need about 4½ lbs (2.25 kg) of pears (8 to 10 large) for this recipe. Use a food processor to finely chop the pears by pulsing on and off; do not purée.

Supermarkets now carry all-natural (or pure-pressed) apple juice, which contains solids. Shake before using.

This spread may also be made with just the sweetener (increase to 1½ cups/375 mL, or to taste) and no sugar.

Variations

Pear Spread with Brown Sugar and Ginger: Omit the vanilla and cinnamon. Stir in ¼ cup (60 mL) minced crystallized ginger after the brown sugar.

Spiced Pear Spread with Brown Sugar: Stir in ¼ tsp (1 mL) ground nutmeg and a pinch of ground cloves with the vanilla and cinnamon.

4 cups	finely chopped peeled pears	1 L
1 cup	all-natural apple juice (see tip, at left) or unsweetened apple cider	250 mL
2 tbsp	lemon juice	30 mL
1	package (1.75 oz/49 g) no-sugar-needed pectin	1
1 cup	Splenda No Calorie Sweetener	250 mL
1 cup	packed brown sugar	250 mL
1 tsp	vanilla extract (optional)	5 mL
¾ tsp	ground cinnamon (optional)	3 mL

1. In a large, deep, heavy-bottomed pot, combine pears, apple juice and lemon juice.

2. Stir in pectin until dissolved. Bring to a full boil over high heat, stirring constantly.

3. Stir in sweetener until dissolved. Add brown sugar, stirring constantly. Return to a full boil, stirring constantly to dissolve sugar. Stir in vanilla and cinnamon (if using). Reduce heat to medium and boil rapidly for 3 minutes, stirring constantly and reducing heat further if the mixture sputters or is sticking on the bottom.

4. Remove from heat and skim off any foam. Stir for 5 to 8 minutes to prevent floating fruit.

5. Ladle into sterilized jars to within ¼ inch (0.5 cm) of rim; wipe rims. Apply prepared lids and rings; tighten just until fingertip-tight.

6. Process jars in boiling water canner for 10 minutes (for details, see page 20). Transfer jars to a towel-lined surface and let rest at room temperature until set. Check seals; refrigerate any unsealed jars for up to 3 weeks.

Raspberry Blueberry Spread

*Here's one of my
favorite mid-summer
dream combos.*

— o o o —

Tips

For 1½ cups (375 mL)
crushed blueberries,
you'll need about 3 cups
(750 mL) whole berries.
Crush blueberries in a food
processor by pulsing on
and off (do not purée), or
use a potato masher.

Use a whisk to blend in
the pectin, sugar and
sweetener.

This spread may also
be made with just the
sweetener (increase to
1½ cups/375 mL, or
to taste) and no sugar.

4 cups	raspberries	1 L
1½ cups	crushed blueberries	375 mL
1 cup	all-natural apple juice (see tip, page 186)	250 mL
1 tbsp	lemon juice	15 mL
1	package (1.75 oz/49 g) no-sugar-needed pectin	1
1 cup	Splenda No Calorie Sweetener	250 mL
1 cup	granulated sugar	250 mL

1. In a large, deep, heavy-bottomed pot, combine raspberries, blueberries, apple juice and lemon juice.

2. Stir in pectin until dissolved. Bring to a full boil over high heat, stirring constantly.

3. Stir in sweetener until dissolved. Add sugar, stirring constantly. Return to a full boil, stirring constantly to dissolve sugar. Reduce heat to medium and boil rapidly for 3 minutes, stirring constantly.

4. Remove from heat and skim off any foam.

5. Ladle into sterilized jars to within ¼ inch (0.5 cm) of rim; wipe rims. Apply prepared lids and rings; tighten rings just until fingertip-tight.

6. Process jars in a boiling water canner for 10 minutes (for details, see page 20). Transfer jars to a towel-lined surface and let rest at room temperature until set. Check seals; refrigerate any unsealed jars for up to 3 weeks.

Raspberry Peach Spread

Here, two popular summer fruits combine as a classic peach Melba duo.

— o o o —

Tips

For 2 cups (500 mL) crushed raspberries, you'll need 4 to 5 cups (1 to 1.25 L) whole berries.

This spread may also be made with just the sweetener (increase to 1½ cups/375 mL, or to taste) and no sugar.

Variations

Raspberry Mango Spread: Replace the peaches with mangos.

Blueberry Peach Spread: Replace the raspberries with blueberries.

2 cups	crushed raspberries	500 mL
2 cups	finely chopped peeled peaches (see tip, page 180)	500 mL
1 cup	white cranberry peach juice or white grape juice	250 mL
2 tbsp	lemon juice	30 mL
1	package (1.75 oz/49 g) no-sugar-needed pectin	1
1 cup	Splenda No Calorie Sweetener	250 mL
1 cup	granulated sugar	250 mL

1. In a large, deep, heavy-bottomed pot, combine raspberries, peaches, peach juice and lemon juice.

2. Stir in pectin until dissolved. Bring to a full boil over high heat, stirring constantly.

3. Stir in sweetener until dissolved. Add sugar, stirring constantly. Return to a full boil, stirring constantly to dissolve sugar. Reduce heat to medium and boil rapidly for 3 minutes, stirring constantly.

4. Remove from heat and skim off any foam.

5. Ladle into sterilized jars to within ¼ inch (0.5 cm) of rim; wipe rims. Apply prepared lids and rings; tighten rings just until fingertip-tight.

6. Process jars in a boiling water canner for 10 minutes (for details, see page 20). Transfer jars to a towel-lined surface and let rest at room temperature until set. Check seals; refrigerate any unsealed jars for up to 3 weeks.

> Splenda is made from sugar and is heat-stable. It provides sweetness but not the preserving properties of sugar, making proper safe canning techniques essential. For a good set, it is also necessary to use special pectins for lower sugar or no sugar, so Splenda is not suitable for long-boil recipes.

Raspberry Pear Spread

Raspberries and pears are partnered here in a yummy spread with a gorgeous color.

— o o o —

Tips

You'll need 4 or 5 large pears for this recipe.

Use a whisk to blend in the pectin, sweetener and sugar.

This spread may also be made with just the sweetener (increase to 1½ cups/375 mL, or to taste) and no sugar.

Variation

Blackberry Pear Spread: Replace the raspberries with blackberries.

3 cups	raspberries	750 mL
2 cups	finely chopped peeled pears	500 mL
2 tbsp	lemon juice	30 mL
1	package (1.75 oz/49 g) no-sugar-needed pectin	1
1 cup	Splenda No Calorie Sweetener	250 mL
1 cup	granulated sugar	250 mL

1. In a large, deep, heavy-bottomed pot, combine raspberries, pears and lemon juice.

2. Stir in pectin until dissolved. Bring to a full boil over high heat, stirring constantly.

3. Stir in sweetener until dissolved. Add sugar, stirring constantly. Return to a full boil, stirring constantly to dissolve sugar. Reduce heat to medium and boil rapidly for 3 minutes, stirring constantly and reducing heat further if the mixture sputters or is sticking on the bottom.

4. Remove from heat and skim off any foam.

5. Ladle into sterilized jars to within ¼ inch (0.5 cm) of rim; wipe rims. Apply prepared lids and rings; tighten just until fingertip-tight.

6. Process jars in a boiling water canner for 10 minutes (for details, see page 20). Transfer jars to a towel-lined surface and let rest at room temperature until set. Check seals; refrigerate any unsealed jars for up to 3 weeks.

Micro-Mini Peach Spread with Stevia

Makes about two 8-ounce (250 mL) jars

Stevia has become more available in stores and is a great alternative sweetener for fruit spreads.

— o o o —

Tips

If you add the granulated sugar (which improves the texture), reduce the peaches to 2¼ cups (550 mL). Adjust the stevia to taste.

See page 159 for helpful information on making micro-mini jams.

A heat-resistant silicone spatula is great for scraping down the sides of the bowl when stirring.

2½ cups	finely chopped peeled peaches (see tips, at left and page 180)	625 mL
1 tbsp	lemon juice	15 mL
3 tbsp	no-sugar-needed pectin	45 mL
3 tbsp	stevia (regular or vanilla-flavored), or to taste	45 mL
½ cup	granulated sugar (optional)	125 mL

1. In a 16-cup (4 L) microwave-safe bowl, combine peaches and lemon juice.

2. Stir in pectin and stevia. Stir in sugar (if using).

3. Microwave, uncovered, on High for 2 minutes; stir to dissolve sugar and scrape down sides of bowl. Microwave on High again for 2 minutes; stir and scrape down sides of bowl. Repeat in 1-minute intervals for another 1 to 3 minutes, or until jam froths up and thickens; stir and scrape down sides each time.

4. Test for setting point (for details, see page 19). Microwave in additional 1-minute intervals as needed.

5. Remove from microwave. Stir slowly until foam subsides; skim off any remaining foam.

6. Ladle into clean jars; wipe rims. Apply metal lids and rings, or use plastic lids; tighten until snug. Transfer to a towel-lined surface and let rest at room temperature until set. Refrigerate for up to 3 weeks.

> Stevia is a sweetener extracted from the leaf of the stevia plant, found in South America, and is about 300 times sweeter than sugar. It doesn't break down and can withstand high cooking temperatures. You can find it in most large supermarkets and health food stores. One brand is called Truvia.

Banana Orange and Date Conserve

Makes about four 8-ounce (250 mL) jars

This super-tasting lower-sugar conserve is perfect on whole-grain breads or bran muffins. Try it in Marmalade Pecan Cookies (page 358), Stuffed French Toast (page 354) or the Fruit Loaf (page 356).

— o o o —

Variations

Banana Orange and Date Conserve with Rum: Stir in 2 tbsp (30 mL) amber rum with the nuts.

Spiced Banana Orange and Date Conserve: Add ½ tsp (2 mL) ground cinnamon and ¼ tsp (1 mL) ground nutmeg with the sugar.

4	large oranges	4
4	large firm ripe bananas, diced	4
1 cup	chopped pitted dates	250 mL
1	package (1.75 oz/49 g) no-sugar-needed pectin	1
1¼ cups	packed brown sugar	300 mL
⅓ cup	chopped pecans (optional)	75 mL

1. Using a fine grater, remove 1 tbsp (15 mL) orange rind; set aside. Peel oranges and remove all pith, seeds and membranes. Chop the fruit and measure to make 1¾ cups (425 mL), including juices.

2. In a Dutch oven or a large, heavy-bottomed pot, combine orange rind, oranges, bananas and dates. Stir in pectin until dissolved. Bring to a boil over medium heat, stirring constantly.

3. Add sugar in a steady stream, stirring constantly. Increase heat to high and bring to a full boil, stirring constantly to dissolve sugar. Reduce heat and boil gently, stirring often for 3 minutes or until thickened.

4. Stir in pecans (if using). Remove from heat and let rest for 1 minute. Stir to distribute dates and nuts.

5. Ladle into sterilized jars to within ½ inch (1 cm) of rim (mixture expands with processing); wipe rims. Apply prepared lids and rings; tighten rings just until fingertip-tight.

6. Process jars in a boiling water canner for 10 minutes (for details, see page 20). Transfer jars to a towel-lined surface and let rest at room temperature until set. Check seals; refrigerate any unsealed jars for up to 3 weeks.

> Dates have been growing in the Middle East for thousands of years, but were introduced to California and Mexico around 1765 by the Spaniards. A *medjhool* date is a large, sweet, succulent variety grown in the U.S., Morocco, Saudi Arabia, Palestine, Israel and Jordan. *Medjhool* is Arabic for "unknown," as the person who first owned it didn't know its species.

Orange Onion Jam with Sage and Thyme

This soft-set jam has a marmalade-like golden color, with a slight tang. If desired, add a bit of finely grated orange rind with the oranges. This jam is excellent with pork, lamb or chicken.

—ooo—

5 cups	thinly sliced sweet onions	1.25 L
1/3 cup	water	75 mL
1	large clove garlic, minced	1
3 cups	finely chopped peeled oranges	750 mL
2 tbsp	finely chopped fresh sage (or 2 tsp/10 mL dried)	30 mL
1 tsp	finely chopped fresh lemon thyme or regular thyme (or 1/2 tsp/ 2 mL dried)	5 mL
1/3 cup	white wine vinegar	75 mL
1/2 tsp	salt	2 mL
Pinch	freshly ground black pepper	Pinch
1	package (1.75 oz/49 or 57 g) powdered pectin	1
3 1/4 cups	granulated sugar	800 mL
3/4 cup	packed brown sugar	175 mL

1. In a Dutch oven or a large, heavy-bottomed pot, combine onions and water. Reduce heat and simmer, covered, stirring occasionally, for about 10 minutes or until very soft.

2. Stir in garlic, oranges, sage and thyme. Increase heat to high and bring to a boil. Reduce heat and simmer, covered, for 8 minutes or until oranges are softened. Stir in vinegar, salt and pepper.

3. Stir in pectin until dissolved. Bring to a full boil over high heat, stirring constantly.

4. Stir in granulated sugar and brown sugar. Return to a full boil, stirring constantly to dissolve sugar. Boil hard for 1 minute.

Use a sweet onion such as Vidalia (Georgia) or Walla Walla (Washington). Alternatively, you can use sweet red onions.

You'll need about 2 large onions and 5 large oranges for this recipe.

5. Remove from heat and skim off any foam. Stir for 5 to 8 minutes to prevent floating fruit.

6. Ladle into sterilized jars to within $\frac{1}{2}$ inch (1 cm) of rim; wipe rims. Apply prepared lids and rings; tighten rings just until fingertip-tight.

7. Process jars in a boiling water canner for 15 minutes (for details, see page 20). Transfer jars to a towel-lined surface and let rest at room temperature until set. Check seals; refrigerate any unsealed jars for up to 3 weeks.

> Onion jams are sweet, savory condiments to enjoy with cheeses, meats or cooked vegetables. Add them to sauces when deglazing the pan after cooking meat, use as a finishing sauce on roasted meats or toss with cooked vegetables.

Tomato Orange Jam with Basil and Saffron

Makes about four 8-ounce (250 mL) jars

This exquisite jam has an interesting blend of flavors. For a touch of heat, add 1/4 tsp (1 mL) hot pepper flakes with the herbs. Serve on cheese with crackers, brush over roasted whole chicken or breasts, or toss with cooked green beans or carrots.

— o o o —

Tips

You'll need about 1 large onion, 2 large shallots, 3 lbs (750 g) of tomatoes and 2 large oranges for this recipe.

How to Peel Tomatoes:
Bring a large pot of water to a boil over high heat. Add several tomatoes and boil for 40 to 60 seconds. Remove tomatoes with a slotted spoon and immediately immerse in a bowl of very cold water. When the tomatoes are cool, the skins will slip off.

2 cups	thinly sliced sweet onions	500 mL
¾ cup	finely chopped shallots	175 mL
¼ cup	water	60 mL
1	clove garlic, minced	1
4 cups	finely chopped peeled seeded plum (Roma) tomatoes	1 L
1 tbsp	finely grated orange rind	15 mL
¾ cup	chopped peeled oranges	175 mL
¼ cup	lemon juice	60 mL
¼ tsp	saffron threads	1 mL
2 tbsp	finely chopped fresh basil (or 2 tsp/10 mL dried)	30 mL
½ tsp	dried oregano	2 mL
1	package (1.75 oz/49 to 57 g) powdered pectin	1
4 cups	granulated sugar	1 L
½ cup	packed brown sugar	125 mL

1. In a Dutch oven or a large, heavy-bottomed pot, combine onions, shallots and water. Reduce heat and simmer, covered, stirring occasionally, for about 10 minutes or until very soft.

2. Stir in garlic; cook for 2 minutes, stirring often.

3. Stir in tomatoes, orange rind, oranges and lemon juice. Increase heat to high and bring to a boil. Reduce heat to medium and boil gently, uncovered, for 15 minutes, stirring often.

4. Stir in saffron, basil and oregano; boil gently for 5 minutes, stirring occasionally.

5. Stir in pectin until dissolved. Bring to a full boil over high heat, stirring often.

6. Stir in granulated sugar and brown sugar. Return to a full boil, stirring constantly to dissolve sugar. Boil hard for 1 minute.

7. Remove from heat and skim off any foam.

8. Ladle into sterilized jars to within ½ inch (1 cm) of rim; wipe rims. Apply prepared lids and rings; tighten rings just until fingertip-tight.

9. Process jars in a boiling water canner for 15 minutes (for details, see page 20). Transfer jars to a towel-lined surface and let rest at room temperature until set. Check seals; refrigerate any unsealed jars for up to 3 weeks.

> Shallots are a member of the allium (onion) family and have a sweet, mild onion flavor and a firm texture. Stored in a cool, dry place, they will keep for up to 6 months.

Strawberry Onion Jam with Balsamic Vinegar and Rosemary

Makes about five 8-ounce (250 mL) jars

Serve this terrific jam on a roast beef sandwich or use to make a hot dressing for Steak Salad with Strawberry Balsamic Dressing (page 352).

——— o o o ———

Tips

You'll need about 2 large onions for this recipe.

To remove rosemary leaves from the stem, grasp the stem at the top end and pull leaves off in the opposite direction to their growth (toward the cut end).

5 cups	thinly sliced sweet onions	1.25 L
1/3 cup	water	75 mL
1	large clove garlic, minced	1
1 tbsp	finely chopped fresh rosemary (or 1 tsp/5 mL dried)	15 mL
2½ cups	finely chopped or mashed strawberries	625 mL
¼ cup	balsamic vinegar	60 mL
1	package (1.75 oz/49 to 57 g) powdered pectin	1
4 cups	granulated sugar	1 L
	Salt and freshly ground black pepper	

1. In a Dutch oven or a large, heavy-bottomed pot, combine onions and water. Reduce heat and simmer, covered, stirring occasionally, for about 10 minutes or until very soft.

2. Stir in garlic and rosemary; cook, covered for 5 minutes, stirring often. Stir in strawberries and vinegar.

3. Stir in pectin until dissolved. Bring to a full boil over high heat, stirring often.

4. Stir in sugar. Season to taste with salt and pepper. Return to a full boil, stirring constantly to dissolve sugar. Boil hard for 1 minute.

5. Remove from heat and skim off any foam. Stir for 5 to 8 minutes to prevent floating fruit.

6. Ladle into sterilized jars to within ½ inch (1 cm) of rim; wipe rims. Apply prepared lids and rings; tighten rings just until fingertip-tight.

7. Process jars in a boiling water canner for 15 minutes (for details, see page 20). Transfer jars to a towel-lined surface and let rest at room temperature until set. Check seals; refrigerate any unsealed jars for up to 3 weeks.

Carrot Apple Mincemeat

This tasty minced fruit mixture is perfect for tarts. Or use it to make Marmalade Pecan Cookies (page 358).

— o o o —

Tip

For information on the best apples to use, see page 25.

4 cups	chopped peeled apples that keep their shape	1 L
3½ cups	packed brown sugar	875 mL
2½ cups	water	625 mL
2 cups	finely grated carrots	500 mL
1 tbsp	finely grated lemon rind	15 mL
2 tbsp	lemon juice	30 mL
1 tsp	ground cinnamon	5 mL
½ tsp	ground nutmeg	2 mL
1 cup	golden raisins	250 mL
½ cup	chopped pecans (optional)	125 mL

1. In a Dutch oven or a large, heavy-bottomed pot, combine apples, brown sugar, water, carrots, lemon rind, lemon juice, cinnamon and nutmeg. Bring to a full boil over high heat, stirring constantly. Reduce heat and boil gently, stirring often and reducing heat further as the mixture thickens, for 30 minutes.

2. Stir in raisins; boil gently, stirring often, for 20 minutes or until mixture reaches a soft, jam-like consistency. Test for doneness (for details, see page 201).

3. Stir in pecans (if using); boil gently for 2 minutes, stirring constantly. Remove from heat and let rest for 1 minute. Stir to distribute raisins and nuts.

4. Ladle into sterilized jars to within ½ inch (1 cm) of rim; remove air pockets and wipe rims. Apply prepared lids and rings; tighten rings just until fingertip-tight.

5. Process jars in a boiling water canner for 10 minutes (for details, see page 20). Transfer jars to a towel-lined surface and let rest at room temperature until cooled. Check seals; refrigerate any unsealed jars for up to 3 weeks.

Pear and Apple Mincemeat

*This flavor-packed
all-fruit mixture can
be spooned directly into
tart shells and baked.*

—○○○—

Tips

You'll need about 5 large pears for this recipe.

For information on the best apples to use, see page 25.

Crystallized ginger and candied ginger are the same thing. Look for it at supermarkets or bulk stores.

If you prefer, you can replace the rum with 1 tsp (5 mL) rum extract.

4 cups	diced peeled pears	1 L
2	large apples that keep their shape, peeled and diced	2
1 tbsp	finely grated orange rind	15 mL
1/3 cup	orange juice	75 mL
1 tbsp	finely grated lemon rind	15 mL
1/4 cup	lemon juice	60 mL
1 1/2 cups	packed brown sugar	375 mL
3/4 cup	raisins	175 mL
1/2 cup	dried currants	125 mL
1/4 cup	minced crystallized ginger	60 mL
3/4 tsp	ground allspice	3 mL
3/4 tsp	ground cinnamon	3 mL
Pinch	salt	Pinch
1/3 cup	chopped pecans (optional)	75 mL
1/4 cup	dark rum (optional)	60 mL

1. In a Dutch oven or a large, heavy-bottomed pot, combine pears, apples, orange rind, orange juice, lemon rind, lemon juice, brown sugar, raisins, currants, ginger, allspice, cinnamon and salt. Bring to a full boil over high heat, stirring constantly.

2. Reduce heat and boil gently, stirring often and reducing heat further as the mixture thickens, for about 45 minutes or until mixture reaches a soft, jam-like consistency. Test for doneness (for details, see page 201).

3. Stir in pecans and rum (if using); simmer for 2 minutes, stirring constantly. Remove from heat and let rest for 1 minute. Stir to distribute fruit and nuts.

4. Ladle into prepared jars to within 1/2 inch (1 cm) of rim; remove air pockets and wipe rims. Apply prepared lids and rings; tighten rings just until fingertip-tight.

5. Process jars in a boiling water canner for 10 minutes (for details, see page 20). Transfer jars to a towel-lined surface and let rest at room temperature until cooled. Check seals; refrigerate any unsealed jars for up to 3 weeks.

Conserves

A conserve is a fruit mixture usually made with two or more fresh fruits, sugar, dried fruit, nuts, and sometimes spices or liquor. It is slightly thinner in consistency than jam, but should mound up on spoon.

About Conserves 200
Tips for Successful Conserves 200
Test for Doneness. 201
Trouble-Shooting 202

Apple Orange Apricot Conserve. 203
Apple Rhubarb Conserve with Goji Berries. 204
Apple Rum Raisin Conserve. 205
Apricot Almond Conserve 206
Apricot Rhubarb Conserve. 207
Spiced Carrot Apple Pineapple Conserve. 208
Cherry Cranberry Orange Conserve with Grand Marnier . . 209
Chunky Cherry Plum Conserve 210
Cherry Raspberry Apple Conserve. 211
Cherry Profusion Conserve 212
Cranberry Pear Conserve with Ginger 214
Fig and Italian Plum Conserve 215
Coronation Grape Orange Conserve 216
Nectarine Apricot Cherry Conserve 217
Pear Maple Walnut Conserve. 218
Caribbean Treasure Conserve 219
Grilled Pineapple Banana Conserve with Kahlúa. 220
Plum Cranberry Orange Conserve 222
Plum Rum and Prune Conserve. 223
Christmas Plum Conserve 224
Rumpot Conserve 225
Strawberry Rhubarb and Pear Conserve 226

About Conserves

At one time, conserves were eaten alone as a dessert. We now typically eat them as we do jams, on our favorite bread, toast, scone or muffin. They can also be used to top cake or ice cream, or stirred into fresh yogurt.

Conserves have a soft, jam-like consistency, but are different from jams. They usually contain dried fruit, such as raisins, apricots, cranberries, cherries or goji berries, and often include chopped or whole nuts. The combination of dried fruit and nuts gives these preserves a bit of a chewy and crunchy texture. Alcohol, in the form of rum or fruit liqueur, enhances the flavor and makes it a little more special for gift-giving. Nuts and liquor can be omitted from any of the recipes.

You can easily alter a conserve to suit individual preferences by varying the type of dried fruit, using whole or toasted nuts, changing the nuts or using a different liqueur. Because every conserve is unique, they are not something you can easily buy.

The pieces of fruit used in conserves are somewhat larger than those used for jams: fruit is halved or sliced instead of chopped, or is coarsely chopped — ½-inch (1 cm) pieces work well.

Conserves are usually cooked down until thickened, so they do not normally require added pectin, nor do they need to be made with high-pectin fruit. Firm, slightly underripe fruit is used because it is higher in natural pectin than riper fruit; overripe fruit is lower in pectin and loses its shape more easily when cooked. In a few recipes, commercial pectin is added to allow the conserve to set without overcooking.

Dried fruit is usually added about halfway through the cooking time to help it retain its texture. Nuts are added near the end, as they need no cooking. Liqueurs are also added at the end so they retain their flavor.

> Refer to the Produce Purchase Guide, page 32, to estimate the amount of fruit and/or vegetables you'll need to purchase for these recipes.

Tips for Successful Conserves

1. Use slightly underripe or firm, just-ripe fruit; avoid soft, overripe fruit. Wash fruit well and pare away any blemishes or bruises.

2. Measure carefully. As with jams, the proper levels of fruit and sugar are important to the final texture.

3. When adding sugar, stir well to ensure that it is completely dissolved, scraping down any that gets on the sides of the pot or the spoon handle. Undissolved sugar can crystallize in your conserve. Heating the mixture a little before stirring in the sugar will help the sugar dissolve more quickly.

4. If desired, soak dried fruit in water overnight; drain well before adding.

5. Watch your conserve while it is cooking and stir frequently. Dried fruit may sink to the bottom and scorch if insufficiently stirred. Conserves are not cooked for as long as jams without added pectin, so watch them and test for doneness (see details below) to avoid overcooking. A silicone spatula, which is heat-resistant, is great for stirring, as you are able to scrape the bottom of the pot to remove bits that might stick.

6. After removing the conserve from the heat, let it rest for 1 minute, then stir to evenly distribute the dried fruit and nuts.

Please read A Primer on Preserving, pages 14 to 37. Things may have changed since you first started making preserves (such as the recent increase in processing time). If you are a beginner, there are a few important things you need to know before getting started. Many instructions are common to all preserves, so once you get it right for one, you'll sail through the others. In the primer, you will also find a handy Preparation Checklist (page 37).

Test for Doneness

Place a spoonful of conserve on a chilled plate. Place in the freezer for a minute or two, until cooled to room temperature. Gently push the mixture with your finger; when done, it will slightly wrinkle and will have the texture of a soft jam. You want it to mound on a spoon but be soft enough to tumble from it. If it becomes sticky, it is overcooked. You can fix this by stirring a little apple juice, orange juice or water into the pot and reheating the mixture, stirring constantly.

Trouble-Shooting

PROBLEM: Conserve is thin and runny.

Conserve likely needs to be cooked longer. If the jars have all sealed properly, the contents are safe. Return conserve to pot, discard used lids and begin cooking and testing again. It may take only a few minutes after it begins to boil. Proceed with sterilized jars and new prepared lids.

PROBLEM: Conserve is too stiff or tough.

Conserve was likely overcooked. If it has not yet been put into jars, thin it by adding a little fruit juice or water, return to a boil and test for doneness. If you find that it is too stiff after you open a jar, try warming it in the microwave and add fruit juice, water or a bit of liqueur to thin it down.

PROBLEM: Conserve has crystals.

You may have added too much sugar, or undissolved sugar may have coated the sides of the pot or the spoon handle. Measure accurately, using dry measuring cups and leveling the top with a straight edge or knife. Stir well during cooking and scrape down the sides of the pot with a rubber scraper, if necessary.

Crystallization may also result from overcooking or from storage in a place that is too warm or has temperature fluctuations.

PROBLEM: Dried fruit or nuts settle to bottom of jar.

Wait a minute or two after removing conserve from the heat, then stir to evenly distribute fruit and/or nuts throughout the mixture.

Apple Orange Apricot Conserve

Makes about six 8-ounce (250 mL) jars

Make this tasty conserve with apples, oranges and dried fruit any time of year. It's great on muffins, or add a dollop to the center of your muffin batter before baking.

—○○○—

Tips

For information on the best apples to use, see page 25.

Fruit-Fresh is an ascorbic acid color-keeper that prevents apples from browning while you chop. Sprinkle over chopped apples and toss to coat. It also adds acidity to the taste, so don't overdo it.

3	large oranges	3
3	large apples that keep their shape	3
2 cups	water	500 mL
4 1/2 cups	granulated sugar	1.125 L
1/2 tsp	ground cinnamon	2 mL
3/4 cup	diced dried apricots	175 mL
3/4 cup	golden raisins	175 mL
1/3 cup	coarsely chopped pecans (optional)	75 mL
1/4 cup	apricot or orange liqueur (optional)	60 mL

1. Slice unpeeled oranges into rounds about 1/8 inch (3 mm) thick; cut each round into 12 to 14 wedges. Peel apples and cut into 1/2-inch (1 cm) pieces.

2. In a Dutch oven or a large, heavy-bottomed pot, combine oranges, apples and water. Bring to a boil over high heat, stirring often. Reduce heat and boil gently, covered, for 30 minutes or until orange rind is softened.

3. Add sugar in a steady stream, stirring constantly. Stir in cinnamon. Bring to a boil over high heat, stirring constantly to dissolve sugar.

4. Reduce heat and boil gently, uncovered, for 15 minutes, stirring often. Stir in apricots and raisins; boil, stirring often, for 10 to 15 minutes or until mixture reaches a soft, jam-like consistency. Test for doneness (for details, see page 201).

5. Stir in pecans and liqueur (if using); boil for 2 minutes, stirring constantly. Remove from heat and let rest for 1 minute. Stir to distribute dried fruit and nuts.

6. Ladle into sterilized jars to within 1/2 inch (1 cm) of rim; wipe rims. Apply prepared lids and rings; tighten rings just until fingertip-tight.

7. Process jars in a boiling water canner for 10 minutes (for details, see page 20). Transfer jars to a towel-lined surface and let rest at room temperature until set. Check seals; refrigerate any unsealed jars for up to 3 weeks.

Apple Rhubarb Conserve with Goji Berries

This conserve has a lovely tart flavor. Freeze rhubarb when it's in abundance and make this conserve any time of year.

— o o o —

Tips

For information on which apples soften and which keep their shape, see page 25.

For the best texture in this conserve, cut the apples and rhubarb into ½-inch (1 cm) pieces.

Goji berries, a variety of *Lycium* berry grown in the valleys of Tibet and Mongolia, have become increasingly popular in North America and can be found in bulk stores and Asian markets. You will find them in dried form; they are generally cooked before eating. They are sweet and tart, taste somewhat like a cross between a cranberry and a cherry, and are rich in vitamins, minerals and antioxidants

4 cups	chopped peeled apples that keep their shape	1 L
2 cups	chopped peeled apples that soften	500 mL
3 cups	chopped rhubarb	750 mL
¾ cup	water	175 mL
1	package (1.75 oz/49 or 57 g) powdered pectin	1
4 cups	granulated sugar	1 L
½ tsp	ground cinnamon	2 mL
½ cup	dried goji berries or dried cranberries	125 mL
¼ cup	brandy or apple liqueur (optional)	60 mL

1. In a Dutch oven or a large, deep, heavy-bottomed pot, combine apples, rhubarb and water. Bring to a boil over high heat. Cover and cook, stirring occasionally, for 5 minutes or until apples are softened.

2. Stir in pectin until dissolved. Bring to a full boil over high heat, stirring constantly.

3. Add sugar in a steady stream, stirring constantly. Stir in cinnamon. Bring to a full boil over high heat, stirring constantly to dissolve sugar. Boil hard for 1 minute.

4. Stir in goji berries and brandy (if using); boil gently, uncovered, for 2 minutes, stirring occasionally. Remove from heat and let rest for 1 minute. Stir to distribute goji berries.

5. Ladle into sterilized jars to within ½ inch (1 cm) of rim; wipe rims. Apply prepared lids and rings; tighten rings just until fingertip-tight.

6. Process jars in a boiling water canner for 10 minutes (for details, see page 20). Transfer jars to a towel-lined surface and let rest at room temperature until set. Check seals; refrigerate any unsealed jars for up to 3 weeks.

Apple Rum Raisin Conserve

Makes about seven 8-ounce (250 mL) jars

Simply delicious — a perfect blend of complementary tastes! Toast the nuts, if desired, before adding them (see tip, page 215).

— o o o —

Tips

For longer storage, keep nuts in a glass jar in the refrigerator. Nuts, such as walnuts, that are high in omega-3 fats can easily go rancid if exposed to heat. Do not use any nuts that have an off or fishy smell.

Supermarkets now carry all-natural (or pure-pressed) apple juice, which contains solids. Shake before using.

Variations

Spiced Apple Raisin Conserve: Omit the rum and add 1 tsp (5 mL) ground cinnamon and ½ tsp (2 mL) ground nutmeg with the brown sugar.

Apple Cranberry Orange Conserve: Replace the raisins with dried cranberries and the rum with Grand Marnier.

8 cups	chopped peeled apples that soften	2 L
4 cups	chopped peeled apples that keep their shape	1 L
1 cup	all-natural apple juice (see tip, at left) or unsweetened apple cider	250 mL
2 tbsp	lemon juice	30 mL
3¾ cups	granulated sugar	925 mL
1½ cups	packed brown sugar	375 mL
1 cup	sultana or golden raisins	250 mL
½ cup	chopped walnuts (optional)	125 mL
⅓ cup	amber rum (or 2 tsp/10 mL rum extract)	75 mL

1. In a Dutch oven or a large, deep, heavy-bottomed pot, combine apples, apple juice and lemon juice. Bring to a boil over high heat. Reduce heat and simmer, covered, for 5 minutes to soften apples.

2. Add granulated sugar in a steady stream, stirring constantly. Stir in brown sugar and raisins. Bring to a full boil, stirring constantly. Reduce heat and boil gently, uncovered, stirring often and reducing heat further as mixture thickens, for 20 to 25 minutes or until mixture reaches a soft, jam-like consistency. Test for doneness (for details, see page 201).

3. Stir in walnuts (if using) and rum; boil gently for 2 minutes, stirring constantly. Remove from heat and let rest for 1 minute. Stir to distribute raisins and nuts.

4. Ladle into sterilized jars to within ½ inch (1 cm) of rim; wipe rims. Apply prepared lids and rings; tighten rings just until fingertip-tight.

5. Process jars in a boiling water canner for 10 minutes (for details, see page 20). Transfer jars to a towel-lined surface and let rest at room temperature until set. Check seals; refrigerate any unsealed jars for up to 3 weeks.

> *Sultanas* are dried from seedless yellow grapes and are softer and sweeter than other raisins. *Golden*, or white, raisins are usually dried from Muscat grapes.

Apricot Almond Conserve

*Fresh apricots, with
their deep orange and
slightly red peels, give a
wonderful flavor to this
lightly spiced conserve.
For a deeper color and
flavor, substitute packed
brown sugar for the
granulated sugar.*

— o o o —

Tip

If you prefer, you can
replace the amaretto with
$1/2$ tsp (2 mL) almond
extract.

3 lbs	ripe apricots, sliced or chopped	1.5 kg
4 cups	granulated sugar	1 L
1 cup	golden raisins	250 mL
$1^1/_2$ tsp	ground cardamom	7 mL
$1/2$ tsp	ground allspice	2 mL
$1/2$ tsp	ground cinnamon	2 mL
$1/3$ cup	blanched whole almonds	75 mL
$1/3$ cup	amaretto (optional)	75 mL

1. In a Dutch oven or a large, heavy-bottomed pot, combine apricots, sugar, raisins, cardamom, allspice and cinnamon. Bring to a boil over high heat, stirring constantly.

2. Reduce heat and boil gently, stirring often, for 30 to 35 minutes or until mixture reaches a soft, jam-like consistency. Test for doneness (for details, see page 201).

3. Stir in almonds and amaretto (if using); boil gently for 2 minutes, stirring constantly. Remove from heat and let rest for 1 minute. Stir to distribute raisins and nuts.

4. Ladle into sterilized jars to within $1/2$ inch (1 cm) of rim; wipe rims. Apply prepared lids and rings; tighten rings just until fingertip-tight.

5. Process jars in a boiling water canner for 10 minutes (for details, see page 20). Transfer jars to a towel-lined surface and let rest at room temperature until set. Check seals; refrigerate any unsealed jars for up to 3 weeks.

> "Blanched" almonds means they have their skins removed.

Apricot Rhubarb Conserve

The addition of dried apricots intensifies the flavor of this tasty fruit combination.

— o o o —

Tips

You'll need about 2 lbs (1 kg) of apricots for this recipe.

For the best texture, cut the fresh apricots and the rhubarb into 1/2-inch (1 cm) pieces.

When rhubarb is in season in the spring, cut small stalks into 1/2-inch (1 cm) pieces, place in freezer bags and remove as much air as possible. Seal and store for up to a year.

In late winter, forced greenhouse rhubarb is available in stores.

4 cups	chopped ripe apricots	1 L
2 cups	chopped rhubarb	500 mL
2/3 cup	diced dried apricots	150 mL
1/3 cup	water	75 mL
1	package (1.75 oz/49 or 57 g) powdered pectin	1
3 1/2 cups	granulated sugar	875 mL
3 tbsp	apricot brandy (optional)	45 mL

1. In a Dutch oven or a large heavy-bottomed pot, combine fresh apricots, rhubarb, dried apricots and water. Bring to a boil over high heat. Reduce heat and simmer, stirring constantly, for 1 minute or until rhubarb is softened.

2. Stir in pectin until dissolved. Bring to a full boil over high heat, stirring constantly.

3. Add sugar in a steady stream, stirring constantly. Return to a full boil, stirring constantly to dissolve sugar. Boil hard for 1 minute.

4. Remove from heat and stir in brandy (if using).

5. Ladle into sterilized jars to within 1/2 inch (1 cm) of rim; wipe rims. Apply prepared lids and rings; tighten rings just until fingertip-tight.

6. Process jars in a boiling water canner for 10 minutes (for details, see page 20). Transfer jars to a towel-lined surface and let rest at room temperature until set. Check seals; refrigerate any unsealed jars for up to 3 weeks.

Originating in western China, Mongolia and Tibet, rhubarb is classified as a vegetable and has been used for over 4,000 years, mainly as a medicine. Seeds were brought to North America in the late 1700s by Ben Franklin and rhubarb was cultivated on the east coast, becoming popular in pies.

Spiced Carrot Apple Pineapple Conserve

*This conserve is excellent
on a bran or oatmeal
muffin. It's so tasty I
kept eating it out of
the sample jar!*

— o o o —

Tips

Varieties of apples that
soften when cooked include
McIntosh, Cortland, Empire
and Russet. See page 25
for more details.

Use a food processor fitted
with a shredder attachment
to shred large quantities
of carrots, especially
when they're in season
and are nice and sweet.
Measure in 2-cup (500 mL)
amounts and freeze in
medium freezer bags for
convenience.

Supermarkets now carry
all-natural (or pure-pressed)
apple juice, which contains
solids. Shake before using.

7 cups	chopped peeled apples that soften	1.75 L
2 cups	finely shredded carrots	500 mL
1 cup	all-natural apple juice (see tip, at left) or unsweetened apple cider	250 mL
2 cups	granulated sugar	500 mL
1 cup	packed brown sugar	250 mL
1 tsp	ground cinnamon	5 mL
1	can (14 oz/398 mL) crushed pineapple with juice	1
½ cup	golden raisins	125 mL
½ cup	chopped pecans (optional)	125 mL
2 tbsp	amber rum (optional)	30 mL

1. In a Dutch oven or a large, deep, heavy-bottomed pot, combine apples, carrots and apple juice. Bring to a boil over high heat, stirring often. Reduce heat and simmer, covered, stirring occasionally, for about 8 minutes or until apples are softened.

2. Add granulated sugar in a steady stream, stirring constantly. Stir in brown sugar, cinnamon and pineapple with juice. Increase heat to high and bring to a full boil, stirring constantly to dissolve sugar. Reduce heat and boil gently, uncovered, stirring often and reducing heat further as mixture thickens, for about 20 minutes or until beginning to thicken.

3. Stir in raisins, pecans and rum (if using); boil gently, stirring often, for 5 minutes or until mixture reaches a soft, jam-like consistency. Test for doneness (for details, see page 201). Remove from heat and let rest for 1 minute. Stir to distribute raisins and nuts.

4. Ladle into sterilized jars to within ½ inch (1 cm) of rim; wipe rims. Apply prepared lids and rings; tighten just until fingertip-tight.

5. Process jars in a boiling water canner for 10 minutes (for details, see page 20). Transfer jars to a towel-lined surface and let rest at room temperature until cool. Check seals; refrigerate any unsealed jars for up to 3 weeks.

Cherry Cranberry Orange Conserve with Grand Marnier

Makes about seven 8-ounce (250 mL) jars

This is a nice blend of flavors — the tang of cranberries with orange and a hint of nutmeg. Orange liqueur lifts the flavor to new heights.

— ○○○ —

Tips

You'll need about 2 lbs (1 kg) of cherries for this recipe.

Bing cherries are a popular dark cherry that would be great in this recipe. Conserve may also be made with Rainier cherries. See page 213 for information on cherry types.

3	large oranges	3
4 cups	coarsely chopped sweet cherries, such as Bing	1 L
4 cups	cranberries	1 L
5½ cups	granulated sugar	1.375 mL
¼ tsp	ground nutmeg	1 mL
¼ cup	Grand Marnier, Triple Sec or cherry brandy	60 mL

1. Using a fine grater, remove 1 tbsp (15 mL) orange rind; set aside. Peel oranges and remove all pith and seeds. Chop the fruit, reserving the juices.

2. In a Dutch oven or a large, deep, heavy-bottomed pot, combine orange rind, oranges with juice, cherries and cranberries. Bring to a boil over high heat, stirring occasionally. Reduce heat and simmer, covered, for 5 minutes. Use a potato masher to further break down fruit.

3. Add sugar in a steady stream, stirring constantly. Stir in nutmeg. Increase heat to high and bring to a full boil, stirring constantly to dissolve sugar. Reduce heat and boil gently, uncovered, stirring often and reducing heat further as mixture thickens, for 20 to 25 minutes or until mixture reaches a soft, jam-like consistency. Test for doneness (for details, see page 201).

4. Stir in Grand Marnier; simmer for 1 minute.

5. Ladle into sterilized jars to within ½ inch (1 cm) of rim; wipe rims. Apply prepared lids and rings; tighten rings just until fingertip-tight.

6. Process jars in a boiling water canner for 10 minutes (for details, see page 20). Transfer jars to a towel-lined surface and let rest at room temperature until set. Check seals; refrigerate any unsealed jars for up to 3 weeks.

Chunky Cherry Plum Conserve

This is a lovely red conserve with a rich cherry flavor.

— o o o —

Tip
You'll need about 2 lbs (1 kg) of cherries for this recipe.

Recipe Suggestion
Use conserve in sauce for pork chops, duck or chicken. Remove browned meat from skillet, use water, wine, apple juice, orange juice or cranberry juice to deglaze the pan, then stir in conserve and a little chopped fresh rosemary. Add meat back to pan and simmer, covered, for about 5 minutes.

4 cups	coarsely chopped sweet cherries, such as Bing	1 L
4 cups	chopped red plums	1 L
¾ cup	granulated sugar	175 mL
1 cup	coarsely chopped dried sour cherries	250 mL
⅓ cup	cherry brandy (optional)	75 mL

1. In a Dutch oven or a large, deep, heavy-bottomed pot, combine cherries and plums. Add sugar in a steady stream, stirring constantly. Bring to a full boil over high heat, stirring constantly to dissolve sugar.

2. Reduce heat and boil gently, stirring often, for 15 minutes. Stir in dried cherries; boil, stirring often and reducing heat further as mixture thickens, for about 10 minutes or until mixture reaches a soft, jam-like consistency. Test for doneness (for details, see page 201).

3. Stir in brandy (if using). Remove from heat and let rest for 1 minute. Stir to distribute dried cherries.

4. Ladle into sterilized jars to within ½ inch (1 cm) of rim; wipe rims. Apply prepared lids and rings; tighten rings just until fingertip-tight.

5. Process jars in a boiling water canner for 10 minutes (for details, see page 20). Transfer jars to a towel-lined surface and let rest at room temperature until set. Check seals; refrigerate any unsealed jars for up to 3 weeks.

Cherry Raspberry Apple Conserve

This deep red conserve will have a nice cherry-almond flavor if you add the almond liqueur or extract. Serve with English muffins.

— o o o —

Tips

Sour cherries are also called red tart cherries. Look for cherries that are medium-firm with a glossy surface. Store in a plastic bag in the refrigerator.

Cherry pitters are available in most gourmet kitchen shops.

For information on the best apples to use, see page 25.

If you prefer, you can replace the amaretto with ½ tsp (2 mL) almond extract.

3 cups	halved or coarsely chopped sour (tart) cherries	750 mL
2 cups	raspberries	500 mL
2	large apples that keep their shape, peeled and chopped into ½-inch (1 cm) pieces	2
4½ cups	granulated sugar	1.125 L
1 tbsp	grated lemon rind	15 mL
1 tbsp	lemon juice	15 mL
⅓ cup	slivered blanched almonds (optional)	75 mL
¼ cup	amaretto or cherry liqueur (optional)	60 mL

1. In a Dutch oven or a large, heavy-bottomed pot, combine cherries, raspberries, apples, sugar, lemon rind and lemon juice. Bring to a boil over high heat, stirring constantly.

2. Reduce heat and boil gently, stirring often and reducing heat further as mixture thickens, for 25 to 30 minutes or until mixture reaches a soft jam-like consistency. Test for doneness (for details, see page 201).

3. Stir in nuts and amaretto (if using); simmer for 2 minutes, stirring occasionally. Remove from heat and let rest for 1 minute. Stir to distribute nuts.

4. Ladle into sterilized jars to within ½ inch (1 cm) of rim; wipe rims. Apply prepared lids and rings; tighten rings just until fingertip-tight.

5. Process jars in a boiling water canner for 10 minutes (for details, see page 20). Transfer jars to a towel-lined surface and let rest at room temperature until cooled. Check seals; refrigerate any unsealed jars for up to 3 weeks.

Cherry Profusion Conserve

**Makes about four
8-ounce (250 mL) jars**

*I loved the idea of doing a
jam for cherry aficionados
like my friend Sonja. It
uses sweet, sour and
dried cherries for a fusion
of cherry-liciousness!*

— o o o —

Tip

You'll need about 1 lb
(500 g) of sweet cherries
and 1½ lbs (750 g) of sour
(tart) cherries for this recipe.

2 cups	chopped sweet cherries, such as Bing	500 mL
3 cups	chopped sour (tart) cherries	750 mL
2 tbsp	lemon juice	30 mL
4 cups	granulated sugar	1 L
½ cup	coarsely chopped dried sour cherries	125 mL
⅓ cup	blanched whole almonds (optional)	75 mL
2 tbsp	Kirsch, cherry brandy or amaretto (optional)	30 mL

1. In a Dutch oven or a large, deep, heavy-bottomed pot, combine sweet cherries, tart cherries and lemon juice. Add sugar in a steady stream, stirring constantly. Bring to a full boil over high heat, stirring constantly to dissolve sugar.

2. Reduce heat and boil gently, stirring often and reducing heat further as mixture thickens, for 20 to 22 minutes or until mixture reaches a soft, jam-like consistency. Test for doneness (for details, see page 201).

3. Stir in dried cherries, almonds and Kirsch (if using); boil gently for 2 minutes, stirring occasionally. Remove from heat, skim off any foam and let rest for 1 minute. Stir to distribute dried cherries and nuts.

4. Ladle into sterilized jars to within ½ inch (1 cm) of rim; wipe rims. Apply prepared lids and rings; tighten rings just until fingertip-tight.

5. Process jars in a boiling water canner for 10 minutes (for details, see page 20). Transfer jars to a towel-lined surface and let rest at room temperature until set. Check seals; refrigerate any unsealed jars for up to 3 weeks.

Tips

Chop sweet cherries coarsely with a knife or by pulsing in a food processor fitted with a metal blade, being sure not to purée them. (Beware of stray pits.) Sour (tart) cherries are best chopped with a knife so they don't get too mushed up. Drain juice from sour cherries from the pail. (The juice can be used to make jelly.)

For preserves containing cherries, check for stray pits when skimming off any foam — the pits will float.

Bing cherries are the most popular dark sweet cherry. They are grown primarily in Washington, Oregon and British Columbia. This cultivar was developed in Oregon in the 1870s by Seth Lewelling and is named for his Chinese foreman, Ah Bing.

Rainier cherries are yellow with a red blush and a sweet flavor. They are named after Mount Rainier in Washington State, where they grow. They are a cultivar of a Bing and a Van cherry and were created in 1952 at Washington State University.

Montmorency cherries are the most common sour (tart) cherry. They are grown in Michigan and Wisconsin, and in the Niagara area in Canada. Ideal for jams, they can be found fresh, pitted in large pails during their harvest, then frozen afterwards. (You may have to ask the produce manager for them.)The juice from pitted cherries is drained off and can be used to make jellies. Montmorency are also used to make dried sour cherries.

Cranberry Pear Conserve with Ginger

Makes about seven 8-ounce (250 mL) jars

Because I've added powdered pectin, this recipe is a little quicker to make than the long-boil method usually used for conserves. The fruit keeps a bit of chunkiness as a result. Freeze an extra bag of cranberries around the holidays so you'll have them on hand to make this. Pears are usually available in supermarkets year-round.

— o o o —

Tips

You'll need about 4 lbs (2 kg) of pears (about 5 large) for this recipe.

Try flavored dried cranberries, such as cherry or orange.

2 cups	cranberries	500 mL
½ cup	water	125 mL
4 cups	finely chopped peeled pears	1 L
1	package (1.75 oz/49 or 57 g) powdered pectin	1
5 cups	granulated sugar	1.25 L
¾ cup	dried cranberries	175 mL
¼ cup	finely chopped crystallized ginger	60 mL

1. In a Dutch oven or a large, deep, heavy-bottomed pot, combine fresh cranberries and water. Bring to a boil over high heat. Reduce heat and simmer for 5 minutes. Use a potato masher to further break down cranberries.

2. Stir in pears. Stir in pectin until dissolved. Increase heat to high and bring to a full boil, stirring constantly.

3. Add sugar in a steady stream, stirring constantly. Return to a full boil, stirring constantly to dissolve sugar. Stir in dried cranberries and ginger. Boil hard for 1 minute.

4. Remove from heat and skim off any foam. Stir for 5 minutes to prevent floating fruit.

5. Ladle into sterilized jars to within ½ inch (1 cm) of rim; wipe rims. Apply prepared lids and rings; tighten rings just until fingertip-tight.

6. Process jars in a boiling water canner for 10 minutes (for details, see page 20). Transfer jars to a towel-lined surface and let rest at room temperature until set. Check seals; refrigerate any unsealed jars for up to 3 weeks.

Fig and Italian Plum Conserve

Makes about five 8-ounce (250 mL) jars

This conserve has a wonderful mixture of rich Mediterranean flavors and a beautiful deep red color. Toasted pine nuts add a unique touch.

— o o o —

Tips

Buy fresh figs that are slightly soft and sweet-smelling, with undamaged skin. They can be stored in the refrigerator for several days, but use them as soon after purchase as possible.

How to Toast Nuts: Place nuts in an ungreased skillet over low heat. Stir constantly until lightly toasted. You will begin to see glistening on the outside of the nuts as the natural oils warm.

Toasting nuts enhances their nuttiness and gives them a crisp texture (moisture may have softened them during storage, especially once the package is opened).

2 lbs	Italian (prune) purple plums, coarsely chopped or sliced	1 kg
1 lb	ripe fresh figs, coarsely chopped or sliced	500 g
2 1/2 cups	granulated sugar	625 mL
1/2 cup	liquid honey	125 mL
1/2 cup	sweet sherry	125 mL
2 tsp	finely grated lemon rind	10 mL
1/4 cup	lemon juice	60 mL
1	piece (6 inches/15 cm) cinnamon stick, broken into 3 pieces	1
1/3 cup	toasted pine nuts (optional)	75 mL

1. In a Dutch oven or a large, heavy-bottomed pot, combine plums, figs, sugar, honey, sherry, lemon rind, lemon juice and cinnamon. Bring to a boil over high heat, stirring constantly.

2. Reduce heat and boil gently, stirring often and reducing heat further as mixture thickens, for 50 to 60 minutes or until mixture reaches a soft, jam-like consistency. Test for doneness (for details, see page 201).

3. Stir in pine nuts (if using); boil gently for 2 minutes, stirring constantly. Remove from heat and let rest for 1 minute. Stir to distribute nuts.

4. Ladle into sterilized jars to within 1/2 inch (1 cm) of rim; wipe rims. Apply prepared lids and rings; tighten rings just until fingertip-tight.

5. Process jars in a boiling water canner for 10 minutes (for details, see page 20). Transfer jars to a towel-lined surface and let rest at room temperature until set. Check seals; refrigerate any unsealed jars for up to 3 weeks.

> Figs have soft flesh with many tiny, edible seeds. Calimyrna is a variety of fig grown in California that has green skin and white flesh. Any fresh fig may be used in this recipe.

Coronation Grape Orange Conserve

In this conserve, I have joined together grapes, wine and raisins — ode to the vine! It has an almost cranberry-like tart flavor.

—ooo—

Recipe Suggestion

Serve on top of cheese (or Baked Brie, page 345) at your next wine and cheese gathering.

Coronation grapes are small, bluish-colored eating grapes (sometimes called blue grapes) that are usually seedless. Their flavor is different from the Concord grape jelly taste you may be familiar with. You will find them in stores and markets from late August to mid-September.

2½ lbs	Coronation table grapes	1.25 kg
2	large oranges	2
¼ cup	red wine, such as Shiraz or Cabernet	60 mL
1	package (1.75 oz/49 or 57 g) powdered pectin	1
½ cup	sultana raisins	125 mL
4 cups	granulated sugar	1 L

1. Carefully remove grapes from stems. (Check well for small stem bits before processing.) Using a food processor fitted with a metal blade, coarsely chop grapes, in batches, by pulsing on and off. Measure 4 cups (1 L).

2. Using a fine grater, remove 1 tbsp (15 mL) orange rind; set aside. Peel oranges and remove all pith, seeds and membranes. Finely chop the fruit and measure to make 1 cup (250 mL), including juices.

3. In a Dutch oven or a large, deep, heavy-bottomed pot, combine grapes, orange rind and oranges. Bring to a boil over high heat, stirring occasionally. Reduce heat and simmer, covered, for about 20 minutes or until grape skins are softened.

4. Stir in wine. Stir in pectin until dissolved. Stir in raisins. Increase heat to high and bring to a full boil, stirring constantly.

5. Add sugar in a steady stream, stirring constantly. Return to a full boil, stirring constantly to dissolve sugar. Boil hard for 1 minute.

6. Remove from heat, skim off any foam and let rest for 1 minute. Stir to distribute raisins.

7. Ladle into sterilized jars to within ½ inch (1 cm) of rim; wipe rims. Apply prepared lids and rings; tighten rings just until fingertip-tight.

8. Process jars in a boiling water canner for 10 minutes (for details, see page 20). Transfer jars to a towel-lined surface and let rest at room temperature until set. Check seals; refrigerate any unsealed jars for up to 3 weeks.

Nectarine Apricot Cherry Conserve

Makes about six 8-ounce (250 mL) jars

I developed this conserve for my friend Wendi, who loves nectarines. Dried cherries, which can be found at bulk stores, add a bit of tartness. It has turned out to be one of my favorites.

— o o o —

Tip

Choose nectarines that have a smooth skin with red and yellow coloring. Nectarines should give slightly to the touch. Place slightly underripe fruit in a paper bag and leave at room temperature for a couple of days to ripen. Avoid fruit that is overly hard or green.

8 cups	chopped nectarines (unpeeled)	2 L
1 tbsp	finely grated lemon rind	15 mL
$\frac{1}{4}$ cup	lemon juice	60 mL
$4\frac{1}{2}$ cups	granulated sugar	1.125 L
1 cup	sliced dried apricots	250 mL
1 cup	dried cherries	250 mL
2 tbsp	apricot brandy (optional)	30 mL

1. In a Dutch oven or a large, heavy-bottomed pot, combine nectarines, lemon rind and lemon juice. Bring to a boil over high heat, stirring constantly. Reduce heat and simmer, covered, for 12 to 15 minutes or until softened.

2. Add sugar in a steady stream, stirring constantly. Stir in apricots and cherries; return to a boil, stirring constantly to dissolve sugar. Reduce heat and boil gently, uncovered, stirring often and reducing heat further as mixture thickens, for 25 to 30 minutes or until mixture reaches a soft, jam-like consistency. Test for doneness (for details, see page 201).

3. Stir in brandy (if using); simmer for 1 minute. Remove from heat and let rest for 1 minute. Stir to distribute dried fruit.

4. Ladle into sterilized jars to within $\frac{1}{2}$ inch (1 cm) of rim; wipe rims. Apply prepared lids and rings; tighten rings just until fingertip-tight.

5. Process jars in a boiling water canner for 10 minutes (for details, see page 20). Transfer jars to a towel-lined surface and let rest at room temperature until set. Check seals; refrigerate any unsealed jars for up to 3 weeks.

Pear Maple Walnut Conserve

*Here, maple-walnut flavor
is combined with pears
for a sensational taste.
Pears are low in natural
pectin, so the powdered
pectin in this recipe
helps it to set without
overcooking.*

— o o o —

Recipe Suggestions

Stir into plain yogurt and
top with granola for a great
snack.

Dot over apples in a pie or
an apple crisp, or use in
turnovers.

4½ cups	chopped peeled pears	1.125 L
1 tbsp	lemon juice	15 mL
1	package (1.75 oz/49 or 57 g) powdered pectin	1
3½ cups	granulated sugar	875 mL
¾ cup	pure maple syrup	175 mL
¼ cup	chopped walnuts or pecans	60 mL

1. In a Dutch oven or a large, heavy-bottomed pot, combine pears and lemon juice. Stir in pectin until dissolved. Bring to a full boil over high heat, stirring constantly.

2. Add sugar in a steady stream, stirring constantly. Return to a full boil, stirring constantly to dissolve sugar. Boil hard for 1 minute.

3. Remove from heat and stir in maple syrup and nuts. Skim off any foam. Stir for 5 to 8 minutes to prevent floating fruit.

4. Ladle into sterilized jars to within ½ inch (1 cm) of rim; wipe rims. Apply prepared lids and rings; tighten rings just until fingertip-tight.

5. Process jars in a boiling water canner for 10 minutes (for details, see page 20). Transfer jars to a towel-lined surface and let rest at room temperature until set. Check seals; refrigerate any unsealed jars for up to 3 weeks.

Caribbean Treasure Conserve

Makes about six 8-ounce (250 mL) jars

This conserve brings you the taste of the tropics.

— o o o —

Tips

To prepare the papaya before puréeing it, peel off the skin with a vegetable peeler, cut the flesh in half lengthwise and scoop out the seeds with a spoon.

If you prefer, you can replace the rum with 1 tsp (5 mL) coconut extract or rum extract.

For information on how to section citrus fruit, see page 26.

Recipe Suggestions

Thin conserve with a little orange juice and serve over ice cream.

Use to make Fried Bananas Caribbean (page 366), Caribbean Chicken (page 350) or Fruit Loaf (page 356).

> Papaya flesh is juicy and tastes like a musky cantaloupe. Papayas are often green when purchased, but the skin will be yellow when ripe. The seeds are edible (though not used in this recipe) and taste a bit like black pepper.

2	medium oranges	2
1	can (19 oz/540 mL) crushed pineapple with juice	1
2 cups	puréed papaya	500 mL
1½ cups	diced mango	375 mL
¼ cup	lime or lemon juice	60 mL
½ tsp	ground allspice	2 mL
½ tsp	ground cinnamon	2 mL
4½ cups	granulated sugar	1.125 L
⅓ cup	amber or coconut rum (optional)	75 mL
⅓ cup	toasted slivered almonds (optional)	75 mL

1. Using a fine grater, remove 2 tbsp (30 mL) orange rind; set aside. Peel and section oranges, removing all pith, seeds and membranes, and chop the fruit, reserving any juices.

2. In a Dutch oven or a large, heavy-bottomed pot, combine orange rind, oranges with juice, pineapple with juice, papaya, mango, lime juice, allspice and cinnamon. Bring to a boil over high heat, stirring constantly. Reduce heat and boil gently for 5 minutes, stirring often.

3. Add sugar in a steady stream, stirring constantly. Increase heat to high and bring to a full boil, stirring constantly to dissolve sugar. Reduce heat and boil gently, stirring often and reducing heat further as mixture thickens, for 30 to 40 minutes or until mixture reaches a soft, jam-like consistency. Test for doneness (for details, see page 201).

4. Stir in rum and almonds (if using); boil gently for 2 minutes, stirring constantly. Remove from heat and let rest for 1 minute. Stir to distribute nuts.

5. Ladle into sterilized jars to within ½ inch (1 cm) of rim; wipe rims. Apply prepared lids and rings; tighten rings just until fingertip-tight.

6. Process jars in a boiling water canner for 10 minutes (for details, see page 20). Transfer jars to a towel-lined surface and let rest at room temperature until set. Check seals; refrigerate any unsealed jars for up to 3 weeks.

Grilled Pineapple Banana Conserve with Kahlúa

Makes about five 8-ounce (250 mL) jars

Warm this conserve in a small bowl in the microwave and use it as a dip for chicken, shrimp or pork kebabs. It also makes a tasty topping for ice cream (top with a maraschino cherry!) or cheesecake.

— ○○○ —

Tips

For convenience, purchase a peeled and cored pineapple.

Pineapple slices can be placed on a baking sheet and browned under the broiler instead of using a barbecue.

• Preheat barbecue grill to medium-high

1	large fresh extra-sweet gold pineapple	1
2 cups	chopped peeled apples that soften	500 mL
¼ cup	lemon juice	60 mL
2 cups	finely chopped firm ripe bananas	500 mL
½ cup	all-natural apple juice (see tip, at right) or water	125 mL
1	package (1.75 oz/49 or 57 g) powdered pectin	1
3½ cups	granulated sugar	875 mL
½ cup	packed brown sugar	125 mL
2 tbsp	Kahlúa or amber rum	30 mL

1. Trim a slice from top and bottom of pineapple. Cut rind off sides and remove "eyes." Do not remove core. Slice into 8 rounds, about ½ inch (1 cm) thick.

2. Place pineapple rounds on grill, close lid and grill for about 3 minutes on each side or until softened and golden brown. Let cool. Trim off any charred or dry pieces. Finely chop pineapple, cutting away and discarding core. Measure 1 cup (250 mL).

3. In a Dutch oven or a large, deep, heavy-bottomed pot, combine pineapple, apples and lemon juice. Bring to a boil over high heat. Reduce heat and simmer, covered, for 5 minutes.

4. Stir in bananas and apple juice. Stir in pectin until dissolved. Increase heat to high and bring to a full boil, stirring constantly.

Cored grilled pineapple can be finely chopped in a food processor by pulsing on and off. Just be sure not to purée it.

Varieties of apples that soften when cooked include McIntosh, Cortland, Empire and Russet. See page 25 for more details.

Supermarkets now carry all-natural (or pure-pressed) apple juice, which contains solids. Shake before using.

5. Add granulated sugar in a steady stream, stirring constantly. Stir in brown sugar. Return to a full boil, stirring constantly to dissolve sugar. Boil hard for 1 minute.

6. Remove from heat and skim off any foam. Stir in Kahlúa.

7. Ladle into sterilized jars to within $\frac{1}{2}$ inch (1 cm) of rim; wipe rims. Apply prepared lids and rings; tighten rings just until fingertip-tight.

8. Process jars in a boiling water canner for 10 minutes (for details, see page 20). Transfer jars to a towel-lined surface and let rest at room temperature until set. Check seals; refrigerate any unsealed jars for up to 3 weeks.

Plum Cranberry Orange Conserve

This conserve has a lovely plum and orange flavor, with dried cranberries and whole almonds dispersed throughout.

— o o o —

Tips

You'll need about 1½ lbs (750 g) of plums for this recipe.

For a different taste, lightly toast the almonds (see tip, page 215) to enhance their flavor.

4 cups	sliced or quartered small yellow plums	1 L
	Finely grated rind and juice of 3 large oranges	
3½ cups	granulated sugar	875 mL
¾ cup	dried cranberries	175 mL
¼ cup	blanched whole almonds (optional)	60 mL
2 tbsp	amaretto or orange liqueur (optional)	30 mL

1. In a Dutch oven or a large, heavy-bottomed pot, combine plums, orange rind, orange juice, sugar and dried cranberries. Bring to a boil over high heat, stirring constantly.

2. Reduce heat and boil gently, stirring often and reducing heat further as mixture thickens, for 20 to 30 minutes or until mixture reaches a soft, jam-like consistency. Test for doneness (for details, see page 201).

3. Stir in almonds and liqueur (if using); boil gently for 2 minutes, stirring constantly. Remove from heat and let rest for 1 minute. Stir to distribute cranberries and nuts.

4. Ladle into sterilized jars to within ½ inch (1 cm) of rim; wipe rims. Apply prepared lids and rings; tighten rings just until fingertip-tight.

5. Process jars in a boiling water canner for 10 minutes (for details, see page 20). Transfer jars to a towel-lined surface and let rest at room temperature until set. Check seals; refrigerate any unsealed jars for up to 3 weeks.

> Yellow plums (sometimes called sugar plums) are available in early to mid-summer (depending on the weather). The flesh can be sweet, but the skins are tart, especially if picked a bit green. Look for yellow fruit that has a bit of orange to pink blush and a sweet fragrance.

Plum Rum and Prune Conserve

Makes about four 8-ounce (250 mL) jars

This conserve is rich and delicious. Try it in the Apricot Ladder Braid (page 365) in place of apricot jam.

— o o o —

Tips

You'll need about 3 lbs (1.5 kg) of plums (about 8 large) for this recipe.

For the best texture, cut the plums into 1/2-inch (1 cm) pieces.

Variations

Sour Cherry Plum Rum Conserve: Replace half or all of the prunes with chopped dried sour cherries. If desired, replace the rum with cherry brandy.

Apricot Plum Rum Conserve: Replace half or all of the prunes with chopped dried apricots. If desired, replace the rum with apricot brandy.

Ginger Plum Rum Conserve: Add 1 tbsp (15 mL) finely grated gingerroot with the plums.

Spiced Plum Rum Conserve: Add 1/2 tsp (2 mL) ground cinnamon and 1/4 tsp (1 mL) ground nutmeg or cardamom with the prunes.

6 cups	chopped red plums	1.5 L
1 tbsp	finely grated orange rind (optional)	15 mL
1/2 cup	orange juice, strong brewed tea or Marsala wine	125 mL
3 1/4 cups	granulated sugar	800 mL
1/2 cup	coarsely chopped pitted prunes	125 mL
2 tbsp	rum or amaretto	30 mL

1. In a Dutch oven or a large, deep, heavy-bottomed pot, combine plums, orange rind (if using) and orange juice. Add sugar in a steady stream, stirring constantly. Bring to a full boil over high heat, stirring constantly to dissolve sugar. Reduce heat and boil gently, stirring often and reducing heat further as mixture thickens, for 25 minutes.

2. Stir in prunes; boil gently, stirring often, for 5 to 10 minutes or until mixture reaches a soft, jam-like consistency. Test for doneness (for details, see page 201).

3. Remove from heat and skim off any foam. Stir in rum. Let rest for 1 minute. Stir to distribute prunes.

4. Ladle into sterilized jars to within 1/2 inch (1 cm) of rim; wipe rims. Apply prepared lids and rings; tighten rings just until fingertip-tight.

5. Process jars in a boiling water canner for 10 minutes (for details, see page 20). Transfer jars to a towel-lined surface and let rest at room temperature until set. Check seals; refrigerate any unsealed jars for up to 3 weeks.

> Prunes are actually dried prune plums.

Christmas Plum Conserve

This deep-colored conserve, made with Italian plums, is part of my jam- and marmalade-making friend Larry McGuire's family tradition. He eats it year-round, but it is well suited to the festive table.

—o o o—

Tip
This is a very large recipe that can easily be halved.

4 lbs	Italian (prune) purple plums, halved	2 kg
½ cup	water	125 mL
6½ cups	granulated sugar	1.625 L
3 cups	Thompson raisins	750 mL
	Grated rind and juice of 2 oranges	
	Grated rind and juice of 1 lemon	
1 cup	chopped walnuts or pecans (optional)	250 mL

1. In a Dutch oven or a large, heavy-bottomed pot, combine plums and water. Bring to a boil over high heat, stirring often. Add sugar in a steady stream, stirring constantly. Stir in raisins, orange rind, orange juice, lemon rind and lemon juice; return to a boil, stirring constantly to dissolve sugar.

2. Reduce heat and boil gently, stirring often and reducing heat further as mixture thickens, for 45 minutes.

3. Stir in nuts (if using); simmer, stirring often, for 10 to 15 minutes or until mixture reaches a soft, jam-like consistency. Test for doneness (for details, see page 201). Remove from heat and let rest for 1 minute. Stir to distribute raisins and nuts.

4. Ladle into sterilized jars to within ½ inch (1 cm) of rim; wipe rims. Apply prepared lids and rings; tighten rings just until fingertip-tight.

5. Process jars in a boiling water canner for 10 minutes (for details, see page 20). Transfer jars to a towel-lined surface and let rest at room temperature until set. Check seals; refrigerate any unsealed jars for up to 3 weeks.

> Small, oval-shaped, bluish-purple Italian (prune) plums are usually available in stores and markets in September. They are often dried to make prunes, which is why they are sometimes called prune plums.

Tangerine and Honey Marmalade (page 247)

front to back: Blood Orange Marmalade
(page 242), Apple Lemon Marmalade (page 236)
and Lime Coconut Marmalade (page 241)

Vanilla Jelly Roll (page 368)
with Rhubarb Jelly (page 277)

Blackberry Plum Jelly (page 262)

Rumpot Conserve

When my friend Sylvia L. was making Rumpot to serve to her family over the holidays, I thought it would be a great idea for a conserve! It is a little chunkier than most jams and conserves, but is less thick. Because it is a soft-set conserve, it is easy to spoon over ice cream, frozen yogurt or cake. It should still move slightly in the jars after cooling. If you want to use it as a spread, cook it longer, until the desired consistency is reached.

—ooo—

Tips

Freeze small leftover bits of excess fruit and make this conserve when you have collected enough. Supplement with store-bought frozen fruit if you don't have quite enough. Measure the volume of fruit while frozen, then let thaw before adding to the pot.

Some conserves have a tendency to sputter when they start to thicken. If this happens, reduce the heat. Wear oven mitts to prevent burns.

4 cups	assorted berries (preferably half dark and half red), such as raspberries, blueberries, blackberries, black and/or red currants, gooseberries, sliced strawberries	1 L
3 cups	finely chopped pitted tree fruits, such as apricots, nectarines, plums or sour (tart) or sweet cherries	750 mL
6 cups	granulated sugar	1.5 L
¼ cup	amber rum	60 mL

1. Place berries in a Dutch oven or a large, deep, heavy-bottomed pot. Bring to a boil over high heat; reduce heat and simmer for 3 minutes. Use a potato masher to crush berries. Stir in tree fruits.

2. Add sugar in a steady stream, stirring constantly. Increase heat to high and bring to a full boil, stirring constantly to dissolve sugar. Reduce heat and boil rapidly, stirring often and reducing heat further as mixture thickens, for 12 to 14 minutes or until mixture reaches a soft, jam-like consistency. Test for doneness (for details, see page 201).

3. Remove from heat and stir in rum. Skim off any foam.

4. Ladle into sterilized jars to within ½ inch (1 cm) of rim; wipe rims. Apply prepared lids and rings; tighten rings just until fingertip-tight.

5. Process jars in a boiling water canner for 10 minutes (for details, see page 20). Transfer jars to a towel-lined surface and let rest at room temperature until set. Check seals; refrigerate any unsealed jars for up to 3 weeks.

> Rumpot, or Rumtopf, is a German fruit and rum preserve traditionally served at Christmas. It is made by layering each fruit in a large jar or crock as it comes into season. Sugar is stirred in, then it's topped off with rum. The fruity liqueur can be drunk in glasses, and the boozy fruit served over cake or vanilla ice cream.

Strawberry Rhubarb and Pear Conserve

Makes about six 8-ounce (250 mL) jars

In this conserve, pear is added to the classic strawberry-rhubarb combination.

— o o o —

Tips

Cut up your rhubarb and freeze in 4-cup (1 L) portions in freezer bags to use in this conserve.

Make this recipe with frozen strawberries, if desired. Measure fruit while still frozen then let thaw slightly before adding to pot.

Recipe Suggestion

Use to make Easy Coffee Cake (page 355).

4 cups	chopped rhubarb ($\frac{1}{2}$-inch/1 cm pieces)	1 L
3 cups	chopped or sliced strawberries	750 mL
3 cups	chopped peeled pears	750 mL
$\frac{1}{3}$ cup	lemon juice	75 mL
6 cups	granulated sugar	1.5 L

1. In a Dutch oven or a large, heavy-bottomed pot, combine rhubarb, strawberries, pears and lemon juice. Add sugar in a steady stream, stirring constantly. Bring to a full boil over high heat, stirring constantly to dissolve sugar.

2. Reduce heat and boil gently, stirring often and reducing heat further as mixture thickens, for 30 to 40 minutes or until mixture reaches a soft, jam-like consistency. Test for doneness (for details, see page 201).

3. Ladle into sterilized jars to within $\frac{1}{2}$ inch (1 cm) of rim; wipe rims. Apply prepared lids and rings; tighten rings just until fingertip-tight.

4. Process jars in a boiling water canner for 10 minutes (for details, see page 20). Transfer jars to a towel-lined surface and let rest at room temperature until cooled. Check seals; refrigerate any unsealed jars for up to 3 weeks.

Marmalades

Marmalades are spreads made with one or more citrus fruits, or citrus fruits mixed with other fruits or vegetables. Fruit pulp and juice and citrus rind are cooked with sugar and set with naturally present pectin or added commercial pectin. In the final product, small pieces of citrus rind are suspended in a transparent jelly.

About Marmalade 228
A Word on Peel and Rind 228
Tips for Successful Marmalades. 229
Trouble-Shooting 231

Lemon Ginger Marmalade 233
Honey Lemon Marmalade 234
Lemon and Mint Marmalade with Calendula Petals. 235
Apple Lemon Marmalade. 236
Wild Blueberry Lemon Marmalade 237
Raspberry Lemonade Marmalade 238
Lemon Lime Marmalade 239
Lime Marmalade 240
Lime Coconut Marmalade 241
Blood Orange Marmalade 242
Clementine Marmalade 243
Orange Marmalade with Earl Grey Tea 244
Seville Orange Marmalade 245
Tangelo Marmalade 246
Tangerine and Honey Marmalade. 247
Cranberry Orange Marmalade 248
Peach Orange Marmalade 249
Carrot Orange Marmalade 250
Zucchini Orange Marmalade 251
Pink Grapefruit and Pomegranate Marmalade 252
Pineapple Citrus Marmalade 253
Three-Fruit Marmalade. 254

About Marmalade

The word "marmalade" comes from the Portuguese *marmelo*, meaning "quince." Quinces used to be popular for jelly-making because of their high pectin level. (You can still find quinces at farmers' markets, usually in the fall. They taste a bit like a cross between an apple and a pear and are used to make jams and jellies, sometimes in combination with other fruits, such as apples. The texture tends to be dry and the flavor tart, so they are generally not eaten raw.)

One interesting myth about the origin of the word says that Mary, Queen of Scots, asked for an orange preserve when she was sick (she had eaten it when living in France as a young girl); thus, "Marie-malade" (*malade* is French for "ill"). Although fiction, this story is a fun way to remember the name, and eating some marmalade when you are sick is sure to make you feel a little better!

A Scottish family was credited with making the first commercial marmalade, similar to those we know today. Because it includes grated, finely chopped or sliced citrus rind, marmalade is known for its bitter-tart flavor.

In this chapter, you'll find recipes for some of your favorites, such as Lime Marmalade (page 240) and Seville Orange Marmalade (page 245), as well as interesting combinations with blueberries, cranberries, peaches, raspberries, carrots or zucchini. Many of these marmalades can be made year-round, using fresh oranges and lemons and a variety of fresh or frozen fruits. Some recipes use finely grated rind, which will appeal to those who find traditional marmalade too heavy with thick rind. And in some recipes, I have used sweet, seedless oranges, which have rinds that soften with minimal cooking.

Most of the recipes have been simplified to make them as easy as possible, using commercial pectin to significantly cut down on prep and cooking time. Seville Orange Marmalade, a classic, does take a bit more work. It is made in January or February, when Seville oranges are available.

> The marmalades in this book were tested for sugar content using a refractometer, so no more sugar was added than was needed for a good set. Acidity was tested with a pH meter to ensure sufficient acid for gelling.

> Refer to the Produce Purchase Guide, page 32, to estimate the amount of fruit and/or vegetables you'll need to purchase for these recipes.

A Word on Peel and Rind

The words "peel" and "rind" are often used interchangeably, but there is a difference: peel includes the white pith, while rind is just the colored part of the peel, with the pith removed. Pith adds a bitter taste that some people enjoy in a marmalade.

People sometimes dislike marmalades that have too much peel. I have found that about ¾ cup (175 mL) is a good amount of peel when you're making five or six 8-ounce (250 mL) jars of marmalade. If you like lots of peel, increase to about 1 cup (250 mL) and use a thicker cut that includes the pith. If you don't much like peel, try ½ cup (125 mL) and go for thinly sliced fine rind. A bit of peel adds appeal! You may even convert some people who think they don't like marmalade, especially if you serve them Carrot Orange Marmalade (page 250) or Zucchini Orange Marmalade (page 251).

Feel free to change the way the peel is prepared in any of these recipes. To suit your own taste, it can range from extra-fine rind to thick peel.

- For *extra-fine rind*, use a citrus zester or a fine grater to remove the rind.

- For *fine rind*, use a vegetable peeler to remove strips of rind.

- For *medium peel*, use a sharp paring knife to remove strips of rind and a bit of pith.

- For *thick peel*, use a large knife to remove large strips of peel, all the way to the flesh.

Slice strips of peel or rind crosswise into pieces about ⅛ inch (3 mm) thick. (You can slice them thicker, if you prefer.) If your strips are fairly thin, you'll get longer slices if you cut the strips on the diagonal; discard any small or odd-shaped pieces at the ends.

Tips for Successful Marmalades

1. Scrub citrus fruit well with warm, soapy water (remove any stickers first, or they will be harder to get off). Rinse well and dry with paper towels.

2. Be meticulous in your preparation of the fruit, particularly the cutting of the peel or rind to achieve thin, even pieces. Make sure your knife is sharp. Discard all excess membranes and pith (unless you're using them in the recipe, as with Seville Orange Marmalade). It's not usually recommended to chop fruit (pulp) in a food processor, as pieces will at best be of uneven size and at worst may be puréed. If you do want to use a food processor, pulse only a few times and scrape down the sides of the work bowl in between.

3. Measure all ingredients carefully and use a knife to level the top of the measuring cup (don't just shake it). Measure sugar into a large bowl before you start cooking.

4. A large, wide pot, such as a Dutch oven with a heavy bottom (preferably stainless steel), is recommended to allow the mixture to evaporate more quickly and retain better color and flavor. Make sure the pot is deep enough to prevent boilovers.

5. Heat the fruit a little bit before stirring in the sugar. This will help the sugar dissolve more quickly. When adding the sugar, stir well to ensure that it is completely dissolved, scraping down any that gets on the sides of the pot or the spoon handle. Undissolved sugar can crystallize in your marmalade afterwards.

6. Stir and watch your marmalade. Pectin-added marmalades require a full boil, stirred constantly, for the entire cooking time. Marmalades with natural pectin will thicken as they cook; reduce the heat as they thicken, stirring constantly to prevent sticking and scorching.

7. Before beginning to cook pectin-added marmalades, check the expiration date on the box of pectin (especially liquid pectin); do not use if it's past the date. Liquid pectin and powdered pectin (pectin crystals) are not interchangeable; if you substitute one for the other in a recipe, it will not set. Powdered pectin must be added before the sugar, or it will not set. Mix in pectin well. The timing should be exact — use a timer. When in doubt, go by the manufacturer's instructions for boiling time. For example, no-sugar-needed pectin is boiled hard for 3 minutes instead of 1 minute.

8. For marmalades without added pectin, the timing will vary depending on the amount of pectin in the fruit and peels, how accurately you measure, how the fruit is chopped or sliced, and the diameter of your pot. These marmalades must be tested to determine when they have reached the setting point (see Test for the Setting Point, page 19). Be sure to leave the test plate in the freezer long enough for the marmalade to cool and give an idea of the set. Do not put too much on the plate, just a spoonful. Always remove the pot from the heat to stop cooking the marmalade while you do the test.

9. To prevent floating of the fruit pieces, stir the mixture slowly for 5 to 8 minutes after removing it from the heat. This step can sometimes take longer, especially if fruit or rind pieces are on the large side, or if the cooking time was on the short side (especially for recipes using liquid pectin). Ladle the mixture into one jar only, leave it for a minute or two, then check. If pieces of fruit or rind start to slowly migrate to the top, pour the marmalade back into the pot and stir for a few more minutes. Processing may also cause the mixture to heat up and become thinner, in which case floating may start after you remove the jars from the boiling water canner. If this happens, let jars cool for about 30 minutes, check to make sure they are sealed, then, without tipping them upside down, gently rotate the jars to redistribute the floating bits.

10. Skim off any foam with a large metal spoon before ladling marmalade into jars. (Not all marmalades will have foam.)

11. After they have cooled, let the jars of marmalade rest, without disturbing them, for about 1 week. Marmalades, particularly those made without added pectin, may take a little longer to set than some jams.

12. Always store sealed preserves in a cool, dry, dark place. This will help them keep their color and flavor the longest. Preserves are best eaten within a year. Store any unsealed jars in the refrigerator and eat the contents within about 3 weeks.

> Please read A Primer on Preserving, pages 14 to 37. Things may have changed since you first started making preserves (such as the recent increase in processing time). If you are a beginner, there are a few important things you need to know before getting started. Many instructions are common to all preserves, so once you get it right for one, you'll sail through the others. In the primer, you will also find a handy Preparation Checklist (page 37).

Trouble-Shooting

PROBLEM: Marmalade does not set or is thin and runny.

Marmalades may take up to a week to set. Let the jars rest, undisturbed. If your marmalade has not set after this time, check your recipe. If it is a pectin-added recipe, check the expiration date on the pectin box. You may wish to contact the manufacturer of the pectin, using the toll-free number or the website on the box; they may have a solution for their particular product.

For a marmalade without added pectin, you may need to cook it a little longer. If the jars have all sealed properly, the contents are safe. Return the marmalade to the pot, discard the used lids and begin cooking and testing for the setting point. It may take only another couple of minutes for it to reach the setting point. When it does, proceed with sterilized jars and new prepared lids.

PROBLEM: Marmalade is stiff or tough.

This can occur when fruit is high in natural pectin or when too much pectin was added. Likely your marmalade was overcooked. To salvage it, dilute it with fruit juice or a little liqueur and warm it in the microwave just before serving, to make it more spreadable. Or warm a little in maple syrup for pancakes or waffles.

PROBLEM: Peel or rind is tough.

Likely, the peel or rind was not precooked long enough to soften. To salvage the marmalade, warm it to thin it, then press it through a strainer and discard the solids (the flavor will still be in the marmalade). Reheat and process, or store in the refrigerator.

PROBLEM: Floating peel or rind.

To prevent floating, stir the mixture slowly for 5 to 8 minutes after removing it from the heat. Then ladle it into the first jar and leave it for a minute or two. If solids still float, pour the marmalade back into the pot and stir for a few more minutes. The pieces will usually become suspended as the mixture begins to set. If not, you may want to retest it for the setting point to ensure that it has been cooked long enough.

Lemon Ginger Marmalade

This is a lovely yellow marmalade with the essence of ginger.

— o o o —

Recipe Suggestions

Toss a little of this marmalade with cooked green beans to glaze them.

When cooking winter squash, replace the brown sugar with marmalade to taste.

Use to make Fruit Loaf (page 356).

Variation

Lemon Lavender Marmalade: Omit the crystallized ginger and add 2 tbsp (30 mL) dried organic lavender flowers to the cheesecloth in Step 1.

- Cheesecloth
- Kitchen string

3	large lemons (approx.)	3
4½ cups	water	1.125 mL
4¾ cups	granulated sugar	1.175 mL
⅓ cup	thinly sliced crystallized ginger	75 mL

1. Cut lemons in half and squeeze out juice; measure ¾ cup (175 mL) juice. Remove seeds and place in a square of several layers of cheesecloth. Cut lemons in half again. Scrape membranes from peels, add to cheesecloth and tie with string. Thinly slice peel.

2. In a medium saucepan, combine peel, juice, water and cheesecloth bag. Bring to a full boil over high heat. Reduce heat and simmer, covered, for 15 to 20 minutes or until peel is softened.

3. Transfer rind with liquid to a Dutch oven or a large, heavy-bottomed pot. Squeeze liquid from cheesecloth bag into pot; discard bag.

4. Add sugar in a steady stream, stirring constantly. Stir in ginger; heat over medium heat, stirring constantly to dissolve sugar. Increase heat to high and bring to a full boil, stirring constantly. Boil rapidly, stirring often, for 12 to 15 minutes or until marmalade thickens. Test for setting point (for details, see page 19).

5. Remove from heat and skim off any foam. Stir for 5 to 8 minutes to prevent floating rind.

6. Ladle into sterilized jars to within ¼ inch (0.5 cm) of rim; wipe rims. Apply prepared lids and rings; tighten rings just until fingertip-tight.

7. Process jars in a boiling water canner for 10 minutes (for details, see page 20). Transfer jars to a towel-lined surface and let rest at room temperature until set. Check seals; refrigerate any unsealed jars for up to 3 weeks. This marmalade is best served after resting for 1 week.

Honey Lemon Marmalade

**Makes about five
8-ounce (250 mL) jars**

*The right balance of tart
and sweet comes through
in this golden-colored jelly
with finely sliced rind.*

— o o o —

Tip
This mixture will boil up very
high, so make sure to use
a deep pot. Reduce heat to
medium-high if necessary.

Recipe Suggestion
Stir a spoonful or two into hot
tea when you have a cold.

Variations
*Honey Lemon Tea
Marmalade:* Replace
water with 1 1/2 cups
(375 mL) strong steeped
tea (steep 3 to 4 bags of
orange pekoe, Earl Grey,
green or jasmine tea for
about 5 minutes; remove
bags or leaves). Measure
the exact amount; if short,
add more water.

Meyer Lemon Marmalade:
Use 6 large Meyer lemons
in place of the regular
lemons.

Lemon Marmalade:
Replace the honey
with granulated sugar
(total sugar equal to
4 1/4 cups/1.05 L).

6	large lemons	6
1 1/2 cups	water	375 mL
2 3/4 cups	granulated sugar	675 mL
1 1/2 cups	liquid honey	375 mL
1	pouch (3 oz/85 mL) liquid pectin	1

1. Using a vegetable peeler, remove rind from several of the lemons in wide strips; thinly slice to make 3/4 cup (175 mL).

2. In a small saucepan, combine rind and water. Bring to a boil over high heat. Reduce heat and simmer, covered, for 15 to 20 minutes or until rind is softened. Set aside.

3. Remove remaining peel and pith from lemons. Finely chop lemons, discarding seeds and any connective membranes. Place in a 4-cup (1 L) measure with any juice. Squeeze any juice from peel into the measure; discard peel. Add cooked rind with liquid and enough water to make 3 cups (750 mL) total.

4. In a Dutch oven or a large, heavy-bottomed pot, combine lemon mixture and sugar. Bring to a full boil over high heat, stirring constantly to dissolve sugar. Stir in honey. Return to a full boil, stirring constantly.

5. Immediately stir in pectin; return to a full boil. Boil hard for 1 minute, stirring constantly.

6. Remove from heat and skim off any foam. Stir for 5 to 8 minutes to prevent floating rind.

7. Ladle into sterilized jars to within 1/4 inch (0.5 cm) of rim; wipe rims. Apply prepared lids and rings; tighten rings just until fingertip-tight.

8. Process jars in a boiling water canner for 10 minutes (for details, see page 20). Transfer jars to a towel-lined surface and let rest at room temperature until set. Check seals; refrigerate any unsealed jars for up to 3 weeks. This marmalade is best served after resting for 1 week.

Lemon and Mint Marmalade with Calendula Petals

Makes about five 8-ounce (250 mL) jars

You may substitute dandelion or marigold petals for the calendula flower petals (or leave them out altogether). Ensure that flowers were not sprayed with herbicides or pesticides. Rinse well to remove any insects.

—o o o—

Tip
For information on mint, see page 304.

Variations
Lemon Tarragon Marmalade: Omit the flower petals and substitute tarragon for the mint.

Lemon Lavender Marmalade: Omit the mint and substitute 2 tbsp (30 mL) fresh lavender flowers for the calendula.

10	large lemons (approx.)	10
½ cup	water	125 mL
6 cups	granulated sugar	1.5 L
1	pouch (3 oz/85 mL) liquid pectin	1
½ cup	chopped fresh mint	125 mL
⅓ cup	organically grown yellow or orange calendula petals	75 mL

1. Using a vegetable peeler, remove rind from lemons in wide strips; thinly slice to make 1¾ cups (425 mL). Cut lemons in half and squeeze out juice; measure 2 cups (500 mL).

2. In a medium saucepan, combine rind, juice and water. Bring to a full boil over high heat. Reduce heat and simmer, covered, for 15 to 20 minutes or until rind is softened.

3. Transfer rind with liquid to a Dutch oven or a large, heavy-bottomed pot. Add sugar in a steady stream, stirring constantly. Bring to a full boil over high heat, stirring constantly to dissolve sugar.

4. Immediately stir in pectin; return to a full boil. Boil hard for 1 minute, stirring constantly.

5. Remove from heat and skim off any foam. Stir in mint and calendula petals; stir for 5 to 8 minutes to prevent floating rind, mint and petals.

6. Ladle into sterilized jars to within ¼ inch (0.5 cm) of rim; wipe rims. Apply prepared lids and rings; tighten rings just until fingertip-tight.

7. Process jars in a boiling water canner for 10 minutes (for details, see page 20). Transfer jars to a towel-lined surface and let rest at room temperature until set. Check seals; refrigerate any unsealed jars for up to 3 weeks.

Apple Lemon Marmalade

Deliciously tangy! This marmalade is perfect on banana bran bread or bran muffins.

— o o o —

Tips

You'll need about 2¼ lbs (1.125 kg) of apples for this recipe. For information on the best types of apples to use, see page 25.

As you chop the apples, pour some of the measured lemon juice over them to keep them from browning.

Variations

Lemon Apple Mint Marmalade: Stir in ¼ cup (60 mL) finely chopped fresh spearmint, apple mint or orange mint leaves after adding the pectin.

Lemon Apple Orange Marmalade: Replace half of the lemon juice and rind with orange juice and rind.

Lemon Pear Marmalade: Replace the apples with peeled, cored, chopped pears.

Spiced Lemon Apple Marmalade: Add 1 tsp (5 mL) ground cinnamon, ½ tsp (2 mL) ground nutmeg and a pinch each of ground ginger and cloves when cooking the apples.

4	large lemons	4
1¾ cups	water	425 mL
5 or 6	medium apples that soften	5 or 6
4½ cups	granulated sugar	1.125 L
1	pouch (3 oz/85 mL) liquid pectin	1

1. Using a paring knife, remove peel from lemons in large strips, taking some of the white pith if desired; thinly slice to make ¾ cup (175 mL).

2. In a medium saucepan, combine peel and water. Bring to a boil over high heat. Reduce heat and simmer, covered, for about 15 minutes or until peel is softened. Set aside.

3. Cut lemons in half and squeeze out juice; measure to make 1 cup (250 mL).

4. Peel, core and finely chop apples; measure to make 4 cups (1 L). In a Dutch oven or a large, heavy-bottomed pot, combine apples and lemon juice. Bring to a full boil over high heat. Reduce heat and simmer, covered, for about 3 minutes or until apples are softened. Stir in cooked peel with liquid.

5. Add sugar in a steady stream, stirring constantly. Bring to a full boil over high heat, stirring constantly to dissolve sugar.

6. Immediately stir in pectin; return to a full boil. Boil hard for 1 minute, stirring constantly.

7. Remove from heat and skim off any foam. Stir for 5 to 8 minutes to prevent floating rind.

8. Ladle into sterilized jars to within ¼ inch (0.5 cm) of rim; wipe rims. Apply prepared lids and rings; tighten rings just until fingertip-tight.

9. Process jars in a boiling water canner for 10 minutes (for details, see page 20). Transfer jars to a towel-lined surface and let rest at room temperature until set. Check seals; refrigerate any unsealed jars for up to 3 weeks.

Wild Blueberry Lemon Marmalade

Makes about five 8-ounce (250 mL) jars

Wild blueberries are best for this marmalade, as their flavor is more intense than cultivated ones. Pick your own when they're in season and freeze them. Some stores sell frozen wild blueberries.

— o o o —

Tips

"Sections" refer to only the fleshy part of the fruit, not the inner membranes. For instructions on sectioning citrus fruit, see page 26.

When crushing blueberries, do not leave any whole berries. Mash further, if needed, after mixture starts to boil and berries start to soften (before adding pectin). Remove the pot from the heat while doing this.

Blueberries are rich in anthocyanins, which are powerful antioxidants.

5 or 6	large lemons	5 or 6
1 cup	water	250 mL
3 cups	wild or regular blueberries	750 mL
5 cups	granulated sugar	1.25 L
1	pouch (3 oz/85 mL) liquid pectin	1

1. Using a vegetable peeler, remove rind from 3 or 4 of the lemons in wide strips; thinly slice to make ¾ cup (175 mL).

2. In a small saucepan, combine rind and water. Bring to a boil over high heat. Reduce heat and simmer, covered, for 10 minutes or until rind is softened. Set aside.

3. Remove and discard remaining peel and pith from lemons. Section lemons, discarding any seeds and connective membranes, and place in a 1-cup (250 mL) measure. Add enough juice to make 1 cup (250 mL). Add sections and juice to rind mixture in saucepan; return to a boil. Reduce heat and simmer, covered, for 10 minutes or until rind is softened. Transfer to a 4-cup (1 L) measure and add water, if necessary, to make 3½ cups (875 mL).

4. In a large bowl or flat pan, using a potato masher, crush blueberries, one layer at a time; measure to make 1½ cups (375 mL).

5. In a Dutch oven or a large, heavy-bottomed pot, combine cooked rind mixture and blueberries. Add sugar in a steady stream, stirring constantly. Bring to a full boil over high heat, stirring constantly to dissolve sugar.

6. Immediately stir in pectin; return to a full boil. Boil hard for 1 minute, stirring constantly.

7. Remove from heat and skim off any foam.

8. Ladle into sterilized jars to within ¼ inch (0.5 cm) of rim; wipe rims. Apply prepared lids and rings; tighten rings just until fingertip-tight.

9. Process jars in a boiling water canner for 10 minutes (for details, see page 20). Transfer jars to a towel-lined surface and let rest at room temperature until set. Check seals; refrigerate any unsealed jars for up to 3 weeks.

Raspberry Lemonade Marmalade

*The idea for this recipe
came from a lemon
marmalade recipe in a
book I have on lemons.
I like pink lemonade
and decided to add
raspberries as a twist.*

— o o o —

Tips

When using frozen fruit,
measure whole berries
before thawing. Let thaw
slightly before adding to
the pot.

To make this recipe
seedless, start with 6 cups
(1.5 L) raspberries. Crush
and press berries through a
fine-mesh sieve and discard
seeds. This may have to be
done a few times to remove
most of the seeds. Rinse
the strainer in between
each time.

3 or 4	large lemons	3 or 4
2 cups	water	500 mL
4 cups	raspberries	1 L
1	package (1.75 oz/49 or 57 g) powdered pectin	1
5 cups	granulated sugar	1.25 L

1. Using a vegetable peeler, remove rind from lemons in wide strips; thinly slice to make $3/4$ cup (175 mL).

2. In small saucepan, combine rind and water. Bring to a boil over high heat. Reduce heat and simmer, covered, for 10 minutes or until rind is softened. Set aside.

3. Remove and discard remaining peel and pith from lemons. Finely chop lemons, discarding seeds and any connective membranes. Measure to make $3\frac{1}{2}$ cups (875 mL), including juices.

4. In a Dutch oven or a large, heavy-bottomed pot, combine chopped lemons, cooked rind with liquid and raspberries.

5. Stir in pectin until dissolved. Bring to a full boil over high heat, stirring constantly.

6. Add sugar in a steady stream, stirring constantly. Return to a full boil, stirring constantly to dissolve sugar. Boil hard for 1 minute.

7. Remove from heat and skim off any foam. Stir for 5 to 8 minutes to prevent floating rind.

8. Ladle into sterilized jars to within $1/4$ inch (0.5 cm) of rim; wipe rims. Apply prepared lids and rings; tighten rings just until fingertip-tight.

9. Process jars in a boiling water canner for 10 minutes (for details, see page 20). Transfer jars to a towel-lined surface and let rest at room temperature until set. Check seals; refrigerate any unsealed jars for up to 3 weeks.

Lemon Lime Marmalade

This citrus duo makes a superb-tasting marmalade that is lovely and tart.

— o o o —

Tip
Some limes and lemons can be dry and yield less juice, so buy a few extra.

Recipe Suggestion
Use as an ingredient in Lime Phyllo Tarts (page 364).

- Cheesecloth
- Kitchen string

4	medium limes (approx.)	4
3	medium lemons (approx.)	3
7½ cups	water	1.875 L
7 cups	granulated sugar	1.75 L

1. Cut limes and lemons in half and squeeze out juice; measure ⅔ cup (150 mL) lime juice and ¾ cup (175 mL) lemon juice. Remove seeds and place in a square of several layers of cheesecloth. Cut limes and lemons in half again. Scrape membranes from peels, add to cheesecloth and tie with string. Thinly slice peel.

2. In a medium saucepan, combine peel, juice, water and cheesecloth bag. Bring to a full boil over high heat. Reduce heat and simmer, covered, for 15 to 20 minutes or until peel is softened.

3. Transfer peel with liquid to a Dutch oven or a large, heavy-bottomed pot. Squeeze liquid from cheesecloth bag into pot; discard bag.

4. Add sugar in a steady stream, stirring constantly. Heat over medium heat, stirring constantly to dissolve sugar. Increase heat to high and bring to a full boil, stirring constantly. Boil rapidly, stirring often, for 20 to 25 minutes or until marmalade thickens. Test for setting point (for details, see page 19).

5. Remove from heat and skim off any foam. Stir for 5 to 8 minutes to prevent floating rind.

6. Ladle into sterilized jars to within ¼ inch (0.5 cm) of rim; wipe rims. Apply prepared lids and rings; tighten rings just until fingertip-tight.

7. Process jars in a boiling water canner for 10 minutes (for details, see page 20). Transfer jars to a towel-lined surface and let rest at room temperature until set. Check seals; refrigerate any unsealed jars for up to 3 weeks. This marmalade is best served after resting for 1 week.

Lime Marmalade

10 to 12	large limes	10 to 12
4 cups	water	1 L
5 cups	granulated sugar	1.25 mL

This lime marmalade has the mouth-puckering tartness of British-style marmalade and was contributed by Paul Barrie (see Contributors, page 12).

— o o o —

Tip

Feel free to change the way the rind is prepared in this recipe. To suit your own taste, it can range from extra-fine rind to thick peel. See page 229 for more information.

1. Using a vegetable peeler, remove rind from limes in wide strips; thinly slice to make $1\frac{1}{2}$ cups (375 mL). Cut limes in half and squeeze out juice; measure to make 2 cups (500 mL). Discard any remaining peel, pith and seeds.

2. In a medium saucepan, combine rind, juice and water. Bring to a boil over high heat. Reduce heat and simmer, covered, for 15 to 20 minutes or until rind is softened.

3. Transfer rind with liquid to a Dutch oven or a large, heavy-bottomed pot. Add sugar in a steady stream, stirring constantly. Heat over medium heat, stirring constantly to dissolve sugar. Increase heat to high and bring to a full boil, stirring constantly. Boil rapidly, stirring often, for 15 to 20 minutes or until marmalade thickens. Test for setting point (for details, see page 19).

4. Remove from heat and skim off any foam. Stir for 5 to 8 minutes to prevent floating rind.

5. Ladle into sterilized jars to within $\frac{1}{4}$ inch (0.5 cm) of rim; wipe rims. Apply prepared lids and rings; tighten rings just until fingertip-tight.

6. Process jars in a boiling water canner for 10 minutes (for details, see page 20). Transfer jars to a towel-lined surface and let rest at room temperature until set. Check seals; refrigerate any unsealed jars for up to 3 weeks. This marmalade is best served after resting for 1 week.

Lime Coconut Marmalade

This delightful marmalade (de lime and de coconut) is nice and tart and sports tiny specks of green.

Tips

Some limes can be dry and yield less juice, so buy a few extra.

To obtain more juice from limes, microwave them on High for 15 to 20 seconds, roll them on the counter, then extract juice.

Microplane (rasp-type) graters make it easy to remove citrus rind. They are available with fine or coarse blades.

Recipe Suggestions

Serve over strawberry cream cheese on a cracker. If desired, add a small slice of fresh strawberry.

Spoon into baked mini tart shells and top with a few small blueberries and raspberries.

6	large limes	6
1¾ cups	piña colada drink mix	425 mL
1	package (1.75 oz/49 or 57 g) powdered pectin	1
4 cups	granulated sugar	1 L
¾ cup	coconut rum (or ½ cup/125 mL amber rum)	175 mL

1. Using a fine grater, grate lime rind to make ¼ cup (50 mL). Cut limes in half and squeeze out juice; measure to make 1 cup (250 mL). Discard any peel, pith and seeds.

2. In a Dutch oven or a large, heavy-bottomed pot, combine rind, juice and piña colada drink mix. Stir in pectin until dissolved. Bring to a full boil over high heat, stirring constantly.

3. Add sugar in a steady stream, stirring constantly. Return to a full boil, stirring constantly to dissolve sugar. Boil hard for 1 minute.

4. Remove from heat and skim off any foam. Stir in rum. Stir for 5 minutes to prevent floating rind.

5. Ladle into sterilized jars to within ¼ inch (0.5 cm) of rim; wipe rims. Apply prepared lids and rings; tighten rings just until fingertip-tight.

6. Process jars in a boiling water canner for 10 minutes (for details, see page 20). Transfer jars to a towel-lined surface and let rest at room temperature until set. Check seals; refrigerate any unsealed jars for up to 3 weeks.

> Piña colada drink mix is sold in bottles, and is available at most supermarkets, often in the soft drinks aisle. Do not substitute coconut milk or coconut cream; due to their high fat content, they are not safe for preserving.

Blood Orange Marmalade

*Blood oranges are
available from December
to May from places such
as Spain and California.
Their flesh is deep red
with some orange, and
there is also sometimes
red in the rind, which
gives this marmalade
its alluring appearance.
Healthful nutrients called
anthocyanins are found
in the deep reddish-
purple pigment.*

— o o o —

Recipe Suggestions

Make a fruit salad containing
some sliced blood oranges
(or regular oranges). Thin
marmalade with a little
orange juice or water and
stir into salad or drizzle
over top.

Use in place of sugar to
sweeten a grapefruit half.
Spread on cut half and
microwave until warm.

12 to 14	medium blood oranges	12 to 14
1½ cups	water	375 mL
3 tbsp	lemon juice	45 mL
1	package (1.75 oz/49 or 57 g) powdered pectin	1
5 cups	granulated sugar	1.25 L

1. Using a paring knife, remove peel from several of the oranges in large strips, taking some of the white pith if desired; thinly slice to make ¾ cup (175 mL).

2. In a small saucepan, combine peel and water. Bring to a full boil over high heat. Reduce heat and simmer, covered, for 15 to 20 minutes or until peel is softened. Set aside.

3. Remove and discard remaining peel and pith from oranges. Finely chop oranges, discarding seeds. Measure to make 3 cups (750 mL), including juices.

4. In a Dutch oven or a large, heavy-bottomed pot, combine chopped oranges and lemon juice. Add cooked peel with liquid. Bring to a boil over high heat; reduce heat and simmer for 5 minutes.

5. Stir in pectin until dissolved. Bring to a full boil over high heat, stirring constantly.

6. Add sugar in a steady stream, stirring constantly. Return to a full boil, stirring constantly to dissolve sugar. Boil hard for 1 minute.

7. Remove from heat and skim off any foam. Stir for 5 to 8 minutes to prevent floating rind.

8. Ladle into sterilized jars to within ¼ inch (0.5 cm) of rim; wipe rims. Apply prepared lids and rings; tighten rings just until fingertip-tight.

9. Process jars in a boiling water canner for 10 minutes (for details, see page 20). Transfer jars to a towel-lined surface and let rest at room temperature until set. Check seals; refrigerate any unsealed jars for up to 3 weeks. This marmalade is best served after resting for 1 week.

Clementine Marmalade

*Clementines are a type
of mandarin orange with
thin skins and very little
pith. They are almost
always seedless.*

—○○○—

Tip
Ten large clementines will
weigh about 3 lbs (1.5 kg).

Variation
*Clementine Marmalade
with Maple Syrup:*
Replace ¾ cup (175 mL)
of the sugar with pure
maple syrup. Omit the
whiskey.

3 lbs	large clementines	1.5 kg
½ cup	water	125 mL
⅓ cup	lemon juice	75 mL
1	package (1.75 oz/49 or 57 g) powdered pectin	1
3½ cups	granulated sugar	875 mL
2 tbsp	whiskey, such as Jack Daniels (optional)	30 mL

1. Trim a small slice from the top of each of 5 of the clementines; set slices aside. Slice clementines horizontally into thin rounds. Cut each slice into 8 to 10 wedges, discarding seeds and any connective membranes. Place in a 4-cup (1 L) liquid measure, along with any juice. Squeeze any pulp and juice from reserved top slices into the measure, using thumbs to remove pulp, then discard top slices.

2. Cut remaining clementines in half and squeeze out juice; add to measuring cup to make 4 cups (1 L) total pulp, peel and juice.

3. In a Dutch oven or a large, heavy-bottomed pot; combine prepared clementines, water and lemon juice. Bring to a full boil over high heat. Reduce heat and simmer, covered, for 15 minutes or until peel is softened.

4. Stir in pectin until dissolved. Bring to a full boil over high heat, stirring constantly.

5. Add sugar in a steady stream, stirring constantly. Return to a full boil, stirring constantly to dissolve sugar. Boil hard for 1 minute.

6. Remove from heat and stir in whiskey (if using). Skim off any foam. Stir for 5 to 8 minutes to prevent floating rind.

7. Ladle into sterilized jars to within ¼ inch (0.5 cm) of rim; wipe rims. Apply prepared lids and rings; tighten rings just until fingertip-tight.

8. Process jars in a boiling water canner for 10 minutes (for details, see page 20). Transfer jars to a towel-lined surface and let rest at room temperature until set. Check seals; refrigerate any unsealed jars for up to 3 weeks. This marmalade is best served after resting for 1 week.

Orange Marmalade with Earl Grey Tea

*Oil from the rind of the
bergamot orange, grown
primarily in southern
Italy, is used to flavor
Earl Grey tea and gives
a wonderful flavor to
this marmalade.*

———o o o———

Tip
To test for floating at the end
of Step 7, ladle marmalade
into one of the jars and
leave it for a minute or two.
If necessary, pour it back
into the pot and stir for a
few more minutes.

5	large navel oranges or tangelos	5
2 cups	water	500 mL
5	Earl Grey tea bags	5
1	package (1.75 oz/49 or 57 g) powdered pectin	1
4½ cups	granulated sugar	1.125 L

1. Using a vegetable peeler, remove rind from 3 of the oranges in wide strips; thinly slice to make ¾ cup (175 mL).

2. In a small saucepan, combine rind and water. Bring to a full boil over high heat. Reduce heat and simmer, covered, for 15 to 20 minutes or until rind is softened. Remove from heat.

3. Add tea bags to hot rind mixture; let steep for 5 minutes. Discard tea bags, squeezing out liquid into saucepan.

4. Remove remaining peel and pith from oranges. Finely chop oranges, discarding seeds. Measure to make 3½ cups (875 mL), including juices.

5. In a Dutch oven or a large, heavy-bottomed pot, combine chopped oranges and cooked rind with liquid. Stir in pectin until dissolved. Bring to a full boil over high heat, stirring constantly.

6. Add sugar in a steady stream, stirring constantly. Return to a full boil, stirring constantly to dissolve sugar. Boil hard for 1 minute.

7. Remove from heat and skim off any foam. Stir for 5 to 8 minutes to prevent floating rind.

8. Ladle into sterilized jars to within ¼ inch (0.5 cm) of rim; wipe rims. Apply prepared lids and rings; tighten rings just until fingertip-tight.

9. Process jars in a boiling water canner for 10 minutes (for details, see page 20). Transfer jars to a towel-lined surface and let rest at room temperature until set. Check seals; refrigerate any unsealed jars for up to 3 weeks. This marmalade is best served after resting for 1 week.

Seville Orange Marmalade

Makes about seven 8-ounce (250 mL) jars

Seville oranges, grown in the Mediterranean, are bitter and unsuitable for eating, but make delicious marmalades and popular liqueurs such as Grand Marnier, Cointreau, Triple Sec and Curaçao. Larry McGuire (see Contributors, page 12) hosts annual marmalade-making bees with his friends in January, when these oranges are in season. What a great way to start off the new year! He shares his recipe here in this traditional method.

— o o o —

Variations

Orange Ginger Marmalade: Replace 1 cup (250 mL) of the sliced peel with thinly sliced crystallized ginger.

If desired, add about 1 tsp (5 mL) orange liqueur or whiskey to each jar before filling with marmalade.

- Cheesecloth
- Kitchen string

6	large Seville oranges	6
	Water	
	Granulated sugar	

1. Cut oranges in half and squeeze out juice. Remove seeds and place in a square of several layers of cheesecloth. Cut oranges in half again. Scrape membranes from peels and add to cheesecloth; tie with string. Slice peel sliver-thin.

2. Measure combined volume of juice and peel; you should get about 6 cups (1.5 L). Place in a Dutch oven or a large, heavy-bottomed pot. Add an equal volume of water. Place cheesecloth bag in center of pot and bring to a boil over high heat. Reduce heat and simmer, stirring occasionally and squeezing cheesecloth bag several times, for about 2 hours or until peel is very soft.

3. Measure the peel and liquid, squeezing cheesecloth bag; discard bag. Stir in an equal volume of sugar. Bring to a boil over medium heat, stirring constantly to dissolve sugar. Boil rapidly, stirring often, for 10 to 15 minutes or until marmalade thickens. Test for the setting point (for details, see page 19).

4. Remove from heat and skim off any foam. Stir for 5 to 8 minutes to prevent floating rind.

5. Ladle into sterilized jars to within $\frac{1}{4}$ inch (0.5 cm) of rim; wipe rims. Apply prepared lids and rings; tighten rings just until fingertip-tight.

6. Process jars in a boiling water canner for 10 minutes (for details, see page 20). Transfer jars to a towel-lined surface and let rest at room temperature until set. Check seals; refrigerate any unsealed jars for up to 3 weeks. This marmalade is best served after resting for 1 week.

Tangelo Marmalade

Makes about five 8-ounce (250 mL) jars

A tangelo is a cross between a tangerine and either a pomelo or a grapefruit. The skin is easy to remove, and tangelos have a distinctive-looking bump on the stem end. They are juicy and sweet-tasting.

— o o o —

Recipe Suggestion

Spoon marmalade into melted chocolate for fondue.

7	large tangelos	7
1 cup	water	250 mL
1	package (1.75 oz/49 or 57 g) powdered pectin	1
4 1/2 cups	granulated sugar	1.125 L
2 tbsp	whiskey or Grand Marnier (optional)	30 mL

1. Using a vegetable peeler, remove rind from about 3 of the tangelos in wide strips; thinly slice to make 3/4 cup (175 mL).

2. In a small saucepan, combine rind and water. Bring to a full boil over high heat. Reduce heat and simmer, covered, for 15 to 20 minutes or until rind is softened. Pour into a liquid measuring cup; add more water if necessary to make 1 cup (250 mL).

3. Remove and discard remaining peel and pith from tangelos. Finely chop tangelos, discarding seeds. Measure to make 3 1/2 cups (875 mL), including juices.

4. In a Dutch oven or a large, heavy-bottomed pot, combine chopped tangelos and cooked rind with liquid. Bring to a full boil over high heat; reduce heat and simmer for 5 minutes.

5. Stir in pectin until dissolved. Bring to a full boil over high heat, stirring constantly.

6. Add sugar in a steady stream, stirring constantly. Return to a full boil, stirring constantly to dissolve sugar. Boil hard for 1 minute.

7. Remove from heat and stir in whiskey (if using). Skim off any foam. Stir for 5 to 8 minutes to prevent floating rind.

8. Ladle into sterilized jars to within 1/4 inch (0.5 cm) of rim; wipe rims. Apply prepared lids and rings; tighten rings just until fingertip-tight.

9. Process jars in a boiling water canner for 10 minutes (for details, see page 20). Transfer jars to a towel-lined surface and let rest at room temperature until set. Check seals; refrigerate any unsealed jars for up to 3 weeks. This marmalade is best served after resting for 1 week.

Tangerine and Honey Marmalade

Makes about five 8-ounce (250 mL) jars

Tangerines, a type of mandarin orange, get their name from Tangier, a sea port of Morocco from which they were first shipped. I like to use honey tangerines in this marmalade, and I also add honey to create an interesting blend of flavors.

— o o o —

Tip

If your liquid honey has become crystallized, warm it briefly in the microwave or in a saucepan.

8	large honey tangerines	8
1½ cups	water	375 mL
1	package (1.75 oz/49 or 57 g) powdered pectin	1
4 cups	granulated sugar	1 L
½ cup	liquid honey	125 mL

1. Using a paring knife, remove peel from 2 or 3 of the tangerines in large strips, taking some of the white pith if desired; thinly slice to make ¾ cup (175 mL).

2. In a small saucepan, combine peel and water. Bring to a full boil over high heat. Reduce heat and simmer, covered, for 15 minutes or until peel is softened. Set aside.

3. Remove and discard peel and pith from remaining tangerines. Finely chop tangerines, discarding seeds. Measure to make 3 cups (750 mL), including juices.

4. Place chopped tangerines in a Dutch oven or a large, heavy-bottomed pot. Stir in pectin until dissolved. Bring to a full boil over high heat, stirring constantly; reduce heat to low and simmer for 5 minutes, stirring often.

5. Add sugar in a steady stream, stirring constantly. Stir in honey and cooked rind with liquid. Return to a full boil, stirring constantly to dissolve sugar. Boil hard for 1 minute.

6. Remove from heat and skim off any foam. Stir for 5 to 8 minutes to prevent floating rind.

7. Ladle into sterilized jars to within ¼ inch (0.5 cm) of rim; wipe rims. Apply prepared lids and rings; tighten rings just until fingertip-tight.

8. Process jars in a boiling water canner for 10 minutes (for details, see page 20). Transfer jars to a towel-lined surface and let rest at room temperature until set. Check seals; refrigerate any unsealed jars for up to 3 weeks. This marmalade is best served after resting for 1 week.

Cranberry Orange Marmalade

This classic taste combination produces a delicious marmalade that is deep red with lots of orange rind.

— o o o —

Recipe Suggestions

Use to glaze poultry or to make Fruit Loaf (page 356).

Use in place of sugar to sweeten a grapefruit half. Spread on cut half and microwave until warm.

4	medium seedless oranges (approx.)	4
1 cup	water	250 mL
2¼ cups	cranberry cocktail	550 mL
3 tbsp	lemon juice	45 mL
3½ cups	granulated sugar	875 mL
1 cup	coarsely chopped cranberries	250 mL

1. Cut oranges in half and squeeze out juice; measure 2⅔ cups (650 mL) juice. Cut oranges in half again. Scrape membranes from peels and discard. Thinly slice peel; measure ¾ cup (175 mL).

2. In a Dutch oven or a large, heavy-bottomed pot, combine orange juice, peel and water. Bring to a boil over high heat. Reduce heat and simmer, covered, for about 20 minutes or until peel is softened.

3. Stir in cranberry cocktail and lemon juice. Add sugar in a steady stream, stirring constantly. Heat over medium heat, stirring constantly to dissolve sugar. Increase heat to high and bring to a full boil, stirring constantly. Boil rapidly for 5 minutes, stirring often. Stir in cranberries; cook, stirring often, for 5 to 10 minutes or until marmalade thickens. Test for setting point (for details, see page 19).

4. Remove from heat and skim off any foam. Stir for 5 to 8 minutes to prevent floating rind.

5. Ladle into sterilized jars to within ¼ inch (0.5 cm) of rim; wipe rims. Apply prepared lids and rings; tighten rings just until fingertip-tight.

6. Process jars in a boiling water canner for 10 minutes (for details, see page 20). Transfer jars to a towel-lined surface and let rest at room temperature until set. Check seals; refrigerate any unsealed jars for up to 3 weeks. This marmalade is best served after resting for 1 week.

Peach Orange Marmalade

Makes about eight 8-ounce (250 mL) jars

Sharon Evans (see Contributors, page 12) sells her preserves at her shop, called Country Jams. This unique marmalade has a wonderful summery peach taste, accented with citrus. If you plan to present it as a gift, you may wish to add the optional liqueur.

— o o o —

Tips

Eight large peaches will weigh about 2 lbs (1 kg).

How to Peel Peaches: Bring a pot of water to boil over high heat. Place peaches in water two at a time; boil for 20 to 30 seconds. Remove peaches with a slotted spoon and immediately immerse in a bowl of cold water. Repeat with remaining peaches. When peaches are cool enough to handle, slit down side of peel with a paring knife and slip off peel. Cut peaches in half and remove pits.

2	medium lemons	2
1	medium orange	1
1 cup	water	250 mL
2 tbsp	lemon juice	30 mL
2 lbs	peaches, peeled (see tip at left) and finely chopped	1 kg
1	package (1.75 oz/49 or 57 g) powdered pectin	1
7 cups	granulated sugar	1.75 L
2 tbsp	orange liqueur or peach schnapps (optional)	30 mL

1. Cut lemons and orange into quarters. Thinly slice or finely chop fruit and peel, discarding seeds.

2. In a medium saucepan, combine prepared citrus fruit with any juice, water and additional lemon juice. Bring to a full boil over high heat. Reduce heat and simmer, covered, for 15 to 20 minutes or until peel is softened.

3. In a Dutch oven or a large, heavy-bottomed pot, combine peaches and cooked citrus fruit with liquid. Stir in pectin until dissolved. Bring to a full boil over high heat, stirring constantly.

4. Add sugar in a steady stream, stirring constantly. Return to a full boil, stirring constantly to dissolve sugar. Boil hard for 1 minute.

5. Remove from heat and stir in orange liqueur (if using). Skim off any foam. Stir for 5 to 8 minutes to prevent floating rind.

6. Ladle into sterilized jars to within $1/4$ inch (0.5 cm) of rim; wipe rims. Apply prepared lids and rings; tighten rings just until fingertip-tight.

7. Process jars in a boiling water canner for 10 minutes (for details, see page 20). Transfer jars to a towel-lined surface and let rest at room temperature until set. Check seals; refrigerate any unsealed jars for up to 3 weeks.

Carrot Orange Marmalade

3 cups	finely shredded carrots	750 mL
	Finely grated rind and juice of 3 medium lemons	
	Finely grated rind and juice of 2 large seedless oranges	
1 cup	water	250 mL
7 cups	granulated sugar	1.75 L
2	pouches (each 3 oz/85 mL) liquid pectin	2

1. In a Dutch oven or a large, heavy-bottomed pot, combine carrots, lemon rind, lemon juice, orange rind, orange juice and water. Bring to a full boil over high heat. Reduce heat and simmer, covered, for about 15 minutes or until carrots and rind are softened.

2. Add sugar in a steady stream, stirring constantly. Bring to a full boil over high heat, stirring constantly to dissolve sugar.

3. Immediately stir in pectin; return to a full boil. Boil hard for 1 minute, stirring constantly.

4. Remove from heat and skim off any foam. Stir for 5 to 8 minutes to prevent floating carrots and rind.

5. Ladle into sterilized jars to within $1/4$ inch (0.5 cm) of rim; wipe rims. Apply prepared lids and rings; tighten rings just until fingertip-tight.

6. Process jars in a boiling water canner for 10 minutes (for details, see page 20). Transfer jars to a towel-lined surface and let rest at room temperature until set. Check seals; refrigerate any unsealed jars for up to 3 weeks.

Zucchini Orange Marmalade

This delightful, unusual marmalade is easy to make year-round and has an intense, fresh orange flavor.

— o o o —

Tip

For convenience, use a food processor to shred the zucchini and a citrus zester to remove rind in shreds.

	Finely grated rind of 4 large seedless oranges	
2 cups	orange juice	500 mL
4 cups	lightly packed shredded zucchini	1 L
7 cups	granulated sugar	1.75 L
1/4 cup	lemon juice	60 mL
2	pouches (each 3 oz/85 mL) liquid pectin	2

1. In a small saucepan, combine orange rind and juice. Bring to a simmer over high heat. Reduce heat and simmer, covered, for 10 minutes or until rind is softened. Set aside.

2. In a Dutch oven or a large, heavy-bottomed pot over medium heat, cook zucchini, stirring frequently, for 5 minutes or until softened (water will come out of zucchini as it begins to cook).

3. Add sugar in a steady stream, stirring constantly. Stir in lemon juice and cooked orange rind and juice. Bring to a full boil over high heat, stirring constantly to dissolve sugar.

4. Immediately stir in pectin; return to a full boil. Boil hard for 1 minute, stirring constantly.

5. Remove from heat and skim off any foam. Stir for 5 to 8 minutes to prevent floating rind and zucchini.

6. Ladle into sterilized jars to within 1/4 inch (0.5 cm) of rim; wipe rims. Apply prepared lids and rings; tighten rings just until fingertip-tight.

7. Process jars in a boiling water canner (for details, see page 20) for 10 minutes. Transfer jars to a towel-lined surface and let rest at room temperature until set. Check seals; refrigerate any unsealed jars for up to 3 weeks.

Pink Grapefruit and Pomegranate Marmalade

**Makes about six
8-ounce (250 mL) jars**

This pretty in pink marmalade has a tasty tartness. Pomegranate juice is now widely available in supermarkets and comes in flavor combinations such as cherry pomegranate. Any can be used in this recipe, but make sure to choose one that is 100% fruit juice (no sugar added).

— o o o —

Tip

Feel free to change the way the rind is prepared in this recipe. To suit your own taste, it can range from extra-fine rind to thick peel. See page 229 for more information.

3 or 4	large pink grapefruit	3 or 4
1 cup	water	250 mL
1 cup	unsweetened pomegranate juice	250 mL
1	package (1.75 oz/49 or 57 g) powdered pectin	1
4½ cups	granulated sugar	1.125 L

1. Using a paring knife, remove peel from grapefruit in large strips, taking a bit of white pith if desired; thinly slice to make ¾ cup (175 mL).

2. In a small saucepan, combine peel and water. Bring to a full boil over high heat. Reduce heat and simmer, covered, for 15 to 20 minutes or until peel is softened. Set aside.

3. Remove and discard any remaining peel and pith from grapefruit. Finely chop grapefruit, discarding seeds and any connective membranes. Measure to make 3 cups (750 mL), including juices.

4. In a Dutch oven or a large, heavy-bottomed pot, combine chopped grapefruit, cooked peel with liquid and pomegranate juice. Bring to a full boil over high heat; reduce heat and simmer for 5 minutes, stirring occasionally.

5. Stir in pectin until dissolved. Bring to a full boil over high heat, stirring constantly.

6. Add sugar in a steady stream, stirring constantly. Return to a full boil, stirring constantly to dissolve sugar. Boil hard for 1 minute.

7. Remove from heat and skim off any foam. Stir for 5 to 8 minutes to prevent floating rind.

8. Ladle into sterilized jars to within ¼ inch (0.5 cm) of rim; wipe rims. Apply prepared lids and rings; tighten rings just until fingertip-tight.

9. Process jars in a boiling water canner for 10 minutes (for details, see page 20). Transfer jars to a towel-lined surface and let rest at room temperature until set. Check seals; refrigerate any unsealed jars for up to 3 weeks. This marmalade is best served after resting for 1 week.

Pineapple Citrus Marmalade

You'll enjoy the refreshing tartness of this bright-colored marmalade.

— o o o —

Tips

One medium pineapple should yield 4 cups (1 L) finely chopped.

"Sections" refer to only the fleshy part of the fruit, not the inner membranes. For instructions on sectioning citrus fruit, see page 26.

Recipe Suggestion

Use as an ingredient for Fried Bananas Caribbean (page 366).

2	medium lemons	2
1	medium orange	1
1 cup	water	250 mL
4 cups	finely chopped fresh pineapple	1 L
4½ cups	granulated sugar	1.125 L

1. Using a vegetable peeler, remove rind from lemons and orange in wide strips; thinly slice.

2. In a medium saucepan, combine rind and water. Bring to a full boil over high heat. Reduce heat and simmer, covered, for 15 to 20 minutes or until rind is softened. Set aside.

3. Section lemons and orange. Finely chop lemon and orange sections, discarding seeds and any connective membranes.

4. In a Dutch oven or a large, heavy-bottomed pot, combine chopped lemon and orange with any juice, cooked rind with liquid and pineapple.

5. Add sugar in a steady stream, stirring constantly. Bring to a boil over high heat, stirring constantly to dissolve sugar. Bring to a full boil, stirring constantly. Boil rapidly, stirring constantly, for 15 to 20 minutes or until marmalade thickens. Test for setting point (for details, see page 19).

6. Remove from heat and skim off any foam. Stir for 5 to 8 minutes to prevent floating rind.

7. Ladle into sterilized jars to within ¼ inch (0.5 cm) of rim; wipe rims. Apply prepared lids and rings; tighten rings just until fingertip-tight.

8. Process jars in a boiling water canner for 10 minutes (for details, see page 20). Transfer jars to a towel-lined surface and let rest at room temperature until set. Check seals; refrigerate any unsealed jars for up to 3 weeks. This marmalade is best served after resting for 1 week.

Three–Fruit Marmalade

*This is a classic fruit trio
marmalade with a deep
orange color and intense
citrus flavor.*

— o o o —

Recipe Suggestion
Use to make Marmalade
Pecan Cookies (page 358).

- Cheesecloth
- Kitchen string

4	medium lemons	4
3	large oranges	3
2	small pink grapefruit	2
4 cups	water	1 L
7½ cups	granulated sugar	1.875 L

1. Using a vegetable peeler, remove rind from lemons, oranges and grapefruit in wide strips; thinly slice and pack to make 3 cups (750 mL) total. Line a large strainer with several layers of cheesecloth and place over a medium bowl. Cut lemons, oranges and grapefruit in half and squeeze out juice; pour juice through cheesecloth to catch the seeds. Measure juice to make 3 cups (750 mL). Place squeezed fruit halves in cheesecloth with seeds; tie securely with string.

2. In a Dutch oven or a large, heavy-bottomed pot, combine rind, juice, water and cheesecloth bag. Bring to a full boil over high heat. Reduce heat and simmer, covered, for 25 to 30 minutes or until rind is softened. Squeeze liquid from cheesecloth bag into pot; discard bag.

3. Add sugar in a steady stream, stirring constantly. Heat over medium heat, stirring constantly to dissolve sugar. Increase heat to high and bring to a full boil, stirring constantly. Boil rapidly, uncovered, stirring often, for 20 to 25 minutes or until marmalade thickens. Test for setting point (for details, see page 19).

4. Remove from heat and skim off any foam. Stir for 5 to 8 minutes to prevent floating rind.

5. Ladle into sterilized jars to within ¼ inch (0.5 cm) of rim; wipe rims. Apply prepared lids and rings; tighten rings just until fingertip-tight.

6. Process jars in a boiling water canner (for details, see page 20) for 10 minutes. Transfer jars to a towel-lined surface and let rest at room temperature until set. Check seals; refrigerate any unsealed jars for up to 3 weeks. This marmalade is best served after resting for 1 week.

Jellies

Jellies are sparkling, clear gels made with strained fruit juice (or other liquids, such as wine) and sugar. They are cooked with or without added commercial pectin. Jelly holds its shape but is tender enough to quiver, and it spreads easily. For convenience, I've divided the recipes into two sections. The first, Fruit Jellies, contains jellies that have only sweet ingredients, while the second, Savory Jellies, has recipes with both sweet and savory ingredients.

About Jellies 255
How to Use a Jelly Bag 256
Tips for Successful Jellies 256
Trouble-Shooting 257

Fruit Jellies 259
Savory Jellies 281

About Jellies

Jellies are different from jams in that they are clear and are made with only liquids: the juices of fruits; wine, vinegar or water; or liquid infused with herbs. (Some jellies do, however, have flowers, herbs or peppers suspended in them.) Some people prefer the texture of jellies over jams, or like to use jellies as clear glazes for fruit flans or meats.

Jellies are the ideal choice when you want to make preserves from fruits that have a lot of seeds or pits (since they'll get strained out with little effort on your part) or to capture the flavor of garlic or hot peppers. In some ways, jellies are easier to make than jams, as they do not usually require peeling or much preparation of the fruit. With some jellies, you don't even have to do any cooking. And you can add unique infused flavors to them for a taste surprise.

Jellies made from fruit with high natural pectin or a combination of high- and low-pectin fruit will gel without added commercial pectin. When the extracted juice is very thick, it is rich in pectin. Keep water to a minimum while the fruit is cooking for flavorful, thick juice.

These jellies were tested for sugar content using a refractometer, so no more sugar was added than was needed for a good set. Acidity was tested with a pH meter to ensure sufficient acid for gelling.

Many jellies do require the addition of pectin, either liquid or powdered, because they lack enough natural pectin. Indeed, wine jellies would not be possible without added pectin, nor would the savory jellies infused with herbs or garlic.

How to Use a Jelly Bag

Place the jelly bag in its holder. Rinse the bag by pouring about 2 cups (500 mL) boiling water over it; let drain. (This also helps to keep juice from soaking into the bag.) Set the jelly bag over a large bowl or pot; pour in cooked fruit and juice. Cover and let juice drip slowly through the jelly bag overnight. Most of the juice will have dripped through after about 4 hours; longer dripping will yield about $\frac{1}{2}$ cup (125 mL) more liquid. Discard contents of bag, wash the bag with warm, soapy water and let it dry; store in a plastic bag to keep it clean.

If you don't have a jelly bag, you can use several layers of cheesecloth layered in a fine-mesh strainer, but the jelly may not be as clear.

> Refer to the Produce Purchase Guide, page 32, to estimate the amount of fruit you'll need to purchase for these recipes.

Tips for Successful Jellies

1. Choose just-ripe fruit; about a quarter of it can be slightly underripe (underripe fruit is higher in pectin). Cook fruit just until softened; do not overcook or the pectin will be destroyed.

2. Do not squeeze the jelly bag or jelly will be cloudy.

3. Use the exact amount of liquid specified in the recipe; using extra may result in a jelly that does not set. Juice may be frozen and used to make jelly later.

4. Check the expiration date on the box of pectin before beginning.

5. Measure sugar accurately and stir well to ensure that it is completely dissolved, scraping down any that gets on the sides of the pot or the spoon handle. Bringing the liquid to a full boil before stirring in the sugar will help the sugar dissolve more quickly.

6. Jellies require a full boil to evaporate the liquid and to concentrate the sugar and pectin. Your pot should be at least four times as deep as the liquid, measured from the inside. Do not double recipes or add more liquid than is called for. The liquid will likely bubble right to the top of the pot. I recommend using the deepest pot you have or, if you make jellies often, investing in one that is at least 6 inches (15 cm) deep, with an inner diameter of at least 9 inches (23 cm). Sticky hot jelly makes a real mess and can cause burns!

7. The timing for pectin-added jellies should be exact; use a timer.

8. Jellies *without* added pectin must be checked for the setting point (see Test for the Setting Point, page 19). Always remove the pot from the heat to stop the cooking before testing.

9. Use strained freshly squeezed lemon juice (no pulp) or bottled lemon juice for clear jellies.

10. Skim any foam from the top of jelly using a large metal spoon (not all jellies will have foam). I do not like to add butter to my jellies to prevent foaming, as suggested in some recipes you may come across. To remove small bits of foam that sink or are hard to get with your spoon, pour jelly through a fine-mesh strainer.

11. Work quickly with jellies, as they may set quickly. I often pour them from the pot into a sterilized 4-cup (1 L) glass measure, then pour the mixture quickly into jars (it is faster than ladling). If it begins to set, you may get small bubbles in your jelly.

12. For rose petal jelly, you may add petals to the mixture in the glass measure (described in tip #11) and stir slowly with a sterilized skewer until they look suspended, then pour the mixture into jars.

13. Pepper jellies benefit from being stirred for 5 to 8 minutes to prevent floating.

14. Do not seal jellies with paraffin wax. This practice is no longer considered safe, as air may still get under the wax. It cannot replace the safety you get with two-piece metal lids and boiling water processing.

15. Do not invert jars after they have sealed.

> Please read A Primer on Preserving, pages 14 to 37. Things may have changed since you first started making preserves (such as the recent increase in processing time). If you are a beginner, there are a few important things you need to know before getting started. Many instructions are common to all preserves, so once you get it right for one, you'll sail through the others. In the primer, you will also find a handy Preparation Checklist (page 37).

Trouble-Shooting

PROBLEM: Jelly does not set or is soft.

Some jellies will set as soon as they are cooled, while others may take 24 hours or longer. If it is an added-pectin recipe, check the expiration date on the pectin box. You may wish to contact the manufacturer of the pectin, using the toll-free number or website on the box; they may have a solution for their particular product.

For jellies without added pectin, you may need to cook the mixture a little longer. If the jars have all sealed properly, the contents are safe. Return the jelly to the pot, discard the used lids and begin boiling and testing for the setting point. It may take only another couple of minutes after it begins to boil for it to reach the setting point. Then proceed with sterilized jars and new prepared lids.

It is also possible that the jelly was overcooked or cooked too slowly for too long, or that the fruit was naturally low in pectin or overripe. In this case, you can still use the jelly as a syrup to pour over pancakes or ice cream, or to sweeten fruit salads or compotes.

PROBLEM: Jelly is stiff or tough.

This can happen when fruit is high in natural pectin or when too much pectin is added. Likely the jelly was overcooked; this happens when there is not enough sugar and the mixture takes too long to reach the setting point. To salvage it, dilute it with fruit juice or a little liqueur and warm it in the microwave just before serving, to make it more spreadable; stir well. It can then be used to pour over pancakes or ice cream, or to sweeten fruit salads or compotes.

PROBLEM: Jelly weeps.

This occurs when liquid seeps from the jelly. Weeping is caused by too much acid in the juice, not enough pectin, or storage in a place that is too warm or has temperature fluctuations. If your jelly weeps, pour out or blot off excess liquid. The gel will be weak, but it will likely still be edible. Warm it to use as a sauce or glaze for fruit, toss it with hot cooked vegetables, or use it to deglaze the pan after cooking meat.

PROBLEM: Jelly has small bubbles.

Some jellies begin to set very quickly. If they do, you may get small air bubbles trapped in your jelly. Work quickly, keeping everything hot, and pour the mixture quickly into jars.

PROBLEM: Jelly has crystals.

This can occur when too much sugar has been added or when there is undissolved sugar on the sides of the pan or the spoon handle. Stir well during cooking and scrape down the sides with a rubber scraper, if necessary.

Crystallization may also result from overcooking or from storage in a place that is too warm or has temperature fluctuations.

PROBLEM: Jelly is cloudy.

Thoroughly wash fruit before cooking. Do not overcook fruit; cook just until tender. If you squeeze the jelly bag, the jelly will become cloudy when cooked.

Fruit Jellies

*This section contains single-fruit and mixed-fruit jellies, as well as
one made with jasmine green tea (you'll love it!).*

Beet Plum Jelly 260

Black Currant Jelly. 261

Blackberry Plum Jelly. 262

Crabapple Jelly 263

Cranberry Orange and Ginger Jelly 264

Cran-Raspberry Jelly 265

Elderberry Jelly 266

Concord Grape Jelly 267

Jasmine Green Tea Jelly with Ginger and Lemon 268

Clementine Orange Lemon Jelly. 269

Peach Vanilla Jelly 270

Pomegranate Jelly. 271

Raspberry Jelly 272

Red Currant Jelly. 273

Red Currant Raspberry Jelly 274

Red Plum Jelly. 275

Red Plum Orange Jelly 276

Rhubarb Jelly 277

Rose Hip Jelly 278

Rhuberry Jelly 280

Beet Plum Jelly

**Makes about five
8-ounce (250 mL) jars**

*Beets have a strong flavor
and benefit from being
combined with plums.
Alternatively, if desired,
use only beets and
combine 2 cups (500 mL)
of the beet juice with
2 cups (500 mL) sour
cherry juice to make up
the 4 cups (1 L) of liquid.*

—ooo—

Tips

You'll need about 3 lbs
(1.5 kg) of beets and 4 lbs
(2 kg) of plums for this
recipe.

Before chopping beets,
scrub them and trim off the
stem and root end; there's
no need to peel them.

This jelly may take 24 hours
or longer to set fully. Let rest
undisturbed.

Recipe Suggestions

Use this jelly as a glaze
for diced cooked beets or
chopped cooked carrots.

Add a couple of spoonfuls
to a salad dressing for mixed
salad greens or baby spinach
leaves, roasted beets, blue
cheese or goat cheese and
toasted walnuts. (Warm the
jelly in the microwave so
it blends into the dressing
more easily.)

- Jelly bag

8 cups	chopped beets	2 L
8 cups	chopped pitted black or red plums	2 L
2 cups	water	500 mL
1	package (1.75 oz/49 or 57 g) powdered pectin	1
5¼ cups	granulated sugar	1.3 L

1. In a large, deep, heavy-bottomed pot, combine beets, plums and water. Bring to a boil over high heat. Reduce heat and simmer for about 15 minutes or until beets are softened. Use a potato masher to further break down beets and plums; simmer for 2 minutes.

2. Pour into prepared jelly bag and let drip overnight, without squeezing (for details, see page 256).

3. Measure exactly 4 cups (1 L) of liquid (add water if there's not enough liquid); pour into clean pot. Stir in pectin until dissolved. Bring to a full boil over high heat, stirring constantly.

4. Add sugar in a steady stream, stirring constantly. Return to a full boil, stirring constantly to dissolve sugar. Boil hard for 1 minute.

5. Remove from heat and skim off any foam.

6. Ladle quickly into sterilized jars to within ¼ inch (0.5 cm) of rim; wipe rims. Apply prepared lids and rings; tighten just until fingertip-tight.

7. Process jars in a boiling water canner for 10 minutes (for details, see page 20). Transfer jars to a towel-lined surface and let rest at room temperature until set. Check seals; refrigerate any unsealed jars for up to 3 weeks.

Variations

Beet, Plum and Orange Jelly: Add strips of orange rind from 1 large orange with the beets.

Beet, Plum and Ginger Jelly: Add 2 tbsp (30 mL) grated gingerroot with the beets.

Black Currant Jelly

*Black currants have
plenty of natural pectin
and make a splendid jelly.*

—— o o o ——

• Jelly bag

4 lbs	black currants	2 kg
3 cups	water	750 mL
4 cups	granulated sugar	1 L

1. In a large, deep, heavy-bottomed pot, combine currants and water. Bring to a boil over high heat. Reduce heat and simmer, covered, for 8 to 10 minutes or until currants are softened. Use a potato masher to further break down currants and release juice.

2. Pour into prepared jelly bag and let drip overnight, without squeezing (for details, see page 256).

3. Measure exactly 4 cups (1 L) of liquid (add water if there's not enough liquid); pour into clean pot. Bring to a full boil over high heat, stirring constantly.

4. Add sugar in a steady stream, stirring constantly. Return to a full boil, stirring constantly to dissolve sugar. Boil, without stirring, reducing heat a bit if it starts to boil over, for 5 to 8 minutes or until setting point is reached (for details, see page 19).

5. Remove from heat and skim off any foam.

6. Ladle quickly into sterilized jars to within $1/4$ inch (0.5 cm) of rim; wipe rims. Apply prepared lids and rings; tighten just until fingertip-tight.

7. Process jars in a boiling water canner for 10 minutes (for details, see page 20). Transfer jars to a towel-lined surface and let rest at room temperature until set. Check seals; refrigerate any unsealed jars for up to 3 weeks.

> Black currants are a very rich source of vitamin C, second only to rose hips. Even after cooking, they retain high levels of vitamin C. They are also rich in anthocyanins and other important minerals, such as potassium. Black currants have a little "beard" on the blossom end that must be removed for jam, but that step is unnecessary when you're making jelly.

Blackberry Plum Jelly

*This dark jelly has a very
rich, intense flavor.*

— o o o —

Tip
Be careful when pouring the
liquid into the jelly bag — it
can stain (clothes, counter,
etc.).

Recipe Suggestion
Heat with an equal amount
of maple syrup, whisking to
blend, and serve as a sauce
over pancakes or waffles.

• Jelly bag

3 lbs	plums	1.5 kg
3 cups	blackberries	750 mL
1	small lemon	1
3 cups	water	750 mL
5 cups	granulated sugar	1.25 L

1. Halve plums and remove pits. Cut each plum into
   8 wedges. In a large, deep, heavy-bottomed pot,
   combine plums and blackberries. Cut lemon into
   wedges. Squeeze juice into pot; place squeezed wedges
   in pot. Stir in water.

2. Bring to a boil over high heat. Reduce heat and simmer,
   covered, for 10 minutes or until fruit is softened. Use
   a potato masher to further break down fruit; simmer,
   covered, for 5 minutes.

3. Pour into prepared jelly bag and let drip overnight,
   without squeezing (for details, see page 256).

4. Measure exactly 6 cups (1.5 L) of liquid (add water if
   there's not enough liquid); pour into clean pot. Bring
   to a full boil over high heat, stirring constantly.

5. Add sugar in a steady stream, stirring constantly. Return
   to a full boil, stirring constantly to dissolve sugar. Boil,
   without stirring, reducing heat a bit if it starts to boil
   over, for 14 to 16 minutes or until setting point is
   reached (for details, see page 19).

6. Remove from heat and skim off any foam.

7. Ladle quickly into sterilized jars to within 1/4 inch
   (0.5 cm) of rim; wipe rims. Apply prepared lids and
   rings; tighten just until fingertip-tight.

8. Process jars in a boiling water canner for 10 minutes
   (for details, see page 20). Transfer jars to a towel-lined
   surface and let rest at room temperature until set. Check
   seals; refrigerate any unsealed jars for up to 3 weeks.

> This jelly mixture may boil over if the pot is not deep
> enough. If the froth rises to the top of the pot during
> cooking, reduce the heat to prevent it from boiling over.

Crabapple Jelly

Makes about six 8-ounce (250 mL) jars

Tart crabapples make a delicious, deep red jelly. Use this jelly to glaze meats or fruit flans, or spread on fresh-baked scones or muffins.

— o o o —

- Jelly bag

14 cups	crabapples	3.5 L
6 cups	water	1.5 L
4½ cups	granulated sugar	1.125 L

1. Cut crabapples in half through stem, and remove stem and blossom ends. In a large, deep, heavy-bottomed pot, combine crabapples and water. Bring to a boil over high heat. Reduce heat and boil gently for 15 minutes or until crabapples are softened. Use a potato masher to further break down apples; boil gently for 5 minutes.

2. Pour into prepared jelly bag and let drip overnight, without squeezing (for details, see page 256).

3. Measure exactly 6 cups (1.5 L) of liquid (add water if there's not enough liquid); pour into clean pot. Bring to a full boil over high heat, stirring constantly.

4. Add sugar in a steady stream, stirring constantly. Return to a full boil, stirring constantly to dissolve sugar. Boil, without stirring, reducing heat a bit if it starts to boil over, for 8 to 12 minutes or until setting point is reached (for details, see page 19).

5. Remove from heat and skim off any foam.

6. Ladle quickly into sterilized jars to within ¼ inch (0.5 cm) of rim; wipe rims. Apply prepared lids and rings; tighten just until fingertip-tight.

7. Process jars in a boiling water canner for 10 minutes (for details, see page 20). Transfer jars to a towel-lined surface and let rest at room temperature until set. Check seals; refrigerate any unsealed jars for up to 3 weeks.

> Do not seal jellies with paraffin wax. This practice is no longer considered safe. Process in a boiling water canner for a good seal. Do not invert jars after sealing.

Cranberry Orange and Ginger Jelly

Fresh ginger adds zing to this slightly tangy jelly.

— o o o —

Tips

You'll need about 2½ lbs (1.25 kg) of cranberries for this recipe.

Fresh cranberries are easy to freeze when in season. Simply pop the bag they came in into a freezer bag, squeeze out excess air and seal. Measure before thawing.

- Jelly bag

13 cups	cranberries	3.25 L
4	oranges	4
2 tbsp	grated gingerroot	30 mL
4 cups	water	1 L
5 cups	granulated sugar	1.25 L

1. Place cranberries in a large, deep, heavy-bottomed pot. Cut each orange into 8 wedges. Squeeze juice from wedges into pot (it's not necessary to remove seeds); nestle wedges into cranberries. Stir in gingerroot and water.

2. Bring to a boil over high heat. Reduce heat and simmer, covered, for 10 minutes or until cranberries are softened. Use a potato masher to further break down fruit; simmer for 5 minutes.

3. Pour into prepared jelly bag and let drip overnight, without squeezing (for details, see page 256).

4. Measure exactly 4 cups (1 L) of liquid (add water if there's not enough liquid); pour into clean pot. Bring to a full boil over high heat, stirring constantly.

5. Add sugar in a steady stream, stirring constantly. Return to a full boil, stirring constantly to dissolve sugar. Boil, without stirring, reducing heat a bit if it starts to boil over, for 5 to 8 minutes or until setting point is reached (for details, see page 19).

6. Remove from heat and skim off any foam.

7. Ladle quickly into sterilized jars to within ¼ inch (0.5 cm) of rim; wipe rims. Apply prepared lids and rings; tighten just until fingertip-tight.

8. Process jars in a boiling water canner for 10 minutes (for details, see page 20). Transfer jars to a towel-lined surface and let rest at room temperature until set. Check seals; refrigerate any unsealed jars for up to 3 weeks.

Cran–Raspberry Jelly

**Makes about six
8-ounce (250 mL) jars**

*This flavor combination,
popular as a juice drink,
works well as a jelly too.
You can use either fresh
or frozen fruit.*

— o o o —

- Jelly bag

9 cups	raspberries	2.25 L
6 cups	cranberries	1.5 L
4¾ cups	granulated sugar	1.175 L

1. In a large, deep, heavy-bottomed pot, combine raspberries and cranberries. Bring to a boil over high heat, stirring constantly. Reduce heat and simmer, covered, for 10 minutes or until fruit is softened. Use a potato masher to further break down fruit; simmer for 5 minutes.

2. Pour into prepared jelly bag and let drip overnight, without squeezing (for details, see page 256).

3. Measure exactly 5 cups (1.25 L) of liquid (add water if there's not enough liquid); pour into clean pot. Bring to a full boil over high heat, stirring constantly.

4. Add sugar in a steady stream, stirring constantly. Return to a full boil, stirring constantly to dissolve sugar. Boil, without stirring, reducing heat a bit if it starts to boil over, for 5 to 8 minutes or until setting point is reached (for details, see page 19).

5. Ladle quickly into sterilized jars to within ¼ inch (0.5 cm) of rim; wipe rims. Apply prepared lids and rings; tighten just until fingertip-tight.

6. Process jars in a boiling water canner for 10 minutes (for details, see page 20). Transfer jars to a towel-lined surface and let rest at room temperature until set. Check seals; refrigerate any unsealed jars for up to 3 weeks.

> The setting point is the point at which the preserve is done, when the sugar, pectin and acid come together to create a gel that will set upon cooling.

Elderberry Jelly

*Elderberries are dark,
almost black, berries with
large seeds and a taste a
bit like both blackberries
and blueberries. You will
find them growing wild.*

— o o o —

Tips

Use a fork to strip
elderberries from their
stalks; this berry will stain
your hands.

In jellies, always use freshly
squeezed lemon or lime
juice that has been strained.
This will keep the finished
jellies clear.

• Jelly bag

5 cups	elderberries	1.25 L
3 cups	water	750 mL
¼ cup	strained lemon juice (see tip, at left)	60 mL
1	package (1.75 oz/49 or 57 g) powdered pectin	1
6½ cups	granulated sugar	1.625 L

1. In a large, deep, heavy-bottomed pot, combine elderberries and water. Bring to a boil over high heat. Reduce heat and simmer for 15 minutes or until elderberries are softened. Use a potato masher to further break down berries.

2. Pour into prepared jelly bag and let drip overnight, without squeezing (for details, see page 256).

3. Measure exactly 4 cups (1 L) of liquid (add water if there's not enough liquid); pour into clean pot. Stir in lemon juice. Stir in pectin until dissolved. Bring to a full boil over high heat, stirring constantly.

4. Add sugar in a steady stream, stirring constantly. Return to a full boil, stirring constantly to dissolve sugar. Boil hard for 1 minute.

5. Remove from heat and skim off any foam.

6. Ladle quickly into sterilized jars to within ¼ inch (0.5 cm) of rim; wipe rims. Apply prepared lids and rings; tighten just until fingertip-tight.

7. Process jars in a boiling water canner for 10 minutes (for details, see page 20). Transfer jars to a towel-lined surface and let rest at room temperature until set. Check seals; refrigerate any unsealed jars for up to 3 weeks.

European elder is native to central Europe and grows in England as well. In North America, elder grows in hardiness zones 3 through 9 (which include the coastal and southern regions of Canada). Try adding a handful of elderflowers to jams such as apricot, gooseberry, quince, rhubarb or strawberry. Rub flowers between your hands to remove them from their stems and add about 5 minutes before the jam is done cooking. Or tie flowers in a cheesecloth bag; remove bag after cooking.

Concord Grape Jelly

*This is the grape jelly of
the peanut butter and
jelly sandwiches of your
childhood. Look for these
deep bluish-purple grapes
at farmers' markets in
September.*

— ○○○ —

Tips

You'll need about 5½ lbs
(2.75 kg) of grapes for this
recipe.

Tartaric acid (found in
grapes, bananas, mangos
and other fruit) forms
granules after the fruit is
cooked that can cause jelly
to crystallize after it sets.
Do not skip step 3.

- Jelly bag

14 cups	stemmed Concord grapes	3.5 L
1	tart apple, stem and blossom ends removed, sliced	1
2 cups	water	500 mL
3¾ cups	granulated sugar	925 mL

1. In a large, deep, heavy-bottomed pot, combine grapes, apple and water. Bring to a full boil over high heat. Reduce heat to medium-high and boil for 8 minutes or until fruit is softened. Use a potato masher to further break down fruit; boil for 2 minutes.

2. Pour into prepared jelly bag and let drip overnight, without squeezing (for details, see page 256).

3. Refrigerate liquid for 24 hours to allow granules formed by tartaric acid to settle to bottom.

4. Measure exactly 5 cups (1.25 L) of liquid, being careful not to include any of the granules (add water if there's not enough liquid); pour into clean pot. Bring to a full boil over high heat, stirring constantly.

5. Add sugar in a steady stream, stirring constantly. Return to a full boil, stirring constantly to dissolve sugar. Boil, without stirring, reducing heat a bit if it starts to boil over, for 15 to 20 minutes or until setting point is reached (for details, see page 19).

6. Remove from heat and skim off any foam.

7. Ladle quickly into sterilized jars to within ¼ inch (0.5 cm) of rim; wipe rims. Apply prepared lids and rings; tighten just until fingertip-tight.

8. Process jars in a boiling water canner for 10 minutes (for details, see page 20). Transfer jars to a towel-lined surface and let rest at room temperature until set. Check seals; refrigerate any unsealed jars for up to 3 weeks.

Jasmine Green Tea Jelly with Ginger and Lemon

Makes about five 8-ounce (250 mL) jars

This amber-colored jelly has a touch of ginger and a hint of lemon.

— o o o —

Recipe Suggestions

Use this jelly to glaze fruit flans or tarts.

Stir into a hot cup of tea or serve over scones.

Variations

Jasmine Green Tea Jelly: Omit the ginger.

Green Tea Jelly with Honey: Use regular green tea and replace 1/2 cup (125 mL) of the sugar with liquid honey. If desired, omit the ginger.

4 cups	cold water	1 L
2 tbsp	finely grated gingerroot	30 mL
8	jasmine green tea bags (or either jasmine tea or green tea)	8
1/4 cup	strained lemon juice (see tip, page 272)	60 mL
1	package (1.75 oz/49 or 57 g) powdered pectin	1
5 cups	granulated sugar	1.25 L

1. In a large saucepan, combine water and ginger. Bring to a boil over high heat. Reduce heat and simmer, covered, for 2 minutes.

2. Remove from heat and add tea bags. Cover and let steep for 5 minutes.

3. Pour through a fine-mesh sieve; discard ginger and tea bags. Measure exactly 3 1/2 cups (875 mL) of liquid (add water if there's not enough liquid). Pour into a large, deep, heavy-bottomed pot. Stir in lemon juice.

4. Stir in pectin until dissolved. Bring to a full boil over high heat, stirring constantly.

5. Add sugar in a steady stream, stirring constantly. Return to a full boil, stirring constantly to dissolve sugar. Boil hard for 1 minute.

6. Remove from heat and skim off any foam.

7. Ladle quickly into sterilized jars to within 1/4 inch (0.5 cm) of rim; wipe rims. Apply prepared lids and rings; tighten just until fingertip-tight.

8. Process jars in a boiling water canner for 10 minutes (for details, see page 20). Transfer jars to a towel-lined surface and let rest at room temperature until set. Check seals; refrigerate any unsealed jars for up to 3 weeks.

Clementine Orange Lemon Jelly

Makes about five 8-ounce (250 mL) jars

This orange-colored jelly makes a terrific glaze for fruit, cake, tarts and fruit galettes.

— o o o —

Tip
This jelly is best consumed after it sets for a few weeks.

Recipe Suggestion
Warm this jelly and use it as a sauce for pancakes or waffles.

A clementine is a type of (generally) seedless mandarin orange with an easy-to-peel skin. It was named for Father Clément Rodier, who found a chance seedling in the garden of his orphanage in Algeria.

- Jelly bag

6 lbs	clementines	3 kg
2	lemons	2
3 cups	water	750 mL
5½ cups	granulated sugar	1.375 L

1. Chop 3 lbs (1.5 kg) of the clementines and both lemons (all unpeeled); place in a large, deep, heavy-bottomed pot. Halve and squeeze juice from the remaining clementines to measure 2 cups (500 mL). Add juice to pot and pour in water. Cover and let stand for about 8 hours, or overnight.

2. Bring fruit mixture to a boil over high heat. Reduce heat and simmer, covered, for about 1 hour or until rinds are softened.

3. Pour into prepared jelly bag and let drip overnight, without squeezing (for details, see page 256).

4. Measure exactly 4 cups (1 L) of liquid (add water if there's not enough liquid); pour into clean pot. Bring to a full boil over high heat, stirring constantly.

5. Add sugar in a steady stream, stirring constantly. Return to a full boil over high heat, stirring constantly to dissolve sugar. Boil, without stirring, reducing heat a bit if it starts to boil over, for about 25 minutes or until setting point is reached (for details, see page 19).

6. Remove from heat and skim off any foam.

7. Ladle quickly into sterilized jars to within ¼ inch (0.5 cm) of rim; wipe rims. Apply prepared lids and rings; tighten just until fingertip-tight.

8. Process jars in a boiling water canner for 10 minutes (for details, see page 20). Transfer jars to a towel-lined surface and let rest at room temperature until set. Check seals; refrigerate any unsealed jars for up to 3 weeks.

Peach Vanilla Jelly

*A hint of vanilla adds a
nice flavor accent to this
sparkling, orange-colored
jelly. The more red on
the fruit, the deeper the
color will be.*

— o o o —

Tip
Whole vanilla beans can be
found in specialty grocery
stores, packaged in glass
tubes.

Recipe Suggestion
Use to glaze French Apple
Tarts (page 361).

- Jelly bag

5 lbs	peaches, sliced	2.5 kg
1½ cups	water	375 mL
1	vanilla bean, split lengthwise	1
1	package (1.75 oz/49 or 57 g) powdered pectin	1
5¾ cups	granulated sugar	1.425 L

1. In a large, deep, heavy-bottomed pot, combine peaches, water and vanilla bean. Bring to a boil over high heat. Reduce heat and simmer for 15 minutes or until peaches are softened. Use a potato masher to further break down peaches; simmer for 5 minutes.

2. Pour into prepared jelly bag and let drip overnight, without squeezing (for details, see page 256).

3. Measure exactly 4 cups (1 L) of liquid (add water if there's not enough liquid); pour into clean pot. Stir in pectin until dissolved. Bring to a full boil over high heat, stirring constantly.

4. Add sugar in a steady stream, stirring constantly. Return to a full boil, stirring constantly to dissolve sugar. Boil hard for 1 minute.

5. Remove from heat and skim off any foam.

6. Ladle quickly into sterilized jars to within ¼ inch (0.5 cm) of rim; wipe rims. Apply prepared lids and rings; tighten just until fingertip-tight.

7. Process jars in a boiling water canner for 10 minutes (for details, see page 20). Transfer jars to a towel-lined surface and let rest at room temperature until set. Check seals; refrigerate any unsealed jars for up to 3 weeks.

> The tiny seeds of the vanilla bean are known as its caviar.

Pomegranate Jelly

Makes about five 8-ounce (250 mL) jars

3½ cups	unsweetened 100% pomegranate juice	875 mL
2 tbsp	strained lime or lemon juice (see tip, page 272)	30 mL
1	package (1.75 oz/49 or 57 g) powdered pectin	1
4½ cups	granulated sugar	1.125 L

Makes about five 8-ounce (250 mL) jars

This gorgeous crimson jelly is great for Christmas gifts.

— o o o —

Tip
This jelly will bubble up very high while cooking, so use a deep pot. Reduce heat to medium when boiling, if necessary.

1. In a large, deep, heavy-bottomed pot, combine pomegranate juice and lime juice. Stir in pectin until dissolved. Bring to a boil over high heat, stirring constantly.

2. Add sugar in a steady stream, stirring constantly. Return to a full boil, stirring constantly to dissolve sugar. Boil hard for 1 minute.

3. Remove from heat and skim off any foam.

4. Ladle quickly into sterilized jars to within ¼ inch (0.5 cm) of rim; wipe rims. Apply prepared lids and rings; tighten just until fingertip-tight.

5. Process jars in a boiling water canner for 10 minutes (for details, see page 20). Transfer jars to a towel-lined surface and let rest at room temperature until set. Check seals; refrigerate any unsealed jars for up to 3 weeks.

Variations

Pomegranate Rosemary Jelly: Add 2 tbsp (30 mL) finely chopped fresh rosemary to the pomegranate juice. Cover and simmer over low heat for 5 minutes. Strain, discarding rosemary. Measure 3½ cups (875 mL), topping up with more juice or water, if necessary.

Pomegranate Wine Jelly: Replace half of the pomegranate juice with red or white wine.

Pomegranate Cherry Jelly: Replace half of the pomegranate juice with unsweetened 100% cherry juice (made from sour cherries).

Pomegranate Ginger Jelly: Add 2 tbsp (30 mL) grated gingerroot after the lime juice. Cover and simmer over low heat for 5 minutes. Strain, discarding gingerroot. Measure 3½ cups (875 mL), topping up with more juice or water, if necessary.

Raspberry Jelly

A classic jelly with a beautiful color and slight tartness, this recipe will also work for blackberries, boysenberries or loganberries. Jellies are a great way to preserve these fruits, without the seeds!

—ooo—

Tips

If you want to use frozen berries, you'll need about 2½ lbs (1.25 kg) frozen unsweetened whole raspberries.

In jellies, always use freshly squeezed lemon or lime juice that has been strained. This will keep the finished jellies clear.

Variation

Raspberry Lychee Jelly: Add ¼ cup (60 mL) lychee liqueur after skimming the jelly.

- Jelly bag

10 cups	raspberries	2.5 L
2 cups	water	500 mL
3 tbsp	strained lemon juice (see tip, at left)	45 mL
1	package (1.75 oz/49 or 57 g) powdered pectin	1
5¾ cups	granulated sugar	1.425 L

1. In a large, deep, heavy-bottomed pot, combine raspberries and water. Bring to a boil over high heat. Reduce heat and simmer, covered, for 5 minutes. Use a potato masher to further break down berries.

2. Pour into prepared jelly bag and let drip overnight, without squeezing (for details, see page 256).

3. Measure exactly 4 cups (1 L) of liquid (add water if there's not enough liquid); pour into clean pot. Stir in lemon juice. Stir in pectin until dissolved. Bring to a full boil over high heat, stirring constantly.

4. Add sugar in a steady stream, stirring constantly. Return to a full boil, stirring constantly to dissolve sugar. Boil hard for 1 minute.

5. Remove from heat and skim off any foam.

6. Ladle quickly into sterilized jars to within ¼ inch (0.5 cm) of rim; wipe rims. Apply prepared lids and rings; tighten just until fingertip-tight.

7. Process jars in a boiling water canner for 10 minutes (for details, see page 20). Transfer jars to a towel-lined surface and let rest at room temperature until set. Check seals; refrigerate any unsealed jars for up to 3 weeks.

> Loganberries are thought to be a cross between a European red raspberry and the American blackberry, created by an American lawyer and horticulturist, James Harvey Logan, while attempting to cross two varieties of blackberries. Logan accidentally planted them next to an old variety of raspberry, and they all flowered and fruited together.

Red Currant Jelly

**Makes about seven
8-ounce (250 mL) jars**

*Red currants make a
bright red jelly with
a lovely flavor.*

— o o o —

Tips

You'll need about 3½ lbs
(1.75 kg) of currants for
this recipe.

This recipe is great to make
when you have an abundant
supply of red currants. You
can also freeze the fruit or
the juice for jelly-making at
a later date.

Recipe Suggestion

Thin the jelly by adding a
little water, orange juice or
liqueur, and spoon over
cheesecake, use to glaze
a fruit flan or French Apple
Tarts (page 361), or serve
with Baked Brie (page 345).

- Jelly bag

12 cups	red currants	3 L
6 cups	water	1.5 L
6 cups	granulated sugar	1.5 L

1. In a large, deep, heavy-bottomed pot, combine currants and water. Bring to a boil over high heat. Reduce heat and simmer for 10 minutes or until currants are softened. Use a potato masher to further break down currants; simmer for 5 minutes.

2. Pour into prepared jelly bag and let drip overnight, without squeezing (for details, see page 256).

3. Measure exactly 6 cups (1.5 L) of liquid (add water if there's not enough liquid); pour into clean pot. Bring to a full boil over high heat, stirring constantly.

4. Add sugar in a steady stream, stirring constantly. Return to a full boil, stirring constantly to dissolve sugar. Boil, without stirring, reducing heat a bit if it starts to boil over, for 5 to 8 minutes or until setting point is reached (for details, see page 19).

5. Remove from heat and skim off any foam.

6. Ladle quickly into sterilized jars to within ¼ inch (0.5 cm) of rim; wipe rims. Apply prepared lids and rings; tighten just until fingertip-tight.

7. Process jars in a boiling water canner for 10 minutes (for details, see page 20). Transfer jars to a towel-lined surface and let rest at room temperature until set. Check seals; refrigerate any unsealed jars for up to 3 weeks.

Red Currant Raspberry Jelly

*The red currants in this
jelly are set off by a bit
of raspberry flavor. It
makes a terrific glaze for
fruit flans or topping
for cheesecake.*

— o o o —

Tip
You'll need about 2 lbs
(1 kg) of currants for this
recipe.

- Jelly bag

7 cups	red currants	1.75 L
5 cups	raspberries	1.25 L
2 cups	water	500 mL
3¾ cups	granulated sugar	925 mL

1. In a large, deep, heavy-bottomed pot, combine currants, raspberries and water. Bring to a boil over high heat. Reduce heat and simmer for 10 minutes or until fruit is softened. Use a potato masher to further break down fruit; simmer for 5 minutes.

2. Pour into prepared jelly bag and let drip overnight, without squeezing (for details, see page 256).

3. Measure exactly 4 cups (1 L) of liquid (add water if there's not enough liquid); pour into clean pot. Bring to a full boil over high heat, stirring constantly.

4. Add sugar in a steady stream, stirring constantly. Return to a full boil, stirring constantly to dissolve sugar. Boil, without stirring, reducing heat a bit if it starts to boil over, for 8 to 10 minutes or until setting point is reached (for details, see page 19).

5. Remove from heat and skim off any foam.

6. Ladle quickly into sterilized jars to within ¼ inch (0.5 cm) of rim; wipe rims. Apply prepared lids and rings; tighten just until fingertip-tight.

7. Process jars in a boiling water canner for 10 minutes (for details, see page 20). Transfer jars to a towel-lined surface and let rest at room temperature until set. Check seals; refrigerate any unsealed jars for up to 3 weeks.

> Jellies are the ideal choice when you want to make preserves from fruits that have lots of seeds (as both red currants and raspberries do), since they'll get strained out with little effort on your part.

Red Plum Jelly

Makes about four 8-ounce (250 mL) jars

Red plums give a lot of color to this medium-red jelly, which is delicious as a glaze for fruit flans and tarts, such as French Apple Tarts (page 361).

— o o o —

Tip

In jellies, always use freshly squeezed lemon or lime juice that has been strained. This will keep the finished jellies clear.

- Jelly bag

2½ lbs	red plums, pitted and quartered	1.25 kg
	Water	
2 tbsp	strained lemon juice (see tip, at left)	30 mL
3½ cups	granulated sugar	875 mL

1. Place plums in a large, deep, heavy-bottomed pot; add enough water to cover. Bring to a boil over high heat. Reduce heat and simmer, covered, for about 20 minutes or until plums are softened. Use a potato masher to further break down plums; simmer for 5 minutes .

2. Pour into prepared jelly bag and let drip overnight, without squeezing (for details, see page 256).

3. Measure exactly 4 cups (1 L) of liquid (add water if there's not enough liquid); pour into clean pot. Stir in lemon juice. Bring to a full boil over high heat, stirring constantly.

4. Add sugar in a steady stream, stirring constantly. Return to a full boil, stirring constantly to dissolve sugar. Boil, without stirring, reducing heat a bit if it starts to boil over, for 8 to 10 minutes or until setting point is reached (for details, see page 19).

5. Remove from heat and skim off any foam.

6. Ladle quickly into sterilized jars to within ¼ inch (0.5 cm) of rim; wipe rims. Apply prepared lids and rings; tighten just until fingertip-tight.

7. Process jars in a boiling water canner for 10 minutes (for details, see page 20). Transfer jars to a towel-lined surface and let rest at room temperature until set. Check seals; refrigerate any unsealed jars for up to 3 weeks.

> Plums are not peeled for jam- or jelly-making. Their skins contribute a lovely color and flavor.

Red Plum Orange Jelly

**Makes about six
8-ounce (250 mL) jars**

*This jelly has a nice,
slightly tart flavor.*

— o o o —

Tip
Use a whisk to easily blend
in the powdered pectin.

- Jelly bag

3 lbs	red or black plums, chopped	1.5 kg
5	large oranges	5
	Pulp-free orange juice or water	
2 tbsp	strained lemon juice (see tip, page 275)	30 mL
1	package (1.75 oz/49 or 57 g) powdered pectin	1
5½ cups	granulated sugar	1.375 L

1. Place plums in a large, deep, heavy-bottomed pot.

2. Using a paring knife, remove rind from oranges in strips; place in pot. Cut oranges in half and squeeze juice into pot.

3. Bring to a boil over high heat. Reduce heat and simmer, covered, for about 20 minutes or until fruit is softened. Use a potato masher to further break down fruit; simmer for 5 minutes.

4. Pour into prepared jelly bag and let drip overnight, without squeezing (for details, see page 256).

5. Measure exactly 4 cups (1 L) of liquid (add orange juice if there's not enough liquid); pour into clean pot. Stir in lemon juice. Stir in pectin until dissolved. Bring to a full boil over high heat, stirring constantly.

6. Add sugar in a steady stream, stirring constantly. Return to a full boil, stirring constantly to dissolve sugar. Boil hard for 1 minute.

7. Remove from heat and skim off any foam.

8. Ladle quickly into sterilized jars to within ¼ inch (0.5 cm) of rim; wipe rims. Apply prepared lids and rings; tighten just until fingertip-tight.

9. Process jars in a boiling water canner for 10 minutes (for details, see page 20). Transfer jars to a towel-lined surface and let rest at room temperature until set. Check seals; refrigerate any unsealed jars for up to 3 weeks.

Rhubarb Jelly

Makes about five 8-ounce (250 mL) jars

For the best flavor and color, use rhubarb that is very red. If rhubarb is primarily green, add red plums, which will contribute additional color to the jelly.

— o o o —

Tip

One pound (500 g) of raw rhubarb yields about 3 cups (750 mL) chopped.

• Jelly bag

12 cups	chopped red rhubarb (½-inch/1 cm pieces)	3 L
2 cups	water	500 mL
2	red plums, thinly sliced (optional)	2
1	package (1.75 oz/49 or 57 g) powdered pectin	1
6 cups	granulated sugar	1.5 L

1. In a large, deep, heavy-bottomed pot, combine rhubarb, water and plums (if using). Bring to a boil over high heat. Reduce heat and simmer, covered, for 10 minutes or until fruit is softened. Use a potato masher to further break down fruit; simmer for 5 minutes.

2. Pour into prepared jelly bag and let drip overnight, without squeezing (for details, see page 256).

3. Measure exactly 4 cups (1 L) of liquid (add water if there's not enough liquid); pour into clean pot. Stir in pectin until dissolved. Bring to a full boil over high heat, stirring constantly.

4. Add sugar in a steady stream, stirring constantly. Return to a full boil, stirring constantly to dissolve sugar. Boil hard for 1 minute.

5. Remove from heat and skim off any foam.

6. Ladle quickly into sterilized jars to within ¼ inch (0.5 cm) of rim; wipe rims. Apply prepared lids and rings; tighten just until fingertip-tight.

7. Process jars in a boiling water canner for 10 minutes (for details, see page 20). Transfer jars to a towel-lined surface and let rest at room temperature until set. Check seals; refrigerate any unsealed jars for up to 3 weeks.

> Rhubarb, typically used as a fruit, is actually a vegetable of the buckwheat family.

Rose Hip Jelly

Makes about five 8-ounce (250 mL) jars

In the late summer, I came across an abundance of bush roses ripe with shiny red rose hips, the fruit of the rose plant. They have a tangy, tart flavor like cranberries (the taste is not at all like roses) and are rich in vitamin C. The seeds, with their tiny hairs, can be irritating (and it's an irritating job to remove them), so I prefer to make jelly, rather than jam, from rose hips.

— o o o —

Tip

In jellies, always use freshly squeezed lemon or lime juice that has been strained. This will keep the finished jellies clear.

- Jelly bag

16 cups	rose hips	4 L
	Water	
½ cup	strained lemon juice (see tip, at left)	125 mL
1	package (1.75 oz/49 or 57 g) powdered pectin	1
5¾ cups	granulated sugar	1.425 L

1. Rinse rose hips well; trim ends. Place rose hips in a large, deep, heavy-bottomed pot; add enough water to cover. Bring to a boil over high heat. Reduce heat and simmer, covered, for about 1 hour or until rose hips are softened. Use a potato masher to further break down rose hips; simmer for 10 minutes. Mash again.

2. Pour into prepared jelly bag and let drip overnight, without squeezing (for details, see page 256).

3. Measure exactly 4 cups (1 L) of liquid (add water if there's not enough liquid); pour into clean pot. Stir in lemon juice. Stir in pectin until dissolved. Bring to a full boil over high heat, stirring constantly.

4. Add sugar in a steady stream, stirring constantly. Return to a full boil, stirring constantly to dissolve sugar. Boil hard for 1 minute.

5. Remove from heat and skim off any foam.

6. Ladle quickly into sterilized jars to within ¼ inch (0.5 cm) of rim; wipe rims. Apply prepared lids and rings; tighten just until fingertip-tight.

Tips

You'll need about 6 lbs (3 kg) of rose hips for this recipe. Pick rose hips that are deep red and slightly soft. For the best flavor and the most juice, choose the biggest and reddest rose hips.

Some sources recommend picking rose hips after the first frost. If desired, pick when fully ripe, wash and freeze in plastic freezer bags or containers. Freezing helps them to release their juices.

Variations

Rose Hip and Roses Jelly: Follow Wine and Roses Jelly recipe (page 298), using 3 cups (750 mL) rose hip liquid in place of the wine to steep the rose petals in.

Rose Hip and Rose Water Jelly: Add ⅓ cup (75 mL) rose water with the lemon juice, or add 1 tbsp (15 mL) to each jar.

7. Process jars in a boiling water canner for 10 minutes (for details, see page 20). Transfer jars to a towel-lined surface and let rest at room temperature until set. Check seals; refrigerate any unsealed jars for up to 3 weeks.

Rose hips contain very little natural pectin, so commercial pectin is necessary to set jellies and jams made with them.

Rhuberry Jelly

**Makes about six
8-ounce (250 mL) jars**

*This jelly was designed
after a frozen-juice drink
called Rhuberry Frost,
which is no longer on
the market. It makes a
delicious glaze for fruit
flans and tarts.*

—○○○—

Tip

If desired, use frozen fruit for
this recipe. Always measure
fruit while still frozen and
let thaw before adding to
pot. If using frozen sliced
strawberries, increase to
5 cups (1.25 L).

• Jelly bag

6 cups	chopped rhubarb (1/2-inch/1 cm pieces)	1.5 L
4 cups	halved strawberries	1 L
1 1/2 cups	water	375 mL
1	orange, cut into wedges	1
2 tbsp	strained lemon juice (see tip, page 278)	30 mL
1	package (1.75 oz/49 or 57 g) powdered pectin	1
5 1/2 cups	granulated sugar	1.375 L

1. In a large, deep, heavy-bottomed pot, combine
   rhubarb, strawberries and water. Squeeze juice from
   orange wedges into pot; add wedges to pot. Bring
   to a boil over high heat. Reduce heat and simmer,
   covered, for 10 minutes or until fruit is softened. Use a
   potato masher to further break down fruit; simmer for
   5 minutes.

2. Pour into prepared jelly bag and let drip overnight,
   without squeezing (for details, see page 256).

3. Measure exactly 4 cups (1 L) of liquid (add water if
   there's not enough liquid); pour into clean pot. Stir in
   lemon juice. Stir in pectin until dissolved. Bring to a
   full boil over high heat, stirring constantly.

4. Add sugar in a steady stream, stirring constantly.
   Return to a full boil, stirring constantly to dissolve
   sugar. Boil hard for 1 minute.

5. Remove from heat and skim off any foam.

6. Ladle quickly into sterilized jars to within 1/4 inch
   (0.5 cm) of rim; wipe rims. Apply prepared lids and
   rings; tighten just until fingertip-tight.

7. Process jars in a boiling water canner for 10 minutes
   (for details, see page 20). Transfer jars to a towel-lined
   surface and let rest at room temperature until set. Check
   seals; refrigerate any unsealed jars for up to 3 weeks.

Savory Jellies

Savory jellies add a wealth of satisfying flavor that is sometimes lacking in our meals. They make great appetizers and condiments for meats, and can act as special flavoring ingredients in recipes. Although hot or sweet pepper jellies have bits of pepper in them, they are suspended in a clear jelly, so these preserves are classified as jellies. Also included in this section are recipes for garlic jellies, wine jellies and herb jellies (I used purple basil, rosemary, mint, lavender and lemon verbena). Savory jellies make great gifts.

"Campari with a Twist" Jelly 282
Mojito Jelly 283
Sangria Jelly 284
Tequila Sunrise Jelly. 285
Garlic Jelly. 286
Roasted Garlic Wine Jelly 287
Apple Jalapeño Pepper Jelly 288
Hot Cherry Pomegranate Jelly 289
Pineapple Habanero Pepper Jelly. 290
Red and Green Pepper Jelly 291
Fire and Ice Jelly 292
Cabernet Wine Jelly. 293
Kir Royale Jelly 294
Spiced Cranberry and Red Wine Jelly 295
Spiced Port Wine Jelly. 296
Strawberry Fields Wine Jelly. 297
Wine and Roses Jelly. 298
Purple Basil Wine Jelly. 299
Muscat Wine Jelly with Lemon Balm 300
Shiraz-Cabernet and Lemon Thyme Jelly 301
Lavender Jelly 302
Lemon Verbena Jelly 303
Mint Jelly. 304
Pineapple and Mint Jelly 305
Rosemary Apple Cider Jelly 306

"Campari with a Twist" Jelly

**Makes about four
8-ounce (250 mL)
jars or eight 4-ounce
(125 mL) jars**

*This slightly opaque,
strawberry red jelly has
an herbal taste. A half-
slice of lime is added to
the top to give recipients
a surprise when they
open the jar. If using the
smaller jars, increase
the lime halves to eight.*

— o o o —

Tip

For the orange juice, you
can use fresh-squeezed,
not from concentrate,
concentrate or pulp-free
from concentrate. Straining
the juice of pulp will help
keep the finished jelly from
looking cloudy.

1²⁄₃ cups	Campari	400 mL
1 cup	strained orange juice (see tip, at left)	250 mL
¼ cup	strained lime juice (see tip, page 278)	60 mL
2 tbsp	strained lemon juice	30 mL
2	thin lime slices (with peel), cut in half	2
3½ cups	granulated sugar	875 mL
1	pouch (3 oz/85 mL) liquid pectin	1
2 tbsp	brandy or orange liqueur (optional)	30 mL

1. In a large, deep, heavy-bottomed pot, combine Campari, orange juice, lime juice, lemon juice, lime halves and sugar. Bring to a full boil over high heat, stirring constantly.

2. Immediately stir in pectin; return to a full boil. Boil hard for 1 minute, stirring constantly.

3. Remove from heat and skim off any foam. Stir in brandy (if using). Use tongs or a fork to remove lime halves to a clean bowl.

4. Ladle quickly into sterilized jars to within ¼ inch (0.5 cm) of rim; wipe rims. Carefully place a half-slice of lime on the top of each jelly; submerge slightly to cover with jelly. Apply prepared lids and rings; tighten just until fingertip-tight.

5. Process jars in a boiling water canner for 10 minutes (for details, see page 20). Transfer jars to a towel-lined surface and let rest at room temperature until set. Check seals; refrigerate any unsealed jars for up to 3 weeks.

> Campari is a slightly bitter-tasting Italian aperitif, normally served with appetizers.

Mojito Jelly

A mojito (pronounced mo-hee-toe) is a popular Cuban drink made with fresh mint and rum. This pretty jelly is a variation on classic mint jelly, typically served with lamb.

— o o o —

Tip
See page 304 for info on mint varieties.

Recipe Suggestions
Serve this jelly as a condiment with shrimp, chicken or pork.

Place a dollop of Mojito Jelly on top of cream cheese spread on crackers.

Variations
Mexican Mojito Jelly: Use tequila in place of the rum.

Mint Julep Jelly: Use bourbon whiskey or brandy in place of the rum.

2 cups	loosely packed chopped fresh mint leaves	500 mL
3 cups	water	750 mL
1 tsp	finely grated lime rind (optional)	5 mL
½ cup	lime juice (with pulp)	125 mL
½ cup	white rum	125 mL
1	package (1.75 oz/49 to 57 g) powdered pectin	1
4¾ cups	granulated sugar	1.175 L
1 tbsp	finely chopped fresh mint	15 mL

1. In a large, deep, heavy-bottomed pot, combine the 2 cups (500 mL) chopped mint and water. Bring to a boil over high heat. Reduce heat and simmer, covered, for 15 minutes. Strain over a bowl, squeezing leaves; reserve liquid and discard leaves.

2. Measure exactly 2½ cups (625 mL) of liquid (add water if there's not enough liquid); pour into clean pot. Stir in lime rind (if using), lime juice and rum. Stir in pectin until dissolved. Bring to a full boil over high heat, stirring constantly.

3. Add sugar in a steady stream, stirring constantly. Return to a full boil, stirring constantly to dissolve sugar. Boil hard for 1 minute.

4. Remove from heat and skim off any foam. Stir in the 1 tbsp (15 mL) finely chopped mint. Stir for 5 to 8 minutes to prevent floating mint.

5. Ladle quickly into sterilized jars to within ¼ inch (0.5 cm) of rim; wipe rims. Apply prepared lids and rings; tighten just until fingertip-tight.

6. Process jars in a boiling water canner for 10 minutes (for details, see page 20). Transfer jars to a towel-lined surface and let rest at room temperature until set. Check seals; refrigerate any unsealed jars for up to 3 weeks.

Sangria Jelly

This fruity red wine jelly tastes like the delicious drink it is named after. Serve over cream cheese on crackers.

— o o o —

Variation

Sangria Blanco Jelly: Use a fruity, unoaked Chardonnay in place of the red wine. Replace the orange juice with white grape juice or peach-flavored white cranberry juice.

1½ cups	dry full-bodied red wine, such as Burgundy or Cabernet	375 mL
¾ cup	strained orange juice (see tip, page 282)	175 mL
2 tbsp	strained lemon or lime juice (see tip, page 285)	30 mL
3¼ cups	granulated sugar	800 mL
1	pouch (3 oz/85 mL) liquid pectin	1
2 tbsp	brandy or orange liqueur	30 mL

1. In a large, deep, heavy-bottomed pot, combine wine, orange juice, lemon juice and sugar. Bring to a full boil over high heat, stirring constantly.

2. Immediately stir in pectin; return to a full boil. Boil hard for 1 minute, stirring constantly.

3. Remove from heat and skim off any foam. Stir in brandy.

4. Ladle quickly into sterilized jars to within ¼ inch (0.5 cm) of rim; wipe rims. Apply prepared lids and rings; tighten just until fingertip-tight.

5. Process jars in a boiling water canner for 10 minutes (for details, see page 20). Transfer jars to a towel-lined surface and let rest at room temperature until set. Check seals; refrigerate any unsealed jars for up to 3 weeks.

> Taking its name from the Spanish word meaning "bloody," due to the dark red wine it is made from, sangria is a popular summer beverage in southern Portugal and Spain, as well as in Mexico. It is served in large pitchers with chopped fruit, brandy and ice.

Tequila Sunrise Jelly

**Makes about six
8-ounce (250 mL) jars**

*A tequila sunrise is
a cocktail that has a
graduated color effect,
starting with red at the
bottom, then orange
through the middle and
yellow toward the top.
This jelly tastes and looks
like its counterpart.*

— o o o —

Tip

In jellies, always use freshly
squeezed lemon or lime
juice that has been strained.
This will keep the finished
jellies clear.

3½ cups	strained orange juice (see tip, page 282)	875 mL
¾ cup	tequila	175 mL
½ cup	strained lime juice (see tip, at left)	75 mL
5½ cups	granulated sugar	1.375 L
2	pouches (each 3 oz/85 mL each) liquid pectin	2
¼ cup	grenadine syrup	60 mL

1. In a large, deep, heavy-bottomed pot, combine orange juice, tequila and lime juice. Bring to a full boil over high heat.

2. Add sugar in a steady stream, stirring constantly. Return to a full boil, stirring constantly to dissolve sugar.

3. Immediately stir in pectin; return to a full boil. Boil hard for 1 minute, stirring constantly.

4. Remove from heat and skim off any foam.

5. Ladle quickly into sterilized jars to within ¼ inch (0.5 cm) of rim. Add about 2 tsp (10 mL) grenadine syrup to each jar (it will sink to the bottom). Stir slightly with a small spoon to get the sunrise effect. Wipe rims. Apply prepared lids and rings; tighten just until fingertip-tight.

6. Process jars in a boiling water canner for 10 minutes (for details, see page 20). Transfer jars to a towel-lined surface and let rest at room temperature until set. Check seals; refrigerate any unsealed jars for up to 3 weeks.

Garlic Jelly

Makes about four 8-ounce (250 mL) jars or eight 4-ounce (125 mL) jars

My sister-in-law Joanne was mad for this jelly after tasting it, so she and her sisters made it to give as Christmas gifts one year. It's a great condiment for chicken, beef or pork, or it can be used to deglaze the pan — just add wine to create a tasty sauce. If desired, place a sprig of rosemary in each jar before adding the jelly.

— o o o —

Tip
A food processor makes finely mincing the large amount of garlic an easy task.

Recipe Suggestions
Use this jelly to glaze roast chicken or to make Garlic Chicken Portobello (page 351).

Serve with cream cheese on crackers.

2 cups	unsweetened apple juice, white wine or water	500 mL
1 cup	cider vinegar or white wine vinegar	250 mL
1/4 cup	finely minced garlic	60 mL
4 cups	granulated sugar	1 L
1	pouch (3 oz/85 mL) liquid pectin	1

1. In a large, deep, heavy-bottomed pot, combine apple juice, vinegar and garlic. Bring to a boil over high heat. Reduce heat and simmer, covered, for 5 minutes.

2. Measure exactly $2\frac{1}{2}$ cups (625 mL) of liquid (adding water if there's not enough liquid); pour into clean pot. Bring to a full boil over high heat, stirring constantly.

3. Add sugar in a steady stream, stirring constantly. Return to a full boil, stirring constantly to dissolve sugar.

4. Immediately stir in pectin; return to a full boil. Boil hard for 1 minute, stirring constantly.

5. Remove from heat and skim off any foam. Stir for 5 to 8 minutes to prevent floating garlic (some garlic may settle to the bottom as it cools).

6. Ladle quickly into prepared jars to within $\frac{1}{4}$ inch (0.5 cm) of rim; wipe rims. Apply prepared lids and rings; tighten just until fingertip-tight.

7. Process jars in a boiling water canner for 10 minutes (for details, see page 20). Transfer jars to a towel-lined surface and let rest at room temperature until set. Check seals; refrigerate any unsealed jars for up to 3 weeks.

Roasted Garlic Wine Jelly

*Roasting garlic makes it
mellow, and this opaque
savory jelly has a mild
garlic flavor. The amount
of garlic can be increased
to 1/2 cup (125 mL) for
a more intense taste. I
used a Gewürztraminer
wine with the description
"complements pâtés,
cheeses and desserts…
spicy aroma and exotic
taste of peach and
mango." Choose a wine
you would enjoy drinking
that also complements the
food it is to be served with.*

— o o o —

Tips

How to Roast Garlic: Slice
about 1/2 inch (1 cm) off
the top of 3 large heads of
garlic to expose the cloves.
Place cut side up on a
double layer of foil; drizzle
with a little olive oil. Fold
foil over to seal. Bake in a
preheated 350°F (180°C)
oven for about 45 minutes,
or until softened. Press
garlic through a fine-mesh
sieve set over a bowl, using
a large spoon or a rubber
or silicone spatula; discard
paper skins.

3 cups	white wine	750 mL
1/4 cup	roasted garlic (see tip, at left), or to taste	60 mL
1	package (1.75 oz/49 or 57 g) powdered pectin	1
3 1/4 cups	granulated sugar	800 mL

1. In a large, deep, heavy-bottomed pot, combine wine and roasted garlic. Stir in pectin until dissolved. Bring to a full boil over high heat, stirring constantly.

2. Add sugar in a steady stream, stirring constantly. Return to a full boil, stirring constantly to dissolve sugar. Boil hard for 1 minute.

3. Remove from heat and skim off any foam.

4. Ladle quickly into sterilized jars to within 1/4 inch (0.5 cm) of rim; wipe rims. Apply prepared lids and rings; tighten just until fingertip-tight.

5. Process jars in a boiling water canner for 10 minutes (for details, see page 20). Transfer jars to a towel-lined surface and let rest at room temperature until set. Check seals; refrigerate any unsealed jars for up to 3 weeks.

> I noticed the mixture bubbling in the jar after I removed this jelly from the canner. If desired, process for 5 minutes only, but ensure that the jars are fully sterilized and that care is taken when bottling to prevent contamination.

Apple Jalapeño Pepper Jelly

*Pepper jelly served
over cream cheese with
crackers is a popular
appetizer at gatherings.
Try this one as a finishing
glaze brushed on pork
or chicken in the latter
stages of cooking,
or as a condiment
alongside them.*

— o o o —

Tips

Supermarkets now carry
all-natural (or pure-pressed)
apple juice, which contains
solids. Shake before using.

As you skim off foam, there
is a tendency to remove
the chopped pepper pieces
along with it. To prevent the
loss of the peppers, spoon
the foam into a mesh sieve
and rinse with hot water.
Blot well with paper towels
and return any peppers to
the pot.

You may have to stir for
longer than 8 minutes to
prevent floating peppers
in this recipe. To test for
floating, fill one jar; let rest
for 1 minute. If peppers
start to float upward, pour
jelly back into pot and keep
stirring; begin again with a
new sterilized jar.

3½ cups	all-natural apple juice (see tip, at left) or unsweetened apple cider (approx.)	875 mL
¾ cup	cider vinegar	175 mL
⅔ cup	finely chopped jalapeño peppers	150 mL
1	package (1.75 oz/49 or 57 g) powdered pectin	1
4¾ cups	granulated sugar	1.175 L

1. In a large, deep, heavy-bottomed pot, combine apple juice, vinegar and jalapeños. Bring to a boil over high heat. Reduce heat and simmer, covered, for 20 minutes.

2. Measure exactly 3¾ cups (925 mL) of liquid (adding more apple juice if there's not enough liquid); pour into clean pot. Stir in pectin until dissolved. Bring to a full boil over high heat, stirring constantly.

3. Add sugar in a steady stream, stirring constantly. Return to a full boil, stirring constantly to dissolve sugar. Boil hard for 1 minute.

4. Remove from heat and skim off any foam. Stir for 5 to 8 minutes to prevent floating peppers (see tip, at left).

5. Ladle quickly into sterilized jars to within ¼ inch (0.5 cm) of rim; wipe rims. Apply prepared lids and rings; tighten just until fingertip-tight.

6. Process jars in a boiling water canner for 10 minutes (for details, see page 20). Transfer jars to a towel-lined surface and let rest at room temperature until set. Check seals; refrigerate any unsealed jars for up to 3 weeks.

Hot Cherry Pomegranate Jelly

*Unsweetened 100%
pomegranate juice is
sold in supermarkets
and has no added sugar.
Alternatively, you can
extract juice from
pomegranate seeds
yourself (see page 29).*

— ○○○ —

Variations

Hot Cherry Jelly: Omit
the pomegranate juice.
Use a total of 4 cups
(1 L) cherry juice.

*Hot Cherry Cinnamon
Jelly:* Add one 5-inch
(12.5 cm) cinnamon
stick with the hot pepper
flakes. Remove the
cinnamon stick after
skimming off foam, or
pour mixture through
a fine-mesh sieve to
remove pepper flakes
too. Alternatively, stir in
2 tbsp (30 mL) cinnamon
liqueur after skimming off
foam.

*Sweet Cherry
Pomegranate Jelly:* Omit
the hot pepper flakes.

*Hot Cherry Balsamic
Jelly:* Replace ¼ cup
(60 mL) of the cherry or
pomegranate juice with
balsamic vinegar.

3 cups	sour cherry juice	750 mL
1 cup	unsweetened 100% pomegranate or apple juice	250 mL
1	package (1.75 oz/49 or 57 g) powdered pectin	1
2 tsp	hot pepper flakes (or 2 tbsp/30 mL minced jalapeño peppers), or to taste	10 mL
5½ cups	granulated sugar	1.375 L

1. In a large, deep, heavy-bottomed pot, combine cherry juice and pomegranate juice. Stir in pectin until dissolved. Stir in hot pepper flakes. Bring to a full boil over high heat, stirring constantly.

2. Add sugar in a steady stream, stirring constantly. Return to a full boil, stirring constantly to dissolve sugar. Boil hard for 1 minute.

3. Remove from heat and skim off any foam. Stir for 5 to 8 minutes to prevent floating pepper flakes. (If desired, pour mixture through a fine-mesh sieve to remove pepper flakes and omit this stirring step.)

4. Ladle quickly into sterilized jars to within ¼ inch (0.5 cm) of rim; wipe rims. Apply prepared lids and rings; tighten just until fingertip-tight.

5. Process jars in a boiling water canner for 10 minutes (for details, see page 20). Transfer jars to a towel-lined surface and let rest at room temperature until set. Check seals; refrigerate any unsealed jars for up to 3 weeks.

> *How to Make Fresh Sour Cherry Juice:* Use 16 cups (4 L) fresh sour (tart) cherries. Remove stems, but leave pits. Place cherries in a large pot and crush slightly with a potato masher to release juices. Add 1 cup (250 mL) water; bring to a boil over high heat. Reduce heat and simmer, covered, for 5 minutes. Crush further with masher; simmer for 5 minutes. Strain through a jelly bag. (Or, if you buy pitted cherries in a pail, simply drain the juice.)

Pineapple Habanero Pepper Jelly

This pretty and potent jelly uses habanero peppers, named after the Cuban city La Habana (Havana in English). You could also use Scotch bonnet peppers. Both peppers come in a variety of solid and variegated colors — red, orange, yellow and green.

— o o o —

Tips

Wear latex gloves while chopping hot peppers, and be careful not to touch your eyes, mouth or skin.

As you skim off foam, there is a tendency to remove the minced pepper pieces along with it. To prevent the loss of the peppers, spoon the foam into a mesh sieve and rinse with hot water. Blot well with paper towels and return peppers to the pot.

Variation

Orange Habanero Pepper Jelly: Use pulp-free frozen orange juice concentrate (thawed) instead of pineapple juice concentrate.

½ cup	finely minced habanero peppers	125 mL
1¼ cups	frozen pineapple juice concentrate, thawed	300 mL
1¼ cups	water	300 mL
½ cup	white vinegar	125 mL
6 cups	granulated sugar	1.5 L
2	pouches (each 3 oz/85 mL) liquid pectin	2

1. In a large, deep, heavy-bottomed pot, combine habaneros, pineapple juice concentrate, water, vinegar and sugar. Bring to a boil over high heat, stirring constantly. Reduce heat and simmer, covered, for 20 minutes, stirring occasionally.

2. Remove lid. Increase heat to high and bring to a full boil, stirring constantly. Immediately stir in pectin; return to a full boil. Boil hard for 1 minute, stirring constantly.

3. Remove from heat and skim off any foam. Stir for 5 to 8 minutes to prevent floating peppers.

4. Ladle quickly into sterilized jars to within ¼ inch (0.5 cm) of rim; wipe rims. Apply prepared lids and rings; tighten just until fingertip-tight.

5. Process jars in a boiling water canner for 10 minutes (for details, see page 20). Transfer jars to a towel-lined surface and let rest at room temperature until set. Check seals; refrigerate any unsealed jars for up to 3 weeks.

> Scoville units (developed by Wilbur Scoville in 1912) indicate the hotness of chile peppers by measuring the amount of capsaicin (pronounced cap-say-sin) they contain. On this scale, habaneros (100,000 to 500,000 units) can be as much as 100 times hotter than jalapeño peppers (5,000 to 10,000 units). On another note, pepper spray, made from capsaicin, has a rating of about 5 million units.

Red and Green Pepper Jelly

*This attractive jelly has
suspended bits of red
and green bell pepper (it
can also be made with all
red or all green peppers).
If you follow these
instructions, you should
have no problem with
floating peppers. Serve
over cream cheese on
crackers as an appetizer
or a snack.*

——— o o o ———

Tip

To test for floating, fill one
jar; let rest for 1 minute. If
peppers start to float upward,
pour jelly back into pot and
keep stirring; begin again
with a new sterilized jar.

1 cup	finely chopped red bell peppers	250 mL
1 cup	finely chopped green bell peppers	250 mL
1 or 2	jalapeño peppers, minced (optional)	1 or 2
1½ cups	cider vinegar	375 mL
½ tsp	hot pepper sauce or (¼ tsp/1 mL hot pepper flakes)	2 mL
6½ cups	granulated sugar	1.625 L
2	pouches (3 oz/85 mL each) liquid pectin	2

1. In a large, deep, heavy-bottomed pot, combine red peppers, green peppers, jalapeño peppers, vinegar, hot pepper sauce and sugar. Bring to a boil over medium heat, stirring constantly. Reduce heat and boil gently for 5 minutes. Remove from heat and let stand for 20 minutes, stirring occasionally.

2. Bring to a full boil over high heat, stirring constantly. Immediately stir in pectin; return to a full boil. Boil hard for 1 minute, stirring constantly.

3. Remove from heat and skim off any foam. Stir for 5 to 8 minutes to prevent floating peppers.

4. Ladle quickly into prepared jars to within ¼ inch (0.5 cm) of rim; wipe rims. Apply prepared lids and rings; tighten just until fingertip-tight.

5. Process jars in a boiling water canner for 10 minutes (for details, see page 20). Transfer jars to a towel-lined surface and let rest at room temperature until set. Check seals; refrigerate any unsealed jars for up to 3 weeks.

> Hot pepper jellies are very popular and make great holiday or host/hostess gifts.

Fire and Ice Jelly

*This delicious hot pepper
jelly uses Canada's
renowned ice wine. Turn
up the heat to suit your
own taste with additional
hot pepper flakes or
cayenne pepper.*

— o o o —

Recipe Suggestions

Serve over cream cheese
and crackers.

Brush over roasted chicken
to glaze it.

Spread on a roast chicken
or turkey sandwich.

¾ cup	minced red bell pepper	175 mL
1	bottle (375 mL) ice wine or sweet dessert wine	1
¼ cup	strained lemon juice (see tip, page 285)	60 mL
2 tsp	hot pepper flakes	10 mL
3½ cups	granulated sugar	875 mL
1	pouch (3 oz/85 mL) liquid pectin	1

1. In a large, deep, heavy-bottomed pot, combine red pepper, wine, lemon juice, hot pepper flakes and sugar. Bring to a full boil over high heat, stirring constantly; boil hard for 1 minute. Remove from heat and let stand for 20 minutes, stirring occasionally.

2. Return to a full boil over high heat, stirring constantly. Immediately stir in pectin; return to a full boil. Boil hard for 1 minute, stirring constantly.

3. Remove from heat and skim off any foam. Stir for 5 to 8 minutes to prevent floating peppers.

4. Ladle quickly into sterilized jars to within ¼ inch (0.5 cm) of rim; wipe rims. Apply prepared lids and rings; tighten just until fingertip-tight.

5. Process jars in a boiling water canner for 10 minutes (for details, see page 20). Transfer jars to a towel-lined surface and let rest at room temperature until set. Check seals; refrigerate any unsealed jars for up to 3 weeks.

> Canada is the largest ice wine producer in the world, due to the consistently cold temperature necessary for its production. The grapes are gathered and pressed at a temperature no higher than 18°F (–8°C). Canada produces more than 2 million bottles of ice wine annually.

Cabernet Wine Jelly

Makes about seven 4-ounce (125 mL) jars

3¼ cups	granulated sugar	800 mL
2 cups	Cabernet wine, or any other red or white wine, divided	500 mL
1	pouch (3 oz/85 mL) liquid pectin	1

This recipe from Shirley McMurray (see Contributors, page 12) uses a Cabernet wine. You may want to choose a wine that matches one you are planning to serve on a special occasion. Shirley says that reserving some of the wine to add after the sugar is dissolved helps the jelly retain the flavor of the wine. Her jellies are sold under the name The Jelly Crate in the Niagara region of Ontario, Canada.

— o o o —

Tip

Serve wine jelly at a wine and cheese gathering with soft cheeses such as Brie or Camembert. Accompany with slices of apples and pears and walnut halves for an inviting platter.

1. In a large, deep, heavy-bottomed pot, combine sugar and 1 cup (250 mL) of the wine. Bring almost to a boil over medium-high heat, stirring constantly to dissolve sugar. When sugar is dissolved, add the remaining wine. Bring to a full boil over high heat, stirring constantly.

2. Immediately stir in pectin; return to a full boil. Boil hard for 1 minute, stirring constantly.

3. Remove from heat and skim off any foam.

4. Ladle quickly into sterilized jars to within ¼ inch (0.5 cm) of rim; wipe rims. Apply prepared lids and rings; tighten just until fingertip-tight.

5. Process jars in a boiling water canner for 10 minutes (for details, see page 20). Transfer jars to a towel-lined surface and let rest at room temperature until set. Check seals; refrigerate any unsealed jars for up to 3 weeks.

Kir Royale Jelly

Makes about nine 4-ounce (125 mL) jars

Kir is a wine cocktail traditionally made with crème de cassis (black currant liqueur) and white wine; Kir Royale uses Champagne instead of wine. This jelly is pleasantly sweet, with a translucent red color. It can be used as a glaze for fruit flans.

— ○ ○ ○ —

Variations

Kir Jelly: Use a dry white wine, such as Chablis, in place of the Champagne.

Kir Imperial Jelly: Use raspberry liqueur, such as Chambord, instead of the crème de cassis.

3 cups	Champagne or sparkling white wine (such as Asti)	750 mL
1/3 cup	crème de cassis or black currant nectar concentrate, such as Ribena	75 mL
1	package (1.75 oz/49 or 57 g) powdered pectin	1
3¾ cup	granulated sugar	925 mL

1. In a large, deep, heavy-bottomed pot, combine Champagne and crème de cassis. Stir in pectin until dissolved. Bring to a full boil over high heat, stirring constantly.

2. Add sugar in a steady stream, stirring constantly. Return to a full boil, stirring constantly to dissolve sugar. Boil hard for 1 minute.

3. Remove from heat and skim off any foam.

4. Ladle quickly into sterilized jars to within ¼ inch (0.5 cm) of rim; wipe rims. Apply prepared lids and rings; tighten just until fingertip-tight.

5. Process jars in a boiling water canner for 10 minutes (for details, see page 20). Transfer jars to a towel-lined surface and let rest at room temperature until set. Check seals; refrigerate any unsealed jars for up to 3 weeks.

> Kir is named after Canon Félix Kir, a priest who was a hero of the French resistance during the Second World War and acted as the mayor of Dijon, in Burgundy, France, from 1945 to 1968 (he died in his 90s).

Spiced Cranberry and Red Wine Jelly

Shirley McMurray (see Contributors, page 12) serves this jelly with her Thanksgiving and Christmas turkeys, chicken or pork chops.

— o o o —

Tip

Jellies can set very quickly. Pour immediately (while still hot) into jars to prevent bubbles from forming in the jelly.

3¼ cups	granulated sugar	800 mL
1 cup	cranberry juice	250 mL
1 tsp	ground cinnamon	5 mL
½ tsp	ground cloves	2 mL
¼ tsp	ground nutmeg	1 mL
1 cup	red wine	250 mL
1	pouch (3 oz/85 mL) liquid pectin	1

1. In a large, deep, heavy-bottomed pot, combine sugar, cranberry juice, cinnamon, cloves and nutmeg. Bring almost to a boil over medium-high heat, stirring constantly to dissolve sugar. When sugar is dissolved, add wine. Bring to a full boil over high heat, stirring constantly.

2. Immediately stir in pectin; return to a full boil. Boil hard for 1 minute, stirring constantly.

3. Remove from heat and skim off any foam.

4. Ladle quickly into sterilized jars to within ¼ inch (0.5 cm) of rim; wipe rims. Apply prepared lids and rings; tighten just until fingertip-tight.

5. Process jars in a boiling water canner for 10 minutes (for details, see page 20). Transfer jars to a towel-lined surface and let rest at room temperature until set. Check seals; refrigerate any unsealed jars for up to 3 weeks.

Spiced Port Wine Jelly

This jelly, created by Shirley McMurray (see Contributors, page 12), is delicious over cream cheese and crackers, served along with a peppercorn pâté.

— o o o —

Variation

Port Wine Jelly: Omit the spices.

3¼ cups	granulated sugar	800 mL
2 cups	port wine, divided	500 mL
¼ tsp	ground cinnamon	1 mL
Pinch	ground cloves	Pinch
Pinch	ground nutmeg	Pinch
1	pouch (3 oz/85 mL) liquid pectin	1

1. In a large, deep, heavy-bottomed pot, combine sugar, 1 cup (250 mL) of the wine, cinnamon, cloves and nutmeg. Bring almost to a boil over medium-high heat, stirring constantly to dissolve sugar. When sugar is dissolved, add the remaining wine. Bring to a full boil over high heat, stirring occasionally.

2. Immediately stir in pectin; return to a full boil. Boil hard for 1 minute, stirring constantly.

3. Remove from heat and skim off any foam.

4. Ladle quickly into sterilized jars to within ¼ inch (0.5 cm) of rim; wipe rims. Apply prepared lids and rings; tighten just until fingertip-tight.

5. Process jars in a boiling water canner for 10 minutes (for details, see page 20). Transfer jars to a towel-lined surface and let rest at room temperature until set. Check seals; refrigerate any unsealed jars for up to 3 weeks.

Strawberry Fields Wine Jelly

Makes about nine 4-ounce (125 mL) jars

Wines made from fruit other than grapes (not fruit-flavored wines) are becoming popular. Strawberry fruit wine has an intense strawberry flavor that shines in this light pink jelly. Use as a glaze for chicken or pork.

—○○○—

Tip

You can substitute other berry wines (blueberry, raspberry, cranberry) or fruit wines (peach, pear and apple) for the strawberry wine in this recipe.

1	bottle (750 mL) strawberry fruit wine	1
4¼ cups	granulated sugar	1.05 L
1	pouch (3 oz/85 mL) liquid pectin	1

1. In a large, deep, heavy-bottomed pot, combine wine and sugar. Bring to a full boil over high heat, stirring constantly to dissolve sugar.

2. Immediately stir in pectin; return to a full boil. Boil hard for 1 minute, stirring constantly.

3. Remove from heat and skim off any foam.

4. Ladle quickly into sterilized jars to within ¼ inch (0.5 cm) of rim; wipe rims. Apply prepared lids and rings; tighten just until fingertip-tight.

5. Process jars in a boiling water canner for 10 minutes (for details, see page 20). Transfer jars to a towel-lined surface and let rest at room temperature until set. Check seals; refrigerate any unsealed jars for up to 3 weeks.

Wine and Roses Jelly

*This attractive jelly, with
rose petals suspended in
a clear pink jelly, makes
a wonderful gift. To fully
appreciate its delicate
flavor and fragrance,
serve it with Cream Tea
Scones (page 353).*

—ooo—

Tips

Use only roses that have
not been sprayed with
pesticides or insecticides.
You may use roses you
grow yourself, but not
commercial roses, unless
they are specifically labeled
as organic.

To test for floating, fill one
jar; let rest for 1 minute. If
petals start to float upward,
pour jelly back into pot and
keep stirring; begin again
with a new sterilized jar.

Variation

*Wine and Roses Jelly
with Rose Water: Add
2 tbsp (30 mL) rose water
with the lemon juice.*

2½ cups	loosely packed organic pink or red rose petals (see tip, at left), white or yellow tips removed, divided	625 mL
3 cups	white wine, rosé wine, white Zinfandel, sparkling wine or Champagne	750 mL
2 tbsp	strained lemon juice (see tip, page 303)	30 mL
3½ cups	granulated sugar	875 mL
1	pouch (3 oz/85 mL) liquid pectin	1

1. In a large, deep, heavy-bottomed pot, combine 2 cups (500 mL) of the rose petals and wine. Bring to a boil over high heat. Reduce heat and simmer, covered, for 5 minutes. Strain over a bowl, squeezing petals; reserve liquid and discard petals.

2. Add lemon juice to liquid. Measure exactly 2½ cups (625 mL) of liquid (add water if there's not enough liquid); pour into clean pot. Bring to a full boil over high heat, stirring constantly.

3. Add sugar in a steady stream, stirring constantly. Return to a full boil, stirring constantly to dissolve sugar.

4. Immediately stir in pectin; return to a full boil. Boil hard for 1 minute, stirring constantly.

5. Remove from heat and skim off any foam. Stir in the remaining rose petals. Stir for 5 to 8 minutes to prevent floating petals.

6. Ladle quickly into sterilized jars to within ¼ inch (0.5 cm) of rim; wipe rims. Apply prepared lids and rings; tighten just until fingertip-tight.

7. Process jars in a boiling water canner for 10 minutes (for details, see page 20). Transfer jars to a towel-lined surface and let rest at room temperature until set. Check seals; refrigerate any unsealed jars for up to 3 weeks.

Purple Basil Wine Jelly

*Purple basil (also called
opal basil or Purple
Ruffles) has deep reddish-
purple leaves. When it
is infused in white wine,
the wine turns a beautiful
red. This herb jelly smells
sweetly of basil, yet the
flavor is more subtle
than that of a jelly made
with Italian (Genovese)
green basil.*

— o o o —

3 cups	dry white wine	750 mL
1½ cups	loosely packed purple basil leaves	375 mL
1 tbsp	white wine vinegar	15 mL
4 cups	granulated sugar	1 L
1	pouch (3 oz/85 mL) liquid pectin	1

1. In a large, deep, heavy-bottomed pot, bring wine to a boil over high heat. Stir in basil. Reduce heat and simmer, covered, for 5 minutes. Remove from heat and let steep for 5 minutes. Strain over a bowl, squeezing leaves; reserve liquid and discard leaves.

2. Measure exactly 3 cups (750 mL) of liquid (add water if there's not enough liquid); pour into clean pot. Stir in vinegar. Bring to a full boil over high heat, stirring constantly.

3. Add sugar in a steady stream, stirring constantly. Return to a full boil, stirring constantly to dissolve sugar.

4. Immediately stir in pectin; return to a full boil. Boil hard for 1 minute, stirring constantly.

5. Remove from heat and skim off any foam.

6. Ladle quickly into sterilized jars to within ¼ inch (0.5 cm) of rim; wipe rims. Apply prepared lids and rings; tighten just until fingertip-tight.

7. Process jars in a boiling water canner for 10 minutes (for details, see page 20). Transfer jars to a towel-lined surface and let rest at room temperature until set. Check seals; refrigerate any unsealed jars for up to 3 weeks.

> Purple basil is often difficult to find in grocery stores but is easy to grow in your garden in the summer. Plant bedding plants (or start indoors from seeds) once the ground is warm enough outside. It likes lots of sun and well-drained soil. Prune to stimulate leaf production and pinch off flower heads as they form to keep up the production of volatile oils in the leaves.

Muscat Wine Jelly with Lemon Balm

Makes about four 8-ounce (250 mL) jars

This jelly's inspiration comes from a refreshing summer drink of white wine and lemon balm leaves over ice. I made it after finding lemon balm growing in my backyard when I moved to a new house.

— o o o —

Tip

Muscat is a slightly sweet white wine with an almost peach-like fragrance. The aromatic Gewürztraminer is also a good wine for this jelly.

Variation

White Grape Jelly with Lemon Balm: Replace the wine with white grape juice.

3 cups	Muscat wine	750 mL
1 cup	loosely packed coarsely chopped fresh lemon balm leaves	250 mL
1	package (1.75 oz/49 or 57 g) powdered pectin	1
4 cups	granulated sugar	1 L
2 tbsp	finely chopped fresh lemon balm leaves	30 mL

1. In a large, deep, heavy-bottomed pot, combine wine and the 1 cup (250 mL) coarsely chopped lemon balm. Bring to a boil over high heat. Reduce heat and simmer, covered, for 5 minutes. Strain over a bowl, squeezing leaves; reserve liquid and discard leaves.

2. Measure exactly 2¾ cups (675 mL) of liquid (add water if there's not enough liquid); pour into clean pot. Stir in pectin until dissolved. Bring to a full boil over high heat.

3. Add sugar in a steady stream, stirring constantly. Return to a full boil, stirring constantly to dissolve sugar. Boil hard for 1 minute.

4. Remove from heat and skim off any foam. Stir in the 2 tbsp (30 mL) finely chopped lemon balm.

5. Ladle quickly into sterilized jars to within ¼ inch (0.5 cm) of rim; wipe rims. Apply prepared lids and rings; tighten just until fingertip-tight.

6. Process jars in a boiling water canner for 10 minutes (for details, see page 20). Transfer jars to a towel-lined surface and let rest at room temperature until set. Check seals; refrigerate any unsealed jars for up to 3 weeks.

> Lemon balm, also called sweet Melissa, is a member of the mint family. Like other mints, it is a perennial. It will take over in your garden if it is not contained!

Shiraz–Cabernet and Lemon Thyme Jelly

Shiraz-Cabernet wine has notes of black pepper and cedar (from the Shiraz) and hints of smoky plum, black currant and vanilla (from the Cabernet). Read the label on the bottle for a flavor description of the wine and choose one that appeals to you.

— o o o —

Tips

Use kitchen scissors to cut lemon thyme into tiny sprigs.

The small jars used for this jelly are great for gift-giving.

3 cups	Shiraz-Cabernet wine	750 mL
1 cup	loosely packed small fresh lemon thyme sprigs (or 1/4 cup/60 mL regular thyme), large stems removed	250 mL
2 tbsp	strained lemon juice (see tip, page 303)	30 mL
1	package (1.75 oz/49 or 57 g) powdered pectin	1
3 1/4 cups	granulated sugar	800 mL

1. In a large, deep, heavy-bottomed pot, combine wine and lemon thyme. Bring to a boil over high heat. Reduce heat and simmer, covered, for 5 minutes, stirring occasionally. Strain over a bowl, squeezing leaves; reserve liquid and discard leaves.

2. Measure exactly 2 1/2 cups (625 mL) of liquid (add water if there's not enough liquid); pour into clean pot. Stir in lemon juice. Stir in pectin until dissolved. Bring to a full boil over high heat, stirring constantly.

3. Add sugar in a steady stream, stirring constantly. Return to a full boil, stirring constantly to dissolve sugar. Boil hard for 1 minute.

4. Remove from heat and skim off any foam.

5. Ladle quickly into sterilized jars to within 1/4 inch (0.5 cm) of rim; wipe rims. Apply prepared lids and rings; tighten just until fingertip-tight.

6. Process jars in a boiling water canner for 10 minutes (for details, see page 20). Transfer jars to a towel-lined surface and let rest at room temperature until set. Check seals; refrigerate any unsealed jars for up to 3 weeks.

Lavender Jelly

*This jelly has a beautiful
mauve color and a
delicate flavor, scented
with lavender. Try it on
scones, stir it into fresh
fruit, or use it to glaze
a fruit flan or tart.*

— o o o —

Tip

The flavor of lavender
goes well with lemons,
oranges, apples, peaches,
strawberries, raspberries
and blueberries.

4 cups	water	1 L
1 cup	fresh organic lavender blossom clusters	250 mL
¼ cup	strained lemon juice (see tip, page 303)	60 mL
1	package (1.75 oz/49 or 57 g) powdered pectin	1
5⅔ cups	granulated sugar	1.65 L

1. In a large, deep, heavy-bottomed pot, combine water and lavender. Bring to a boil over high heat. Reduce heat and simmer, covered, for 20 minutes. Strain over a bowl, squeezing flowers; reserve liquid and discard flowers.

2. Measure exactly 2½ cups (625 mL) of liquid (add water if there's not enough liquid); pour into clean pot. Stir in lemon juice. Stir in pectin until dissolved. Bring to a full boil over high heat, stirring constantly.

3. Add sugar in a steady stream, stirring constantly. Return to a full boil, stirring constantly to dissolve sugar. Boil hard for 1 minute.

4. Remove from heat and skim off any foam.

5. Ladle quickly into sterilized jars to within ¼ inch (0.5 cm) of rim; wipe rims. Apply prepared lids and rings; tighten just until fingertip-tight.

6. Process jars in a boiling water canner for 10 minutes (for details, see page 20). Transfer jars to a towel-lined surface and let rest at room temperature until set. Check seals; refrigerate any unsealed jars for up to 3 weeks.

Lemon Verbena Jelly

Makes about six 4-ounce (125 mL) jars

This clear, lemony herb jelly goes well with chicken, pork, veal or lamb, as a glaze or served alongside. Or stir it into sauces made from pan drippings. It is also tasty on biscuits, as a glaze for fruit flans or tarts, or stirred into hot tea.

— o o o —

Tip

In jellies, always use freshly squeezed lemon juice that has been strained. This will keep the finished jellies clear.

3 cups	water	750 mL
1½ cups	loosely packed torn lemon verbena leaves	375 mL
2 tbsp	strained lemon juice (see tip, at left)	30 mL
1	package (1.75 oz/49 or 57 g) powdered pectin	1
3 cups	granulated sugar	750 mL

1. In a large, deep, heavy-bottomed pot, combine water and lemon verbena leaves. Bring to a boil over high heat. Reduce heat and simmer, covered, for 5 minutes. Strain over a bowl, squeezing leaves; reserve liquid and discard leaves.

2. Measure exactly 2½ cups (625 mL) of liquid (add water if there's not enough liquid); pour into clean pot. Stir in lemon juice. Stir in pectin until dissolved. Bring to a full boil over high heat, stirring constantly.

3. Add sugar in a steady stream, stirring constantly. Return to a full boil, stirring constantly to dissolve sugar. Boil hard for 1 minute.

4. Remove from heat and skim off any foam.

5. Ladle quickly into sterilized jars to within ¼ inch (0.5 cm) of rim; wipe rims. Apply prepared lids and rings; tighten just until fingertip-tight.

6. Process jars in a boiling water canner for 10 minutes (for details, see page 20). Transfer jars to a towel-lined surface and let rest at room temperature until set. Check seals; refrigerate any unsealed jars for up to 3 weeks.

Mint Jelly

Makes about four 8-ounce (250 mL) jars or eight 4-ounce (125 mL) jars

This is a classic mint jelly, typically served with lamb. I usually make it with spearmint, but it can be made with any variety of mint.

— o o o —

2½ cups	water	625 mL
2 cups	loosely packed whole mint leaves	500 mL
¾ cup	cider vinegar	175 mL
1	package (1.75 oz/49 or 57 g) powdered pectin	1
4 cups	granulated sugar	1 L
½ cup	finely chopped mint leaves (optional)	125 mL
	Green food coloring (optional)	

1. In a large, deep, heavy-bottomed pot, combine water and whole mint leaves. Bring to a boil over high heat. Reduce heat and simmer, covered, for 15 minutes. Strain over a bowl, squeezing leaves; reserve liquid and discard leaves.

2. Measure exactly 2 cups (500 mL) of liquid (add water if there's not enough liquid); pour into clean pot. Stir in vinegar. Stir in pectin until dissolved. Bring to a full boil over high heat, stirring constantly.

3. Add sugar in a steady stream, stirring constantly. Return to a full boil, stirring constantly to dissolve sugar. Boil hard for 1 minute.

4. Remove from heat and skim off any foam. Stir in finely chopped mint leaves and food coloring (if using). Stir for 5 to 8 minutes to prevent floating leaves.

5. Ladle quickly into sterilized jars to within ¼ inch (0.5 cm) of rim; wipe rims. Apply prepared lids and rings; tighten just until fingertip-tight.

6. Process jars in a boiling water canner for 10 minutes (for details, see page 20). Transfer jars to a towel-lined surface and let rest at room temperature until set. Check seals; refrigerate any unsealed jars for up to 3 weeks.

> There is a wide variety of mint that can be used to make jelly, such as spearmint (the most common mint you'll find in grocery stores), peppermint, apple mint, pineapple mint, lemon mint, orange mint — even chocolate mint. Look for bedding plants at your local nursery and grow your own. If possible, plant mint in containers, as it will spread in the garden. Mint thrives in moist, well-drained soil and partial sun.

Pineapple and Mint Jelly

Makes about five 8-ounce (250 mL) jars

To make this jelly, pineapple juice is infused with mint. At the end of the cooking, additional mint is stirred in, creating a light yellow jelly with suspended bits of fresh mint. Serve on scones or with lamb or pork.

— o o o —

Variations

Cranberry Mint Jelly: Substitute unsweetened cranberry juice for the pineapple juice.

Pomegranate Mint Jelly: Substitute unsweetened 100% pomegranate juice for the pineapple juice.

4 cups	unsweetened pineapple juice	1 L
1 cup	loosely packed chopped fresh mint leaves	250 mL
2 tbsp	strained lemon juice (see tip, page 303)	30 mL
1	package (1.75 oz/49 or 57 g) powdered pectin	1
4 cups	granulated sugar	1 L
2 tbsp	finely chopped fresh mint	30 mL

1. In a large, deep, heavy-bottomed pot, combine pineapple juice and 1 cup (250 mL) chopped mint leaves. Bring to a boil over high heat. Reduce heat and simmer, covered, for 5 minutes. Strain over a bowl, squeezing leaves; reserve liquid and discard leaves.

2. Measure exactly 3¾ cups (925 mL) of liquid (add water if there's not enough liquid); pour into clean pot. Stir in lemon juice. Stir in pectin until dissolved. Bring to a full boil over high heat, stirring constantly.

3. Add sugar in a steady stream, stirring constantly. Return to a full boil, stirring constantly to dissolve sugar. Boil hard for 1 minute.

4. Remove from heat and skim off any foam. Stir in 2 tbsp (30 mL) finely chopped mint. Stir for 5 to 8 minutes to prevent floating mint.

5. Ladle quickly into sterilized jars to within ¼ inch (0.5 cm) of rim; wipe rims. Apply prepared lids and rings; tighten just until fingertip-tight.

6. Process jars in a boiling water canner for 10 minutes (for details, see page 20). Transfer jars to a towel-lined surface and let rest at room temperature until set. Check seals; refrigerate any unsealed jars for up to 3 weeks.

Rosemary Apple Cider Jelly

Makes about five 8-ounce (250 mL) jars

This jelly is one of my favorites, and one I have frequent requests for.

— o o o —

Tips

Supermarkets now carry all-natural (or pure-pressed) apple juice. Jelly made with it will be slightly cloudy.

For gift-giving, place a small sprig of fresh rosemary in each jar before pouring in the jelly.

Recipe Suggestion

Brush this savory jelly over roasted chicken, lamb or pork in the last 10 minutes of roasting, or serve it alongside.

Variation

Cranberry Rosemary Jelly: Substitute cranberry cocktail or cranberry juice blend for the apple cider.

4 cups	unsweetened apple cider or all-natural apple juice (see tip, at left)	1 L
½ cup	loosely packed coarsely chopped fresh rosemary	125 mL
4½ cups	granulated sugar	1.25 L
1	package (1.75 oz/49 or 57 g) powdered pectin	1

1. In a large, deep, heavy-bottomed pot, combine apple cider and rosemary. Bring to a boil over high heat. Reduce heat and simmer, covered, for 20 minutes. Strain over a bowl, squeezing leaves; reserve liquid and discard leaves.

2. Measure exactly 3½ cups (875 mL) of liquid (add additional cider or water if there's not enough liquid); pour into clean pot. Stir in pectin until dissolved. Bring to a full boil over high heat, stirring constantly.

3. Add sugar in a steady stream, stirring constantly. Return to a full boil, stirring constantly to dissolve sugar. Boil hard for 1 minute.

4. Remove from heat and skim off any foam.

5. Ladle quickly into prepared jars to within ¼ inch (0.5 cm) of rim; wipe rims. Apply prepared lids and rings; tighten rings just until fingertip-tight.

6. Process jars in a boiling water canner for 10 minutes (for details, see page 20). Transfer jars to a towel-lined surface and let rest at room temperature until set. Check seals; refrigerate any unsealed jars for up to 3 weeks.

Fruit Butters

Fruit butters are smooth spreads made from puréed fruit, sugar and sometimes spices. They are slowly cooked down to thicken naturally to a spreadable consistency.

About Fruit Butters 307
Tips for Successful Fruit Butters. 308
Test for Doneness. 309
Trouble-Shooting 309

Spiced Apple Butter 310
Spiced Apricot Butter 311
Apricot Orange Butter 312
Blueberry Apple Butter. 313
Blueberry Maple Butter 314
Carrot Apple Butter 315
Cran-Apple Butter 316
Mango Butter 317
Peach Rum Butter. 318
Spiced Pear Butter 320
Plum Good Apple Butter 321
Rhubarb Apple Butter 322

About Fruit Butters

Fruit butters are fairly simple to make. The fruit is often cooked unpeeled; then it is pressed through a sieve or puréed and cooked down with sugar and spices until it is thick and spreadable. It's pretty hard to go wrong. The hardest part is the stirring and the time it takes to cook, but even that can be done in two stages. First, cook the fruit and prepare the purée; refrigerate it overnight. Then cook the fruit butter and put it into jars the next day.

Most of the fruit butters in this collection were made using apples, so make them when apples are abundant in the fall or when your supply of apples is no longer crunchy. They are also a great option when you simply have lots of ripe fruit around. The Apricot Orange Butter (page 312) is made with dried apricots and can be made any time of the year, as can Carrot Apple Butter (page 315).

You can use frozen cranberries to make Cran-Apple Butter (page 316) and frozen rhubarb to make Rhubarb Apple Butter (page 322).

Despite their name, fruit butters *don't contain any butter* — they are named for their smooth, buttery consistency. They have slightly less sugar than other sweet preserves. They will not keep long-term unless processed. Fruit butters are delicious on muffins and toast, or stirred into plain yogurt and topped with crunchy granola.

> Refer to the Produce Purchase Guide, page 32, to estimate the amount of fruit and/or vegetables you'll need to purchase for these recipes.

Tips for Successful Fruit Butters

1. Use ripe fruit and wash it well. Overripe fruit can be used, as long as it is still in good condition; trim away any very soft parts, bruises or blemishes. Fruit is not usually peeled or seeded if it is to be put through a sieve or food mill. The recipe will specify to peel and seed if the fruit will be puréed rather than strained.

2. Cook fruit until very soft, stirring frequently and crushing it with a potato masher after it has cooked for a while or as directed in the recipe; this will further break down the pieces of fruit.

3. Ensure that there are no lumps of fruit by pressing it through a mesh sieve (strainer) or puréeing it well, according to the recipe.

4. Stir often while the mixture is cooking with the sugar and spices, especially as the butter thickens; reduce the heat as it thickens, but keep it bubbling. Place a metal star underneath the pot, if desired, to even out heat and prevent hot spots. The greater the diameter of the pot, the more quickly fruit butter will thicken. A Dutch oven is ideal for cooking fruit butters, as it also has a heavy bottom.

5. Test for doneness (see details opposite) when the mixture becomes very thick. Testing will save you time in the long run and will prevent runny or gluey butters. Unless you test, it is hard to judge what the consistency will be like when cool.

6. Fill jars to within ½ inch (1 cm) of the rim, rather than ¼ inch (0.5 cm) as for other preserves. I find that butters expand in the jar if everything was really hot when you bottled it.

7. Process 8-ounce (250 mL) jars for 10 minutes and pint (500 mL) jars for 15 minutes. I prefer 8-ounce (250 mL) jars because you can use them up faster and you have more jars to give away.

Please read A Primer on Preserving, pages 14 to 37. Things may have changed since you first started making preserves (such as the recent increase in processing time). If you are a beginner, there are a few important things you need to know before getting started. Many instructions are common to all preserves, so once you get it right for one, you'll sail through the others. In the primer, you will also find a handy Preparation Checklist (page 37).

Test for Doneness

Place a spoonful of fruit butter on a plate. Let stand for a few minutes. If there is no liquid seeping from the edges, it is done. It should be thick enough to mound on a spoon. If you leave some in a small spoon set on a dish to cool, it will set slightly and hold its shape.

Trouble-Shooting

PROBLEM: Fruit butter is too soft or liquid seeps from it.

Likely butter has not been cooked long enough. Continue to cook for 3 to 5 minutes and test for doneness again. I recommend proper testing before you ladle the butter into jars. It does thicken more once it's cooled, though. If you open a jar later on and discover this problem, it may help to place it in the refrigerator to chill before using.

PROBLEM: Fruit butter is stiff.

This can result from overcooking, too much sugar or insufficient stirring (as the mixture thickens on the bottom of the pot). If it is overcooked, add a little more liquid, such as water or apple cider, and stir well; reheat before placing in jars and processing. If there is too much sugar due to inaccurately measured sugar or fruit, try cooking another apple (or other fruit) with a bit of water, press through a strainer and add. (Or add some commercial applesauce.) Remember to stir often, and reduce heat to prevent butter from overcooking or scorching on the bottom.

PROBLEM: Fruit butter is sticking (overcooking) on the bottom.

If the mixture has not yet scorched, remove it from the heat and immediately transfer to a clean pot, taking care not to scrape the bottom of the pot. You may need to add a little more liquid if it has thickened too much. Cook over low heat until it tests done. If it has already scorched (it will smell scorched and look very dark on the bottom of the pot), the flavor will have gotten into your butter and the butter will have to be discarded. To prevent scorching, watch the mixture carefully and stir often. Place a metal star or ring under your pot if it is still sticking over the lowest heat.

Spiced Apple Butter

**Makes about four
8-ounce (250 mL) jars**

When you cook this butter, your house will smell like you are baking an apple pie. This is a good recipe for using up large quantities of apples, especially when they are no longer crisp.

— o o o —

Tips

You'll need about 12 medium apples for this recipe. Apples that soften when cooked (those that are good for applesauce) are best for fruit butters. Varieties of apples that soften include McIntosh, Cortland, Empire and Russet. See page 25 for more details.

No peeling needed here!

Supermarkets now carry all-natural (or pure-pressed) apple juice, which contains solids. Shake before using.

4 lbs	apples that soften	2 kg
1½ cups	unsweetened apple cider or all-natural apple juice (see tip, at left)	375 mL
3½ cups	packed brown sugar	875 mL
2 tbsp	lemon juice	30 mL
1 tsp	ground cinnamon	5 mL
¼ tsp	ground nutmeg	1 mL
¼ tsp	ground cloves	1 mL

1. Cut apples into quarters; remove stems and blossom ends. Slice each quarter into 4 or 5 slices.

2. In a Dutch oven or a large, deep, heavy-bottomed pot, combine apples and cider. Bring to a boil over high heat. Reduce heat and boil gently, covered, for about 15 minutes or until apples are very soft.

3. Ladle fruit and liquid into a mesh sieve and press pulp through; discard peel and seeds (or extract pulp using a food mill). Return pulp to clean Dutch oven.

4. Add sugar in a steady stream, stirring constantly. Stir in lemon juice and spices; cook over low heat, stirring constantly to dissolve sugar. Increase heat to high and bring to a boil, stirring constantly. Reduce heat and boil gently, uncovered, stirring often and reducing heat further as mixture thickens, for about 1 hour or until thickened. Test for doneness (for details, see page 309).

5. Ladle into sterilized jars to within ½ inch (1 cm) of rim; wipe rims. Apply prepared lids and rings; tighten just until fingertip-tight.

6. Process jars in a boiling water canner for 10 minutes (for details, see page 20). Transfer jars to a towel-lined surface and let rest at room temperature until cool. Check seals; refrigerate any unsealed jars for up to 3 weeks.

Spiced Apricot Butter

*Tangy and fresh, this
butter has just a hint
of spice, highlighting
the fruit taste.*

— o o o —

Tips

Use the back of a soup
spoon to press pulp through
the sieve.

Do not worry if any foam
appears during cooking —
it will subside on its own
once the mixture is finished
cooking.

Recipe Suggestions

Stir into plain yogurt to
sweeten, and eat with
fresh berries.

Layer in a parfait glass,
interspersed with granola
clusters or bran cereal.

Variations

If desired, replace
1 cup (250 mL) of the
granulated sugar with
1 cup (250 mL) packed
brown sugar.

Replace the spices with
1/2 tsp (2 mL) pumpkin
pie spice.

3 lbs	ripe apricots	1.5 kg
1 cup	water	250 mL
3 1/2 cups	granulated sugar	875 mL
1/4 tsp	ground cinnamon	1 mL
1/4 tsp	ground cardamom or ground nutmeg	1 mL

1. Cut apricots in half along crease; remove pit. Trim away any dark or bruised areas. Chop coarsely.

2. In a Dutch oven or a large, deep, heavy-bottomed pot, combine apricots and water. Bring to a boil over high heat. Reduce heat to medium-low and boil gently for about 20 minutes or until apricots are very soft.

3. Ladle fruit and liquid into a large mesh sieve and press pulp through; discard skins (or extract pulp using a food mill). Return pulp to clean Dutch oven.

4. Add sugar in a steady stream, stirring constantly. Stir in cinnamon and cardamom; bring to a boil over high heat, stirring constantly to dissolve sugar. Reduce heat and boil gently, stirring often and reducing heat further as mixture thickens, for 25 to 30 minutes or until thickened. Test for doneness (for details, see page 309).

5. Ladle into sterilized jars to within 1/2 inch (1 cm) of rim; wipe rims. Apply prepared lids and rings; tighten just until fingertip-tight.

6. Process jars in a boiling water canner for 10 minutes (for details, see page 20). Transfer jars to a towel-lined surface and let rest at room temperature until cool. Check seals; refrigerate any unsealed jars for up to 3 weeks.

Apricot Orange Butter

*This butter is a perky
yellow-orange color and
has a strong apricot
flavor and a refreshing
touch of orange flavor. It
can be made year-round.*

—○○○—

Tip
Some bulk stores carry
good-quality dried apricots.

4 cups	dried apricots	1 L
3½ cups	water	875 mL
2⅔ cups	granulated sugar	650 mL
1 tbsp	finely grated orange rind	15 mL
⅔ cup	orange juice	150 mL

1. In a large bowl, combine dried apricots and water. Cover bowl with plastic wrap and let stand for about 12 hours.

2. Transfer apricots and any liquid to a Dutch oven or a large, deep, heavy-bottomed pot. Bring to a boil over high heat. Reduce heat and simmer, covered, for about 15 minutes or until apricots are very soft.

3. Using a food processor fitted with a metal blade, purée apricots and liquid until very smooth. Return purée to Dutch oven.

4. Add sugar in a steady stream, stirring constantly. Stir in orange rind and orange juice; cook over low heat, stirring constantly to dissolve sugar. Increase heat to high and bring to a boil, stirring constantly. Reduce heat and boil gently, uncovered, stirring often and reducing heat further as mixture thickens, for 15 to 20 minutes or until thickened. Test for doneness (for details, see page 309).

5. Ladle into sterilized jars to within ½ inch (1 cm) of rim; wipe rims. Apply prepared lids and rings; tighten just until fingertip-tight.

6. Process jars in a boiling water canner for 10 minutes (for details, see page 20). Transfer jars to a towel-lined surface and let rest at room temperature until cool. Check seals; refrigerate any unsealed jars for up to 3 weeks.

> Dried apricots are rich in beta carotene, iron and potassium. They are a source of the powerful antioxidant lycopene, which may help to reduce free radical damage and prevent disease, and are a good source of fiber, with 2 grams per 5 medium halves.

Blueberry Apple Butter

Makes about four 8-ounce (250 mL) jars

This butter has a lovely deep purple color. Try it on pancakes or waffles, or put a little in muffin batter to replace some of the fat.

— o o o —

Tips

Use wild blueberries if you can — the flavor is more intense. You can find frozen wild blueberries in the supermarket or pick your own and freeze for later use.

You'll need about 7 medium apples for this recipe. Varieties of apples that soften when cooked include McIntosh, Cortland, Empire and Russet. See page 25 for more details.

4 cups	wild or cultivated blueberries	1 L
8 cups	chopped peeled apples that soften	2 L
1 cup	water	250 mL
3 cups	granulated sugar	750 mL
1 tsp	ground cinnamon	5 mL
1/4 tsp	ground nutmeg	1 mL

1. In a Dutch oven or a large, deep, heavy-bottomed pot, crush blueberries with a potato masher. Add apples and water. Bring to a boil over high heat. Reduce heat and boil gently, stirring occasionally, for about 20 minutes or until apples are very soft.

2. In a food processor fitted with a metal blade, purée blueberry mixture until very smooth. Return purée to clean Dutch oven.

3. Add sugar in a steady stream, stirring constantly. Stir in cinnamon and nutmeg; cook over low heat, stirring constantly to dissolve sugar. Increase heat to high and bring to a boil, stirring constantly. Reduce heat and boil gently, stirring often and reducing heat further as mixture thickens, for 45 to 60 minutes or until thickened. Test for doneness (for details, see page 309).

4. Ladle into sterilized jars to within 1/2 inch (1 cm) of rim; wipe rims. Apply prepared lids and rings; tighten just until fingertip-tight.

5. Process jars in a boiling water canner for 10 minutes (for details, see page 20). Transfer jars to a towel-lined surface and let rest at room temperature until cool. Check seals; refrigerate any unsealed jars for up to 3 weeks.

> Blueberries are rich in the antioxidant anthocyanin.

Blueberry Maple Butter

Makes about five 8-ounce (250 mL) jars

12 cups	blueberries	3 L
2 tbsp	lemon juice	30 mL
3 cups	granulated sugar	750 mL
¾ cup	pure maple syrup	175 mL

This recipe saves time because you purée the berries before cooking them — no need to mash them or pass them through a sieve.

— o o o —

Tips

You'll need about 3 lbs (1.5 kg) of blueberries for this recipe.

For completely smooth butter, after cooking is complete, pass it through a fine-mesh sieve in batches, rinsing away the tiny seeds in between batches.

Recipe Suggestion

Warm this butter in the microwave and drizzle it on pancakes or waffles, stir it into yogurt or use it to top ice cream, cake or sliced peaches.

1. In a food processor fitted with a metal blade, purée blueberries in 3 or 4 batches, scraping down sides.

2. In a Dutch oven or a large, deep, heavy-bottomed pot, combine puréed blueberries and lemon juice.

3. Add sugar in a steady stream, stirring constantly. Stir in maple syrup; cook over low heat, stirring constantly to dissolve sugar. Increase heat to high and bring to a boil, stirring constantly. Reduce heat and boil gently, stirring often and reducing heat further as mixture thickens, for 35 to 40 minutes or until thickened. Test for doneness (for details, see page 309).

4. Ladle into sterilized jars to within ½ inch (1 cm) of rim; wipe rims. Apply prepared lids and rings; tighten just until fingertip-tight.

5. Process jars in a boiling water canner for 10 minutes (for details, see page 20). Transfer jars to a towel-lined surface and let rest at room temperature until cool. Check seals; refrigerate any unsealed jars for up to 3 weeks.

Variations

Spiced Blueberry Maple Butter: Add ½ tsp (2 mL) ground cinnamon and ¼ tsp (1 mL) ground nutmeg with the maple syrup.

Blueberry Orange Butter: Omit the maple syrup and increase the sugar to 4 cups (1 L). Add wide strips of rind (left whole) from 1 large orange; remove and discard the rind after cooking.

Carrot Apple Butter

*This yummy butter has
just a hint of cinnamon
and vanilla.*

— o o o —

Tips

You'll need about 3 lbs
(1.5 kg) of apples (about
6 large) for this recipe.
Varieties of apples that
soften when cooked include
McIntosh, Cortland, Empire
and Russet. See page 25
for more details.

Add the lemon juice to the
chopped apples as you
chop, to prevent browning.

To prevent lumps, the
carrots must be fully
cooked. This recipe does
not work with shredded
carrots.

Variations

Omit the vanilla and add
½ tsp (2 mL) ground
cardamom.

Use orange juice in place
of the apple juice.

1½ lbs	carrots, cut into ½-inch (1 cm) pieces	750 g
8 cups	chopped peeled apples that soften	2 L
1 cup	all-natural apple juice (see tip, page 310) or unsweetened apple cider	250 mL
2 tbsp	lemon juice	30 mL
2 cups	granulated sugar	500 mL
1 cup	packed brown sugar	250 mL
1¼ tsp	ground cinnamon	6 mL
½ tsp	vanilla extract	2 mL

1. Place carrots in a large pot and add enough water to cover. Cover and bring to a boil over high heat. Reduce heat and simmer for about 12 minutes or until softened. Drain well and return to pot. Using a potato masher, mash until smooth (or use a food processor fitted with a metal blade to purée). Set aside.

2. In a Dutch oven or a large, deep, heavy-bottomed pot, combine apples, apple juice and lemon juice. Bring to a boil over high heat. Reduce heat and simmer, covered, for about 7 minutes or until softened.

3. Stir in mashed carrots. Add granulated sugar in a steady stream, stirring constantly. Stir in brown sugar, cinnamon and vanilla; boil gently, uncovered, stirring often and reducing heat further as mixture thickens, for 20 to 25 minutes or until thickened. Use a potato masher to break down fruit and eliminate lumps. Test for doneness (for details, see page 309).

4. Ladle into sterilized jars to within ½ inch (1 cm) of rim; wipe rims. Apply prepared lids and rings; tighten just until fingertip-tight.

5. Process jars in a boiling water canner for 10 minutes (for details, see page 20). Transfer jars to a towel-lined surface and let rest at room temperature until cool. Check seals; refrigerate any unsealed jars for up to 3 weeks.

Cran–Apple Butter

Makes about five 8-ounce (250 mL) jars

2 lbs	apples that soften	1 kg
3 cups	cranberries	750 mL
2 cups	unsweetened apple cider	500 mL
2 tbsp	grated orange rind	30 mL
3 cups	granulated sugar	750 mL
$1/4$ tsp	ground nutmeg	1 mL

Two fall favorites partner in this cranberry red butter. Spread on apple, carrot or bran muffins or loaf slices.

— o o o —

Tips

You'll need about 6 medium apples for this recipe.

Apples that soften when cooked (those that are good for applesauce) are best for fruit butters. Varieties of apples that soften include McIntosh, Cortland, Empire and Russet. See page 25 for more details.

Cranberries can be easily frozen. Buy them when they're abundant during the holiday season, place each bag in a plastic freezer bag to protect it, and put them right into the freezer.

1. Cut apples into quarters; remove stems and blossom ends. Slice each quarter into 4 or 5 slices.

2. In a Dutch oven or a large, deep, heavy-bottomed pot, combine apples, cranberries, cider and orange rind. Bring to a boil over high heat. Reduce heat and boil gently, covered, for about 15 minutes or until apples are very soft.

3. Ladle fruit and liquid into a mesh sieve and press pulp through; discard peel and seeds (or extract pulp using a food mill). Return pulp to clean Dutch oven.

4. Add sugar in a steady stream, stirring constantly. Stir in nutmeg; cook over low heat, stirring constantly to dissolve sugar. Increase heat to high and bring to a boil, stirring constantly. Reduce heat and boil gently, uncovered, stirring often and reducing heat further as mixture thickens, for 20 to 25 minutes or until thickened. Test for doneness (for details, see page 309).

5. Ladle into sterilized jars to within $1/2$ inch (1 cm) of rim; wipe rims. Apply prepared lids and rings; tighten just until fingertip-tight.

6. Process jars in a boiling water canner for 10 minutes (for details, see page 20). Transfer jars to a towel-lined surface and let rest at room temperature until cool. Check seals; refrigerate any unsealed jars for up to 3 weeks.

Mango Butter

**Makes about five
8-ounce (250 mL) jars**

*Choose fragrant mangos
to make this delicious
butter. Whisk some into
your favorite vinaigrette
for a salad of mixed
greens, sliced oranges
and toasted almonds,
or into yogurt dressing
for fruit salad.*

— ○ ○ ○ —

Tips
You'll need 5 or 6 medium
mangos for this recipe.

*How to Get the Most Flesh
from a Mango:* Slice the
mango before peeling.
First, stand it on its stem
end and slice along the
wider sides, along the seed.
You will get two "cheeks"
that flesh can be scooped
from, or you can score the
flesh in a grid pattern, push
the skin from the bottom to
"pop" pieces up, then cut
the flesh from the skin in
small cubes. Cut or scrape
flesh from the seed.

4 lbs	firm ripe mangos, peeled and chopped	2 kg
1⅓ cups	unsweetened apple cider, orange juice or water	325 mL
4 cups	granulated sugar	1 L
2 tbsp	finely grated lemon rind	30 mL
⅓ cup	lemon juice	75 mL

1. In a Dutch oven or a large, deep, heavy-bottomed pot, combine mangos and cider. Bring to a boil over high heat. Reduce heat to low and simmer, stirring occasionally, for 15 to 20 minutes or until mangos are very soft.

2. Press through a mesh sieve, put through a food mill or purée in a food processor fitted with a metal blade until very smooth; return purée to Dutch oven.

3. Add sugar in a steady stream, stirring constantly. Stir in lemon rind and juice; cook over low heat, stirring constantly to dissolve sugar. Increase heat to high and bring to a boil, stirring constantly. Reduce heat and boil gently, stirring often and reducing heat further as mixture thickens, for 35 to 40 minutes or until thickened. Test for doneness (for details, see page 309).

4. Ladle into sterilized jars to within ½ inch (1 cm) of rim; wipe rims. Apply prepared lids and rings; tighten just until fingertip-tight.

5. Process jars in a boiling water canner for 10 minutes (for details, see page 20). Transfer jars to a towel-lined surface and let rest at room temperature until cool. Check seals; refrigerate any unsealed jars for up to 3 weeks.

Peach Rum Butter

This recipe may also be made with nectarines (also unpeeled). You can leave out the rum, but it does add nicely to the flavor.

— ooo —

3½ lbs	unpeeled firm ripe peaches	1.75 kg
¾ cup	water	175 mL
½ cup	amber rum	125 mL
3 cups	granulated sugar	750 mL
½ cup	packed brown sugar	125 mL

1. Cut peaches in half; twist to separate halves. Cut halves containing pit in half again; hold and twist pit to remove it. Cut peaches into large wedges.

2. In a Dutch oven or a large, deep, heavy-bottomed pot, combine peaches and water. Cover and bring to a boil over high heat. Reduce heat and simmer, stirring often, for about 22 minutes or until peaches are very soft.

3. Ladle fruit and liquid into a large mesh sieve and press pulp through; discard skins (or extract pulp using a food mill). Return pulp to clean Dutch oven. Stir in rum.

4. Add granulated sugar in a steady stream, stirring constantly. Stir in brown sugar; cook over low heat, stirring constantly to dissolve sugar. Increase heat to high and bring to a boil, stirring constantly. Reduce heat and boil gently, stirring often and reducing heat further as mixture thickens, for 50 to 60 minutes or until thickened. Test for doneness (for details, see page 309).

5. Ladle into sterilized jars to within ½ inch (1 cm) of rim; wipe rims. Apply prepared lids and rings; tighten just until fingertip-tight.

6. Process jars in a boiling water canner for 10 minutes (for details, see page 20). Transfer jars to a towel-lined surface and let rest at room temperature until cool. Check seals; refrigerate any unsealed jars for up to 3 weeks.

Tips

You'll need about 10 large peaches for this recipe.

Ripe peaches yield when lightly pressed with your thumb. To speed the ripening of hard peaches, place them in a paper bag, or place them on a tray lined with one layer of paper towels and cover with newspaper. Leave for a couple of days in a cool place, checking each day and removing any ripe peaches.

Variations

Peach Amaretto Butter: Replace the rum with amaretto (almond-flavored liqueur), omit the brown sugar and increase the granulated sugar to 4 cups (1 L).

Peach Marsala Butter: Replace the rum with $1/4$ cup (60 mL) sweet Marsala wine, omit the brown sugar and increase the granulated sugar to 4 cups (1 L).

Spiced Peach Butter: Omit the rum. Stir in 1 tsp (5 mL) ground cinnamon, $1/2$ tsp (2 mL) ground nutmeg and a pinch of ground cloves with the sugar.

Peach Orange Butter: Use orange juice in place of the water and replace the rum with $1/4$ cup (60 mL) Grand Marnier.

Spiced Pear Butter

*This caramel-colored
butter has a lovely pear
flavor and a hint of spice.*

— o o o —

Tips

Bartlett or Packham pears
are good choices for fruit
butters, as they have soft
flesh that breaks down
during cooking.

Pears ripen well after being
picked, so they are picked
green for better quality
in transporting. To speed
ripening, place them in a
paper bag. When ripe, a
pear yields to light pressure
near the bottom of the neck.

Variation

Pear Orange Butter:
Substitute orange juice
for the apple cider and
replace the cinnamon
and ginger with $\frac{1}{2}$ tsp
(2 mL) ground nutmeg.

10 lbs	ripe pears	5 kg
2$\frac{1}{2}$ cups	unsweetened apple cider	625 mL
4$\frac{1}{2}$ cups	granulated sugar	1.125 L
1 tsp	ground cinnamon	5 mL
1 tsp	ground ginger	5 mL

1. Cut pears lengthwise into quarters and remove stems,
   blossom ends and cores (do not peel); coarsely chop.

2. In a Dutch oven or a large, deep, heavy-bottomed pot,
   combine pears and cider. Bring to a boil over high
   heat. Reduce heat and boil gently, covered, for about
   40 minutes or until pears are very soft, using a potato
   masher after about 30 minutes to break down pieces
   further.

3. Ladle fruit and liquid into a large mesh sieve and press
   pulp through; discard peel (or extract pulp using a food
   mill). Return pulp to clean Dutch oven.

4. Add sugar in a steady stream, stirring constantly. Stir
   in cinnamon and ginger; cook over low heat, stirring
   constantly to dissolve sugar. Increase heat to high and
   bring to a boil, stirring constantly. Reduce heat and
   boil gently, uncovered, stirring often and reducing
   heat further as mixture thickens, for 35 to 40 minutes
   or until thickened. Test for doneness (for details, see
   page 309).

5. Ladle into sterilized jars to within $\frac{1}{2}$ inch (1 cm) of rim;
   wipe rims. Apply prepared lids and rings; tighten just
   until fingertip-tight.

6. Process jars in a boiling water canner for 10 minutes
   (for details, see page 20). Transfer jars to a towel-lined
   surface and let rest at room temperature until cool.
   Check seals; refrigerate any unsealed jars for up to
   3 weeks.

Pineapple Habanero Pepper Jelly (page 290)

Carrot Apple Butter (page 315)

Tomato Apple Chipotle Chutney (page 340)

Plum Good Apple Butter

*I developed a pie recipe
using this combination
of fruit and thought I
would try it as a butter —
it's just as delicious. It's
excellent on muffins or
stirred into plain yogurt.*

— o o o —

Tips

You'll need about 6
medium apples and 16 to
18 medium plums for this
recipe.

Varieties of apples that
soften when cooked include
McIntosh, Cortland, Empire
and Russet. See page 25
for more details.

Supermarkets now carry
all-natural apple juice, which
contains solids. Shake
before using.

2 lbs	apples that soften	1 kg
2 lbs	red plums, pitted and sliced	1 kg
1½ cups	unsweetened apple cider or all-natural apple juice (see tip, at left)	375 mL
3 cups	granulated sugar	750 mL
1 tsp	ground cinnamon	5 mL

1. Cut apples into quarters; remove stems and blossom ends. Slice each quarter into 4 or 5 slices.

2. In a Dutch oven or a large, deep, heavy-bottomed pot, combine apples, plums and cider. Bring to a boil over high heat. Reduce heat and simmer, covered, for about 20 minutes or until fruit is very soft.

3. Ladle fruit and liquid into a mesh sieve and press pulp through; discard peel and seeds (or extract pulp using a food mill). Return pulp to clean Dutch oven.

4. Add sugar in a steady stream, stirring constantly. Stir in cinnamon; cook over low heat, stirring constantly to dissolve sugar. Increase heat to high and bring to a boil, stirring constantly. Reduce heat and boil gently, uncovered, stirring often and reducing heat further as mixture thickens, for 45 to 50 minutes or until thickened. Test for doneness (for details, see page 309).

5. Ladle into sterilized jars to within ½ inch (1 cm) of rim; wipe rims. Apply prepared lids and rings; tighten just until fingertip-tight.

6. Process jars in a boiling water canner for 10 minutes (for details, see page 20). Transfer jars to a towel-lined surface and let rest at room temperature until cool. Check seals; refrigerate any unsealed jars for up to 3 weeks.

Rhubarb Apple Butter

**Makes about four
8-ounce (250 mL) jars**

*Once rhubarb gets going
in your garden, all of a
sudden it seems there's
too much! Cut it up and
freeze it to make this fruit
butter in the fall, for that
special flavor you crave.*

— o o o —

Tip

Apples that soften when
cooked (those that are good
for applesauce) are best
for fruit butters. Varieties of
apples that soften include
McIntosh, Cortland, Empire
and Russet. See page 25
for more details.

Variation

*Strawberry Rhubarb
Apple Butter:* Add a
quart (1 L) of chopped
strawberries with the
rhubarb and omit the
orange rind and juice.
(This is a good use for
frozen strawberries,
which lose their texture
when frozen and then
thawed.)

4	large apples that soften	4
6 cups	chopped rhubarb	1.5 L
½ cup	water	125 mL
	Grated rind and juice of 1 large orange	
5½ cups	granulated sugar	1.375 L

1. Cut apples into quarters; remove stems and blossom ends. Slice each quarter into 4 or 5 slices.

2. In a Dutch oven or a large, deep, heavy-bottomed pot, combine apples, rhubarb, water, orange rind and orange juice. Bring to a boil over high heat. Reduce heat and boil gently, covered, stirring occasionally, for about 15 minutes or until fruit is very soft.

3. Ladle fruit and liquid into a mesh sieve and press pulp through; discard peel and seeds (or extract pulp using a food mill). Return pulp to clean Dutch oven.

4. Add sugar in a steady stream, stirring constantly. Cook over low heat, stirring constantly to dissolve sugar. Increase heat to high and bring to a boil, stirring constantly. Reduce heat and boil gently, uncovered, stirring often and reducing heat further as mixture thickens, for 45 to 60 minutes or until thickened. Test for doneness (for details, see page 309).

5. Ladle into sterilized jars to within ½ inch (1 cm) of rim; wipe rims. Apply prepared lids and rings; tighten just until fingertip-tight.

6. Process jars in a boiling water canner for 10 minutes (for details, see page 20). Transfer jars to a towel-lined surface and let rest at room temperature until cool. Check seals; refrigerate any unsealed jars for up to 3 weeks.

> Commercially grown (greenhouse) rhubarb, available in late winter, is usually much rosier in color than most garden varieties and makes a butter with a lovely color.

Chutneys

A condiment of East Indian origin, chutney is a tangy-sweet, mild to hot mixture of fruit and/or vegetables, sugar, vinegar and spices. It has a thick, jam-like consistency. The name comes from the Hindi word chatni.

About Chutneys 324
Tips for Successful Chutneys 324
Test for Doneness 325
Trouble-Shooting 325

Apple Chutney 326
Golden Apple Plum Chutney 327
Apricot Chutney 328
Apricot Mango Chutney 329
Cran-Apple Sage and Thyme Chutney 330
Date Orange Chutney 331
Mango Chutney 332
Mango Peach Chutney 333
Peach Plum Chutney 334
Pear Cranberry Chutney 335
Pineapple Chutney 336
Plum Pear Chutney 337
Sweet Pepper Apple Chutney 338
Green Tomato Apple Chutney 339
Tomato Apple Chipotle Chutney 340

About Chutneys

Chutneys are delicious condiments to serve with curries, hot and cold meats, meat pies, egg dishes, cheese and crackers, or in wraps. Stir some into stuffing mixtures for poultry or pork loin roast. They have the sweetness and consistency of jam and contain fruit, but border on a relish with their savory, hot and spicy ingredients.

Chutneys are slowly simmered until thickened, so they do not require added pectin. All the ingredients are stirred together and cooked down, uncovered. The consistency is soft and spoonable, and the pieces of fruit tend to be larger than they are in jam, as in a conserve.

The flavor of chutney improves with age; most are best after resting for at least a month. The flavor is a balance of sweetness from the fruit and sugar with acid from vinegar, citrus juice or apple cider. I have added herbs in some of the recipes for enhanced flavor, and have used a variety of dried fruit for color, flavor and texture.

You may vary the type of vinegar used in the recipes, choosing from white, malt, apple cider, red or white wine, etc. You may also replace up to half of the granulated sugar with brown sugar for a deeper color and flavor.

Hotness may be adjusted to suit your taste. Turn up the heat with fresh chile peppers, such as jalapeños, red finger chiles, habaneros, hot pepper flakes (also called crushed red chiles), cayenne pepper or hot pepper sauce. For a smoky flavor, use chipotle peppers (smoked jalapeños), found in a can, often in a tomato (adobo) sauce.

> Refer to the Produce Purchase Guide, page 32, to estimate the amount of fruit and/or vegetables you'll need to purchase for these recipes.

Tips for Successful Chutneys

1. Choose top-quality, firm, ripe fruit and trim off any bad spots or blemishes. Chop coarsely or slice into larger pieces than you would for jam — $\frac{1}{2}$-inch (1 cm) chunks work well for chutneys.

2. Ensure that spices are fresh by smelling them to see if the aroma is strong. Adjust the heat level according to taste.

3. Stir often to prevent the mixture from scorching, especially as the chutney thickens. Reduce the heat as it thickens, but keep it gently bubbling. If desired, place a wire star under the pot to even out heat and prevent hot spots. The key to great chutney is the long, slow cooking. The greater the diameter of the pot, the more evenly chutney will cook. A Dutch oven with a heavy bottom is a good choice.

4. Begin to test for doneness (see details below) when chutney starts to thicken.

5. Fill jars to within ½ inch (1 cm) of the rim, then slide a *non-metal* tool, such as a narrow rubber scraper or a plastic bubble remover, between the jar and the chutney to remove air pockets. Process for 10 minutes.

> Please read A Primer on Preserving, pages 14 to 37. Things may have changed since you first started making preserves (such as the recent increase in processing time). If you are a beginner, there are a few important things you need to know before getting started. Many instructions are common to all preserves, so once you get it right for one, you'll sail through the others. In the primer, you will also find a handy Preparation Checklist (page 37).

Test for Doneness

Place a spoonful of chutney on a plate. Draw a small spoon through the center. Chutney is done when no liquid seeps into the space. Chutney will thicken more as it cools and should not be overly thick. It should mound on a spoon but fall gently from it.

Trouble-Shooting

PROBLEM: Chutney shrinks in the jar.

Chutney was likely overcooked or stored in too warm a place. Store in a cool, dark, dry place.

PROBLEM: Liquid on the surface.

The chutney was not cooked long enough to evaporate liquid. Ensure complete cooking by testing for doneness.

Apple Chutney

*This is a great chutney
to make during apple
harvest. It is especially
delicious with roast pork
or in a pork or chicken
sandwich.*

— o o o —

Tips

For information on which
apples soften and which
keep their shape, see
page 25.

Gingerroot, or fresh ginger,
is a knobby root with a
thin, tan-colored skin that
is removed before use.
It has a slightly sweet,
peppery flavor with a touch
of hotness. Avoid ginger
with wrinkled skin. Store
unpeeled ginger, tightly
wrapped in plastic, in
the refrigerator for up to
3 weeks or in the freezer
up to 6 months.

4 cups	chopped peeled apples that keep their shape	1 L
4 cups	chopped peeled apples that soften	1 L
2 cups	chopped onions	500 mL
2 cups	unsweetened apple cider	500 mL
1½ cups	packed brown sugar	375 mL
1 cup	cider vinegar	250 mL
⅔ cup	golden raisins or dried cranberries	150 mL
2	cloves garlic, minced	2
2 tbsp	finely grated gingerroot	30 mL
1 tsp	salt	5 mL
¾ tsp	ground cinnamon	3 mL
½ tsp	ground coriander	2 mL
½ tsp	hot pepper flakes	2 mL

1. In a Dutch oven or a large, heavy-bottomed pot, combine apples, onions, cider, brown sugar, vinegar, raisins, garlic, ginger, salt, cinnamon, coriander and hot pepper flakes. Bring to a boil over high heat, stirring often.

2. Reduce heat and boil gently, stirring often and reducing heat further as mixture thickens, for 30 to 35 minutes or until thickened. Test for doneness (for details, see page 325).

3. Ladle into sterilized jars to within ½ inch (1 cm) of rim. Remove any air pockets and adjust headspace, if necessary, by adding chutney; wipe rims. Apply prepared lids and rings; tighten rings just until fingertip-tight.

4. Process jars in a boiling water canner for 10 minutes (for details, see page 20). Transfer jars to a towel-lined surface and let rest at room temperature until cooled. Check seals; refrigerate any unsealed jars for up to 3 weeks.

> Ground coriander is made from the seeds of the coriander plant, which is also called cilantro and Chinese parsley.

Golden Apple Plum Chutney

*In this chutney, golden
apples are paired with
yellow plums and golden
raisins. There are no hot
peppers in this recipe, but
feel free to add some.*

— o o o —

Tips

You'll need about 1½ lbs
(750 g) of plums for this
recipe.

Cloves can be an
overpowering spice, so
measure carefully.

Always check the freshness
of your spices by smelling
them. If they smell only
moderately fragrant, it is
likely time to buy fresh ones.

4	large Golden Delicious apples, peeled and chopped	4
4½ cups	thinly sliced yellow plums	1.125 L
2½ cups	granulated sugar	625 mL
2 cups	chopped onions	500 mL
1 cup	golden raisins	250 mL
1 cup	cider vinegar	250 mL
1 tsp	salt	5 mL
¼ tsp	ground cloves	1 mL

1. In a Dutch oven or a large, heavy-bottomed pot, combine apples, plums, sugar, onions, raisins, vinegar, salt and cloves. Bring to a boil over high heat, stirring often.

2. Reduce heat and boil gently, stirring often and reducing heat further as mixture thickens, for 40 to 45 minutes or until thickened. Test for doneness (for details, see page 325).

3. Ladle into sterilized jars to within ½ inch (1 cm) of rim. Remove any air pockets and adjust headspace, if necessary, by adding chutney; wipe rims. Apply prepared lids and rings; tighten rings just until fingertip-tight.

4. Process jars in a boiling water canner for 10 minutes (for details, see page 20). Transfer jars to a towel-lined surface and let rest at room temperature until cooled. Check seals; refrigerate any unsealed jars for up to 3 weeks.

> Small yellow plums are found in the market in mid-summer. For the best flavor, choose those that are yellow with a slight pink blush.

Apricot Chutney

Makes about seven 8-ounce (250 mL) jars

The idea for this chutney was contributed by Larry McGuire (see Contributors, page 12). In his recipe, he leaves the apricots whole, does not add any onions and uses 10 cloves of garlic. When I made it, I decided to slice the apricots, add onions and let up quite a bit on the garlic. Both versions are delicious!

— o o o —

Variation

Substitute 1 head of roasted garlic for the fresh garlic. See page 287 for instructions on roasting garlic.

5 cups	dried apricots	1.25 L
4 cups	boiling water	1 L
2¾ cups	granulated sugar	675 mL
1½ cups	chopped onions (optional)	375 mL
1¼ cups	white vinegar	300 mL
2 tbsp	finely grated gingerroot	30 mL
1 tbsp	crushed or puréed garlic	15 mL
½ tsp	cayenne pepper or hot pepper flakes	2 mL
¼ tsp	pickling or table salt	1 mL
1 cup	raisins	250 mL

1. In a large bowl, combine apricots and boiling water. Cover and let stand for 8 hours or overnight. If desired, drain apricots, reserving soaking liquid, and cut each apricot into 4 slices.

2. In a Dutch oven or a large, heavy-bottomed pot, combine apricots with soaking liquid, sugar, onions (if using), vinegar, ginger, garlic, cayenne and salt. Bring to a boil over high heat, stirring often.

3. Reduce heat and boil gently, stirring often and reducing heat further as mixture thickens, for 45 minutes. Stir in raisins; cook, stirring often, for about 10 minutes or until thickened. Test for doneness (for details, see page 325).

4. Ladle into sterilized jars to within ½ inch (1 cm) of rim. Remove any air pockets and adjust headspace, if necessary, by adding chutney; wipe rims. Apply prepared lids and rings; tighten rings just until fingertip-tight.

5. Process jars in a boiling water canner for 10 minutes (for details, see page 20). Transfer jars to a towel-lined surface and let rest at room temperature until cooled. Check seals; refrigerate any unsealed jars for up to 3 weeks.

Apricot Mango Chutney

*This is a mildly spiced,
slightly tangy chutney.
You can increase the heat
to your preference.*

— o o o —

Tips

You'll need about 1½ lbs
(750 g) of apricots for this
recipe.

If you like a bit more heat,
you can substitute 1 to
2 tbsp (15 to 30 mL) finely
chopped jalapeño peppers
for the cayenne.

Recipe Suggestions

Try using this chutney as
a finishing glaze for baked
chicken breasts. Brush it
over the breasts and cook
for 5 minutes more.

Stir this chutney into
mayonnaise and use as a
dip for chicken or meatballs.

Canada is the world's
largest exporter of
mustard seeds and
among the top five
producers in the world.
Much of its product is
shipped to the United
States.

3 cups	chopped apricots	750 mL
3 cups	chopped mangos	750 mL
2 cups	chopped sweet onions	500 mL
¾ cup	diced red bell pepper	175 mL
2	cloves garlic, minced	2
2¼ cups	granulated sugar	550 mL
½ cup	packed brown sugar	125 mL
¾ cup	white wine vinegar	175 mL
1 tsp	mustard seeds	5 mL
1 tsp	ground cinnamon	5 mL
1 tsp	ground ginger	5 mL
½ tsp	ground coriander	2 mL
¼ tsp	cayenne pepper, or to taste	1 mL
¼ tsp	salt	1 mL
Pinch	ground cardamom or ground cloves (optional)	Pinch

1. In a Dutch oven or a large, deep, heavy-bottomed pot, combine apricots, mangos, onions, red pepper, garlic, granulated sugar, brown sugar, vinegar, mustard seeds, cinnamon, ginger, coriander, cayenne, salt and cardamom (if using). Bring to a boil over high heat, stirring constantly.

2. Reduce heat and boil gently, stirring often and reducing heat further as mixture thickens, for 55 to 60 minutes or until fruits and vegetables are tender and mixture is very thick. Test for doneness (for details, see page 325).

3. Ladle into sterilized jars to within ½ inch (1 cm) of rim. Remove any air pockets and adjust headspace, if necessary, by adding chutney; wipe rims. Apply prepared lids and rings; tighten rings just until fingertip-tight.

4. Process jars in a boiling water canner for 10 minutes (for details, see page 20). Transfer jars to a towel-lined surface and let rest at room temperature until cooled. Check seals; refrigerate any unsealed jars for up to 3 weeks.

Cran–Apple Sage and Thyme Chutney

This is the kind of chutney you'll want to eat with roasted turkey, chicken or pork, or to add to your stuffing. The flavor of herbs is a nice variation on traditional chutneys, which are primarily seasoned with spices and hot peppers.

— o o o —

Tips

For information on which apples soften and which keep their shape, see page 25.

The secret to great chutney is the long, slow cooking. The greater the diameter of the pot, the more evenly it will cook.

3 cups	chopped peeled apples that keep their shape	750 mL
3 cups	chopped peeled apples that soften	750 mL
3 cups	cranberries	750 mL
1½ cups	chopped onions	375 mL
2	cloves garlic, minced	2
2½ cups	granulated sugar	625 mL
2 cups	water	500 mL
1 cup	cider vinegar	250 mL
1 tsp	salt	5 mL
1 tsp	dried sage	5 mL
¾ tsp	dried thyme	3 mL

1. In a Dutch oven or a large, heavy-bottomed pot, combine apples, cranberries, onions, garlic, sugar, water, vinegar, salt, sage and thyme. Bring to a boil over high heat, stirring often.

2. Reduce heat and boil gently, stirring often and reducing heat further as mixture thickens, for 35 to 40 minutes or until thickened. Test for doneness (for details, see page 325).

3. Ladle into sterilized jars to within ½ inch (1 cm) of rim. Remove any air pockets and adjust headspace, if necessary, by adding chutney; wipe rims. Apply prepared lids and rings; tighten rings just until fingertip-tight.

4. Process jars in a boiling water canner for 10 minutes (for details, see page 20). Transfer jars to a towel-lined surface and let rest at room temperature until cooled. Check seals; refrigerate any unsealed jars for up to 3 weeks.

Date Orange Chutney

Makes about five 8-ounce (250 mL) jars

This chutney has a lovely orange-red color and a subtle orange flavor. It is not too sweet and has just a touch of heat, which you may increase if you like. Serve with aged Cheddar cheese on crackers, or with chicken, pork or scrambled eggs.

— o o o —

Tips

You'll need about 1 lb (500 g) of dates and about 4 large oranges for this recipe.

Stir chutney often to prevent scorching. Reduce the heat as it thickens, but keep it gently bubbling. If desired, place a wire star under the pot to even out heat and prevent hot spots.

2 cups	chopped dates	500 mL
2 tbsp	finely grated orange rind	30 mL
2 cups	chopped peeled oranges	500 mL
3¾ cups	packed brown sugar	925 mL
2¾ cups	white wine vinegar	675 mL
2 cups	chopped onions	500 mL
1 cup	golden raisins	250 mL
1 tbsp	minced gingerroot	15 mL
1½ tsp	ground coriander	7 mL
1 tsp	salt	5 mL
¼ tsp	hot pepper flakes	1 mL

1. In a Dutch oven or a large, heavy-bottomed pot, combine dates, orange rind, oranges, brown sugar, vinegar, onions, raisins, ginger, coriander, salt and hot pepper flakes. Bring to a boil over high heat, stirring often.

2. Reduce heat and boil gently, stirring often and reducing heat further as mixture thickens, for 55 to 60 minutes or until thickened. Test for doneness (for details, see page 325).

3. Ladle into sterilized jars to within ½ inch (1 cm) of rim. Remove any air pockets and adjust headspace, if necessary, by adding chutney; wipe rims. Apply prepared lids and rings; tighten rings just until fingertip-tight.

4. Process jars in a boiling water canner for 10 minutes (for details, see page 20). Transfer jars to a towel-lined surface and let rest at room temperature until cooled. Check seals; refrigerate any unsealed jars for up to 3 weeks.

Mango Chutney

*Perhaps the most
popular chutney, mango
chutney is easily found
in supermarkets and
gourmet stores. It is the
perfect accompaniment
to East Indian dishes,
providing sweet, tart
and hot flavors. It's also
nice served with cheese
on crackers.*

— o o o —

Tips
You'll need about 4$\frac{1}{2}$ lbs
(2.25 kg) of mangos (about
5 medium) for this recipe.

To speed ripening, place
mangos in a paper bag.
See page 317 for details
on how to peel mangos.

6 cups	chopped mangos	1.5 L
2 cups	chopped onions	500 mL
$\frac{3}{4}$ cup	diced red bell pepper	175 mL
2 tbsp	grated gingerroot	30 mL
1 tbsp	minced red or green hot chile pepper	15 mL
3	cloves garlic, minced	3
2$\frac{1}{2}$ cups	packed brown sugar	625 mL
1 cup	cider vinegar	250 mL
1 tbsp	lime juice	15 mL
$\frac{1}{2}$ tsp	salt	2 mL
$\frac{1}{4}$ tsp	ground allspice	1 mL
6	whole cloves	6

1. In a Dutch oven or a large, heavy-bottomed pot, combine mangos, onions, red pepper, ginger, chile pepper, garlic, brown sugar, vinegar, lime juice, salt, allspice and cloves. Bring to a boil over high heat, stirring often.

2. Reduce heat and boil gently, stirring often and reducing heat further as mixture thickens, for 50 to 60 minutes or until thickened. Test for doneness (for details, see page 325).

3. Ladle into sterilized jars to within $\frac{1}{2}$ inch (1 cm) of rim. Remove any air pockets and adjust headspace, if necessary, by adding chutney; wipe rims. Apply prepared lids and rings; tighten rings just until fingertip-tight.

4. Process jars in a boiling water canner for 10 minutes (for details, see page 20). Transfer jars to a towel-lined surface and let rest at room temperature until cool. Check seals; refrigerate any unsealed jars for up to 3 weeks.

> The Ataulfo mango, also called honey mango or Manila mango, is small, yellow and kidney-shaped. It has one of the thinnest seeds of any mango and a large proportion of flesh in the "cheeks" for its size. The flesh is stringless and melts in your mouth. Look for those that have no green and that give slightly when gently pressed.

Mango Peach Chutney

*Mango and peach create
a powerful combination
in this hot and spicy
chutney, which is excellent
served with East Indian
dishes, pork chops or
roast chicken.*

— o o o —

Tips

You'll need about 3 lbs
(1.5 kg) of mangos (3 or
4 medium) for this recipe.

All dried herbs and spices
should be stored away from
heat and light to maintain
their flavor.

Recipe Suggestion

Use to top Baked Brie
(see recipe, page 345).

Variation

*Mango Nectarine
Chutney:* Substitute
unpeeled nectarines
for the peaches.

Turmeric, which comes
from the root of a
tropical plant, adds
flavor and an intense
yellow-orange color to
foods it is cooked with.

4 cups	chopped mangos	1 L
4 cups	chopped peeled peaches (see tip, page 249)	1 L
1	large onion, diced	1
1	red bell pepper, diced	1
2	large cloves garlic, minced	2
1½ cups	packed brown sugar	375 mL
1 cup	cider vinegar	250 mL
½ cup	golden raisins or dried cranberries	125 mL
¼ cup	lime juice	60 mL
1 tsp	salt	5 mL
1 tsp	ground allspice	5 mL
1 tsp	ground cinnamon	5 mL
½ tsp	ground ginger	2 mL
½ tsp	ground turmeric	2 mL
⅛ to ¼ tsp	cayenne pepper (or 1 or 2 jalapeño peppers, finely chopped)	0.5 to 1 mL

1. In a Dutch oven or a large, heavy-bottomed pot, combine mangos, peaches, onion, red pepper, garlic, brown sugar, vinegar, raisins, lime juice, salt, allspice, cinnamon, ginger, turmeric and cayenne to taste. Bring to a boil over high heat, stirring often.

2. Reduce heat and boil gently, stirring often and reducing heat further as mixture thickens, for 1 to 1½ hours or until thickened. Test for doneness (for details, see page 325).

3. Ladle into sterilized jars to within ½ inch (1 cm) of rim. Remove any air pockets and adjust headspace, if necessary, by adding chutney; wipe rims. Apply prepared lids and rings; tighten rings just until fingertip-tight.

4. Process jars in a boiling water canner for 10 minutes (for details, see page 20). Transfer jars to a towel-lined surface and let rest at room temperature until cooled. Check seals; refrigerate any unsealed jars for up to 3 weeks.

Peach Plum Chutney

**Makes about five
8-ounce (250 mL) jars**

*Try making this chutney
in late August, when
both of these fruits are
in season. Serve with
poultry or pork.*

— o o o —

Tips

You'll need about 1½ lbs
(750 g) each of plums and
peaches for this recipe.

How to Peel Peaches: Bring
a pot of water to boil over
high heat. Place peaches
in water two at a time;
boil for 20 to 30 seconds.
Remove peaches with
a slotted spoon and
immediately immerse in a
bowl of cold water. Repeat
with remaining peaches.
When peaches are cool
enough to handle, slit down
side of peel with a paring
knife and slip off peel.
Cut peaches in half and
remove pits.

For the best taste, let
chutneys rest for at least a
month before opening to
allow their flavors to fully
develop and blend.

Variation

Nectarine Plum Chutney:
Substitute unpeeled
nectarines for the
peaches.

4 cups	yellow or red plums, chopped	1 L
3 cups	chopped peeled peaches (see tip, at left)	750 mL
2½ cups	packed brown sugar	625 mL
1 cup	diced yellow or red bell pepper	250 mL
1 cup	chopped onion	250 mL
1	large clove garlic, minced	1
1	green or red hot chile pepper, minced (or 1 tsp/5 mL hot pepper flakes)	1
⅔ cup	white wine vinegar	150 mL
2 tbsp	finely grated gingerroot	30 mL
1 tbsp	finely grated lemon rind	15 mL
2 tsp	salt	10 mL
1 tsp	ground cinnamon	5 mL
1 tsp	ground cloves	5 mL
1 tsp	mustard seeds	5 mL
½ tsp	ground coriander	2 mL
½ tsp	ground turmeric	2 mL

1. In a Dutch oven or a large, heavy-bottomed pot, combine plums, peaches, brown sugar, yellow pepper, onion, garlic, chile pepper, vinegar, ginger, lemon rind, salt, cinnamon, cloves, mustard seeds, coriander and turmeric. Bring to a boil over high heat, stirring often.

2. Reduce heat and boil gently, stirring often and reducing heat further as mixture thickens, for 45 to 60 minutes or until thickened. Test for doneness (for details, see page 325).

3. Ladle into sterilized jars to within ½ inch (1 cm) of rim. Remove any air pockets and adjust headspace, if necessary, by adding chutney; wipe rims. Apply prepared lids and rings; tighten rings just until fingertip-tight.

4. Process jars in a boiling water canner for 10 minutes (for details, see page 20). Transfer jars to a towel-lined surface and let rest at room temperature until cooled. Check seals; refrigerate any unsealed jars for up to 3 weeks.

Pear Cranberry Chutney

*This lovely fall chutney
is perfect with roast
turkey or chicken, or
stirred into stuffing.
With the inclusion of
thyme and the exclusion
of hot peppers, it leans
toward the savory.*

— o o o —

Tips

You'll need about 4 lbs
(2 kg) of pears (about
5 large) for this recipe.

To easily remove fresh
thyme leaves from their
stems, pull gently down the
stem against the direction of
growth. For flavor variation,
try using fresh lemon thyme
(which is easy to grow).

5 cups	chopped peeled pears	1.25 L
3 cups	cranberries	750 mL
3 cups	granulated sugar	750 mL
1½ cups	chopped onions	375 mL
1 cup	red wine vinegar	250 mL
1 tbsp	ground ginger	15 mL
½ tsp	dried thyme (or 1 tsp/5 mL finely chopped fresh thyme)	2 mL

1. In a Dutch oven or a large, heavy-bottomed pot, combine pears, cranberries, sugar, onions, vinegar, ginger and thyme. Bring to a boil over high heat, stirring often.

2. Reduce heat and boil gently, stirring often and reducing heat further as mixture thickens, for 45 to 60 minutes or until thickened. Test for doneness (for details, see page 325).

3. Ladle into sterilized jars to within ½ inch (1 cm) of rim. Remove any air pockets and adjust headspace, if necessary, by adding chutney; wipe rims. Apply prepared lids and rings; tighten rings just until fingertip-tight.

4. Process jars in a boiling water canner for 10 minutes (for details, see page 20). Transfer jars to a towel-lined surface and let rest at room temperature until cooled. Check seals; refrigerate any unsealed jars for up to 3 weeks.

Pineapple Chutney

*This colorful chutney
goes well with ham,
roast pork, pork chops
and chicken.*

— o o o —

Tips

One medium pineapple will
yield about 4 cups (1 L)
chopped.

Varieties of apples that
soften when cooked include
McIntosh, Cortland, Empire
and Russet. See page 25
for more details.

Recipe Suggestion

Stir into plain yogurt for an
interesting dip for veggies
or chicken wings.

4 cups	chopped fresh pineapple	1 L
2	large apples that soften, peeled and diced	2
1 1/2 cups	chopped red onion	375 mL
1/3 cup	chopped red bell pepper	75 mL
1/3 cup	chopped green bell pepper	75 mL
1 tbsp	grated gingerroot (or 1/2 tsp/2 mL ground ginger)	15 mL
1 tbsp	minced hot pepper, such as jalapeño	15 mL
1 3/4 cups	packed brown sugar	425 mL
1 cup	cider vinegar	250 mL
1/3 cup	sultana raisins	75 mL
1/2 tsp	ground cloves	2 mL
Pinch	salt	Pinch

1. In a Dutch oven or a large, heavy-bottomed pot, combine pineapple, apples, onion, red pepper, green pepper, ginger, hot pepper, brown sugar, vinegar, raisins, cloves and salt. Bring to a boil over high heat, stirring often.

2. Reduce heat and boil gently, stirring often and reducing heat further as mixture thickens, for 40 to 50 minutes or until thickened. Test for doneness (for details, see page 325).

3. Ladle into sterilized jars to within 1/2 inch (1 cm) of rim. Remove any air pockets and adjust headspace, if necessary, by adding chutney; wipe rims. Apply prepared lids and rings; tighten rings just until fingertip-tight.

4. Process jars in a boiling water canner for 10 minutes (for details, see page 20). Transfer jars to a towel-lined surface and let rest at room temperature until cooled. Check seals; refrigerate any unsealed jars for up to 3 weeks.

> Sweet gold pineapples are less acidic than regular pineapples.

Plum Pear Chutney

In this chutney, pieces of pear are surrounded by a dark, savory mixture. Serve with pork roast or chops.

— o o o —

Tips

You'll need about 1½ lbs (750 g) each of plums and pears for this recipe.

Pears ripen well after being picked, so they are picked green for better quality in transporting. To speed ripening, place them in a paper bag. When ripe, a pear yields to light pressure near the bottom of the neck.

Varieties of apples that keep their shape when cooked include Golden Delicious, Northern Spy and Spartan. See page 25 for more details.

Recipe Suggestion

Stir into sauce for pork tenderloin.

4 cups	sliced red plums	1 L
3 cups	chopped peeled pears	750 mL
1	large apple that keeps its shape, peeled and sliced	1
3½ cups	packed brown sugar	875 mL
1½ cups	chopped onions	375 mL
1½ cups	cider vinegar	375 mL
½ cup	dried cranberries	125 mL
½ tsp	hot pepper flakes	2 mL
½ tsp	ground nutmeg (optional)	2 mL

1. In a Dutch oven or a large, heavy-bottomed pot, combine plums, pears, apple, brown sugar, onions, vinegar, cranberries, hot pepper flakes and nutmeg (if using). Bring to a boil over high heat, stirring often.

2. Reduce heat and boil gently, stirring often and reducing heat further as mixture thickens, for 45 to 60 minutes or until thickened. Test for doneness (for details, see page 325).

3. Ladle into sterilized jars to within ½ inch (1 cm) of rim. Remove any air pockets and adjust headspace, if necessary, by adding chutney; wipe rims. Apply prepared lids and rings; tighten rings just until fingertip-tight.

4. Process jars in a boiling water canner for 10 minutes (for details, see page 20). Transfer jars to a towel-lined surface and let rest at room temperature until cooled. Check seals; refrigerate any unsealed jars for up to 3 weeks.

Sweet Pepper Apple Chutney

Makes about five 8-ounce (250 mL) jars

This beautiful chutney, which is excellent with poultry or pork, contains red and yellow peppers and dried currants. For a different taste, substitute roasted red peppers for the fresh ones.

— o o o —

Tip

You'll need about 2 lbs (1 kg) of apples (about 5 medium) for this recipe. For information on the best apples to use, see page 25.

Variations

Sweet Pepper Peach Chutney: Substitute chopped peeled peaches for the apples.

Roasted Sweet Pepper Peach Chutney: Substitute 1½ cups (375 mL) chopped roasted red bell peppers for the fresh.

5 cups	chopped peeled apples that keep their shape	1.25 L
2 cups	chopped red bell peppers	500 mL
2 cups	packed brown sugar	500 mL
1½ cups	chopped onions	375 mL
1 cup	chopped yellow bell pepper	250 mL
2 or 3	cloves garlic, minced	2 or 3
1 cup	cider vinegar	250 mL
1 tsp	salt	5 mL
½ tsp	ground cloves	2 mL
½ tsp	hot pepper flakes	2 mL
¼ tsp	freshly ground black pepper	1 mL
½ cup	dried currants	125 mL

1. In a Dutch oven or a large, heavy-bottomed pot, combine apples, red peppers, brown sugar, onions, yellow pepper, garlic, vinegar, salt, cloves, hot pepper flakes and black pepper. Bring to a boil over high heat, stirring often.

2. Reduce heat and boil gently, stirring often and reducing heat further as mixture thickens, for 30 minutes. Stir in currants; cook, stirring often, for 15 minutes or until thickened. Test for doneness (for details, see page 325).

3. Ladle into sterilized jars to within ½ inch (1 cm) of rim. Remove any air pockets and adjust headspace, if necessary, by adding chutney; wipe rims. Apply prepared lids and rings; tighten rings just until fingertip-tight.

4. Process jars in a boiling water canner for 10 minutes (for details, see page 20). Transfer jars to a towel-lined surface and let rest at room temperature until cooled. Check seals; refrigerate any unsealed jars for up to 3 weeks.

> Dried currants are dried from tiny, seedless Zante grapes. They have no relation to red and black currants, which are from the gooseberry family. The name "currant" apparently comes from the Anglo-French *raisins de Corauntz*, "raisins of Corinth." Like other dried fruits, dried currants are high in dietary fiber.

Green Tomato Apple Chutney

Make this sensational chutney in early September, when the last of the tomatoes are struggling to ripen and the new harvest of apples appears in the stores. Serve with scrambled eggs, quiche and omelets, stir into hash brown potatoes or serve with cheese or cold meat.

— o o o —

Tips

You'll need about 3 lbs (1.5 kg) of tomatoes for this recipe.

For the best texture in this chutney, cut the tomatoes and apples into ½-inch (1 cm) chunks.

Varieties of apples that soften when cooked include McIntosh, Cortland, Empire and Russet. See page 25 for more details.

7 cups	chopped green or partially ripe tomatoes	1.75 L
4 cups	chopped peeled apples that soften	1 L
1½ cups	chopped onions	375 mL
1½ cups	packed brown sugar	375 mL
1 cup	granulated sugar	250 mL
1 cup	cider vinegar	250 mL
1	large clove garlic, minced	1
2 tbsp	mustard seeds	30 mL
2 tbsp	finely grated gingerroot	30 mL
1 tsp	salt	5 mL
½ tsp	hot pepper flakes or cayenne pepper	2 mL
¼ tsp	ground cloves	1 mL
1 cup	sultana raisins	250 mL

1. In a Dutch oven or a large, heavy-bottomed pot, combine tomatoes, apples, onions, brown sugar, granulated sugar, vinegar, garlic, mustard seeds, ginger, salt, hot pepper flakes and cloves. Bring to a boil over high heat, stirring often.

2. Reduce heat and boil gently, stirring often and reducing heat further as mixture thickens, for 40 to 50 minutes. Stir in raisins; cook, stirring often, for about 15 minutes or until thickened. Test for doneness (for details, see page 325).

3. Ladle into sterilized jars to within ½ inch (1 cm) of rim. Remove any air pockets and adjust headspace, if necessary, by adding chutney; wipe rims. Apply prepared lids and rings; tighten rings just until fingertip-tight.

4. Process jars in a boiling water canner for 10 minutes (for details, see page 20). Transfer jars to a towel-lined surface and let rest at room temperature until cooled. Check seals; refrigerate any unsealed jars for up to 3 weeks.

> The word "vinegar" comes from the French *vin aigre*, meaning "sour wine."

Tomato Apple Chipotle Chutney

The aroma while this chutney is cooking is amazing! I used chipotle peppers, which give it an interesting smoked flavor.

— o o o —

Tip

Varieties of apples that soften when cooked include McIntosh, Cortland, Empire and Russet. See page 25 for more details.

Variations

Tomato Basil Chutney with Sun-Dried Tomatoes: Omit the chipotle peppers, ground cloves and raisins. Add 2 tsp (10 mL) dried basil, 1 tsp (5 mL) dried oregano and ½ cup (125 mL) finely chopped softened sun-dried tomatoes.

Yellow Tomato Chutney: Use yellow tomatoes in place of the plum tomatoes, and replace the chipotle pepper with 1 tbsp (15 mL) finely chopped jalapeño peppers.

4 cups	chopped seeded peeled plum (Roma) tomatoes	1 L
4 cups	chopped peeled apples that soften	1 L
2 cups	chopped onions	500 mL
1½ cups	packed brown sugar	375 mL
¾ cup	granulated sugar	175 mL
1 cup	cider vinegar	250 mL
2	large cloves garlic, minced	2
2 tsp	finely minced drained canned chipotle pepper, or to taste	10 mL
1 tsp	salt	5 mL
⅛ tsp	ground cloves	0.5 mL
¾ cup	golden or sultana raisins	175 mL

1. In a Dutch oven or a large, deep, heavy-bottomed pot, combine tomatoes, apples, onions, brown sugar, granulated sugar, vinegar, garlic, chipotle pepper, salt and cloves. Bring to a boil over high heat, stirring often.

2. Reduce heat and boil gently, stirring often and reducing heat further as mixture thickens, for 45 minutes. Stir in raisins; cook, stirring often, for 15 to 20 minutes or until thickened. Test for doneness (for details, see page 325).

3. Ladle into sterilized jars to within ½ inch (1 cm) of rim. Remove any air pockets and adjust headspace, if necessary, by adding chutney; wipe rims. Apply prepared lids and rings; tighten rings just until fingertip-tight.

4. Process jars in a boiling water canner for 10 minutes (for details, see page 20). Transfer jars to a towel-lined surface and let rest at room temperature until cooled. Check seals; refrigerate any unsealed jars for up to 3 weeks.

> Buy chipotles (smoked jalapeños) with tomato purée in 7-oz (210 mL) cans. You will also see them labeled "in adobo sauce," which is a stewed tomato sauce with vinegar, garlic and spices. If you cannot find chipotle peppers, use any other fresh hot chile pepper you like, or hot pepper flakes to taste.

Recipes Using Preserves

You now have delicious fruit flavors captured in a jar. Jams, jellies, conserves, marmalades and chutneys are wonderful ingredients to add to other recipes. This chapter shows you how to use them in a variety of appetizers, main courses, desserts and baked goods.

Ideas for Using Preserves. 342

Savory Recipes

Baked Brie 345

Cheddar Cheese Thumbprints with Hot Pepper Jelly 346

Coconut Shrimp 347

Purple Basil Salad Dressing 348

Peach Barbecue Sauce 349

Caribbean Chicken 350

Garlic Chicken Portobello. 351

Steak Salad with Strawberry Balsamic Dressing. 352

Sweet Recipes

Cream Tea Scones 353

Stuffed French Toast 354

Easy Coffee Cake 355

Fruit Loaf. 356

Empire Cookies. 357

Marmalade Pecan Cookies 358

Shut Cookies. 359

Fig Bars. 360

French Apple Tarts. 361

Linzertorte. 362

Pineapple Tartlets 363

Lime Phyllo Tarts 364

continued…

Apricot Ladder Braid 365

Fried Bananas Caribbean. 366

Low-Fat Raspberry Mango Frozen Cake 367

Vanilla Jelly Roll 368

Sherry Trifle 369

Ideas for Using Preserves

Here are some suggestions for easy ways to use preserves.

Breakfast

- Stir jam or conserve into plain or vanilla yogurt. Sprinkle with granola.

- Stir jam or fruit butter into hot porridge to sweeten it. Pear Jam with Brown Sugar and Cinnamon (page 66) and Blueberry Maple Butter (page 314) would be particularly good.

- Add a little jelly or marmalade to sweeten grapefruit halves; warm in the microwave. Try Raspberry Jelly (page 272), Black Currant Jelly (page 261), Cranberry Orange Marmalade (page 248) or Wild Blueberry Lemon Marmalade (page 237).

- Stir a peach, apricot or berry preserve into cottage cheese.

- Stir jam into cream cheese to spread on bagels.

- Stir a bit of jam into softened butter; add finely chopped dried cranberries and finely grated orange peel. Spread on hot scones.

- Add jam or orange marmalade to pancake batter in place of some of the sugar and liquid.

- Warm jam or jelly and drizzle over pancakes or waffles.

- Layer crêpes alternately with cream cheese and jam; stack crêpes and cut into wedges. Serve with fresh fruit.

- Add preserves to breakfast shakes or smoothies.

Appetizers and Salads

- Spoon hot pepper jelly over softened or slightly warmed goat cheese.

- Mix a tart jelly, jam or fruit butter with a little vinegar and use as a sweet-and-sour sauce or dip for egg rolls. Try a plum, grape, kiwi, rhubarb or apricot jam, or Plum Good Apple Butter (page 321).

- Use hot pepper jelly as a dip for seafood (crab cakes, bacon-wrapped shrimp) or samosas.

- Stir hot pepper jelly, herb jelly or wine jelly into homemade salad dressing.

- Stir mango chutney into curried chicken salad.

Entrées

- Add wine jelly or garlic jelly to a meat marinade.

- When cooking duck, chicken or pork, use a cherry jam or conserve to deglaze the pan, adding flavor to your sauce or gravy.

- Glaze chicken or pork with herb jelly or hot pepper jelly.

- Brush pineapple, mango or kiwi preserves over ham to glaze.

- Use chutney as a sauce for chicken or pork skewers. Purée to use as a finishing glaze, or serve on the side as a dip.

- Add cranberry, cherry, apricot or plum preserves to a slow cooker sauce for meat or meatballs.

- Stir ginger jam, garlic jelly or orange marmalade into a stir-fry.

Side Dishes

- Brush apricot or pineapple preserves on the surface of winter squash halves before baking.

- Stir a little jelly into cooked vegetables, along with a little butter. Herb jellies are particularly good, or try Beet Plum Jelly (page 260) with carrots or sliced beets, or an apricot jam with carrots or sweet potatoes.

- Use a cranberry jelly or Spiced Carrot Apple Pineapple Conserve (page 208) to sweeten dressing for coleslaw.

continued…

Desserts and Snacks

- Place a spoonful of jam or conserve in the center of sweet batter in half-full muffin pans, top with more batter and bake. Or spoon a bit of jam on top before baking. For cornmeal muffins, use a hot pepper jelly.

- Spoon jam or jelly into the center of thumbprint cookies. For Cheddar Cheese Thumbprints with Hot Pepper Jelly (page 346), use hot pepper or savory jellies.

- Use jam as a filling for cookies such as rugelach.

- Stir about 1/3 cup (75 mL) raspberry, cherry, orange or apricot jam into brownie batter.

- Swirl jam through batter for cheesecake before baking, or glaze the top of cooled cheesecake with jelly.

- Use jam or jelly to fill a layer cake or jelly roll.

- When making trifle, warm jam and stir in a bit of orange or almond liqueur; spoon over sponge cake.

- Make turnovers using jam folded inside puff pastry squares.

- Use jam, conserve or mincemeat to fill mini tart shells.

- Warm jam with a little liqueur, if desired; strain through a fine-mesh sieve and brush over fruit flans or tarts to glaze.

Baked Brie

**Makes about
6 servings**

*This is a quick appetizer
to make — warm, oozing
cheese with a topping.*

— o o o —

Preserve Suggestions

Jams: Pears and Port Jam
(page 70), Fig Strawberry
Jam with Balsamic Vinegar
(page 112), Spiced Peach
Cranberry Jam (page 126)

Conserves: Fig and Italian
Plum Conserve (page 215),
Cherry Cranberry Orange
Conserve with Grand
Marnier (page 209)

Chutneys: Apricot Mango
Chutney (page 329), Cran-
Apple Sage and Thyme
Chutney (page 330)

Onion Jam: Strawberry
Onion Jam with Balsamic
Vinegar and Rosemary
(page 196)

Variation

Bake the Brie without
removing the top, and
serve with Red Currant
Jelly (page 273),
Pineapple Habanero
Pepper Jelly (page 290)
or Fire and Ice Jelly
(page 292).

- Preheat oven to 350°F (180°C)
- Shallow baking dish or foil-lined baking sheet

1	whole 4-inch (10 cm) round Brie (about 8 oz/250 g)	1
1/3 cup	jam, conserve or chutney	75 mL
1/3 cup	coarsely chopped pecans (optional)	75 mL
	Crackers	

1. Carefully slice rind off one flat side of the Brie (this is best done while it's cold from the refrigerator). Place rind side down in baking dish. Top with jam and sprinkle with pecans (if using).

2. Bake in preheated oven for 10 to 12 minutes or until softened. Serve immediately with crackers.

Cheddar Cheese Thumbprints with Hot Pepper Jelly

Makes 28 to 30 savory cookies

These delectable savory cookies are an impressive party hors d'oeuvre. I like to make them with sharp (aged) white Cheddar. These are also good filled with any of the wine jellies.

— o o o —

Tips

If you do not have a food processor, combine butter and cheese in a medium bowl; stir with a wooden spoon to blend well. In a small bowl, combine flour, salt and cayenne; stir into cheese mixture until flour is moistened and mixture begins to stick together. Proceed with step 3.

For nicely shaped, deep indentations, use the end of a wooden spoon instead of your thumb.

Cookies may be baked ahead and stored in an airtight container at room temperature for up to 2 days or in the freezer for up to 3 months. To crisp, heat cookies (thawed if they were frozen) on a baking sheet in a 350°F (180°C) oven for 3 minutes. Let cool on a wire rack. Top with jelly and serve.

- Preheat oven to 375°F (190°C)

1½ cups	all-purpose flour	375 mL
½ tsp	salt	2 mL
Pinch	cayenne pepper	Pinch
⅔ cup	butter, softened	150 mL
2 cups	finely shredded sharp (aged) Cheddar cheese	500 mL
½ cup	Pineapple Habanero Pepper Jelly (page 290), Apple Jalapeño Pepper Jelly (page 288) or Fire and Ice Jelly (page 292)	125 mL

1. In a food processor fitted with a metal blade, combine flour, salt and cayenne. Add butter; pulse several times to combine. Add cheese; pulse until flour is all moistened and mixture begins to stick together.

2. Transfer to a lightly floured surface, knead a few times and form into a ball. Cover with plastic wrap and refrigerate for 30 minutes.

3. Roll dough into 1-inch (2.5 cm) balls, using about 1 tbsp (15 mL) dough for each ball. Place at least 2 inches (5 cm) apart on baking sheets. Using a wooden spoon or your thumb, make an indentation in the center of each ball.

4. Bake in preheated oven, in batches as necessary, for 8 to 10 minutes or until firm and bottoms are golden. Let cool on baking sheets for 1 minute, then lightly press indentations again. Transfer to wire racks and let cool completely.

5. Just before serving, stir jelly slightly and place about 1 tsp (5 mL) in the center of each cookie.

Variations

If desired, roll balls of dough in finely chopped nuts, such as pecans or walnuts, or lightly toasted sesame seeds.

Add ½ tsp (2 mL) paprika or ¼ tsp (1 mL) dry mustard to the flour mixture.

Coconut Shrimp

Here's a tasty appetizer to try. Warmed Piña Colada Jam makes the perfect dip for these scrumptious shrimp.

—ooo—

* Candy/deep-fry thermometer

1	egg yolk	1
½ cup	milk	125 mL
1 cup	unsweetened shredded or medium desiccated coconut, divided	250 mL
½ cup	all-purpose flour	125 mL
½ tsp	salt	2 mL
Pinch	cayenne pepper	Pinch
1 lb	large shrimp, peeled and deveined (leave tails on)	500 g
	Vegetable oil	
½ cup	Piña Colada Jam (page 71) or Lime Coconut Marmalade (page 241)	125 mL

1. In a small bowl, beat egg yolk and milk. Stir in ¼ cup (60 mL) of the coconut, flour, salt and cayenne. Cover and refrigerate for 30 minutes.

2. Dry shrimp well with paper towels. Cover and refrigerate until ready to cook.

3. Preheat oven to 225°F (110°C).

4. Pour oil into a skillet to about 1 inch (2.5 cm) deep. Heat over medium-high heat until it reaches 375°F (190°C).

5. Place the remaining ¾ cup (175 mL) coconut in a shallow bowl or on a plate. Holding shrimp by the tail, dip into batter, then into coconut; shake off excess.

6. Fry about 4 at a time in hot oil for about 30 seconds on each side or until golden brown. Remove with a slotted spoon and drain on paper towels. Keep hot on a baking sheet in preheated oven and repeat with remaining shrimp. Discard any excess batter and coconut.

7. In a small saucepan over low heat or in the microwave, warm jam. Serve hot shrimp with warmed jam for dipping.

Purple Basil Salad Dressing

Makes about ½ cup (125 mL)

Use Purple Basil Wine Jelly to make this delicious vinaigrette to serve over mixed greens. Add sliced oranges or strawberries, thinly sliced red onion, toasted sliced almonds or pecan pieces, and even edible flowers to your salad.

— ○ ○ ○ —

Tip

It's best not to use olive oil in this dressing, as the strong taste will overpower the jelly.

3 tbsp	Purple Basil Wine Jelly (page 299)	45 mL
1 tbsp	white wine vinegar	15 mL
1 tsp	Dijon mustard	5 mL
	Salt and freshly ground black pepper	
¼ cup	vegetable oil	60 mL

1. In a small bowl or glass measuring cup, whisk together jelly, vinegar and mustard until smooth. Season to taste with salt and pepper. Slowly whisk in oil.

2. Use immediately or cover and refrigerate for up to 3 days. Whisk to blend and pour over salad just before serving.

Peach Barbecue Sauce

Makes about 2⅔ cups
(650 mL)

This tasty sauce is perfect for making barbecued chicken or ribs. It's also great on chicken wings, or used as a dip. Turn up the heat by adding hot pepper sauce to taste.

— o o o —

Tip

Brush sauce over chicken or preboiled ribs and marinate in the refrigerator for 3 hours. Brush additional sauce over top while barbecuing.

1 cup	Peach Jam (variation, page 64)	250 mL
1½ cups	chili sauce	375 mL
2 tbsp	white or cider vinegar	30 mL
2 tbsp	Worcestershire sauce	30 mL
1 tsp	ground ginger	5 mL
½ tsp	garlic powder	2 mL

1. In a food processor fitted with a metal blade or a blender, purée jam (or press through a sieve, discarding solids).

2. Add chili sauce, vinegar, Worcestershire sauce, ginger and garlic powder and process until smooth (or whisk ingredients together in a bowl).

3. Use immediately or transfer to an airtight container and refrigerate for up to 1 week.

> Before brushing meat, transfer some sauce to a separate bowl to use as baste on the barbecue or a dip at the table. After coating the meat, make sure to discard any extra sauce that has come into contact with the brush that touched the raw meat.

Caribbean Chicken

Makes 4 servings

Use Caribbean Treasure Conserve or Piña Colada Jam to make this quick chicken dinner. Put some rice on first to go with it; the chicken will be ready in about 20 minutes.

—o o o—

1 lb	boneless skinless chicken breasts	500 g
½ cup	all-purpose flour	125 mL
½ tsp	salt	2 mL
	Freshly ground black pepper	
1	egg	1
2 tbsp	vegetable oil	30 mL
1 tbsp	cornstarch or all-purpose flour	15 mL
1 cup	chicken broth	250 mL
½ cup	Caribbean Treasure Conserve (page 219) or Piña Colada Jam (page 71)	125 mL

1. Cut chicken into bite-size pieces. In a small bowl, combine flour, salt and a few grinds of pepper. In another bowl, lightly beat egg.

2. Dip chicken pieces into egg, then into flour mixture to coat. Discard any excess egg and flour mixture.

3. In a large skillet, heat oil over medium heat. Cook chicken, stirring often, until golden on all sides; transfer to a bowl and set aside.

4. In a small bowl, whisk together cornstarch and broth until well blended. Pour into skillet and cook over medium heat until bubbling, scraping browned bits from bottom of pan. Stir in conserve until blended.

5. Return chicken to pan with any accumulated juices; simmer, stirring occasionally, for 3 to 5 minutes or until chicken is no longer pink inside and sauce is thickened.

Garlic Chicken Portobello

Makes 4 servings

Garlic Jelly is a great ingredient to add to meat dishes for a touch of garlic. Serve this dish with mashed potatoes or fettuccine, and baby carrots and broccoli.

—ooo—

2 tbsp	vegetable oil (approx.)	30 mL
6 oz	stemmed portobello mushrooms, cut into 1/4-inch (0.5 cm) slices	175 g
1 tsp	finely chopped fresh thyme (or 1/4 tsp/1 mL dried)	5 mL
1 lb	boneless skinless chicken breasts	500 g
	Salt and freshly ground black pepper	
1/2 cup	white wine, chicken broth or unsweetened apple cider	125 mL
3 tbsp	Garlic Jelly (page 286) or Roasted Garlic Wine Jelly (page 287)	45 mL
3/4 cup	chicken broth	175 mL
1 tbsp	all-purpose flour	15 mL
2 tbsp	chopped fresh parsley	30 mL

1. In a large skillet, heat oil over medium heat. Add mushrooms and thyme; sauté for 3 minutes or until softened. Transfer to a bowl and set aside.

2. Cut each chicken breast into 3 equal pieces; season to taste with salt and pepper. Add a little more oil to the pan, if needed. Brown chicken on each side, turning once; transfer to a plate and set aside.

3. Add wine and jelly to pan, whisking to combine; cook over medium heat until bubbling, scraping browned bits from bottom of pan. Whisk together chicken broth and flour; whisk into wine mixture. Cook, whisking, for 1 to 2 minutes or until slightly thickened.

4. Return mushrooms and chicken to pan and stir in parsley. Simmer,, stirring occasionally, for 3 to 5 minutes or until chicken is no longer pink inside and sauce is thickened. Serve immediately.

Steak Salad with Strawberry Balsamic Dressing

Makes 4 servings

The strawberry balsamic dressing is a slightly sweet complement to the peppery flavors of the salad, with toasted walnuts adding a pleasant crunch.

— o o o —

Tip

How to Toast Walnuts: One of the easiest ways to do this is to place walnuts in a dry skillet (preferably nonstick). Toast over medium heat, stirring often, until lightly browned. Transfer to a small bowl and let cool. This can be done several hours ahead, if desired.

Variations

For a less sweet dressing, use red wine vinegar instead of balsamic.

Add grilled asparagus, or grilled or roasted red or yellow bell peppers.

Use sweet onions in place of the red onions.

Replace the steak with 10 oz (300 g) goat cheese, crumbled over top of salads.

Add sliced fresh strawberries when they're in season.

- Preheat barbecue grill to high or preheat broiler

4	portions boneless sirloin steak (each about 6 oz/175 g)	4
	Cracked or coarsely ground black pepper	
¼ cup	vegetable oil	60 mL
3 cups	thinly sliced red onions	750 mL
1	large clove garlic, minced	1
¼ cup	strawberry jam	60 mL
¼ cup	balsamic vinegar	60 mL
4 cups	packed mixed greens	1 L
1 cup	packed arugula or baby spinach	250 mL
½ cup	coarsely chopped walnuts, toasted (see tip, at left)	125 mL

1. Coat steaks generously with pepper. Grill or broil to desired doneness. Transfer to a cutting board, tent with foil and let rest for 5 to 10 minutes to allow juices to settle.

2. Meanwhile, in a large nonstick skillet, heat oil over medium heat. Add onions; cook, stirring, for 5 minutes. Stir in garlic; cook, stirring, for 2 minutes or until onions are very soft and lightly browned. Stir in jam and vinegar; heat until bubbling.

3. Divide mixed greens and arugula among four large salad plates. Sprinkle with walnuts. Thinly slice steak on the diagonal and arrange on top. Spoon onion mixture over salad and steak.

Cream Tea Scones

*My favorite way to
enjoy preserves is on
fresh-baked scones. The
recipe for these light,
delicious scones comes
from friend and colleague
Carol Ferguson, former
food editor of* Canadian
Living *and* Homemaker's
*magazines, and author
of* The New Canadian
Basics Cookbook
(Penguin, 1999).

— o o o —

Tip
Reduce the oven
temperature if scones begin
to brown too quickly; your
oven may be hotter than it
says it is.

Variation
For wedges, divide
dough in half and shape
into two rounds about
3/4 inch (2 cm) thick; dust
the top of each lightly
with flour and place on
baking sheet. With a
floured knife, cut each
round into 6 wedges,
but do not separate.
Brush tops with reserved
egg; sprinkle with
sugar. Bake for about
15 minutes or until
golden brown. Makes
12 wedges.

- Preheat oven to 425°F (220°C)
- 2½-inch (6.5 cm) round biscuit or cookie cutter

2 cups	all-purpose flour (or 1 cup/250 mL each all-purpose flour and cake-and-pastry flour)	500 mL
2 tbsp	granulated sugar (approx.)	30 mL
1 tbsp	baking powder	15 mL
½ tsp	salt	2 mL
½ cup	butter, softened	125 mL
1	egg	1
⅔ cup	milk or light (5%) cream	150 mL

1. In a large bowl, combine flour, sugar, baking powder and salt. Using a pastry blender, cut in butter until mixture resembles coarse crumbs.

2. In a small bowl, beat egg; set 1 tbsp (15 mL) aside to brush on top of scones before baking. Stir milk into remaining egg.

3. Using a fork, stir egg mixture into flour mixture to make a light, soft dough. If dough seems too sticky, stir in a bit more flour.

4. Gather dough into a ball and knead lightly a few times on a lightly floured surface until smooth. Flatten with hands or a rolling pin to ¾-inch (2 cm) thickness. Using biscuit cutter, cut into rounds, rerolling scraps or pressing them together to make scones of about the same size. Place on a baking sheet, about 2 inches (5 cm) apart. Brush tops with reserved egg. Sprinkle with a little sugar, if desired.

5. Bake in preheated oven for 10 to 12 minutes or until golden brown. Serve hot.

Stuffed French Toast

Makes 4 servings

This special French toast has a delightful surprise filling. Use jams made from strawberries, peaches, cherries, blueberries, apricots — whatever you like! Serve drizzled with warmed jam or maple syrup and whipped cream.

— o o o —

Tip

For the jam, try Strawberry Jam (page 83), Blueberry Banana Jam (page 101), Sour Cherry Raspberry Jam (page 109) or Spiced Mango Jam (page 62).

8	slices French stick bread, cut diagonally in 1$\frac{1}{2}$-inch (4 cm) thick slices	8
$\frac{1}{2}$ cup	cream cheese, softened	125 mL
1 tbsp	jam	15 mL
4	eggs	4
$\frac{1}{2}$ cup	milk	125 mL
$\frac{1}{2}$ tsp	vanilla extract	2 mL
2 tbsp	vegetable oil (approx.), divided	30 mL

1. Cut a slit into the side of each slice of bread (as though you are making two slices, each $\frac{3}{4}$ inch/2 cm thick), but do not cut all the way through.

2. In a bowl, mash together cream cheese and jam. Spread about 1 tbsp (15 mL) filling evenly into each slit. Press gently to close.

3. In another bowl, whisk together eggs, milk and vanilla. Dip each stuffed bread slice in egg mixture, coating both sides. (If bread is dry, let it soak longer.)

4. In a nonstick skillet, heat 1 tbsp (15 mL) of the oil over medium heat. Cook 4 slices of stuffed bread for 1 to 2 minutes per side or until golden brown. Repeat with the remaining bread, adding more oil as needed.

Easy Coffee Cake

Makes about 8 servings

This cake takes just a few minutes to stir together. Use any of your jams or conserves to give it a special flavor. The nuts will toast as it bakes.

— o o o —

- Preheat oven to 350°F (180°C)
- 8-inch (20 cm) square cake pan, greased

1 1/2 cups	all-purpose flour	375 mL
1/2 cup	granulated sugar	125 mL
2 tsp	baking powder	10 mL
1/2 tsp	salt	2 mL
1	egg	1
3/4 cup	milk	175 mL
1/2 cup	vegetable oil	125 mL
1/2 tsp	vanilla extract	2 mL
1/4 cup	jam	60 mL
2 tbsp	sliced almonds or chopped pecans (optional)	30 mL

1. In a large bowl, combine flour, sugar, baking powder and salt.

2. In another bowl, whisk together egg, milk, oil and vanilla. Stir into flour mixture until just combined.

3. Spoon batter into prepared pan, smoothing top. Dot with jam and sprinkle with nuts (if using).

4. Bake in preheated oven for about 30 minutes or until golden and a tester inserted in the center comes out clean. Serve warm.

Fruit Loaf

**Makes 1 loaf
(about 12 slices)**

Make this loaf with Lemon Ginger Marmalade (page 233), Cranberry Orange Marmalade (page 248), Zucchini Orange Marmalade (page 251), Banana Orange and Date Conserve (page 191), Cherry Cranberry Orange Conserve with Grand Marnier (page 209) or Pear Maple Walnut Conserve (page 218). After cooling the loaf, wrap it well and cut it the next day. It freezes well too.

— o o o —

Tips

Chop peel smaller if marmalade has large pieces.

If using a dark metal loaf pan or a glass loaf dish, reduce the oven temperature to 325°F (160°C) and bake the loaf a little longer.

Variation

Lemon Ginger Poppy Seed Loaf: Use Lemon Ginger Marmalade (page 233) and add 2 tbsp (30 mL) poppy seeds to the flour mixture.

- Preheat oven to 350°F (180°C)
- 9- by 5-inch (23 by 12.5 cm) metal loaf pan, greased and floured

2 cups	all-purpose flour	500 mL
1½ tsp	baking powder	7 mL
½ tsp	salt	2 mL
½ cup	butter, softened	125 mL
½ cup	granulated sugar	125 mL
2	eggs	2
½ tsp	vanilla extract	2 mL
¾ cup	marmalade or conserve	175 mL
⅔ cup	milk	150 mL

Glaze (Optional)

¼ cup	lemon or lime juice	60 mL
¼ cup	granulated sugar	60 mL

1. In a bowl, combine flour, baking powder and salt.

2. In a large bowl, using an electric mixer, beat butter briefly until lightened. Beat in sugar until fluffy. Beat in eggs and vanilla until blended. Beat in marmalade just until combined. Stir in flour mixture alternately with milk, making three additions of flour and two of milk.

3. Pour into prepared pan, smoothing top with a knife. Bake in preheated oven for 50 to 60 minutes or until a tester inserted in the center comes out clean. Let cool in pan on a wire rack for 10 minutes, then turn out onto rack to cool. If glazing, place a baking sheet under the rack to catch drips.

4. *Prepare the glaze (if using):* In a small bowl, whisk together lemon juice and sugar. While the loaf is still warm, prick the surface with a toothpick or skewer; slowly pour glaze over loaf, letting it soak in. Let cool completely.

Empire Cookies

**Makes about
2 dozen cookies**

These are sandwich-style cookies filled with jam. Use cookie cutters with scalloped edges if you can. This recipe is from my friend Pat Moynihan (see Contributors, page 12), who makes them for courses she teaches on teas.

— o o o —

Tip
Press jam with large pieces of fruit through a sieve before spreading on cookies.

Variations
Try any of the apricot jams (pages 46 to 48), Blackberry Jam (page 50), Boysenberry Jam (page 53), Plumcot Orange Jam (page 133) or Strawberry Jam (page 83) instead of Raspberry Jam.

Valentine Cookies: Use a heart-shaped cookie cutter. If desired, use a smaller heart cutter to cut holes in the top halves of the cookies so the jam will show through. Bake the cut-out pieces too and make little heart cookies. Tint the icing with red food coloring, if desired.

Skip the icing and dust the tops of the cookies with confectioner's (icing) sugar.

- 2-inch (5 cm) round cookie cutter

2¼ cups	all-purpose flour	550 mL
1½ tsp	baking powder	7 mL
¼ tsp	salt	1 mL
½ cup	butter, softened	125 mL
¼ cup	shortening, softened	60 mL
¾ cup	granulated sugar	175 mL
2	eggs	2
1 tsp	vanilla extract	5 mL
½ cup	Raspberry Jam (page 78)	125 mL

Icing

1½ cups	sifted confectioner's (icing) sugar	375 mL
¼ tsp	almond extract	1 mL
2 tbsp	hot water (approx.)	30 mL
	Candied cherries (optional)	

1. In a bowl, combine flour, baking powder and salt.

2. In a large bowl, using an electric mixer, beat butter and shortening briefly to lighten. Beat in sugar until fluffy. Beat in eggs and vanilla until blended. Stir in flour mixture until a soft dough forms. Form dough into a ball, wrap in plastic wrap and refrigerate for 1 hour.

3. Preheat oven to 350°F (180°C).

4. On a lightly floured surface, roll out dough to ¼-inch (0.5 cm) thickness. Cut into 2-inch (5 cm) rounds, rerolling scraps. Place on baking sheets, at least 2 inches (5 cm) apart.

5. Bake, in batches as necessary, for 8 to 10 minutes or until lightly browned around the edges. Transfer to wire racks and let cool completely.

6. *Prepare the icing:* In a bowl, combine icing sugar, almond extract and enough of the hot water to make a thin icing.

7. Spread the bottoms of half of the cookies with jam. Ice the tops of the remaining cookies and decorate each with a small piece of candied cherry (if using). Place tops icing side up onto jam-coated bottoms, sandwiching the jam between cookies. Store in a single layer in an airtight container or cookie tin for up to 1 week.

Marmalade Pecan Cookies

Makes 2 to 3 dozen cookies

These soft cookies with a nutty crunch can be made with either marmalade or conserve.

— o o o —

Tip

Try using Seville Orange Marmalade (page 245), Tangerine and Honey Marmalade (page 247), Lemon Ginger Marmalade (page 233), Apple Rum Raisin Conserve (page 205), Apricot Almond Conserve (page 206) or Chunky Cherry Plum Conserve (page 210).

Variations

Caribbean Treasure Cookies: Use Caribbean Treasure Conserve (page 219) and add ½ cup (125 mL) sweetened shredded coconut with the pecans.

Carrot Apple Mincemeat Cookies: Use Carrot Apple Mincemeat (page 197) in place of the marmalade and omit the cinnamon and pecans.

- Preheat oven to 350°F (180°C)
- Baking sheets, greased

2¼ cups	all-purpose flour	550 mL
2 tsp	baking powder	10 mL
½ tsp	ground cinnamon	2 mL
¼ tsp	baking soda	1 mL
¼ tsp	salt	1 mL
½ cup	butter, softened	125 mL
½ cup	packed brown sugar	125 mL
1	egg	1
½ tsp	vanilla extract	2 mL
½ cup	marmalade or conserve	125 mL
¾ cup	coarsely chopped pecans	175 mL

1. In a bowl, combine flour, baking powder, cinnamon, baking soda and salt.

2. In a large bowl, using an electric mixer, beat butter briefly to lighten. Beat in brown sugar until fluffy. Beat in egg and vanilla until blended. Beat in marmalade just until combined. Stir in flour mixture just until combined. Stir in pecans.

3. Drop spoonfuls onto prepared baking sheets, at least 2 inches (5 cm) apart. Bake in preheated oven, in batches as necessary, for 10 to 12 minutes or until lightly browned. Transfer to wire racks and let cool completely. Store in an airtight container or cookie tin for up to 1 week.

Shut Cookies

Makes 36 to 40 sandwich cookies

My grandmother Margaret Stefan made this favorite recipe for us when my five siblings and I visited the farm every summer. I learned to make them with her and my cousin JoAnne. Our cousins (five brothers), who lived on the farm next door, named them "shut" cookies because they were glued shut with the date filling.

— o o o —

Tips

These cookies work best with thick conserves or thick, well-set jam. Try Banana Orange and Date Conserve (page 191), Three-Berry Blend Jam (page 156) or Plum Rum and Prune Conserve (page 223). Purée or strain through a mesh sieve to remove large fruit pieces. They're also great with thick fruit butters, such as Spiced Apricot Butter (page 311).

Use a cookie cutter with a scalloped edge, if desired.

- Preheat oven to 350°F (180°C)
- 2-inch (5 cm) round cookie or biscuit cutter

2½ cups	all-purpose flour (approx.)	625 mL
1 tsp	salt	5 mL
3 cups	quick-cooking rolled oats (not the instant type)	750 mL
1½ cups	butter, softened	375 mL
1 cup	packed brown sugar	250 mL
1 tsp	baking soda	5 mL
2 tsp	hot water	10 mL
1 cup	thick conserve, jam or fruit butter (see tip, at left)	250 mL

1. In a medium bowl, combine flour and salt. Stir in oats. Set aside.

2. In a large bowl, using an electric mixer, cream together butter and brown sugar until fluffy. In a small bowl, combine baking soda and water. Beat into creamed mixture. Using a wooden spoon, stir in flour mixture until well combined. (Dough should be moist but not sticky; add more flour as needed, 1 tbsp/15 mL at a time.)

3. Remove half the dough, form into a ball and place on a lightly floured surface. Roll out to ¼-inch (0.5 cm) thickness. Using cookie cutter, cut into rounds, rerolling scraps. Place at least 1 inch (2.5 cm) apart on baking sheets. Repeat with the remaining dough.

4. Bake in preheated oven, in batches as necessary, for 6 to 8 minutes or until lightly browned around edges. Transfer to wire racks and let cool completely.

5. Spread half of the cookies with a generous teaspoon (5 mL) of conserve. Place another cookie on top of each and press to stick shut. Store in an airtight container at room temperature for up to 1 week.

> My grandma's original recipe says to store the cookies "in a clean ice cream pail," as she used to save and reuse everything! My grandpa loved ice cream, and even poured thick farm cream over it. He lived to 96.

Fig Bars

Makes about 4 dozen cookies

Fig jam makes a quick filling for these classic cookies. I made these especially for Lise Ferguson, who kept insisting on a recipe.

—o o o—

Variations

Orange Fig Bars: Use Fig Orange Jam (page 111) to fill these cookies.

Strawberry Fig Bars: Make Fig Strawberry Jam with Balsamic Vinegar (page 112), omitting the vinegar, and use to fill these cookies.

The Fig Newton, named after a suburb of Boston, was introduced in 1891 by the Kennedy Biscuit Works. James Henry Mitchell is credited with designing a machine that would make and fill a cookie in one step.

- Preheat oven to 350°F (180°C)
- Baking sheets, lightly greased or lined with parchment paper

2 cups	all-purpose flour	500 mL
1 tsp	baking powder	5 mL
½ tsp	salt	2 mL
½ tsp	ground cinnamon	2 mL
¼ tsp	ground nutmeg	1 mL
⅔ cup	butter, softened, or soft shortening (or a combination)	150 mL
1 cup	granulated sugar	250 mL
2	eggs	2
½ tsp	vanilla extract	2 mL
1 cup	Dried Fig Jam (page 57) or Fig Jam (page 56)	250 mL
1	egg, lightly beaten	1

1. In a medium bowl, combine flour, baking powder, salt, cinnamon and nutmeg. Set aside.

2. In a large bowl, using an electric mixer, cream together butter and sugar until fluffy. Beat in the 2 eggs and vanilla until creamy. Using a wooden spoon, stir in flour mixture just until combined. Form into 3 logs, each 8 by 2 inches (20 by 5 cm). Wrap well with plastic wrap and refrigerate for about 1 hour or until slightly firm.

3. On a lightly floured surface, working with one log at a time, roll into a 12- by 7-inch (30 by 18 cm) rectangle, then cut lengthwise into two strips 3½ inches (8.5 cm) wide. Spoon about 2 tbsp (30 mL) jam in a ½-inch (1 cm) strip down the center of each. Fold one long side of dough over jam. Brush lightly beaten egg along the edge of folded dough. Fold the other long side of dough over the egg-brushed edge. Press lightly to seal. Cut each strip into eight 1½-inch (4 cm) long pieces. Place seam side down on prepared baking sheet. Repeat with the remaining dough and jam.

4. Bake in preheated oven, in batches as necessary, for 16 to 18 minutes or until lightly browned. Let cool on pan for 1 minute. Transfer to wire racks and let cool completely. Store in an airtight container or cookie tin at room temperature for up to 1 week.

French Apple Tarts

I developed this recipe for the Ontario Apple Producers, using Apricot Jam mixed with brandy to glaze the fruit after the tarts are baked. Frozen puff pastry makes it easy to prepare this elegant dessert.

— o o o —

Tips

For information on the best apples to use, see page 25.

You can use any of the apricot jams in this book. If your jam has bigger pieces of fruit in it, warm it slightly in the microwave and press through a fine-mesh sieve before brushing it on.

Variations

Replace the apricot jam with Blood Orange Marmalade (page 242), Cranberry Orange Marmalade (page 248), Tangelo Marmalade (page 246), Red Currant Jelly (page 273), Cranberry Orange and Ginger Jelly (page 264), Pomegranate Jelly (page 271) or Kir Royale Jelly (page 294).

• Preheat oven to 400°F (200°C)

1	package (14 to 16 oz/400 to 500 g) frozen puff pastry, thawed	1
4	large apples that hold their shape, peeled and sliced	4
1 tbsp	lemon juice	15 mL
2 tbsp	granulated sugar, divided	30 mL
1/2 tsp	ground cinnamon	2 mL
1/4 cup	apricot jam	60 mL
2 tsp	apricot brandy, orange liqueur or orange juice	10 mL

1. On a lightly floured surface, roll out half of the puff pastry into a 9-inch (23 cm) square. Cut into four 4½-inch (11.5 cm) squares. Place on a baking sheet, about 2 inches (5 cm) apart. Repeat with the remaining pastry on another baking sheet.

2. In a large bowl, toss apple slices with lemon juice. In a small bowl, combine 1 tbsp (15 mL) of the sugar and the cinnamon; stir into apples.

3. Arrange apple slices on pastry, overlapping slightly. Place one of the baking sheets in the refrigerator.

4. Place the other baking sheet in the preheated oven and bake for 15 minutes. Sprinkle half of the remaining sugar over the apples. Rotate baking sheet for even browning and bake for about 10 minutes or until pastry is puffed and golden. Repeat with the second baking sheet, using the remaining sugar.

5. In a small bowl, whisk together jam and brandy. Brush over warm tarts to glaze. Serve warm or at room temperature.

Linzertorte

Makes 8 servings

This delicious jam-filled pastry originated in Linz, Austria, around the early 1700s. It can be made with many different jams, such as black or red currant, apricot or raspberry. I chose to make it with Sweet Cherry and Black Plum Jam (page 108). My simplified version eliminates the lattice top.

— o o o —

Tips

You can make the dough even more quickly by adding the dry ingredients and the sugar to the ground nuts in the food processor. Then pulse in the butter until coarse crumbs form. In a small bowl, lightly beat egg and vanilla; pulse into dough just until well combined. If dough is sticky, add flour as needed, 1 tbsp (15 mL) at a time.

If you do not have a food processor, you can purchase ground almonds or hazelnuts and skip the toasting.

Variations

Replace ¼ cup (60 mL) of the flour with unsweetened cocoa powder.

Substitute hazelnuts for the almonds. Rub off the skins after toasting.

- Preheat oven to 350°F (180°C)
- Fluted 9-inch (23 cm) tart pan, preferably with removable bottom, buttered

1 cup	almonds (whole or slivered), toasted and cooled	250 mL
1¾ cups	all-purpose flour (approx.)	425 mL
2 tsp	finely grated lemon rind	10 mL
¾ tsp	ground cinnamon	4 mL
½ tsp	baking powder	2 mL
½ tsp	salt	2 mL
⅛ tsp	ground cloves	0.5 mL
¾ cup	butter, softened	175 mL
1 cup	granulated sugar	250 mL
1	egg	1
1 tsp	vanilla extract	5 mL
1 cup	jam	250 mL

1. In a food processor fitted with a metal blade, process almonds until finely ground.

2. In a bowl, combine ground almonds, flour, lemon rind, cinnamon, baking powder, salt and cloves. Set aside.

3. In a large bowl, using an electric mixer, cream together butter and sugar until fluffy. Beat in egg and vanilla. Using a wooden spoon, stir in flour mixture until dough comes together. (Dough should not be sticky; add more flour as needed, 1 tbsp/15 mL at a time.) Reserve 1 cup (250 mL) of the dough for the topping.

4. Press the remaining dough into bottom and sides of prepared tart pan, creating a ½-inch (1 cm) thick edge. Stir jam a bit and spread evenly over the crust. Drop reserved dough in small pieces on top, pressing it lightly into the jam.

5. Bake in preheated oven for 25 to 30 minutes or until lightly browned. Transfer to a wire rack and let cool for 1 hour. Remove outer ring and let cool completely before slicing.

Pineapple Tartlets

Makes about 2 dozen mini tarts

This recipe is from my friend Pat Moynihan's Auntie Ev, who makes them every Christmas. They quickly disappear from her cookie tray. They would be good with any jam.

— o o o —

- Preheat oven to 400°F (200°C)
- Mini tart pans (about 1½-inch/4 cm diameter)

2 cups	all-purpose flour	500 mL
4 tsp	baking powder	20 mL
¼ tsp	salt	1 mL
1 cup	butter, softened	250 mL
2 tbsp	granulated sugar	30 mL
1	egg	1
2 tbsp	milk	30 mL
1 tsp	vanilla extract	5 mL
⅓ cup	Piña Colada Jam (page 71) or Pineapple Citrus Marmalade (page 253)	75 mL

1. In a bowl, combine flour, baking powder and salt.

2. In a large bowl, using an electric mixer, cream together butter and sugar. Beat in egg, milk and vanilla. Stir in flour mixture until a soft dough forms.

3. On a lightly floured surface, roll out dough to ¼-inch (0.5 cm) thickness. Cut into 2-inch (5 cm) squares and fit into mini tart pans. Spoon about 1 tsp (5 mL) jam into each tart and fold the four corners of pastry over jam to partially cover.

4. Bake in preheated oven, in batches as necessary, for 8 to 10 minutes or until lightly browned. Transfer to wire racks and let cool completely. Store in an airtight container or cookie tin for up to 5 days.

Lime Phyllo Tarts

Makes 9 tarts

Light, crispy phyllo cups are the perfect containers for a delightfully tart filling, garnished with whipped cream, raspberries and mint.

—ooo—

Tips

If you don't have a food processor, first finely chop the rind in the marmalade into smaller pieces. In a large bowl, using an electric mixer, cream together cream cheese, marmalade and 2 tbsp (30 mL) of the sugar until smooth, then continue with the recipe.

Fill the phyllo cups just before serving, so they stay crisp.

Variation

Lime Pie: Instead of the phyllo cups, use a prepared 9-inch (23 cm) graham or cookie crumb crust. Spread cream cheese mixture into pie crust. Spread remaining whipped cream over top and garnish around the edges with thinly sliced lime wedges. Refrigerate for at least 3 hours, until chilled and set, or for up to 6 hours.

- Two 6-cup muffin tins, 9 cups greased

8 oz	brick-style cream cheese, softened	250 g
1/2 cup	Lime Marmalade (page 240) or Lemon Lime Marmalade (page 239)	125 mL
1/4 cup	granulated sugar, divided	60 mL
1 cup	whipping (35%) cream	250 mL
1/4 tsp	vanilla extract	1 mL
6	sheets frozen phyllo pastry, thawed	6
	Melted butter	
	Raspberries or blueberries	
9	sprigs fresh mint	9

1. In a food processor fitted with a metal blade, process cream cheese, marmalade and 2 tbsp (30 mL) of the sugar until smooth. Transfer to a large bowl.

2. In a separate bowl, whip cream with the remaining sugar and vanilla until firm peaks form. Fold half of the whipped cream into cream cheese mixture. Cover and refrigerate cream cheese mixture and the remaining whipped cream for at least 1 hour, until chilled, or for up to 3 hours.

3. Preheat oven to 375°F (190°C).

4. Stack 2 sheets of phyllo pastry and brush top lightly with melted butter. Cut in half lengthwise, then into three crosswise. Place squares in 6 prepared muffin cups. Repeat, placing a second double-layered square crosswise over each of the first squares. Repeat with 2 more sheets, this time using the 6 squares to make 3 more phyllo cups.

5. Bake on lower rack for 6 minutes or until golden brown. Let cool.

6. When ready to serve, spoon cream cheese mixture into phyllo cups. Top each with a dollop of whipped cream and garnish with fresh raspberries and a sprig of mint.

Apricot Ladder Braid

**Makes 2 loaves
(about 10 slices each)**

This recipe is courtesy of my friend Pat Moynihan, who teaches traditional bread-making and bread-machine courses. If you have a machine, just prepare any 1¹/₂-lb (750 g) sweet dough recipe from the bread machine cookbook or manual, then proceed with step 4.

— o o o —

Tip

Letting the dough rest for 10 minutes in step 3 will make it easier to roll out.

Loaves may be wrapped well in plastic, then overwrapped in foil, and frozen for up to 3 months. Thaw in wrappings at room temperature.

Variation

Use plum, cherry or blueberry jam in place of the apricot.

• Large baking sheet, greased

3 cups	bread or all-purpose flour	750 mL
¼ cup	granulated sugar	60 mL
2 tsp	quick-rising (instant) yeast	10 mL
1 tsp	salt	5 mL
1 cup	milk	250 mL
3 tbsp	butter or margarine, softened	45 mL
1	egg, beaten	1
½ cup	apricot jam, divided	125 mL
1	egg white	1
1 tsp	water	5 mL
½ cup	sliced almonds	125 mL

1. In a large bowl, combine flour, sugar, yeast and salt.

2. In a small saucepan, over medium heat, heat milk and butter until hot to the touch (125 to 130°F/50 to 55°C). Stir milk mixture into flour mixture; stir in egg. Knead until a soft dough forms.

3. Turn dough out onto a floured surface and knead for 8 to 10 minutes or until smooth and elastic. Cover and let rest for 10 minutes.

4. Punch down dough and knead for 2 to 3 minutes. Divide dough in half.

5. On a lightly floured surface, roll half of the dough out into a 12- by 9-inch (30 by 23 cm) rectangle. Spread ¼ cup (60 mL) of the jam lengthwise down the center third. Make diagonal cuts 1 inch (2.5 cm) apart and 3 inches (7.5 cm) long along both long sides. Beginning at one end, fold dough strips over jam (one side, then the other), overlapping in the center. Pinch in ends to seal. Repeat with remaining dough and jam.

6. Place braids on prepared baking sheet; cover with waxed paper and a light tea towel. Let rise in a warm, draft-free place for 30 to 35 minutes or until doubled.

7. Meanwhile, preheat oven to 375°F (190°C).

8. In a bowl, whisk together egg white and water; brush over top of braids. Sprinkle with almonds. Bake for 20 to 25 minutes or until golden brown. Cover loosely with foil if they brown too quickly.

Fried Bananas Caribbean

Here's a quick dessert that uses the Caribbean Treasure Conserve. It's delicious served over vanilla ice cream or frozen yogurt.

— o o o —

Variation

Use Piña Colada Jam (page 71) or Lime Coconut Marmalade (page 241) instead of the Caribbean Treasure Conserve.

2	firm ripe bananas	2
1 tbsp	butter	15 mL
½ cup	Caribbean Treasure Conserve (page 219)	125 mL
1 tbsp	amber or coconut rum, or water	15 mL
	Ice cream	
2 tbsp	slivered almonds, toasted	30 mL

1. Peel bananas and cut in half lengthwise, then into 2-inch (5 cm) pieces.

2. In a large skillet, melt butter over medium heat. Place bananas cut side down in skillet. Reduce heat to medium-low and cook, turning once, for 2 to 3 minutes per side or until just tender.

3. In a small bowl, stir together conserve and rum. Pour over bananas and stir gently to coat. Cook just until heated through.

4. Spoon over ice cream and sprinkle with almonds.

Low-Fat Raspberry Mango Frozen Cake

This low-fat cake is easy to make using frozen fruit ices or frozen yogurt and low-fat pound cake. Mix and match flavors, such as strawberry, orange, vanilla, lemon, lime and so on. Use your favorite jam, mixed with a little liqueur, if desired. This makes a terrific, cool birthday cake!

— o o o —

Tips

This cake can be stored in the freezer for up to 1 month. Wrap the pan well with foil to ensure no loss of moisture or transfer of flavors from other foods in the freezer.

• 8- or 9-inch (20 or 23 cm) springform pan

1	package (about 10 oz/300 g) frozen low-fat pound cake	1
1/3 cup	Raspberry Jam (page 78)	75 mL
2 cups	mango fruit ice	500 mL
2 cups	raspberry fruit ice	500 mL
	Raspberries and/or sliced mango (optional)	

1. Cut cake into slices about ¾ inch (2 cm) thick. Line bottom of pan with cake, trimming to fit and leaving no spaces. Spread jam over cake.

2. Place mango fruit ice in a bowl and let soften slightly at room temperature. Stir just until soft enough to spread. Spread evenly over jam and place pan in the freezer for 10 minutes.

3. Meanwhile, place raspberry fruit ice in a bowl and let soften slightly. Stir just until soft enough to spread. Remove pan from freezer and spread raspberry fruit ice over mango layer. Cover with plastic wrap and freeze for about 3 hours or until firm.

4. To serve, remove sides of pan and let cake warm slightly at room temperature. Using a sharp knife, slice into wedges. Top with fruit (if using).

Variations

In place of the Raspberry Jam, use Raspberry Mango Jam (page 139), Kiwi Raspberry Jam (119), Raspberry Lychee Jam with Lychee Liqueur (page 138) or Seedless Raspberry Lemon Verbena Jam (page 80).

Replace the raspberry fruit ice with vanilla frozen yogurt and use Wild Blueberry Lemon Marmalade (page 237) in place of the Raspberry Jam.

If desired, you can mix the raspberries and/or sliced mango with jam and liqueur (such as orange, lemon, lychee) before topping the cake with them.

Vanilla Jelly Roll

*Jams and jellies are great
fillings for jelly rolls.*

— o o o —

Tips

For the jam or jelly, try
Raspberry Mango Jam
(page 139), Strawberry Kiwi
Jam (page 150), Blackberry
Plum Jelly (page 262) or
Peach Vanilla Jelly (page
270).

If you're making this jelly roll
for the Sherry Trifle (page
369), roll it up from a long
side.

The jelly roll can be prepared
through step 5, wrapped
tightly with plastic wrap and
refrigerated for up to 1 day.

Variation

Chocolate Jelly Roll:
Substitute ½ cup
(125 mL) sifted
unsweetened cocoa
powder for the same
amount of flour. Spread
cake with Ginger Pear
Jam with Crème de
Cacao (page 69) or any
of the cherry jams (pages
54–55 and 104–110).

- Preheat oven to 350°F (180°C)
- 15- by 10-inch (38 by 25 cm) jelly roll pan, lined
  with waxed or parchment paper

1 cup	sifted cake-and-pastry flour	250 mL
1 tsp	baking powder	5 mL
¼ tsp	salt	1 mL
4	eggs	4
1 cup	granulated sugar	250 mL
¼ cup	water	60 mL
1 tsp	vanilla extract	5 mL
	Confectioner's (icing) sugar	
1¼ cups	jam or fruit jelly	300 mL

Topping (Optional)

1 cup	whipping (35%) cream	250 mL
2 tbsp	granulated sugar	30 mL
½ tsp	vanilla extract	2 mL

1. In a bowl, combine flour, baking powder and salt.

2. In a large bowl, using an electric mixer, beat eggs until
   thick and lemon-colored, about 5 minutes. Gradually
   beat in sugar until very thick. Beat in water and vanilla.
   Gently fold in flour mixture.

3. Pour batter into prepared pan, spreading evenly. Bake
   in preheated oven for 15 to 20 minutes, or until cake
   springs back when lightly touched in the center.

4. Place a clean tea towel on a board and lightly sprinkle
   with icing sugar. Loosen edges of cake, turn out onto
   towel and peel off paper. Starting at one short side,
   roll up cake in towel while still warm. Let rest until
   completely cool.

5. Unroll cake and spread with jam. For a smooth finished
   edge, trim a bit of cake, at an angle, off the short side
   you will end with. Reroll cake.

6. *Prepare the topping (if using):* In a bowl, whip cream with
   sugar and vanilla until stiff peaks form.

7. Place cake on a platter, seam side down. Dust with icing
   sugar or spread topping over top. Serve immediately or
   wrap in plastic wrap and refrigerate for up to 1 day.

Sherry Trifle

*This showy dessert
is popular during the
festive season. It is
layered in a large glass
bowl and can be made
ahead. Make the jelly
roll with raspberry,
strawberry, apricot or
red currant jam. When
preparing the jelly roll,
start rolling from the
long side so that you
get a long, thin roll.*

— o o o —

1	jam-filled Vanilla Jelly Roll (undecorated) (page 368)	1
¾ cup	cream sherry, divided	175 mL
3 cups	chilled custard (approx.)	750 mL
3 cups	mixed fruit (such as raspberries, sliced strawberries, blueberries, chopped kiwifruit or mangos, mandarin orange segments)	750 mL
1 cup	whipping (35%) cream	250 mL
2 tbsp	granulated sugar	30 mL
½ tsp	vanilla extract	2 mL
⅓ cup	slivered or sliced almonds, toasted	75 mL

1. Cut jelly roll into ¾-inch (2 cm) slices. Use about two-thirds of the cake to line the inside and bottom of a deep, straight-sided glass bowl. Sprinkle with about ½ cup (125 mL) of the sherry; let soak into cake.

2. Spoon half of the fruit over cake layer. Spoon half of the custard over fruit.

3. Lay the remaining jelly roll slices flat over custard. Sprinkle with the remaining sherry. Spoon in the remaining fruit, then the remaining custard.

4. In a bowl, whip cream with sugar and vanilla until stiff peaks form. Spread over custard. Cover and refrigerate for at least 4 hours, until chilled, or for up to 8 hours. Just before serving, sprinkle with almonds.

Jam Glam:
Jar Decorations
and Gift Ideas

It doesn't take much to turn your little jars of preserves into beautiful gifts. Craft and fabric stores, as well as discount (dollar) stores, have lots of neat things you can use. Check out party packaging, stationery and bulk food stores as well.

Jar Decorations

- Cut pieces of fabric (small prints of fruit or flowers, or seasonal prints) into 5-inch (12.5 cm) circles using regular scissors or pinking shears to give a zigzag edge. Remove the jar ring, place a fabric circle over the lid and screw the ring back down (do not overtighten). Wrap ribbon around the ring and glue it with a hot glue gun or tie it into a bow. (You can also place the fabric over the jar ring, hold it in place with an elastic and tie ribbon over the elastic.)

- Top jars with paper doilies (white, silver or gold) in place of fabric. Apply the rings carefully so you do not tear the paper.

- Cut pieces of brown paper or tissue paper into 5-inch (12.5 cm) circles. Use rubber stamps or small adhesive stickers to decorate the paper with fruit, herb or seasonal images. Stick gold or silver stars on the paper, or draw pictures with metallic ink pens. Place under or on top of the jar ring and tie with raffia or twine.

- Use ribbons or metallic string to tie small festive ornaments, artificial fruit, dried flowers or greenery (such as ivy) onto jars (or hot-glue them to the jar ring).

- Hot-glue lace ribbon around the jar ring, and glue a small fabric rose where the lace meets.

- Print suggested uses for the preserve on a tag, and tie the tag onto the jar with ribbons or raffia.

- Use your computer to print attractive labels. Download free labels from websites such as: www.canadianfreestuff.com/free-canning-label-printables or www.asonomagarden.wordpress.com/2008/07/21/canning-lids-download. For more sites, search on "free canning labels."

Gift Ideas

- Place jars in fancy wine bags or small gift bags, available at discount (dollar) stores or stationery stores. Tie the handles with ribbon.

- Place a single jar in a small clear or decorated cellophane bag and tie with curling ribbon. Use stickers to decorate bags with a seasonal theme. For an added touch, place an antique silver spoon or a spreader with a decorative handle inside the bag.

- Use a small tray, basket or cookie tin to hold a jar of preserve, fresh-baked scones or muffins, a small package of tea or flavored ground coffee, small paper napkins and a small knife and spoon (purchase in packages of four from gourmet kitchen stores or gift stores) or a jam pot with a lid and a serving spoon.

- Bake a loaf of bread, place it in a basket lined with a linen tea towel and add jams, a small cutting board, spreaders and napkins.

- Place chutneys, conserves or savory jellies in a basket with a small cutting board, a cheese knife, napkins, cheese, a box of crackers and a bottle of wine. With chutneys and conserves, include aged (old) Cheddar cheese. With wine, herb or pepper jellies, include cream cheese and pâté. With wine jelly or red currant jelly, include a round of Brie or Camembert (especially attractive in round boxes with lids) and water crackers.

- Package a small tub of spreadable cream cheese and fresh bagels with strawberry jam.

- Line a basket with brightly colored East Indian fabric. Fill with chutney, a small package of basmati rice, naan bread or pappadums, and East Indian sauces such as korma or vindaloo (found in supermarkets). Or simply look for an Indian meal kit and add your homemade chutney to that.

- For festive-season baskets, include cookie cutters, tree ornaments, bells, pinecones sprayed gold, poinsettia napkins and scented candles. Package each jar in a miniature Christmas stocking or wrap several in tissue paper and place in a larger stocking.

Resources

Canning Equipment

Canning equipment and supplies are sold at many grocery stores and hardware stores, as well as online at sites such as www.canningpantry.com.

Jarden Home Brands
Ball (United States)
Canning information, recipes, canning equipment and supplies, pectins
www.freshpreserving.com

Bernardin Ltd. (Canada)
Canning information, recipes, canning equipment and supplies, pectins
www.homecanning.com/can

Pectin
Kraft Foods Inc. (United States)
Sure-Jell powdered pectin, Certo liquid pectin, information, recipes, canning tips
Toll-free phone: 1-800-323-0768
www.kraftfoods.com/surejell

Kraft Canada Inc. (Canada)
Certo powdered and liquid pectin, information, recipes, canning tips
Toll-free phone: 1-800-268-6038
www.kraftcanada.com (search on "Certo")

Free Jar Labels
www.alenkasprintables.com (click on "Labels" under "Misc")
www.asonomagarden.wordpress.com
www.countryclipart.com/countrylabels.htm
www.idityourself.com/2009/10/free-canning-labels
www.marthastewart.com/article.decorative-jam-labels
www.merrimentdesign.com/canning-label-template.php
www.onlinelabels.com (click on "Jar Labels" under "Shop by Category")
www.rainbowrowgraphics.com/printables (click on "Canning Labels")

Dried Organic Lavender
United States
www.lavendergreen.com (Pennsylvania)
www.olympiclavender.com (Washington)
www.purplehazelavender.com (Washington)

Canada
www.happyvalleylavender.com (British Columbia)
www.okanaganlavender.com (British Columbia)
www.stoneyhollowtreasures.com (Ontario)
www.lavendercanada.com (Nova Scotia)

United Kingdom
www.lavender-products.co.uk_gifts_food
www.daisygifts.co.uk (click on "Culinary (cooking) lavender")
www.steenbergs.co.uk (click on "Organic herbs and spices," then "Flowers")

Useful Websites

The United States Department of Agriculture
"The USDA Complete Guide to Home Canning"
foodsafety.cas.psu.edu/canningguide.html

National Center for Home Food Preservation
University of Georgia
Canning information and questions answered
www.uga.edu/nchfp/how/general.html

Many states have extension services that offer canning and food preservation information and recipes. Here are a few.

University of Minnesota Cooperative Extension System
"Using Minnesota's Wild Fruits"
www.extension.umn.edu/distribution/nutrition/DJ1089.html

Ohio State University Extension
"Jams, Jellies and Other Fruit Spreads"
http://ohioline.osu.edu./hyg-fact/500%5350.html

Oregon State University
http://extension.oregonstate.edu/fch/food-preservation

Discussion Groups

Food Preservation: http://groups.google.com/group/preservenation
Jarden Home Brands message board: http://www.freshpreserving.com/phpbb/phpBB3

Library and Archives Canada Cataloguing in Publication

Tremblay, Yvonne (Yvonne M.)
    250 home preserving favorites : from jams & jellies to marmalades & chutneys /
Yvonne Tremblay.

Includes index.
ISBN 978-0-7788-0237-2

    1. Canning and preserving. 2. Jam. 3. Jelly. 4. Marmalade. 5. Chutney.
I. Title. II. Title: Two hundred fifty home preserving favorites.

TX603.T733 2010   641.8'52   C2009-906690-4

Index

A

alcohol. *See* spirits
almonds, 36
  Apricot Almond Conserve, 206
  Apricot Ladder Braid, 365
  Linzertorte, 362
appetizers, 343, 345–47
apple juice and cider. *See also* apples
  Apple Chutney, 326
  Apple Jalapeño Pepper Jelly, 288
  Cran-Apple Butter, 316
  Double Ginger Jam, 58
  Garlic Jelly, 286
  Mango Butter, 317
  Plum Good Apple Butter, 321
  Rosemary Apple Cider Jelly, 306
  Spiced Apple Butter, 310
  Spiced Pear Butter, 320
apples, 25. *See also* apple juice and cider
  Apple Berry Jam, 90
  Apple Chutney, 326
  Apple Lemon Marmalade, 236
  Apple Orange Apricot Conserve, 203
  Apple Rhubarb Conserve with Goji Berries, 204
  Apple Rum Raisin Conserve, 205
  Blackberry Apple Jam, 98
  Blackberry Apple Spread, 182
  Black Currant Apple Jam, 95
  Blueberry Apple Butter, 313
  Carrot Apple Butter, 315
  Carrot Apple Mincemeat, 197
  Cherry Raspberry Apple Conserve, 211
  Cran-Apple Butter, 316
  Cran-Apple Sage and Thyme Chutney, 330
  Cranberry Orange Micro-Mini Jam (variation), 167
  French Apple Tarts, 361
  Golden Apple Plum Chutney, 327
  Green Tomato Apple Chutney, 339
  Grilled Pineapple Banana Conserve with Kahlúa, 220
  Mixed Berry Apple Spread, 184
  Pear and Apple Mincemeat, 198
  Pineapple Chutney, 336
  Plum Good Apple Butter, 321
  Quince Jam (variation), 77
  Rhubarb Apple Butter, 322
  Spiced Apple Butter, 310
  Spiced Carrot Apple Pineapple Conserve, 208
  Sweet Pepper Apple Chutney, 338
  Tomato Apple Chipotle Chutney, 340
Apricot Ladder Braid, 365
apricots, dried
  Apple Orange Apricot Conserve, 203
  Apricot Chutney, 328
  Apricot Orange Butter, 312
  Apricot Rhubarb Conserve, 207
  Dried Apricot Jam, 46
  Nectarine Apricot Cherry Conserve, 217
  Plum Rum and Prune Conserve (variation), 223
apricots, fresh, 25. *See also* plumcots
  Apricot Almond Conserve, 206
  Apricot Almond Jam, 47
  Apricot Cranberry Jam, 91
  Apricot Kiwi Jam, 92
  Apricot Mango Chutney, 329
  Apricot Raspberry Jam, 94
  Apricot Rhubarb Conserve, 207
  Apricot Yellow Plum Jam with Apricot Brandy, 93
  Brandied Apricot Jam, 48
  Sour Cherry Apricot Jam, 104
  Spiced Apricot Butter, 311

B

Baked Brie, 345
balsamic vinegar, 36
bananas, 25
  Banana Orange and Date Conserve, 191
  Blueberry Banana Jam, 101
  Chocolate Banana Micro-Mini Jam, 162
  Fried Bananas Caribbean, 366
  Grilled Pineapple Banana Conserve with Kahlúa, 220
  Kiwi Banana Orange Jam, 116
  Strawberry Banana Micro-Mini Jam, 171
  Strawberry Banana No-Cook Jam, 178
  Tropical Tango Spread, 183
basil (fresh)
  Purple Basil Wine Jelly, 299
  Tomato Orange Jam with Basil and Saffron, 194
beets, 25
  Beet Plum Jelly, 260
berries, 25. *See also specific types of berries*
  Apple Rhubarb Conserve with Goji Berries, 204
  Bumbleberry Jam, 103
  Elderberry Jelly, 266
  Five Berry Jam, 113
  Mixed Berry Apple Spread, 184
  Rumpot Conserve, 225
  Saskatoon Berry Jam, 82
  Strawberry Rhubarb Micro-Mini Jam (variation), 172
  Three-Berry Blend Jam, 156
  Winter Berry Jam, 158
Black and Red Currant Jam, 96

blackberries. *See also* berries
   Apricot Raspberry Jam
    (variation), 94
   Blackberry Apple Jam, 98
   Blackberry Apple Spread,
    182
   Blackberry Blueberry Jam, 99
   Blackberry Blueberry Micro-
    Mini Jam, 163
   Blackberry Jam, 50
   Blackberry Orange Jam, 100
   Blackberry Plum Jelly, 262
   Bumbleberry Jam, 103
   Five Berry Jam, 113
   Kiwi Raspberry Jam
    (variation), 119
   Raspberry Blackberry Jam,
    135
   Raspberry Pear Spread
    (variation), 189
   Seedless Blackberry Jam with
    Cassis, 50
   Sour Cherry Raspberry Jam
    (variation), 109
Black Currant Apple Jam, 95
Black Currant Jam, 49
Black Currant Jelly, 261
Black Currant Rhubarb Jam, 97
Blood Orange Marmalade, 242
blueberries. *See also* berries
   Blackberry Blueberry Jam, 99
   Blackberry Blueberry Micro-
    Mini Jam, 163
   Blueberry Apple Butter, 313
   Blueberry Banana Jam, 101
   Blueberry Mango Micro-Mini
    Jam, 165
   Blueberry Maple Butter, 314
   Blueberry Micro-Mini Jam,
    164
   Blueberry Orange Amaretto
    Jam, 102
   Blueberry Orange No-Cook
    Jam, 176
   Bumbleberry Jam, 103
   Lime Phyllo Tarts, 364
   Nectarine Blueberry Jam, 123
   Peach Blueberry No-Cook
    Jam, 177
   Raspberry Blueberry Jam, 136
   Raspberry Blueberry Spread,
    187
   Raspberry Peach Spread
    (variation), 188

Sweet Cherry and Blueberry
   Jam, 105
Three-Berry Blend Jam, 156
Wild Blueberry Jam with
   Grand Marnier, 52
Wild Blueberry Lemon
   Marmalade, 237
Boysenberry Jam, 53
brandy
   Apricot Yellow Plum Jam
    with Apricot Brandy, 93
   Brandied Apricot Jam, 48
   Brandied Nectarine Jam, 63
   Mojito Jelly (variation), 283
   Plumcot Jam, 75
   Sweet Cherry Jam with
    Kirsch, 55
breakfast ideas, 342, 354
Bumbleberry Jam, 103
butters (fruit), 307–22

C

Cabernet Wine Jelly, 293
"Campari with a Twist" Jelly, 282
canning jars, 15. *See also*
   preserving
   decorating, 370–71
   filling, 18, 23
   lids for, 18–19, 37
   preparing, 18, 37
   processing, 20–21
   rings for, 20, 23
   sterilizing, 18, 20
Caribbean Chicken, 350
Caribbean Treasure Conserve,
   219
carrots, 26
   Carrot Apple Butter, 315
   Carrot Apple Mincemeat,
    197
   Carrot Orange Marmalade,
    250
   Spiced Carrot Apple
    Pineapple Conserve, 208
cheese
   Baked Brie, 345
   Cheddar Cheese
    Thumbprints with Hot
    Pepper Jelly, 346
   Lime Phyllo Tarts, 364
   Steak Salad with Strawberry
    Balsamic Dressing
    (variation), 352
   Stuffed French Toast, 354

cherries, 26. *See also* cherry
   juice
   Cherries Jubilee Jam, 110
   Cherry Cranberry Orange
    Conserve with Grand
    Marnier, 209
   Cherry Profusion Conserve,
    212
   Cherry Raspberry Apple
    Conserve, 211
   Chunky Cherry Plum
    Conserve, 210
   Nectarine Apricot Cherry
    Conserve, 217
   Peach Sour Cherry Jam, 125
   Plum Rum and Prune
    Conserve (variation), 223
   Red Fruit Jam, 144
   Sour Cherry Apricot Jam, 104
   Sour Cherry Jam, 54
   Sour Cherry Pear Jam, 107
   Sour Cherry Raspberry Jam,
    109
   Sweet Cherry and Black
    Plum Jam, 108
   Sweet Cherry and Blueberry
    Jam, 105
   Sweet Cherry Cran-
    Raspberry Jam, 106
   Sweet Cherry Jam with
    Kirsch, 55
   Sweet Cherry Micro-Mini
    Jam, 166
cherry juice. *See also* cherries
   Hot Cherry Pomegranate
    Jelly, 289
   Pomegranate Jelly
    (variation), 271
chicken
   Caribbean Chicken, 350
   Garlic Chicken Portobello,
    351
chocolate, 36
   Chocolate Banana Micro-
    Mini Jam, 162
   Chocolate Raspberry Jam, 79
   Linzertorte (variation), 362
   Raspberry Micro-Mini Jam
    (variation), 170
   Sweet Cherry Micro-Mini
    Jam (variation), 166
   Vanilla Jelly Roll (variation),
    368
Christmas Plum Conserve, 224

Chunky Cherry Plum Conserve, 210
chutneys, 324–40
citrus fruit, 26. *See also specific fruits*
  peel and rind, 228–29
Clementine Marmalade, 243
Clementine Orange Lemon Jelly, 269
cocoa powder. *See* chocolate
Coconut Shrimp, 347
Concord Grape Jelly, 267
conserves, 191, 200–226
conserves (as ingredient)
  Baked Brie, 345
  Caribbean Chicken, 350
  Fried Bananas Caribbean, 366
  Fruit Loaf, 356
  Marmalade Pecan Cookies, 358
  Shut Cookies, 359
cookies, 357–60
Coronation Grape Orange Conserve, 216
crabapples, 26
  Crabapple Jelly, 263
cranberries, dried
  Apple Chutney, 326
  Apple Rhubarb Conserve with Goji Berries, 204
  Apple Rum Raisin Conserve (variation), 205
  Cranberry Pear Conserve with Ginger, 214
  Mango Peach Chutney, 333
  Plum Cranberry Orange Conserve, 222
  Plum Pear Chutney, 337
cranberries, fresh, 26. *See also* cranberry juice
  Apricot Cranberry Jam, 91
  Cherry Cranberry Orange Conserve with Grand Marnier, 209
  Cran-Apple Butter, 316
  Cran-Apple Sage and Thyme Chutney, 330
  Cranberry Orange and Ginger Jelly, 264
  Cranberry Orange Marmalade, 248
  Cranberry Orange Micro-Mini Jam, 167

Cranberry Pear Conserve with Ginger, 214
Cran-Raspberry Jelly, 265
Pear Cranberry Chutney, 335
Spiced Peach Cranberry Jam, 126
Sweet Cherry Cran-Raspberry Jam, 106
Winter Berry Jam, 158
cranberry juice. *See also* cranberries, fresh
  Cranberry Orange Marmalade, 248
  Pineapple and Mint Jelly (variation), 305
  Rosemary Apple Cider Jelly (variation), 306
  Sangria Jelly (variation), 284
  Spiced Cranberry and Red Wine Jelly, 295
cream cheese. *See* cheese
Cream Tea Scones, 353
currants, dried
  Pear and Apple Mincemeat, 198
  Sweet Pepper Apple Chutney, 338
currants, fresh, 26. *See also* berries
  Apple Berry Jam, 90
  Black and Red Currant Jam, 96
  Black Currant Apple Jam, 95
  Black Currant Jam, 49
  Black Currant Jelly, 261
  Black Currant Rhubarb Jam, 97
  Cherries Jubilee Jam, 110
  Five Berry Jam, 113
  Raspberry Gooseberry Red Currant Jam, 137
  Raspberry Red Currant Jam, 141
  Red Currant Jelly, 273
  Red Currant Orange Jam, 143
  Red Currant Raspberry Jelly, 274
  Red Fruit Jam, 144
  Strawberry Red Currant Jam, 154

D
Damson Plum Jam, 73
Damson Plum Raspberry Jam, 131

dates
  Banana Orange and Date Conserve, 191
  Date Orange Chutney, 331
desserts, 344, 355–69
Double Ginger Jam, 58
Dried Apricot Jam, 46
Dried Fig Jam, 57

E
Easy Coffee Cake, 355
Elderberry Jelly, 266
Empire Cookies, 357
entrées, 343, 350–52

F
Fig Bars, 360
figs, 27
  Dried Fig Jam, 57
  Fig and Italian Plum Conserve, 215
  Fig Jam, 56
  Fig Orange Jam, 111
  Fig Strawberry Jam with Balsamic Vinegar, 112
Fire and Ice Jelly, 292
Five Berry Jam, 113
flowers, 36, 266. *See also* lavender
  Lemon and Mint Marmalade with Calendula Petals, 235
  Wine and Roses Jelly, 298
freezer jam. *See* jams, no-cook
French Apple Tarts, 361
French Toast, Stuffed, 354
Fried Bananas Caribbean, 366
fruit. *See also specific fruits*
  dried, 26
  preparing, 22, 24–25
  seasonal, 24–25
fruit butters, 307–22
Fruit-Fresh, 30
Fruit Loaf, 356

G
garlic, 27, 36
  Apricot Chutney (variation), 328
  Garlic Jelly, 286
  Mango Chutney, 332
  Roasted Garlic Wine Jelly, 287
  Sweet Pepper Apple Chutney, 338

garlic (*continued*)
Tomato Apple Chipotle Chutney, 340
Garlic Chicken Portobello, 351
gift ideas, 371
ginger, 27, 36
Apple Chutney, 326
Apricot Chutney, 328
Beet Plum Jelly (variation), 260
Cranberry Orange and Ginger Jelly, 264
Cranberry Pear Conserve with Ginger, 214
Double Ginger Jam, 58
Ginger Pear and Lime Jam, 68
Ginger Pear Jam with Crème de Cacao, 69
Gooseberry Jam (variation), 59
Green Tomato Apple Chutney, 339
Jasmine Green Tea Jelly with Ginger and Lemon, 268
Lemon Ginger Marmalade, 233
Mango Chutney, 332
Peach Plum Chutney, 334
Pear and Apple Mincemeat, 198
Pear Spread with Brown Sugar and Cinnamon (variation), 186
Plum Ginger Jam, 72
Plum Rum and Prune Conserve (variation), 223
Pomegranate Jelly (variation), 271
Prickly Pear and Pear Jam (variation), 134
Rhubarb Jam (variation), 81
Rhubarb Orange Ginger Jam, 145
Seville Orange Marmalade (variation), 245
Goji Berries, Apple Rhubarb Conserve with, 204
Golden Apple Plum Chutney, 327
gooseberries, 27. *See also* berries
Apple Berry Jam, 90
Five Berry Jam, 113
Gooseberry Jam, 59
Gooseberry Orange Jam, 114

Raspberry Gooseberry Red Currant Jam, 137
Strawberry Gooseberry Jam, 148
grapefruit, 26
Pink Grapefruit and Pomegranate Marmalade, 252
Strawberry Red Grapefruit Jam, 149
Three-Fruit Marmalade, 254
grape juice. *See also* grapes
Muscat Wine Jelly with Lemon Balm (variation), 300
Sangria Jelly (variation), 284
grapes, 27. *See also* grape juice
Concord Grape Jelly, 267
Coronation Grape Orange Conserve, 216
Spiced Black Grape Jam, 60
Green Tomato Apple Chutney, 339
Grilled Pineapple Banana Conserve with Kahlúa, 220

H
headspace, 23
herbs, 36. *See also specific herbs*
honey, 36, 175
Dried Fig Jam (variation), 57
Fig Jam (variation), 56
Honey-Do Citrus Jam, 115
Honey Lemon Marmalade, 234
Honey Pear and Vanilla Bean Jam, 67
Jasmine Green Tea Jelly with Ginger and Lemon (variation), 268
Prickly Pear and Pear Jam (variation), 134
Quince Jam (variation), 77
Tangerine and Honey Marmalade, 247
Hot Cherry Pomegranate Jelly, 289

J
jams
about, 39–43
micro-mini, 41, 159–72, 190
mixed-fruit, 90–158
no-cook (freezer), 174, 176–81

onion, 175, 192–94
single-fruit, 46–87
tips, 41–42
trouble-shooting, 42
jams (as ingredient)
Apricot Ladder Braid, 365
Baked Brie, 345
Caribbean Chicken, 350
Coconut Shrimp, 347
Easy Coffee Cake, 355
Empire Cookies, 357
Fig Bars, 360
French Apple Tarts, 361
Fried Bananas Caribbean, 366
Low-Fat Raspberry Mango Frozen Cake, 367
Peach Barbecue Sauce, 349
Pineapple Tartlets, 363
Shut Cookies, 359
Steak Salad with Strawberry Balsamic Dressing, 352
Stuffed French Toast, 354
Vanilla Jelly Roll, 368
jars. *See* canning jars
Jasmine Green Tea Jelly with Ginger and Lemon, 268
jellies, 255–306
fruit, 260–80
savory, 282–306
jellies (as ingredient)
Cheddar Cheese Thumbprints with Hot Pepper Jelly, 346
French Apple Tarts, 361
Garlic Chicken Portobello, 351
Purple Basil Salad Dressing, 348
Vanilla Jelly Roll, 368
jelly bags, 256

K
Kir Royale Jelly, 294
kiwifruit, 27
Apricot Kiwi Jam, 92
Kiwi Banana Orange Jam, 116
Kiwi Jam, 61
Kiwi Mango Jam, 117
Kiwi Pineapple Orange Jam, 118
Kiwi Raspberry Jam, 119
Kiwi Watermelon Jam, 120

Raspberry Kiwi Light No-Cook Jam, 181
Raspberry Micro-Mini Jam (variation), 170
Strawberry Kiwi Jam, 150

L

lavender
Lavender Jelly, 302
Lemon and Mint Marmalade with Calendula Petals (variation), 235
Lemon Ginger Marmalade (variation), 233
Peach Lavender Jam, 65
Strawberry Lavender Jam, 84
lemon, 26
Apple Lemon Marmalade, 236
Carrot Orange Marmalade, 250
Clementine Orange Lemon Jelly, 269
Ginger Pear and Lime Jam (variation), 68
Honey Lemon Marmalade, 234
Jasmine Green Tea Jelly with Ginger and Lemon, 268
Lemon and Mint Marmalade with Calendula Petals, 235
Lemon Ginger Marmalade, 233
Lemon Lime Marmalade, 239
Peach Orange Marmalade, 249
Pineapple Citrus Marmalade, 253
Raspberry Lemonade Marmalade, 238
Three-Fruit Marmalade, 254
Wild Blueberry Lemon Marmalade, 237
Lemon Balm, Muscat Wine Jelly with, 300
lemon verbena
Lemon Verbena Jelly, 303
Seedless Raspberry Lemon Verbena Jam, 80
lime juice. See also limes
Mojito Jelly, 283
Strawberry Mango Daiquiri Jam, 151
Strawberry Margarita Jam, 86
Tequila Sunrise Jelly, 285

Lime Phyllo Tarts, 364
limes, 26. See also lime juice
"Campari with a Twist" Jelly, 282
Ginger Pear and Lime Jam, 68
Lemon Lime Marmalade, 239
Lime Coconut Marmalade, 241
Lime Marmalade, 240
Linzertorte, 362
liqueurs
Apple Rum Raisin Conserve (variation), 205
Apricot Almond Jam (variation), 47
Apricot Yellow Plum Jam with Apricot Brandy, 93
Blackberry Apple Jam (variation), 98
Blueberry Orange Amaretto Jam, 102
Cherry Cranberry Orange Conserve with Grand Marnier, 209
Ginger Pear Jam with Crème de Cacao, 69
Grilled Pineapple Banana Conserve with Kahlúa, 220
Kir Royale Jelly, 294
Peach Rum Butter (variation), 318
Plum Rum and Prune Conserve, 223
Prickly Pear Jam with Triple Sec, 76
Raspberry Blackberry Jam (variation), 135
Raspberry Jelly (variation), 272
Raspberry Lychee Jam with Lychee Liqueur, 138
Raspberry Micro-Mini Jam (variation), 170
Seedless Blackberry Jam with Cassis, 50
Seville Orange Marmalade (variation), 245
Strawberry Jam (variation), 83
Strawberry Margarita Jam, 86
Sweet Cherry Jam with Kirsch, 55
Wild Blueberry Jam with Grand Marnier, 52

Low-Fat Raspberry Mango Frozen Cake, 367
lychees, 27
Raspberry Lychee Jam with Lychee Liqueur, 138

M

mango, 27–28
Apricot Mango Chutney, 329
Blueberry Mango Micro-Mini Jam, 165
Caribbean Treasure Conserve, 219
Kiwi Mango Jam, 117
Mango Butter, 317
Mango Chutney, 332
Mango Orange Jam with Mint Green Tea, 121
Mango Passion Fruit Jam, 122
Mango Peach Chutney, 333
Orange Passion Fruit Micro-Mini Jam (variation), 168
Peach Papaya Orange Spread (variation), 185
Pineapple Mango Jam, 130
Raspberry Mango Jam, 139
Raspberry Peach Spread (variation), 188
Spiced Mango Jam, 62
Strawberry Mango Daiquiri Jam, 151
Tropical Tango Spread, 183
maple syrup
Blueberry Maple Butter, 314
Blueberry Micro-Mini Jam (variation), 164
Clementine Marmalade (variation), 243
Pear Maple Walnut Conserve, 218
Strawberry Maple No-Cook Jam, 179
marmalades, 228–54
marmalades (as ingredient)
Coconut Shrimp, 347
French Apple Tarts, 361
Fried Bananas Caribbean, 366
Fruit Loaf, 356
Lime Phyllo Tarts, 364
Low-Fat Raspberry Mango Frozen Cake, 367
Marmalade Pecan Cookies, 358
Pineapple Tartlets, 363

melon, 28
  Honey-Do Citrus Jam, 115
  Strawberry Cantaloupe Jam, 147
Micro-Mini Peach Spread with Stevia, 190
mincemeats, 175, 197–98
mint (fresh)
  Apple Lemon Marmalade (variation), 236
  Lemon and Mint Marmalade with Calendula Petals, 235
  Lime Phyllo Tarts, 364
  Mango Orange Jam with Mint Green Tea (variation), 121
  Mint Jelly, 304
  Mojito Jelly, 283
  Pineapple and Mint Jelly, 305
  Rhubarb Jam (variation), 81
  Spiced Mango Jam (variation), 62
  Strawberry Cantaloupe Jam (variation), 147
Mixed Berry Apple Spread, 184
Mojito Jelly, 283
mold, 14
Muscat Wine Jelly with Lemon Balm, 300

N

nectarines, 28
  Brandied Nectarine Jam, 63
  Mango Peach Chutney (variation), 333
  Nectarine Apricot Cherry Conserve, 217
  Nectarine Blueberry Jam, 123
  Nectarine Plum Jam, 124
  Peach Lavender Jam (variation), 65
  Peach Plum Chutney (variation), 334
  Peach Pomegranate Jam (variation), 128
  Peach Sour Cherry Jam (variation), 125
  Spiced Peach Cranberry Jam (variation), 126
nuts. See also almonds
  Cheddar Cheese Thumbprints with Hot Pepper Jelly (variation), 346

Marmalade Pecan Cookies, 358
Pear Maple Walnut Conserve, 218
Steak Salad with Strawberry Balsamic Dressing, 352

O

onions, 28, 36
  Apple Chutney, 326
  Apricot Mango Chutney, 329
  Cran-Apple Sage and Thyme Chutney, 330
  Date Orange Chutney, 331
  Golden Apple Plum Chutney, 327
  Green Tomato Apple Chutney, 339
  Mango Chutney, 332
  Mango Peach Chutney, 333
  Orange Onion Jam with Sage and Thyme, 192
  Peach Plum Chutney, 334
  Pear Cranberry Chutney, 335
  Pineapple Chutney, 336
  Plum Pear Chutney, 337
  Steak Salad with Strawberry Balsamic Dressing, 352
  Strawberry Onion Jam with Balsamic Vinegar and Rosemary, 196
  Sweet Pepper Apple Chutney, 338
  Tomato Apple Chipotle Chutney, 340
  Tomato Orange Jam with Basil and Saffron, 194
orange juice. See also oranges
  "Campari with a Twist" Jelly, 282
  Mango Butter, 317
  Orange Passion Fruit Micro-Mini Jam, 168
  Peach Papaya Orange Spread, 185
  Peach Rum Butter (variation), 318
  Pineapple Habanero Pepper Jelly (variation), 290
  Sangria Jelly, 284
  Spiced Pear Butter (variation), 320
  Tequila Sunrise Jelly, 285
  Tropical Tango Spread, 183

oranges, 26. See also orange juice
  Apple Lemon Marmalade (variation), 236
  Apple Orange Apricot Conserve, 203
  Apricot Orange Butter, 312
  Banana Orange and Date Conserve, 191
  Beet Plum Jelly (variation), 260
  Blackberry Orange Jam, 100
  Blood Orange Marmalade, 242
  Blueberry Maple Butter (variation), 314
  Blueberry Micro-Mini Jam (variation), 164
  Blueberry Orange Amaretto Jam, 102
  Blueberry Orange No-Cook Jam, 176
  Caribbean Treasure Conserve, 219
  Carrot Orange Marmalade, 250
  Cherry Cranberry Orange Conserve with Grand Marnier, 209
  Clementine Marmalade, 243
  Clementine Orange Lemon Jelly, 269
  Coronation Grape Orange Conserve, 216
  Cranberry Orange and Ginger Jelly, 264
  Cranberry Orange Marmalade, 248
  Cranberry Orange Micro-Mini Jam, 167
  Date Orange Chutney, 331
  Dried Apricot Jam (variation), 46
  Dried Fig Jam (variation), 57
  Fig Jam (variation), 56
  Fig Orange Jam, 111
  Gooseberry Orange Jam, 114
  Honey-Do Citrus Jam, 115
  Kiwi Banana Orange Jam, 116
  Kiwi Pineapple Orange Jam, 118
  Mango Orange Jam with Mint Green Tea, 121

Orange Marmalade with Earl Grey Tea, 244
Orange Onion Jam with Sage and Thyme, 192
Peach Orange Marmalade, 249
Pineapple Citrus Marmalade, 253
Plumcot Orange Jam, 133
Plum Cranberry Orange Conserve, 222
Red Currant Orange Jam, 143
Red Plum Orange Jelly, 276
Rhubarb Orange Ginger Jam, 145
Seville Orange Marmalade, 245
Spiced Black Grape Jam (variation), 60
Strawberry Maple No-Cook Jam, 179
Strawberry Red Grapefruit Jam (variation), 149
Strawberry Rhubarb Orange Jam, 155
Tangelo Marmalade, 246
Tangerine and Honey Marmalade, 247
Three-Fruit Marmalade, 254
Tomato Orange Jam with Basil and Saffron, 194
Zucchini Orange Marmalade, 251

P

papayas, 28
Caribbean Treasure Conserve, 219
Kiwi Banana Orange Jam (variation), 116
Peach Papaya Orange Spread, 185
Pineapple Mango Jam (variation), 130
passion fruit, 28
Mango Passion Fruit Jam, 122
Orange Passion Fruit Micro-Mini Jam, 168
Peach Barbecue Sauce, 349
peaches, 28
Blueberry Mango Micro-Mini Jam (variation), 165

Brandied Nectarine Jam (variation), 63
Mango Passion Fruit Jam (variation), 122
Mango Peach Chutney, 333
Micro-Mini Peach Spread with Stevia, 190
Nectarine Blueberry Jam (variation), 123
Nectarine Plum Jam (variation), 124
Peach Blueberry No-Cook Jam, 177
Peach Lavender Jam, 65
Peach Micro-Mini Jam, 169
Peach Orange Marmalade, 249
Peach Papaya Orange Spread, 185
Peach Pear Jam, 127
Peach Plum Chutney, 334
Peach Pomegranate Jam, 128
Peach Raspberry Jam, 129
Peach Raspberry Light No-Cook Jam, 180
Peach Rum Butter, 318
Peach Sour Cherry Jam, 125
Peach Vanilla Jelly, 270
Raspberry Peach Spread, 188
Spiced Peach Cranberry Jam, 126
Spiced Peach Jam, 64
Sweet Pepper Apple Chutney (variation), 338
pears, 28. See also prickly pears
Apple Lemon Marmalade (variation), 236
Cranberry Pear Conserve with Ginger, 214
Ginger Pear and Lime Jam, 68
Ginger Pear Jam with Crème de Cacao, 69
Honey Pear and Vanilla Bean Jam, 67
Peach Pear Jam, 127
Pear and Apple Mincemeat, 198
Pear Cranberry Chutney, 335
Pear Jam with Brown Sugar and Cinnamon, 66
Pear Maple Walnut Conserve, 218

Pears and Port Jam, 70
Pear Spread with Brown Sugar and Cinnamon, 186
Plum Pear Chutney, 337
Prickly Pear and Pear Jam, 134
Raspberry Pear Spread, 189
Sour Cherry Pear Jam, 107
Spiced Pear Butter, 320
Strawberry Rhubarb and Pear Conserve, 226
pectin, 22, 37, 40
commercial, 34, 40
natural, 34–35
peppers, bell, 28
Apricot Mango Chutney, 329
Fire and Ice Jelly, 292
Mango Chutney, 332
Mango Peach Chutney, 333
Peach Plum Chutney, 334
Pineapple Chutney, 336
Red and Green Pepper Jelly, 291
Steak Salad with Strawberry Balsamic Dressing (variation), 352
Sweet Pepper Apple Chutney, 338
peppers, hot, 28–29
Apple Jalapeño Pepper Jelly, 288
Apricot Mango Chutney (tip), 329
Hot Cherry Pomegranate Jelly, 289
Mango Chutney, 332
Mango Peach Chutney, 333
Peach Plum Chutney, 334
Pineapple Habanero Pepper Jelly, 290
Strawberry Jam (variation), 83
Tomato Apple Chipotle Chutney, 340
pineapple, 29. See also pineapple juice
Caribbean Treasure Conserve, 219
Grilled Pineapple Banana Conserve with Kahlúa, 220
Kiwi Pineapple Orange Jam, 118
Piña Colada Jam, 71
Pineapple Chutney, 336

pineapple (*continued*)
Pineapple Citrus Marmalade, 253
Pineapple Mango Jam, 130
Rhubarb Pineapple Jam, 146
Spiced Carrot Apple Pineapple Conserve, 208
Strawberry Pineapple Jam, 152
pineapple juice. *See also* pineapple
Pineapple and Mint Jelly, 305
Pineapple Habanero Pepper Jelly, 290
Pineapple Tartlets, 363
Pink Grapefruit and Pomegranate Marmalade, 252
plumcots, 29
Plumcot Jam, 75
Plumcot Orange Jam, 133
plums, 29
Apricot Yellow Plum Jam with Apricot Brandy, 93
Beet Plum Jelly, 260
Blackberry Plum Jelly, 262
Christmas Plum Conserve, 224
Chunky Cherry Plum Conserve, 210
Damson Plum Jam, 73
Damson Plum Raspberry Jam, 131
Fig and Italian Plum Conserve, 215
Golden Apple Plum Chutney, 327
Nectarine Plum Jam, 124
Peach Micro-Mini Jam (variation), 169
Peach Plum Chutney, 334
Plumcot Orange Jam, 133
Plum Cranberry Orange Conserve, 222
Plum Ginger Jam, 72
Plum Good Apple Butter, 321
Plum Pear Chutney, 337
Plum Rum and Prune Conserve, 223
Raspberry Plum Jam, 140
Red Plum Jelly, 275
Red Plum Orange Jelly, 276

Red Plum Rhubarb Jam, 132
Sweet Cherry and Black Plum Jam, 108
Yellow Plum Jam, 74
pomegranate, 29
Hot Cherry Pomegranate Jelly, 289
Orange Passion Fruit Micro-Mini Jam (variation), 168
Peach Pomegranate Jam, 128
Pineapple and Mint Jelly (variation), 305
Pink Grapefruit and Pomegranate Marmalade, 252
Pomegranate Jelly, 271
port. *See* wine
preserves. *See also* preserving; *specific types of preserves*
cooking, 22
flavor additions, 36
gift ideas, 371
ideas for using, 342–44
labeling, 21
no-cook, 21, 174, 176–81
nutritional content, 14
processing, 20–21
setting, 19, 20, 23
storing, 21
preserving. *See also* canning jars; pectin
equipment, 15–17
at high altitudes, 21
ingredients, 22, 32–33
preparation checklist, 37
processing times, 20–21
safety, 14
terminology, 23
tips, 22–23
yields, 22
prickly pears, 29
Prickly Pear and Pear Jam, 134
Prickly Pear Jam with Triple Sec, 76
Prune Conserve, Plum Rum and, 223
Purple Basil Salad Dressing, 348
Purple Basil Wine Jelly, 299

Q

quinces, 30
Quince Jam, 77

R

raisins
Apple Chutney, 326
Apple Orange Apricot Conserve, 203
Apple Rum Raisin Conserve, 205
Apricot Chutney, 328
Carrot Apple Mincemeat, 197
Christmas Plum Conserve, 224
Coronation Grape Orange Conserve, 216
Date Orange Chutney, 331
Golden Apple Plum Chutney, 327
Green Tomato Apple Chutney, 339
Mango Peach Chutney, 333
Pear and Apple Mincemeat, 198
Pineapple Chutney, 336
Spiced Carrot Apple Pineapple Conserve, 208
raspberries. *See also* berries
Apple Berry Jam, 90
Apricot Raspberry Jam, 94
Bumbleberry Jam, 103
Cherry Raspberry Apple Conserve, 211
Chocolate Raspberry Jam, 79
Cranberry Orange Micro-Mini Jam (variation), 167
Cran-Raspberry Jelly, 265
Damson Plum Raspberry Jam, 131
Five Berry Jam, 113
Kiwi Raspberry Jam, 119
Lime Phyllo Tarts, 364
Peach Raspberry Jam, 129
Peach Raspberry Light No-Cook Jam, 180
Raspberry Blackberry Jam, 135
Raspberry Blueberry Jam, 136
Raspberry Blueberry Spread, 187
Raspberry Gooseberry Red Currant Jam, 137
Raspberry Jam, 78
Raspberry Jelly, 272
Raspberry Kiwi Light No-Cook Jam, 181

Raspberry Lemonade
  Marmalade, 238
Raspberry Lychee Jam with
  Lychee Liqueur, 138
Raspberry Mango Jam, 139
Raspberry Micro-Mini Jam,
  170
Raspberry Peach Spread,
  188
Raspberry Pear Spread, 189
Raspberry Plum Jam, 140
Raspberry Red Currant Jam,
  141
Raspberry Rhubarb Jam, 142
Red Currant Raspberry Jelly,
  274
Red Fruit Jam, 144
Seedless Raspberry Lemon
  Verbena Jam, 80
Sour Cherry Raspberry Jam,
  109
Strawberry Raspberry Jam,
  153
Sweet Cherry Cran-
  Raspberry Jam, 106
Three-Berry Blend Jam, 156
Watermelon Raspberry Jam,
  157
Red and Green Pepper Jelly,
  291
Red Currant Jelly, 273
Red Currant Orange Jam, 143
Red Currant Raspberry Jelly,
  274
Red Fruit Jam, 144
Red Plum Jelly, 275
Red Plum Orange Jelly, 276
Red Plum Rhubarb Jam, 132
rhubarb, 30
  Apple Rhubarb Conserve
    with Goji Berries, 204
  Apricot Rhubarb Conserve,
    207
  Black Currant Rhubarb Jam,
    97
  Bumbleberry Jam, 103
  Raspberry Rhubarb Jam, 142
  Red Plum Rhubarb Jam, 132
  Rhubarb Apple Butter, 322
  Rhubarb Jam, 81
  Rhubarb Jelly, 277
  Rhubarb Orange Ginger Jam,
    145
  Rhubarb Pineapple Jam, 146

Rhuberry Jelly, 280
Strawberry Rhubarb and Pear
  Conserve, 226
Strawberry Rhubarb Micro-
  Mini Jam, 172
Strawberry Rhubarb Orange
  Jam, 155
Roasted Garlic Wine Jelly, 287
rose hips, 30
  Rose Hip Jelly, 278
rosemary (fresh)
  Pomegranate Jelly
    (variation), 271
  Rosemary Apple Cider Jelly,
    306
  Strawberry Onion Jam with
    Balsamic Vinegar and
    Rosemary, 196
rose water
  Gooseberry Jam (variation),
    59
  Plum Ginger Jam (variation),
    72
  Rhubarb Jam (variation), 81
  Strawberry Jam with Rose
    Water, 85
  Wine and Roses Jelly
    (variation), 298
rum
  Apple Rum Raisin Conserve,
    205
  Banana Orange and Date
    Conserve (variation), 191
  Dried Fig Jam (variation),
    57
  Grilled Pineapple Banana
    Conserve with Kahlúa, 220
  Lime Coconut Marmalade,
    241
  Mojito Jelly, 283
  Peach Rum Butter, 318
  Piña Colada Jam, 71
  Plum Rum and Prune
    Conserve, 223
  Quince Jam (variation), 77
  Rumpot Conserve, 225
  Strawberry Mango Daiquiri
    Jam, 151

S
Sage and Thyme, Orange
  Onion Jam with, 192
salads and dressings, 343, 348,
  352

Sangria Jelly, 284
Saskatoon Berry Jam, 82
Seedless Blackberry Jam with
  Cassis, 50
Seedless Raspberry Lemon
  Verbena Jam, 80
Seville Orange Marmalade,
  245
shallots, 30
  Tomato Orange Jam with
    Basil and Saffron, 194
sherry
  Fig and Italian Plum
    Conserve, 215
  Sherry Trifle, 369
Shiraz-Cabernet and Lemon
  Thyme Jelly, 301
Shrimp, Coconut, 347
Shut Cookies, 359
side dishes, 343
snacks, 344
Sour Cherry Apricot Jam, 104
Sour Cherry Jam, 54
Sour Cherry Pear Jam, 107
Sour Cherry Raspberry Jam,
  109
Spiced Apple Butter, 310
Spiced Apricot Butter, 311
Spiced Black Grape Jam, 60
Spiced Carrot Apple Pineapple
  Conserve, 208
Spiced Cranberry and Red
  Wine Jelly, 295
Spiced Mango Jam, 62
Spiced Peach Cranberry Jam,
  126
Spiced Peach Jam, 64
Spiced Pear Butter, 320
Spiced Port Wine Jelly, 296
spices, 36
spirits, 36. *See also* liqueurs;
  wine; *specific spirits*
  "Campari with a Twist" Jelly,
    282
Splenda, 174
spreads
  low-sugar, 174, 184–91
  no-sugar, 174, 182–83
Steak Salad with Strawberry
  Balsamic Dressing, 352
stevia, 174
strawberries. *See also* berries
  Apple Berry Jam, 90
  Bumbleberry Jam, 103

strawberries (*continued*)
Fig Strawberry Jam with Balsamic Vinegar, 112
Raspberry Lychee Jam with Lychee Liqueur (variation), 138
Rhubarb Apple Butter (variation), 322
Rhuberry Jelly, 280
Steak Salad with Strawberry Balsamic Dressing (variation), 352
Strawberry Banana Micro-Mini Jam, 171
Strawberry Banana No-Cook Jam, 178
Strawberry Cantaloupe Jam, 147
Strawberry Gooseberry Jam, 148
Strawberry Jam, 83
Strawberry Jam with Rose Water, 85
Strawberry Kiwi Jam, 150
Strawberry Lavender Jam, 84
Strawberry Mango Daiquiri Jam, 151
Strawberry Maple No-Cook Jam, 179
Strawberry Margarita Jam, 86
Strawberry Onion Jam with Balsamic Vinegar and Rosemary, 196
Strawberry Pineapple Jam, 152
Strawberry Raspberry Jam, 153
Strawberry Red Currant Jam, 154
Strawberry Red Grapefruit Jam, 149
Strawberry Rhubarb and Pear Conserve, 226
Strawberry Rhubarb Micro-Mini Jam, 172
Strawberry Rhubarb Orange Jam, 155
Three-Berry Blend Jam, 156
Strawberry Fields Wine Jelly, 297
Stuffed French Toast, 354
sugar, 40, 175
Sweet Cherry and Black Plum Jam, 108

Sweet Cherry and Blueberry Jam, 105
Sweet Cherry Cran-Raspberry Jam, 106
Sweet Cherry Jam with Kirsch, 55
Sweet Cherry Micro-Mini Jam, 166
Sweet Pepper Apple Chutney, 338

T
Tangelo Marmalade, 246
Tangerine and Honey Marmalade, 247
tarts, 361, 364
tea, 36
Honey Lemon Marmalade (variation), 234
Jasmine Green Tea Jelly with Ginger and Lemon, 268
Mango Orange Jam with Mint Green Tea, 121
Orange Marmalade with Earl Grey Tea, 244
tequila
Mojito Jelly (variation), 283
Strawberry Margarita Jam, 86
Tequila Sunrise Jelly, 285
Three-Berry Blend Jam, 156
Three-Fruit Marmalade, 254
thyme (fresh)
Garlic Chicken Portobello, 351
Orange Onion Jam with Sage and Thyme, 192
Shiraz-Cabernet and Lemon Thyme Jelly, 301
tomatoes, 30
Green Tomato Apple Chutney, 339
Tomato Apple Chipotle Chutney, 340
Tomato Orange Jam with Basil and Saffron, 194
Tropical Tango Spread, 183

V
vanilla, 36
Vanilla Jelly Roll, 368
vegetables, 24. *See also specific vegetables*
vinegar, balsamic, 36

W
watermelon, 28
Kiwi Watermelon Jam, 120
Watermelon Jam, 87
Watermelon Raspberry Jam, 157
whiskey
Brandied Nectarine Jam (variation), 63
Mojito Jelly (variation), 283
Seville Orange Marmalade (variation), 245
Wild Blueberry Jam with Grand Marnier, 52
Wild Blueberry Lemon Marmalade, 237
wine
Cabernet Wine Jelly, 293
Coronation Grape Orange Conserve, 216
Fig and Italian Plum Conserve, 215
Fire and Ice Jelly, 292
Garlic Jelly, 286
Kir Royale Jelly, 294
Muscat Wine Jelly with Lemon Balm, 300
Peach Rum Butter (variation), 318
Pears and Port Jam, 70
Pomegranate Jelly (variation), 271
Purple Basil Wine Jelly, 299
Roasted Garlic Wine Jelly, 287
Sangria Jelly, 284
Sherry Trifle, 369
Shiraz-Cabernet and Lemon Thyme Jelly, 301
Spiced Cranberry and Red Wine Jelly, 295
Spiced Port Wine Jelly, 296
Strawberry Fields Wine Jelly, 297
Wine and Roses Jelly, 298
Winter Berry Jam, 158

Y
Yellow Plum Jam, 74

Z
zucchini, 30
Zucchini Orange Marmalade, 251